TO: NANAY AND TATAY, WITH ALL
OF OUR LOVE,

REDEEM & DEAN.

HOPE YOU ENJOY THESE READINGS.

DOROTHY MINCHIN·COMM

Glimpses of God

Daily
Meditations
for Adults

REVIEW AND HERALD® PUBLISHING ASSOCIATION
HAGERSTOWN, MD 21740

The author assumes full responsibility for the accuracy of all
facts and quotations as cited in this book.

This book was
Edited by Gerald Wheeler
Copyedited by William Cleveland and James Cavil
Designed by Helcio Deslandes
Cover photo by PhotoDisc
Typeset: 10/13 Stempel Schneidler

PRINTED IN U.S.A.

02 01 00 99 98   5 4 3 2 1

R&H Cataloging Service
Minchin-Comm, Dorothy Belle, 1929-
    Glimpses of God

    1. Devotional calendars—Seventh-day Adventists.
2. Devotional literature.   3. Religious art and symbolism.
I. Title.

242.64

ISBN 0-8280-1349-7

*D*EDICATED
TO MY STUDENTS
WITH WHOM I HAVE SPENT
ALMOST 50 YEARS
ADVENTURING
IN THE WORLD
OF IDEAS.

Contents

Introduction

The ideas in this book have formed in many places around the world. Discussions in my literature and writing classes have nurtured them, and they have been aired in conversations with friends and colleagues for many years.

I now invite you to spend the next 365 days looking through the windows Jesus has opened in order to show us new aspects of His character and ministry. What is God like? Surely not *that!* you say. But don't be too sure. Be prepared for a "shock of recognition" as you move through this gallery of pictures, old and new.

Scripture reveals the realities of human experience to us in symbols. Suspicious and fearful of anything approaching idolatry, the Hebrews and first Christians filled their writings with vivid *verbal* images. "God the imager" has, therefore, presented Christ in a varied and colorful field of imagery. Such a tapistry of the divine personality is an extremely rich one. For instance, Christ is the Word as well as the Spirit and the Life. We see Him "made flesh" and also glorified in heaven. He shows both loving-kindness and stern judgment. Christ is the Lamb on the cross and the King on the throne. The Holy Spirit came as a dove and leaping flames of fire.

David the warrior touched upon a vital point in our relationship with God when he exuberantly sang: "The Lord [is] my rock, my fortress, my stronghold and my deliverer, my shield" (Ps. 144:1, 2, RSV). The secret lies in the pronoun *my*. Therefore, by the end of the year, I hope, we will each be able to paint our own portrait of the Master, understanding the many ways by which He can supply our most unique needs.

Special appreciation goes to Virchel Wood, M.D., my orthopedic surgeon friend who read the entire manuscript. He gave useful suggestions not only on scientific matters but also on religious and social issues. And then there is my longtime friend and writing critic, Olivine Nadeau-Bohner. Her help included the final preparation of the manuscript for publication.

Dorothy Minchin-Comm
Professor of English
La Sierra University
Riverside, California

THE UNIVERSAL LIGHT

The slight, pensive man sat by the fire, his study windows overlooking the cottage garden and the rambling street beyond. An exile from London, he had chosen the quiet village of Chalfont St. Giles as a refuge. Untiringly he had supported the republican cause of Oliver Cromwell, but with the return of the king he had given up the turbulent political and social concerns that had occupied most of his life. Fixing his sightless eyes upon God, he now spent his days composing the most exalted and magnificent poetry the English language had produced since Shakespeare. The man's name was John Milton.

GOD IS LIGHT AND IN HIM IS NO DARK- NESS AT ALL.

1 JOHN 1:5, NKJV.

The theme of light flashes through Milton's poetry in brilliant shafts of insight. Through the lofty themes of *Paradise Lost,* the poet passed from the limitations of his own physical blindness to the mysteries of God's purposes. He sang of the "essential light" that is God's own creative energy and power. Then he described the daily "material light" that illuminated and warmed the earth. Finally he celebrated that "inner light" by which the Christian sees inwardly.

> "But thou [Light]
> Revisit'st not these eyes, that roll in vain
> To find thy piercing ray, and find no dawn. . . .
> Seasons return, but not to me returns
> Day, or the sweet approach of even or morn. . . .
> So much the rather thou, celestial Light,
> Shine inward, . . . that I may see and tell
> Of things invisible to mortal sight."*

The first element of Creation, light, is a universally understood symbol. It speaks of the spirit. Physicists can—and have—written volumes on the functions of light: its speed, its life-giving properties, its power. When all is said and done, however, it took a blind Milton to help us comprehend the God of light. Humanity instinctively yearns for Him, as naturally as a sunflower must turn to the sun.

"Arise, shine," the prophet cried, "for your light has come, and the glory of the Lord has risen upon you" (Isa. 60:1, RSV). Here, then, is a resolve for the new year. *Arise* to catch as much of the Light as possible. *Reflect* it! *Shine* so that others may share the gift.

> [*I stand at the gate of the new year, Lord. Let Your light illuminate the unknown path before me.*]

Paradise Lost, III, 22-55.

THE DARKNESS

Most of us can remember being afraid of the dark. Although we were not born with such a fear, the media, the tales we heard at school, and a hundred other influences have nurtured our anxieties. Were we to be perfectly honest with one another, many of us as children would have to confess to looking in the closet and under the bed before going to sleep, and then lying in a cold sweat while familiar shapes in the corners of the room took on horrific forms. Then, hoping that some little sliver of comforting light could reach us, we'd plead, "Please, Mom. Leave the door open just a crack."

THE PEOPLE STOOD AFAR OFF, WHILE MOSES DREW NEAR TO THE THICK DARKNESS WHERE GOD WAS.

EX. 20:21, RSV.

Assuredly, our world *is* dark. We pass through many nights of doubt. The night of bereavement comes to us repeatedly. And no one is spared nights of discouragement over failures, both real and imagined. At times we seem to be standing on the very brink of one of those great black holes of the universe.

God is light, certainly. But John's declaration that in God there "is no darkness at all" (1 John 1:5, NKJV) needs some qualification. While there is no darkness in *Him*, the Lord may be found *in* "the thick darkness." We often sense Him there—strongly. Is it a darkness of mystery? Yes, God does have His secrets, but we learn to trust and to accept them rather than give ourselves up to fear. Is it the darkness of trials? God is in there, too, so we need not be afraid to enter whatever difficulty lies before us. Is it the darkness of desertion? There—especially—we can share Gethsemane with our Lord.

In fifteenth-century Italy the Florentine artist Leonardo da Vinci pioneered the use of chiaroscuro—a painting technique using light and shade in contrast. He produced marvelous three-dimensional effects by throwing highlights on a dark canvas. Likewise for us, finding God in the darkness will reveal treasures available to us nowhere else.

"What then? Shall we sit idly down and say
'The night hath come; it is no longer day?' . . .
Yet, as the evening twilight fades away,
The sky is filled with stars, invisible to day."

I've often been discouraged, Father, when shadows have fallen across my way. Should a dark experience overtake me today, teach me to discover Your presence even there.

THE LIGHT OF THE WORLD

The earth *is* dark—and millennia of sin have made it increasingly so. No wonder that the winter festival customs in many cultures call for candles, lanterns, and twinkling chains of light. The festive lights and the tinsel of Christmas are our rather tawdry echo of what Jesus' birth was all about. He arrived in the world in a burst of light, the star for the Wise Men, the choir of shining angels for the shepherds. The startled peasants on the hills of Bethlehem stared at those angels, who trailed only a little of heaven's light. Even so, it was almost more than the men could endure.

"WHILE I AM IN THE WORLD I AM THE LIGHT OF THE WORLD."

JOHN 9:5, NEB.

Later the aged Simeon, prophesying in the Temple courtyard, pointed out to anyone who would listen the significance of the light-bearing Child, Jesus, being brought in to the Temple for consecration. "Mine eyes have seen thy salvation . . . , a light for revelation to the Gentiles, and for glory to thy people Israel" (Luke 2:30-32, RSV).

Too often we see the future as *night*, assuming that the present somehow ought to be *day*. The suffering Job anticipated his trip to "the land of gloom and chaos, where light is as darkness" (Job 10:22, RSV). The Christian, however, needs to lay hold on hope and reverse that sequence "Let us then cast off the works of darkness and put on the armor of light; let us conduct ourselves becomingly as in the day" (Rom. 13:12, 13, RSV). Those who have accepted salvation walk forever in the light. Indeed, no darkness anywhere can overcome them. "The Lord is my light and my salvation; whom shall I fear?" (Ps. 27:1, NKJV).

Unfortunately, we've become accustomed to earth's night. Often exhausted with work and stress, we welcome the rest of the night—even as the aged and the terminally ill finally accept the dark rest of death itself. John the revelator, however, breathlessly describes the New Jerusalem. A different system operates there, for weariness and death are forever left behind in the darkness. Instead, "the glory of God" is the "radiance" of heaven, and above all, "there shall be no night there" (Rev. 21:11, 25, RSV). God's energizing light will sustain us throughout eternity.

[*I want to be a bearer of light in my circle of activity today, however small. In order to reflect joy to others I must have Your light within my life first, Lord.*]

THE SUN OF RIGHTEOUSNESS

Sun worship, in one form or another, has appeared in virtually every culture. The ancients created myths describing the sun's chariot procession across the sky by day. Ahkenaton, the monotheistic pharaoh of Egypt, wrote a hymn to the sun that portrays the creator god in whom he believed. In India 3,500 years ago the Aryan priests sang their Sanskrit hymns to the sun, "maker of light . . . illuming all the shining space." Even a beachcomber, decadent though he or she may be, instinctively turns to worship the sun—if with nothing else than his or her body! During every day of fine weather we rejoice and throw open our windows to the light. One of the most exuberant lines King David ever sang pictures the sun "like a bridegroom coming forth from his pavilion" (Ps. 19:5, NIV).

> THE SUN OF RIGHTEOUS-NESS SHALL ARISE WITH HEALING IN HIS WINGS.
>
> MAL. 4:2, NKJV.

One never sees the sun to better advantage than from an airplane. Although it may drizzle, rain, or hail on the ground, in moments you can climb to where the sun works its will. Watch that fiery face rising into a violet sky and turning the gray cloud floor blood-red. At 35,000 feet you feel effects that you can never know down below where earth's landscapes and humanity's playthings trivialize the sun's energy. Up there you stand timidly at the threshold of heaven, so to speak, and look into God's mighty workroom. Little wonder that so many air and space travelers come home believers in a higher power.

The sun first appeared in Eden's clear skies. Then, through symbol and parable, it moved across the gloom of suffering and into the storm clouds of sin. At the end of the Old Testament, however, full sunshine burst forth again when the prophet announced the rising of the Sun of Righteousness. With Him comes the heat that cleanses and the purity that heals. Since then, more centuries of darkness have settled upon us. Sometimes we have had only the promise, the forecast, of sunshine. Yet those promises have repeatedly broken through the clouds in bright golden shafts—just when we needed the guidance. Thus our faith lives and warms itself in the light of the Sun of Righteousness.

May every rising of the sun upon Your earth, God, remind me of the gift of the Sun of Righteousness.

THE DAYSPRING

All of us, even children, have experienced enough of illness to know how long a dark, sleepless night can be. Then as we grow older, our causes for worry multiply—and sometimes overwhelm us. Problems that we might have coped with during the day become huge, oppressive fears that consume us at night. The mind churns, and scarcely knowing what to ask for, we pray for the dawn. Like Solomon's anxious bride repeatedly calling to her lover, we cling to the hope of the dawn: "Until the day breaks and the shadows flee away, turn, my beloved . . ." (S. of Sol. 2:17, NKJV).

> THE DAYSPRING FROM ON HIGH HAS VISITED US.
>
> LUKE 1:78, NKJV.

Instinctively we move Godward in the dark hours. Our heavy eyes turn repeatedly to our bedroom window, searching for that first cast of silver gray that tells us that the sun will soon rise. When we see it, we instinctively feel encouraged. Everything looks better with the coming of light—even the first faint hint of it. Strength returns and gives us the will to arise and face the demands of our day.

The appearance of the morning light, the dayspring, is, however, noiseless. Likewise, when the mighty Sun of Righteousness comes upon us, His touch is as gentle as the arrival of the dawn. When God's love lights the soul, it always moves from less to more—from the first streaks in the predawn darkness to the full light of understanding at high noon. Only a few Christians can identify the precise moment of their conversion. For most it did not occur in a blinding flash of light, as it did to Paul on the road to Damascus. Rather it came as a long, slow dawning—one that may well last a lifetime. All we know is that we were once in darkness and are now in light.

It is now more than 450 years since William Tyndale's unorthodox and annotated translation of the Scriptures first shocked ecclesiastical Britain. Because he paid with his life for his beliefs, we appreciate all the more the hope that rings through his quaint sixteenth-century English rendering of Luke's joyous exclamation: "The day springe from an hye hath visited us" (Luke 1:78). Amazement, wonder—our day has sprung! Earth's night is forever broken.

[*Walk with me today, Lord. May my spiritual journey bring me from darkness to the threshold of Your dawning light.*]

THE MORNING STAR

L ong ago a little boy lived on a remote farm in
Western Australia. He passed through the usual
little boyhood ambitions of the time—to drive a
train, to ride on a fire engine, and so forth. But most of
all he wanted to study the stars. Out there in the rolling
fields under the eucalyptus trees, he could see them
clearly. Alone one night with his father, he confided that
he was in love with the stars. "I know, I know, my boy.
I've seen it," his father said. His hardworking, undemon-
strative parent knew? Amazing! Indeed, my father was
"in love with the stars" all of his life. Just two years before his premature death, we gave him a telescope.
What a pity that he had to wait 60 years to have it!

UNTIL THE
DAY BREAKS
AND THE
MORNING
STAR RISES
TO ILLUMI-
NATE YOUR
MINDS.
2 PETER 1:19, NEB.

Fascination with the stars is embedded deeply within us. Astrology, the
belief in star power, is as old as the history of humanity. In various ways
we have all followed the starry trail of the Wise Men of the East toward
spiritual illumination. The Greeks read mythic wisdom into the star constel-
lations. The Buddha reaches "enlightenment" after his many days of fasting
and meditation. Hindu deities dance in flaming hoops of light. Painted
Christian saints wear halos and light rays to indicate illumination and piety.
Some wear halos of stars.

Against this diverse background of shining light, of spiritual insight and
practice, God declared Himself to John the revelator: "I, Jesus, have sent My
angel to testify to you these things. . . . I am . . . the Bright and Morning
Star" (Rev. 22:17, NKJV). Or in the quaint language of the Wycliffe translation, the "day sterre springe in your hearts" (2 Peter 1:19).

As the Bright Star, Jesus then is the very beginning of enlightenment in
darkness. He is not the evening star at the end of the day, lovely as that
may be. Nor is He any of the stars invisible during the daylight of our
workaday world. Instead, He is the morning star, the herald of the dawn,
the one that announces the coming end of darkness. He intends to shine,
single and focused, in the mind of every believer.

[*Like a mariner navigating unknown seas, I look
to You, the Morning Star, to guide me this day.*]

THE DAWN

L ying in bed and waiting for the sun to come up is much too passive for me. I prefer to stand on the back patio to see the early-morning desert transformation. The empty hills slowly soften with pure light—gold etching the landscape lines. Rabbits consort in the sagebrush, magnified so clearly that you can almost see their whiskers. Processions of quail march purposefully along the trails. And a coyote stands on a boulder, watching me with yellow eyes. Sunrise will, of course, blot out those brief, delicate moments that belong only to the dawn.

"BEFORE THE DAWN COMES AND THE SHADOWS FLEE AWAY, COME TO ME, MY BELOVED."

S. OF SOL. 2:17, TLB.

Just as I was about to write on this symbol of the ministry of Christ, I received a letter from a contemplative artistic friend. She captures the mysteriousness of dawn.

"It is dark.
But now lightness overtakes the night.
Imperceptibly, gradually, at first, the darkness thins.
    At what point during dawn can it be said,
    'That is night—but this is day.'
        Who can say?
This is a painless passing.
No sudden splitting of the sky.
No bright flashings yet.
Rather a slow flow sweetening the air.
Wave upon wave as an ascending tide
Upon the pebbles of a quiet bay,
The sun extends himself.
Shadows creep away.
They seep into the cracks of the rocks,
Or fall asleep in icy caves.
    Only then may the trumpets blare
    For the sunrise a brilliant fanfare,
        'Behold! The Day!'"
                —Donna May Peck

Jesus, the divine lover in Solomon's song, calls us to meet Him while "the day breathes and the shadows flee" (S. of Sol. 2:17, RSV). What a gentle moment He chose for us!

Thank You, Lord, for the delicate, loving way in which You open each day for me.

17 ❋ ASTRONOMY

THE SUNRISE

The summer I joined an archaeology team for a dig in Israel, I discovered a piece of trivia from medieval history. Yet it *wasn't* trivia. The French crusaders who died in the wars at Caesarea Maritima made their burials a unique profession of faith. My "dig square" turned out to be a mixed cemetery, and in six weeks we took out 70 skeletons. The Muslims lay on their sides, knees flexed, facing toward Mecca. The Christians lay on their backs in crude stone crypts. Arms folded in the form of the cross on their chests, they were positioned with their heads to the west, feet to the east. Thus in the resurrection they could rise up from their graves, facing toward the east and the sunrise.

FROM THE RISING OF THE SUN EVEN TO ITS GOING DOWN, MY NAME SHALL BE GREAT AMONG THE GENTILES.

MAL. 1:11, NKJV.

Seeing a great sunrise is a breathtaking experience. Even those who are by nature night people will from time to time be persuaded to get out of bed in time to see one. First the sun sends golden shafts of light up through wispy clouds into the pale blue air. Then perhaps it splinters itself on the crest of a hill and rushes down into the valley.

To the last day of earth's history, we can depend on the coming of the dawn. "Let us press on to know the Lord; his going forth is sure as the dawn" (Hosea 6:3, RSV). At the end of the day earth turns slowly away from the face of the sun. By midnight, therefore, we look out into the abyss of empty space—opposite to the sun's light. A moment later, however, we start revolving back toward the sun—which has remained unchanged. It simply waits for the earth to turn back to it.

Similarly, we can still move back toward Jesus, even when we have gone as far as possible from Him. Never varying, He does not move when we turn away. He is waiting for us right there all the time. Facing the sunrise, we realize anew that "the path of the righteous is like the light of dawn, which shines brighter and brighter until full day" (Prov. 4:18, RSV).

[*I praise You, the Creator, for Your gift of daily sunrises. You designed them to diminish the fears and despair of the nights that so often precede them.*]

THE SUNSET

The island of Luzon, in the Philippines, has one unique feature—the most glorious sunsets to be seen anywhere in the world. They are, moreover, an almost nightly event.

Some years ago it became a weekly excursion for my family and me to drive across the city of Manila (an hour's effort, at the least) to see the sunset over Manila Bay. Since we had little access to air-conditioning, we found it worth the labor to pack a picnic supper and eat it in Luneta Park. There we sat on the retaining walls, feet dangling over the rocky shore below, while the breeze off the water cooled our heated faces and rustled the palms overhead. Perched in a row, we waited for curtain time.

FROM THE RISING OF THE SUN TO ITS GOING DOWN. OUT OF ZION, THE PERFECTION OF BEAUTY, GOD WILL SHINE FORTH.
PS. 50:1, NKJV.

The show was different every Saturday night. On clear evenings the sun would drop behind the silhouettes of Corregidor Island and the Bataan Peninsula in a splash of color, its departure mirrored in a blinding trail of light over the waters of the bay. Again, the action might all be in the sky, with feathery white-trimmed layers of cloud superimposed over bands of crimson, yellow, and violet. Then out of the horizon, shafts of light, like flaming swords, would pierce the blue dome overhead. At other times the whole sky would catch fire, an inferno in every direction.

Since then, I'll hear someone say, "Ah, just look at that gorgeous sunset!" When I look, I'll think, *Not bad.* But I always add to myself, *But you've never been down to Manila Bay at sunset, or you wouldn't say so.*

The sunrise and the east have long been a symbol of beginnings and resurrection. The sunset and the west have signified endings and death. Isaiah quoted God: "That men may know, from the rising of the sun and from the west, that there is none besides me" (Isa. 45:6, RSV). Asaph, the psalm writer, described the whole cycle as the very "perfection of beauty"—God Himself will "shine forth" at both the beginning *and* the end (Ps. 50:2, NKJV).

[*How wise and kind You are, Lord, to make our endings as beautiful as our beginnings.*]

THE DEW

Dew is a delicate thing. For Israel, it became a part of the gentle gift of manna. "In the morning there was a layer of dew around the camp. When the dew was gone, thin flakes like frost on the ground appeared on the desert floor" (Ex. 16:13, 14, NIV). During his final blessing on the 12 tribes, Moses prayed that the Promised Land would be a place "where the skies drip with dew" (Deut. 33:28, NEB). Imaginative photographers win prizes for catching a single dewdrop on a rose petal, or beads of dew on a blade of grass.

> I WILL BE LIKE THE DEW TO IS-RAEL; HE WILL BLOS-SOM LIKE A LILY.
>
> HOSEA 14:5, NIV.

An important part of the Holy Land's water supply, dew makes the difference between total barrenness and sufficient vegetation to graze flocks. In the summer heat of the desert, when the days are fiercely hot and clear and the nights cool, heavy dew distills from the moisture in the atmosphere.

When Isaac blessed his two sons, the presence or absence of dew was an integral part of the legacy. The birthright for the deceiving Jacob promised "dew from heaven and the richness of the earth" (Gen. 27:28, NEB). Esau, on the other hand, would live by his sword "far from the richness of the earth, far from the dew of heaven above" (verse 39, NEB). A vivid symbol of God's blessing, dew withheld meant God's displeasure. Thus Elijah's prophecy against King Ahab represented a complete environmental disaster. "There shall be neither dew nor rain these coming years unless I give the word" (1 Kings 17:1, NEB).

Isaiah, however, carries the imagery of dew to its most thrilling application. "They that sleep in the earth will awake and shout for joy; for thy dew is a dew of sparkling light, and the earth will bring those long dead to birth again" (Isa. 26:19, NEB).

Dew, not rain, was God's original plan for watering the earth (Gen. 2:5, 6). Had sin not entered the world, His dealings with His creatures could always have had the grace and gentleness of dew. Forced to live lives of perpetual crisis, however, we must now cry for *showers* of blessing. Daily we cope with challenges that would otherwise overpower us. Meanwhile, the dew, forming imperceptibly in the night, awaits us each new day.

> *My God, while I pray for Your blessings to come in showers, let me never fail to find the quiet refreshment of Your heavenly dew morning by morning.*

THE RAIN

Cynics in southern California like to say that two inches of rain there means that the raindrops are two inches apart on the ground. Like them, I tend to scorn weathercasters who speak anxiously of a "storm" that in the end produces hardly one decent roll of thunder or one fork of lightning.

One has to live near the equator to understand real rain, the kind of rain that produces truly lush plant life. I never wanted to miss the excitement of a rainstorm in the Philippines. In the middle of the bright afternoon sun, glossing the fronds of the palm trees, would come first the sound of the rain. I would rush to the door to watch. To the east would move a gray wall, absorbing sunlight and landscape as it approached. At 100 yards I could see the silver sheen of the wall of water. The roar would increase until the vertical flood hit the house in a burst of fury, blotting out the sun in a single instant. Now, *that* is serious rain. And yet the long-drawn-out drizzle of an English spring is also vital. In any form, rain is a life-giver—if it comes at the right time.

Human beings have universally seen the management of rain as a province of divine power. Every desert-bound culture has its rain god—with endless songs, dances, and even human sacrifices designed to appease him. Prophets and medicine men everywhere have prayed for rain. The Bible narrative, from the Flood onward, attributes the gift of rain to Jehovah. "For he says to . . . the rainstorms, 'Be fierce.' And when his voice is heard, the floods of rain pour down unchecked" (Job 37:6, NEB). The Old Testament even made rain contingent upon obedience. "If you conform to my statutes, . . . I will give you rain at the proper time" (Lev. 26:3, 4, NEB). (The "proper time" in Palestine was October for the "early rain" and May for the "latter rain.")

The psalmist compares God to the rain. This poetic idea turns upon two features. First, rain abundantly nourishes the land. Second, it must be timely. When we ask for the "showers of blessing," we must trust Him to do precisely the right thing at the right time.

> HE SHALL BE LIKE RAIN FALLING ON EARLY CROPS, LIKE SHOWERS WATERING THE EARTH.
>
> PS. 72:6, NEB.

[*I praise You, Master of the weather. Make me receptive to Your heavenly rains, be they soft showers or tropical downpours. I want to grow in just the way You have planned for me.*]

HEAT

Summer by summer, Americans and their foreign visitors swarm by the millions through the great national parks of Utah and Arizona. They come to view the high textured domes of Zion and the red pinnacles of Bryce, carved out by ice, water, and wind. More flock to see the dizzying chasm of the Grand Canyon. Vast stretches of sagebrush plains, twisted patches of Joshua trees, and heaps of boulders, flat-headed mesas, and gray-green stands of trees wetting their feet at almost-dry creek beds line the parks. Western deserts in the summer are hot—115°F and more being the rule rather than the exception. The blazing heat seems to deter no one. Why?

I WILL LOOK FROM MY DWELLING PLACE LIKE CLEAR HEAT IN SUN-SHINE, LIKE A CLOUD OF DEW IN THE HEAT OF HARVEST.

ISA. 18:4, NKJV.

The explorers and pioneers who passed this way, of course, are long gone. Nowadays we sightseers flit through the same canyons and across the plains in air-conditioned cars. The heat waves still dance on the road ahead, but we don't feel them. When we stop for a drink, our water is cold. At night we know where to find a shower and a clean bed. What can we know of the unbearable heat and hardships endured by those who traveled in covered wagons? Modern technology has provided relief from the heat.

Palestine also has a dramatic change of seasons, the summer being very hot. In his poetic prophecies concerning foreign nations, Isaiah sang of the God who remained the omnipotent watcher of human affairs year in, year out. The prophet wished to show that treaties with Egypt, Assyria, or anyone else could bring no security, for God alone is in charge of history.

Therefore, He is changeless, whatever the season and weather conditions. In Isaiah's vivid picture of heat shimmering in the summer sun, God looks down upon us all. Heat waves are particularly devastating for those who have no defenses against them. Seeing us trapped in an unforgiving desert of sin, God knows that we are subject to death-dealing heatstroke. He understands our exhaustion and stands ready to quench our all-consuming thirsts. God is the "technology" that enables us to endure the heat. Only in Him can we find the relief that will save our lives.

[*Dear Lord, we find this desert we are traveling through to be very, very hot. We long for the relief and refreshment that only You can give.*]

COLD

One year the residents of Alberta, Canada, endured the most severe cold weather of the century. For two weeks we had a wind-chill factor of –100°F. A square inch of exposed human flesh would freeze in about 20 seconds. When you walked on the streets, you could identify no one unless you happened to recognize the clothes they were bundled up in. The standard greeting was, "I'll tell you who I am if you tell me who you are."

HE HURLS DOWN HIS HAIL LIKE PEBBLES. WHO CAN WITHSTAND HIS ICY BLAST?

PS. 147:17, NIV.

In your car you were only slightly better off. The highways were sheets of ice. Provided you managed to stay on the road, when you opened your door to step out, your feet were more than likely to skid right out from under you. We survived simply because Canadian homes are warm. Knowing the ruthlessness of the climate, the builders use insulation and every known device for conserving heat. Such provisions require both planning and considerable expense. Heavy equipment for clearing the roads is in constant readiness so that normal life can go on.

There is cold, *cold,* and **cold!** Northern Canada, to be sure, offers you the experience of "third degree cold." It reminds you that intense cold can be a discipline.

Hot as they are, the Palestinian deserts can also have severe cold spells. They did not come often, nor did they last long. Therefore, people were never prepared for them. They had little provision other than huddling around a small fire in a brazier. That's what Peter was doing when he denied his Lord in the courtyard of the high priest. "The servants and the police had made a charcoal fire, because it was cold, and were standing round it warming themselves. And Peter too was standing with them, sharing the warmth" (John 18:18, NEB). Might poor Peter have done better if he had had less discomfort? Who knows?

Nonetheless, cold is good discipline. It forces us to look ahead, to be diligent. To this end "the cold [comes] from the driving winds. The breath of God produces ice, and the broad waters become frozen" (Job 37:9, 10, NIV). The natural world challenges us to self-discipline.

> *Dear Maker of cold, let me not complain of the cold in Your natural world, nor of coldness in the hearts of my neighbors. Light a fire of love within me that those around me may warm themselves.*

THE SNOW

Changes of season in Canada can be dramatic. The first timid crocuses in spring meadows and water dripping off the edges of Rocky Mountain glaciers to form milky lakes below hint at spring. Summers explode under high-domed blue skies. Hailstorms punctuate golden autumns in the harvest fields. But the winters really outdo themselves.

"WASH ME, AND I WILL BE WHITER THAN SNOW."

PS. 51:7, NIV.

First of all, you must adjust yourself to spending a certain amount of time every day pulling on heavy clothes and boots, and then later taking them all off. Your car has a block heater that you plug into an electric socket overnight so that the vehicle can sustain the shock of having the ignition turned on in the morning. Always you carry a snow shovel and broom in the trunk, because many times, if you leave your car for a few hours in a parking lot, it will have become a huge mound of snow. You identify it only by remembering exactly where you left it. All inconvenience aside, however, winter has wonderful rewards. Stars sharp as laser beams in the night sky and the aurora borealis (northern lights), a shimmering curtain of color across the heavens. The morning after an ice storm every twig will be encased in crystal. But most of all, it's the enchantment of the snow.

Palestinians only rarely had firsthand experience with snow. That's why David's warrior Benaiah's encounter with a lion in the Jordan Valley "on a snowy day" (2 Sam. 23:20, NEB) merited special mention—the only nonsymbolic reference to snow that we have in Scripture. Israelites generally viewed snow at a distance, seeing it on the slopes of Mount Hermon or in the mountains of Edom, east of Jordan. Still, they understood the mechanics of snowfall. Job compared the desertion of his friends to "streams that overflow when darkened by thawing ice and swollen with melting snow . . . that cease to flow in the dry season" (Job 6:16, NIV).

Usually, however, Israel regarded snow as an awesomely magnificent symbol of God. "He covers the earth with snow like a white wool blanket. He sprinkles nature with frost like ornaments of silver" (Ps. 147:16, Clear Word). Snow hides everything that is unsightly. It softens hard lines. Above all, its intense whiteness symbolizes innocence and purity of both earth and of the human heart.

[*Jesus, send Your divine snowfall upon my soul. I pray for the refreshment (even if painful) it will bring as it hides the ugly things in my life.*]

THE CLOUDS

The craving for light is such a deep-lying instinct within us that favorite tourist destinations are usually located in sun-belt lands. Of course, overexposure to sunlight has recently had a great deal of bad publicity. Years ago, however, children who grew up in sunny places regularly endured severe sunburns. Engrossed in outdoor games and beach frolics, we would come in, broiled scarlet, wearing our skins like brittle leather underwear—so sensitive that it hurt even to breathe. Mother would anoint us with salve.

HE COVERS THE SKY WITH CLOUDS; HE SUPPLIES THE EARTH WITH RAIN.

PS. 147:8, NIV.

Then we would go to bed in tears—but planning to repeat the episode the next chance we got. David knew many cloudy days. But he too was in love with sunshine. In old age he praised the God who is "like the sun shining forth upon a cloudless morning" (2 Sam. 23:4, RSV).

But clouds worry us, and amateurs that we are, we study the morning skies for news. Woolly cumulus clouds heap themselves up in fanciful mountains. The long sturdy bars of stratus clouds lie low to the horizon. Huge, gray nimbus clouds roll in, heavy with rain. Or the wispy, high-flying cirrus clouds shine with silver ice crystals. They all tell a story. As changeable as an English springtime, our lives move continually on through shade and light, sorrow and joy. Our earthly weather forecast (both physical and spiritual) calls for both sunshine and clouds.

Sunlight comes to youth—before the clouds gather. Again, in old age the clouds disperse in the life of a saint secure and strong in faith. In between we have a great deal of uncertain weather. Not only do the clouds sometimes open up and break violent storms over our heads, but from time to time dank clouds and fog rise up around us from the marshlands of our everyday problems. Because the air always clears after the rain, however, we cannot despair.

In fact, cloud-free living results only in arid deserts. Then when the nurturing rains of blessing *do* fall, the ground, unable to accept the water, gives way to floods and mudslides. Our gray days, when we shelter quietly under God's protective cloud cover, are the times when we learn to know Him best.

[*Dear God of both sunlight and shadow, keep me strong today, whatever the weather. Should clouds darken my day, shelter me until Your light breaks through.*]

THE PILLAR OF CLOUD

A trans-Pacific flight will likely give you one of the most spectacular air shows available anywhere in the world. You will never feel more humble than when you look out your window at the skyscape. Through frayed gaps in the cloud floor you see the dark, landless ocean tens of thousands of feet below. What rivets your attention, however, are the massive cloud towers set like rocky sentinels all the way out to the horizon. Instead of the earth tones of the desert, however, the decor up here is pure white and blue. By day those towers are shot through with shafts of sunlight. At night—if you have chosen the right time—moonlight sculpts the cloud shapes into abstract ivory statues displayed on an indigo-blue stage.

FOR THE CLOUD OF THE LORD WAS ABOVE THE TABERNACLE BY DAY.

EX. 40:38, NKJV.

During the wilderness wanderings of Israel the natural canopy of clouds contained a supernatural "visitor." Jehovah's unique "pillar of cloud" served Israel both day and night. It rested on the ark and preceded the travelers as they marched along (Ex. 13:21; 40:36). The cloud often behaved in very purposeful ways—as in the confrontation at the Red Sea, for instance. The angel of God took up the vanguard position, leaving the cloud free to move *behind* the people. There it became a wall of darkness, separating and protecting them from the pursuing Egyptians (Ex. 14:20).

We wonder, Was that cloud like one of those great free-form shapes out over the Pacific? Or did the Creator choose a more regular, crafted form? Either way, He had everything easily in hand, turning out whatever He chose from His weather workshop. "I am the Lord," He says. "I make the light, I create darkness" (Isa. 45:6, 7, NEB). Engineering is no problem to Him, and He thoroughly programmed His cloud for our benefit.

Since God has identified Himself as the guiding "pillar of cloud," we must learn to trace His pathway designed to lead us out of our wilderness of sin.

> *Let the ever-moving, ever-changing clouds overhead, Lord, help me*
> *remember Your intimate and immediate involvement in my daily life.*

THE PILLAR OF FIRE

A FIRE SHONE WITHIN THE CLOUD BY NIGHT, FOR ALL THE HOUSE OF ISRAEL TO SEE.
EX. 40:38,
JERUSALEM.

Fire myths abound in every culture, because fire fascinates us. Even the sick mind of the arsonist attests to its hypnotic power. Sacred fire consumed sacrifices. Eternal flames burn on the graves of heroes. Volcanoes and uncurbed forest fires hold us hostage. Earthquakes and bombs ignite devastating fires. Meanwhile, we can control fire for our simple domestic needs. Finally, we savor that social moment, gathered about a fire with friends. Or in the fireplace glow, we sit alone with our thoughts.

God has often imaged His presence in fire and smoke. In the wilderness the daily transformation of the pillar of cloud into the pillar of fire must have been a marvelously impressive event. Undoubtedly, the fire was always present in the heart of the cloud, shining through visibly as darkness drew on. Perhaps it blazed up like a natural torch. Or perhaps it glowed like a shaded lamp that did not keep people awake at night. Obviously versatile, it may have taken various forms. In any case, one wonders how, with such concrete evidence of divine guidance, the Hebrews could so repeatedly have lost faith and courage.

Spiritually speaking, God's dwelling place is wide enough to include the whole universe and narrow enough to enclose us in an intimate circle. Long associated with the ministry of the Holy Spirit, heavenly fire illuminates us in three ways. First, the pillar of cloud and fire led the nation of Israel (Num. 9:17-23). That is, as Guide of the church, God directs and infuses His Spirit into each assembly of His people. Next, He hovers over each individual home (Ex. 40:38). Every believing family has the potential for becoming His temple and for knowing the same presence. A too rare but nonetheless thrilling possibility! Finally, God "spreads his tabernacle," as it were, over each individual believer. At Pentecost the Holy Spirit divided Himself to appear as tiny licks of flame on the heads of *each* of the believers (Acts 2:3).

The kingdom of peace, for Isaiah, included just such a comprehensive blessing. "The Lord will create over . . . her assemblies a cloud by day, and smoke and the shining of a flaming fire by night" (Isa. 4:5, RSV).

[
My nights are often lonely and dark. Provide me with Your
divine "ring of fire" for protection. I dare not live alone without it.
]

THE SHEKINAH GLORY*

Civilization has long been obsessed with light. Artists have experimented with it. Photography has utilized it for marvelous visual effects. The fine science of optics has given us eyeglasses, preserving so much of our world for those with failing eyesight. Then with a variety of lenses it has opened up the cosmos through the telescope, bringing heavenly bodies stunningly near. Finally the microscope probes other mysteries of the invisible world around us. One common denominator binds such visual wonders together. With very few exceptions, all of these views depend on external primary or secondary sources of light.

But one light is unlike any other. A glory from outer space, it has been glimpsed only rarely. Our classifying the "Shekinah glory" under "weather" might seem strained. Yet it had the unusual characteristic of being visible and abstract at the same time. First appearing above the ark in the wilderness tabernacle, it filled the Holy of Holies and spilled out into the holy place and on beyond into the courtyard. The mystic, self-powered light spread from the inside out, a "crown of glory" to the people (Isa. 28:5, NKJV). In vision the prophet first mourned the Shekinah cloud's departure from the doomed Temple in Jerusalem (Eze. 9, 10). Later he exulted when the "glory of the Lord" once more filled His house (Eze. 43:5, NKJV).

The good news is that if we have caused the Shekinah to leave us, it *can* return. Through renewed faith and grace, that holy fire that flames out from inside the soul becomes visible in Christian lives—a consecrated church, a loving home, a converted individual.

Mercifully, Jesus veiled His glory when He left heaven for the "shadowlands" of earth. We could not otherwise have been able to bear His presence. In her devotional book *When the Candle Burns,* Rita Snowden writes: "The light of every soul burns upward." As God's "candles" here on earth, we too often show only small, fitful spurts of light—nothing near the magnificent, pervasive "glory of the Lord."

> MOSES COULD NOT ENTER THE TENT OF MEETING BECAUSE THE CLOUD HAD SETTLED UPON IT, AND THE GLORY OF THE LORD FILLED THE TABERNACLE.
>
> EX. 40:35, NIV.

[*In my imperfection, Lord, I am but a small candle. Yet I pray that You enable me to live for You, to burn in such a way that I can catch a spark of the Shekinah.*]

---

*Shekinah is a Hebrew word meaning "resting place." It is not found in Scripture, but later Jews used it to designate the visible symbol of God's presence in the tabernacle (and later the Temple).

THE WIND

Wind produces the rustle of palm fronds on tropical beaches, the Santa Anas blowing reckless balls of tumbleweed down California highways, or the sassy little dust devils dancing through Nebraska cornfields. Can you imagine living in everlasting calm, with never a breeze, never a whisper in the forest, never a ripple on a lake?

From the beginning of time people have been fascinated with the invisible wind, associating it with the creative "breath of God" and with the Holy Spirit. The first Christians understood this connection very well. A "rushing mighty wind" that filled the whole house where the believers waited heralded the coming of the Holy Spirit at Pentecost (Acts 2:2, NKJV).

Jesus must have loved the winds. One can imagine Him as a boy, racing over the hills of Nazareth, the wind in His hair. He remembered that, no doubt, when He sat with a man on a rooftop in the middle of the night and spoke to him of God's entrance into the human heart. "The wind blows (breathes) where it will; and though you hear its sound, yet you neither know where it comes from nor where it goes. So it is with every one who is born of the Spirit" (John 3:8, Amplified).

Thus the wind cleanses, bringing down dead trees and sweeping the pavements bare. The Holy Spirit does the same thing.

"God, keep a clean wind blowing through my heart night and day,
Cleanse it with sunlight—let the silver rain
Wash away cobwebs and the smothering dust that the years leave, I pray.
God, keep a clean wind blowing through my heart;
Wind from far, green pastures,
And from shaded pools where still waters are;
Wind from spaces out beyond the first twilight star.
Bitterness can have no place in me, nor grief stay—
When the winds of God rush through and sweep them away;
God, keep a clean wind blowing through my heart night and day."*

> THERE CAME FROM THE SKY A NOISE LIKE THAT OF A STRONG DRIVING WIND, WHICH FILLED THE WHOLE HOUSE WHERE THEY WERE SITTING.
>
> ACTS 2:2, NEB.

[*Lord of the elements, I never want to stagnate, to perish under a load of preconceived prejudices. Keep my mind flexible, always open to Your leading.*]

*Rita F. Snowden, *The Winds Blow* (London: Epworth Press, 1940), Introduction.

THE WHIRLWIND

G od's wonderful winds are *not* always gentle. Anyone who has lived in the tropics knows what He keeps in His arsenal when "He brings the wind out of His treasuries" (Ps. 135:7, NKJV).

BEHOLD, HE SHALL COME UP LIKE CLOUDS, AND HIS CHARIOTS LIKE A WHIRLWIND.

JER. 4:13, NKJV.

We had been in the Philippines six weeks when the "typhoon of the century" struck. Cataracts of rain fell in a cold gray dawn, with the earth in a strange, nervous agitation. The winds lashed the campus, stripped the trees bare, and wrenched off the limbs. Our electricity flickered and went out as the power lines came down. We nailed the windows shut, stuffed towels around the sills, and fought the gale blowing through the house in a continuous roar. The men rushed to the elementary school to rescue the children, trees falling on all sides, with their roots tossed high in the air. In the run for safety, the little ones literally became airborne. Two hours later the eye of the storm passed overhead. A weird band of clear sky appeared in the south, balancing the blackness to the north. Half an hour of ominous yellow-gray calm, and then the winds tore in again, ripping the roof off the house next door. On the other side our neighbor's walls sagged like wet cardboard and the gutter pipes peeled off like straw. Like David, we prayed for relief. "I would haste to find me a shelter from the raging wind and tempest" (Ps. 55:8, RSV).

But we had no place to go. We could only huddle under the furniture and wait.

Indeed, God does have "His way in the whirlwind and in the storm, and the clouds are the dust of His feet" (Nahum 1:3, NKJV). When He appears in the whirlwind, His dealings seem terrible. As He "raises dust," the clouds often conceal Him from us. Yet He is present in every crisis. The horrendous obstacles that so terrify us are but trifling to Him.

At the time of God's own choosing the rain *will* cease. His soft, healing winds will blow away our difficulties—just when we thought we could not endure another moment. Only then do we realize how much we have grown. We are stronger and have survived!

[*I cannot tell what this day holds for me. If it is calm, I am thankful. But if a whirlwind strikes, give me strength to reach out and grasp Your hand, Lord.*]

THE THUNDERSTORM

Thunder startles us. It shatters our sleep. Babies cry and dogs hide under the bed. Not surprisingly, most ancient cultures believed a thunderstorm to be the voice of a god. As the Greeks' supreme divinity, "Zeus, the cloud gatherer," used thunderbolts to keep humans and gods alike in submission. Thor, the Norse god of thunder and war, had a magic hammer to dispatch his foes. A resounding storm merely indicated that Thor was busy at work.

The God of Israel also spoke like thunder. Wishing to know why he had to endure such suffering, Job requested an interview with the Lord. First, the storm swept in over the desert. Then God spoke to Job out of the whirlwind, proposing 88 questions (Job 37-41). Job could answer none of them, for the Lord of the storm is above and beyond challenge. "Have you an arm like God," Deity inquired, "and can you thunder with a voice like his?" (Job 40:9, RSV).

THE GOD OF GLORY THUNDERS: THE VOICE OF THE LORD ECHOES OVER THE WATERS. . . . THE VOICE OF THE LORD . . . SPLINTERS THE CEDARS OF LEBANON.

PS. 29:3-6, NEB.

David's twenty-ninth psalm has been called "The Song of the Seven Thunders." Nothing else among the psalms, nor in all of Scripture, for that matter, quite matches it for drama. So intense is the feeling that the description of its wild landscape leaves the reader almost breathless. So vivid is the imagery that one virtually hears the thunders—"the voice of the Lord . . . full of majesty" (verse 4, RSV)—as they come in a series of seven explosions. We track the progress of the storm. It sweeps in from the sea and crashes through the trees. The whole mountain shakes. Then as suddenly as it appeared, the storm roars on out into the wilderness.

The poet begins his glorious song with a call to worship the Lord of the storm. After the tempest passes over him, David comprehends even more of heavenly power. Enthroned on land and sea, God will strengthen and "bless his people with peace" (verse 11, RSV).

While we often refer to His speaking with the "still, small voice," we also need to be ready to hear Him in the voice of thunder. Herein, however, lies an amazing, divine paradox. The God of the thunderstorm is the one who brings His people *peace!*

[*God of the thunders, grant that I may account the storms in my life simply as manifestations of Your power to deliver. Herein, I pray to find Your peace.*]

THE LIGHTNING

Growing up in the tropics, I took violent storms for granted. Indeed, my little friends and I made the daily downpour of rain in equatorial Singapore an occasion to scramble into our bathing suits and rush outside to play in the storm drains. And I remember standing around with the neighbors one morning, looking at the great gash lightning had made in a huge durian tree. The long black scar and tattered bark were impressive. Lightning had also, with an ear-splitting crash, once torn a drainpipe off of our house.

THE VOICE OF THE LORD MAKES FLAMES OF FIRE BURST FORTH.
PS. 29:7, NEB.

Then a week later, in the middle of our usual cloudburst, I ran home from the neighbor's house. Halfway along, a huge fireball bounced down and rolled along the wire clothesline under which I raced. "Mum!" I shouted as I shot through the front door. "Guess what! A funny big ball of fire chased me!" She looked startled, hugged me close, and didn't say much. Storms were too common for us to live in perpetual apprehension. Consequently, I grew up with much more curiosity than fear about violent weather.

The electrical aspect of storms, however, is more than a matter of curiosity. Here is elemental power, capable of destruction swift and certain. David describes the thunder and lightning sequence: "The voice of the Lord flashes forth flames of fire" (Ps. 29:7, RSV). That electrical show never fails to fascinate us. When we put on a celebration of fireworks, we are trying to imitate—maybe even improve upon—lightning. We do clever things, of course, but we can't touch the *power*. In the final analysis, our efforts are quite pathetic.

On ordinary days we feel more or less in control of our lives, and in bold moments, of our environment, too. Caught in the middle of a great storm, however, we experience awe akin to worship. Now we see what *God* can do—though it is but little compared to what He *could* show us. For the Lord of the storm it is but a small demonstration. But it forces us to stand before even His small demonstrations of power helpless as ants scattered out of their anthill. The Lord of the storm would have us remember how tiny we really are.

[*I respect and honor Your power, my God. Let me never take You for granted in any way.*]

A FLASH OF LIGHTNING

The parts of the world most subject to violent weather are the regions that provide us with the most dramatic sky shows. You will never know any feeling quite like looking into the murky yellow eye of a West Indian hurricane. And you cannot better a sunrise over the floodplains of Bangladesh. The God of storms seems to have made certain locations in His world His weather workshops, places where He invites us to learn about His capabilities and preview His plans.

"LIKE LIGHTNING FROM THE EAST, FLASHING AS FAR AS THE WEST, WILL BE THE COMING OF THE SON OF MAN."

MATT. 24:27, NEB.

Drama in the heavens is an everyday affair on the island of Luzon. Here Jehovah seems to have written His textbook on meteorology. The most magnificent sunsets on earth (without exception) spread before you as you sit on the harborside wall in Luneta Park. No matter how often you watch them—those great silent fireworks, an extravaganza of light and wild design—they will leave you awed and worshipful.

You do not, however, have to go all the way down to Manila Bay. One of the most memorable nights of my entire life I spent in my own front yard in a Manila suburb. During a moonlit night we had a massive lightning storm. Excruciatingly beautiful, it proceeded in absolute silence, too far away for us to hear the "voice of the Lord" in thunder. But we *saw* Him. Indeed we did!

My family and I dragged chairs out onto the lawn to watch. The moon illuminated the shiny fronds of our palm trees with almost noontime brilliance. (That was just the stage setting.) Above, the lightning leaped from horizon to horizon. It zigged. It zagged. It knifed through layers of cloud low to the skyline. Then it exploded within billowy towers, seeming to shatter the clouds into fragments. The show went on and on, without intermission, for almost an hour. We sat transfixed, scarcely wanting to breathe.

"Like lightning . . . will be the coming of the Son of Man!" That thought burned itself into our minds, and we could almost imagine that the Coming had actually begun!

Lord of the storm, sometimes in our impatience with Your time schedule we forget how decisive You can be. Your identifying Yourself with the lightning must always keep us on our guard.

THE FIRESTORM

The last week of October 1993 will be remembered by many southern Californians as the time of the great firestorm (a disaster duplicated and magnified in Australia only a few weeks later). In a place where brushfires are a seasonal event, no one at first took the initial announcement of the Ventura fire seriously. Everyone knew of the courage and knowhow of the firefighters and the excellent technology they had. And wherever they couldn't reach the fire on land, skillful pilots could scoop water out of the ocean and airdrop it on the conflagration. They even had heavy chemicals to suffocate the blaze. Not to worry.

PUNISH-
MENT SHALL
COME FROM
THE LORD
OF HOSTS
. . . WITH
STORM AND
TEMPEST
AND A
FLAME OF
DEVOURING
FIRE.

ISA. 29:6, NEB.

In a few hours, however, complacency gave way to terror. At least 17 fires raged at once. When we looked out at the smoke rising over our own hills—it was pink! We began to take inventory of what possessions we would take in case of evacuation. People turned their cars around in the driveway, facing outward for speedy departure. For three days the major TV channels abandoned regular programming to track the escalating crisis. The devouring fires took on a life of their own, leaping over whole streets to incinerate wholly unexpected places.

One could easily view such disasters as punishment (except that arsonists also become part of the equation). Moreover, God can—and sometimes does—perform a miracle to block the outworking of His own natural laws. Also, He permits Satan to harvest rebellious persons for his infernal kingdom by natural—or even unnatural—disasters. Without the insights of omniscience, it is impossible for us to analyze the "why" behind such tragedies.

We are better employed seeing them simply as part of our sinful human condition. Our responsibility then is to learn and grow through suffering. Even so, the message never reaches some minds. At the height of the crisis at least one obtuse viewer telephoned the television station to find out when a certain soap opera would be aired—because it was "about time."

For the spiritually minded, however, faith matures in adversity, not prosperity. As we have already noted, the God of the storm is the only one with the power to lead His people to ultimate peace.

[*Judge of humanity, I pray not just for safety from physical destruction. More important, keep me in readiness for Your final day of reckoning.*]

THE WELLSPRING OF LIFE

The Spanish explorer Ponce de León accompanied Christopher Columbus on his second voyage to America and became governor of Puerto Rico. Next, history gives way to fantasy. Having heard Indian legends of the island of Bimini and its "fountain of youth," Ponce de León set out to find it. Those magical waters would tempt jaded European royalty just as surely as the lust for gold had aroused them.

On Easter Sunday, 1513, Ponce de León landed near the site of present-day St. Augustine, claiming the "island" as *Pascua Florida* ("flowery Easter"). Time passed while he subdued a native rebellion in Puerto Rico and ascertained that Florida was *not* an island. Finally, eight years later, with 200 colonizers and herds of domestic animals, Ponce de León set out to tame Florida and find the fabled fountain. A vicious encounter with Indians left him severely wounded, and his ships withdrew to Cuba. There he died at age 61, far from discovering the "spring of life" he had sought.

Instinctively, everyone looks for a fountain of youth. Multivitamins, cosmetics, bizarre health practices—all seek to connect us with that elusive "essence of life." Science has searched also. We have studied the structures of DNA. If only we knew how to manipulate them so they would reverse our natural aging. Supporters of cryogenics have speculated that we could resurrect a frozen body at some later time—when we have worked all the problems out. But what they have, to put it crudely, is nothing but freezers full of dead meat. The essence of life is forever just beyond our grasp. Experimentation reaches a certain point, and then the door slams shut.

Nonetheless, Ponce de León was not entirely wrong. There *is* a whole river of life to be found (Rev. 22:1, 2). He was just looking in the wrong place. God's recipe for life? The "Word became flesh" and *"in him was life"* (John 1:4, 14, NIV). We simply have to nourish ourselves at the true Source.

> **THROUGH HIM ALL THINGS WERE MADE. . . . IN HIM WAS LIFE, AND THAT LIFE WAS THE LIGHT OF MEN.**
>
> JOHN 1:3, 4, NIV.

[*Dear Founder of Life, let me never wander from the source that sustains both my body and my spirit.*]

THE HEAD OF THE CHURCH

Visiting the headhunters along the jungle rivers of Borneo is not what it used to be. Tourists with bizarre tastes have now carried away the heads for souvenirs. Not so in those more elemental times before World War II. I was no more than 7 years old when my uncle, pioneer missionary Gus Youngberg, took me and my parents up the Tatau River in Sarawak to visit the longhouses. The crocodiles sunning themselves on the banks were but a mild preview of what was to come. The chief received us in the dark, smoky "head house." Up under the eaves rows of heads hung like dry coconuts, trophies of the chief's forays among his neighbors. But they were not coconuts. Even I could see that. Standing close to my dad for protection, I peered up at the hollow eyes watching me. Some of the heads, being rather fresh, looked down upon us with real eyes.

HE . . . AP-POINTED HIM AS SUPREME HEAD TO THE CHURCH, WHICH IS HIS BODY.

EPH. 1:22, NEB.

A severed head is always chillingly impressive. The removal of the head offers proof positive of the finality of a sentence of execution. Hence, Salome, in behalf of her mother, asked for the head of John the Baptist on a platter. Certain South American tribes have shrunken heads as mementoes of their conquests. An "aristocratic" form of death in England and France—beheading—allowed the heads of the fallen mighty to be displayed on bridges and in marketplaces. (Persons of lesser rank were hanged.)

The head contains the brain, the control tower of the body. Concentrated in that three-pound lump of gray tissue is our mind, emotions, moral discipline, and all sources of physical power. From the brain electrical impulses govern every movement of life. To be the "head" of any operation, then, is symbolically to be the intelligence and the lifeline that keeps a group alive. Loss of the head guarantees instant death to the body—either physical or corporate.

Execution calls for the removal of the head from the body. Spiritually speaking, however, some Christians have reversed the process. In choosing to separate themselves from Christ, they execute themselves. He, the head of the church (being the source of all life), lives on, but they cut themselves off and perish.

[*Lord, even as the body cannot survive without its head, let me never allow that fatal separation to occur in my spiritual life.*]

THE SHINING FACE

In the ancient East anointing with oil accompanied the bath and denoted affluence. The psalmist praised "wine that gladdens the heart of man, [and] oil to make his face shine" (Ps. 104:15, NIV). The important "shining face" of Scripture, however, is much more than a cosmetic consideration. If a sad face is hard to hide, a happy one is equally obvious. Genuine happiness and sincere love *will* shine through from the inside out.

> HE WAS TRANSFIGURED BEFORE THEM, AND HIS FACE SHONE LIKE THE SUN, AND HIS GARMENTS BECAME WHITE AS LIGHT.
>
> MATT. 17:2, RSV.

At Christ's transfiguration, the disciples learned what the shining face of God looked like (this, even though Peter came up with the useless "cosmetic" suggestion of capturing the experience by building "three shelters" for Jesus, Moses, and Elijah [Matt. 17:4, NIV]). Moses forecast this electrifying moment in his poem recited at his death on Mount Nebo. "The Lord came from Sinai . . . ; He shone forth from Mount Paran" (Deut. 33:2, NKJV).

Repeatedly Scripture describes God's benevolent watch care in terms of His shining face. For thousands of years believers have prayed: "Make Your face shine upon Your servant, and teach me Your statutes" (Ps. 119:135, NKJV). Our favorite benediction reads: "The Lord make his face shine upon you and be gracious to you" (Num. 6:25, NIV).

By the same token, the Christian's face must also shine. I had an uncle who in his youth was skeptical about his mother and sisters becoming Seventh-day Adventists. He'd come home and say, "Well, I saw another Adventist on the train today."

"How could you know if he didn't tell you?" the family would ask.

"Easy," the teenager would reply. "He looked so miserable and unhappy, I knew he had to be an Adventist."

A serious matter this. Many of us—for a great variety of reasons—do *not* like to have our picture taken. The difficulty lies in the fact that the camera *does* heartlessly tell all. (Being but a machine, it can hardly do otherwise.) Therefore, we resort to touch-ups to avoid the harsh truth.

Is the face you show the world shining with love and confidence—with joy that comes from within? If not, apply immediately to the studio of the divine Portrait Maker. He knows how to get the lighting exactly right.

> Lord, use me to let Your face shine upon my family and neighbors. Do the touch-up necessary to create a perfect picture.

THE NOSTRILS

The nose is one of our more peculiar possessions. Useful, but odd—and sometimes troublesome. When very young, my sister (already
experienced in ocean travel) became inexplicably obsessed with the noses of the ship's passengers. She
kept up a running commentary on what she saw. This
one "sticks up between his eyes," that one "is going to
bite his nose with his teeth," or the other one "has
really big portholes, doesn't he, Mum?"

The sense of smell gets far less attention than it
deserves. On the one hand, we revel in the pleasures
of sweet odors—flowers, perfumes, spices, herbs,
fresh bread, clean laundry, and so forth. On the other,
probably no people in the world are more preoccupied
than Americans with cleanliness and deodorants. We spare no pains to
eradicate or at least mask smells we deem unsuitable.

Our functions of smell and of respiration are essential in many ways.
Inability to detect an odor, for instance, is as dangerous as being unable to
feel pain. Also, I have a highly experienced doctor friend who is an excellent diagnostician. His conclusions often seem almost uncanny. "How do
you figure *that* out?" I ask.

"Oh, in various ways," he'll say offhandedly. "Sometimes I can just
smell it." At first I thought he was joking. But he wasn't.

When we exhale, what we breathe out is polluted. Naturally, then, we
have produced fanciful legends of fire-breathing dragons and fair ladies
whose breath, however sweet, is lethal. It is our air *intake* that must purify
our bodies. In contrast, the breath of God is pure and life-giving. Actually,
this is an important, providentially planned arrangement. When God created Adam, He formed him of the earth and then "breathed life-giving
breath into his nostrils and the man began to live" (Gen. 2:7, TEV).

The pervasive breath of God has the power to give life and also to take
it away. This leaves us with just two choices. We allow the breath of God's
Spirit to sustain us now. Or we face Him on judgment day, when "by the
breath of God [the wicked] perish, and by the blast of his anger they are
consumed" (Job 4:9, RSV).

> "THE FOUN-
> DATIONS OF
> THE WORLD
> WERE
> UNCOVERED
> ... AT THE
> BLAST OF
> THE BREATH
> OF HIS
> NOSTRILS."
>
> 2 SAM. 22:16, NKJV.

[*"Breathe on me, breath of God, fill me with life anew, that I
may love what Thou dost love, and do what Thou wouldst do."**]

---

*Edwin Hatch (1835-1889) (Oxford University Press).

THE STRONG ARM

In Alberta, Canada, youngsters take to ice skating as naturally as walking. One year I went to high school there in the land of the northern lights. As Indian summer gave way to autumn colors and the days began to be crisp and nippy around the edges, the whole campus started talking about preparing the skating rink down in the hollow of two little hills.

> AWAKE, AWAKE, PUT ON YOUR STRENGTH, O ARM OF THE LORD.
>
> ISA. 51:9, NEB.

Social life, I discovered, more or less centered on the rink—and it *does* matter to a 16-year-old girl which boy carries her skates down the hill. Ah, and then the skating itself! Out in the dry winter air, under the floodlights, your breath freezing on the fur lining of your parka, you and your partner sweep around the rink in huge graceful circles, like high-flying snowbirds.

This, I say, is the way skating is *supposed* to be. A child growing up on a tropical island, however, has little chance to develop ice-skating skills. Even though I had never seen ice skating before, I determined not to be left out. Bruised and battered, I finally learned to stay on my feet—most of the time. Still, I never became a good skater, nor even an average one. On a scale of 1 to 10 (10 being highest) I tottered somewhere between 1 and 2.

Yet I had wonderful experiences down there on the rink. They occurred when some tall, muscular Canadian invited me to skate with him. Clinging to his strong arm, I actually skated! I too swung around the rink in wide, exhilarating circles, darting through the crowd and trying to avoid being run over by some athletic hockey player doing grand solo figures. My pathetic disabilities disappeared, becoming imperceptible to the other people and even to me. (I never had courage to ask any of my skating partners how *they* felt about my performance, but like true gentlemen, they never complained.)

The difference, of course, lay in that strong arm—the arm that lifted me above my insufficiencies and supplied what I could not do for myself. All of which says a good deal about the strong "arm of the Lord" and how He perfects us for salvation.

[*Never let pride prevent me from grasping Your strong arm, Lord.*
Only with You can my life be full and free, as You designed it to be.]

THE MUSCULAR ARM

Hard, bulging upper arms contribute much to our concept of masculinity. All males, large and small, seem driven to develop such muscles. Little boys in the schoolyard at recess time like to compare biceps. Later would-be athletes work out faithfully in bodybuilding programs—until their lean, sculpted bodies glow like bronze artworks (which, of course, they are).

> O LORD . . .
> WE WAIT
> FOR THEE.
> BE OUR
> ARM EVERY
> MORNING.
>
> ISA. 33:2, RSV.

Considering this basic need, then, we find the story of the man with the withered hand particularly touching. The Greek translation implies that both his hand and arm had atrophied—perhaps from an accident or a disease such as cerebral palsy, polio, or a stroke. Of the three Gospel writers who tell the story, Luke the physician is the one who observes that it is the *right* arm that was incapacitated (Luke 6:6). According to Jerome, the older apocryphal Gospel According to the Hebrews identified the man as a stonemason, dependent on his hands for a livelihood. This would heighten the drama, as Jesus draws the embarrassed man out into the middle of the room, where all can see what will happen (verses 7, 8). Now the man appeals to Jesus for healing so that he might be saved from the shame of becoming a beggar.

Jesus chose to do the nonemergency healing in the synagogue on the Sabbath. The Gospels describe about 20 specific cases of healing, and one third of them happened on the Sabbath. Invariably, priests, scribes, and Pharisees protested loudly. The man probably understood little of the argument that followed that electric moment when his right arm and hand came alive—muscular, sensitive, and healthy. He simply went off rejoicing.

Among the 88 cosmic questions God put to Job, one of them touched directly on the very masculine need for muscular arms. "Have you an arm like God?" (Job 40:9, RSV). Well . . . er . . . no. An arm strong enough to snatch us out of Satan's grasp? An arm firm enough for us to lean upon in the dark, lonely passages of our lives? Not really!

"Lord, be our arm every morning." What an exquisite morning prayer this is. Whatever else you may forget in your prayer, remember to ask for the strong, compassionate arm of Jesus.

[*Mighty God, remember the ones I love, far and near. I cannot be by their side to give them strength today. But You can—and that is even better.*]

THE OUTSTRETCHED ARM

In a Protestant Cathedral in Copenhagen, Denmark, a special statue stands behind the altar. After many weeks of studio work the Danish sculptor Albert Bertel Thorvaldsen (1770-1844) created a majestic figure of Jesus. It was all that he had envisioned—powerful arms raised in a gesture of command, the fine head thrown back triumphantly. Then Thorvaldsen closed his studio so that the clay might set before it went off to the foundry for casting in bronze.

THE LORD BROUGHT US OUT OF EGYPT WITH A MIGHTY HAND AND AN OUT-STRETCHED ARM.

DEUT. 26:8, RSV.

When he returned he stared in horror at what he saw. During a heavy rainstorm moisture had seeped into the room and damaged the statue. The powerful physique drooped, the proud head bent forward, and the outstretched arms fell low. The despairing sculptor seized a hammer to smash the statue, but he looked again and could not destroy it. He fled in remorse.

Weeks later he returned with a friend, ready to try again and recapture the likeness of the Strong Man of Galilee. The two men stood at the door, transfixed. Bathed in light from the high window, the Christ now portrayed gentle compassion. The arms reached out as if to embrace humankind. The bowed head seemed to say, "Come! I understand your needs." Here stood a compassionate Saviour, not a defeated Christ!

Outstretched arms are a natural—even automatic—gesture of love and welcome. Next time you're caught waiting in an airport, get checked in and then go up to the arrival/departure gate and watch the people greet one another. Recently, as I waited for my son to disembark from a flight from Honolulu, I saw a young man with a large and very lovely bouquet of flowers plus a balloon reading "Welcome Home, Tess." He sat quietly, eyes fixed on the door of the jetway as the crowds streamed off the Boeing 747. Hadn't she come after all? My heart ached for him. Finally she appeared, virtually the last person off the plane. She dropped her bags, and in tears and laughter they rushed into each other's arms, crushing the flowers between them. Whatever had separated them, all was now well.

Although it takes the strong hand to bring us out of our Egyptian captivity, the outstretched arms wait to enfold us in safety.

[*My Lord, I need Your strong hand of deliverance. But I also depend on the comfort of Your arms, outstretched to receive me.*]

THE GENEROUS HAND

Do you know about the medical problem called Dupuytren's contracture? Probably not. You would be painfully aware of it, however, if your fingers had drawn up and permanently closed your hand into a semi-fist. Or if the condition was extremely severe and your fourth finger had been amputated to enable you to open your hand again.

Medical writers described the condition as early as the time of the ancient Greek physician Hippocrates. It remained, however, for the French baron Guilliaume Dupuytren (1777-1835) to study the disease with such persistence that it now bears his name.* He first observed it in 1811 among the merchants and cart men handling heavy wine casks on the docks. Investigation has shown, however, that the disease results from too little rather than too much activity of the hand. Also, it is almost exclusive to the Caucasian race, being prevalent in northern Europe and the British Isles. Twice as many men as women suffer from Dupuytren's contracture, and epileptics, alcoholics, and chronic invalids have an above-normal risk for it.

A closed hand is forbidding. It may hide a weapon, withhold a gift, cover up a theft, or threaten violence. In contrast, the open hand indicates safety—perhaps even innocence.

The open hand gives as well as receives. The reason that courting couples so much enjoy holding hands is no doubt because the joining of two *open* hands is a strongly reassuring experience. Nothing is hidden or withheld. Strength and support, joy and freedom, lie in the joining.

When celebrating the glories of Creation, the psalmist found God's "open hand" to be one of His most admirable attributes, supplying the needs of every one of His creatures. In His earthly ministry Christ's hands were always open—to give, comfort, and heal. If we have difficulty keeping our hands open, we may be suffering from spiritual Dupuytren's contracture. Severe or chronic cases may call for surgery—some even amputation.

> THE EARTH IS FULL OF THY CREATURES. . . . WHEN THOU OPENEST THY HAND, THEY ARE FILLED WITH GOOD THINGS.
>
> PS. 104:24-28, RSV.

[*Christ of the generous hands, let me not close my hands against anyone today, for I want to accomplish the work You have given me to do.*]

*M. Dupuytren, *Lecons Orales de Clinique Chirugicale.* See J. T. Hueston, *Dupuytren's Contracture* (Edinburgh: E. and S. Livingstone Ltd., 1963).

THE HELPING HAND

T he medical writings of the Greek physician Galen (A.D. 130-200) dominated medicine for 1,400 years. Before becoming court physician to Marcus Aurelius, he served as doctor for the gladiators in his home city of Pergamum. Although dissection of dead bodies was taboo in his society, Galen learned much from examining the wounds of the fighters in the arena and from dissection of animals. He wrote voluminously about a variety of medical procedures, producing some 500 treatises. His philosophical manuscript *On the Usefulness of the Parts of the Body* alone fills some 700 printed pages. In it he eulogizes the wonder of the human hand: "Thus man is the most intelligent of the animals and so, also, hands are the instruments most suitable for an intelligent animal. . . . [They] are an instrument, as the lyre is the instrument of the musician. . . . Every soul has through its very essence certain faculties." And without such an implement as the hand, a person cannot accomplish what "nature disposed [him or her] to accomplish."*

LET THY HAND BE READY TO HELP ME, FOR I HAVE CHOSEN THY PRECEPTS.

PS. 119:173, RSV.

Greek philosophy aside, however, we have only to look at our own hands to realize the marvel of their structure, their versatility and skill, and the fineness of their control. They surpass animal paws in every respect— even the nimble fingers of monkeys. No wonder we so frequently say, "Lend me a hand, will you?" The hand is forever both the physical and symbolic instrument of helping.

In his poetic portrait of old age, the wise man touchingly describes the plight of the elderly when "the keepers of the house tremble" (Eccl. 12:3, NIV). The loss of the use of a hand, however, is utterly shattering. The habits of the whole body, the timing of tasks, the necessary compensations to make up for the missing hand—all alter one's life forever.

One of the believer's most reassuring promises is the knowledge that God's hand is always outstretched to help. Although He must correct and sometimes destroy, He far more frequently reaches out to give and to heal. Above all, He is ready to *help*—whatever the circumstances from which we call to Him.

[*Loving Friend, I will need Your help today. And when I ask "Would You give me a hand with this problem, Lord?" I know that You will hear.*]

*Cited in Daniel J. Boorstin, *The Discoverers* (New York, 1983), p. 346.

THE BUSY HAND

A striking little story is told about a shattered German village at the end of World War II.* Instead of asking the American occupation forces quartered there to provide food, farm equipment, or money, the townspeople requested help in restoring a statue. For many years the lovely piece of artwork, their most precious possession, had stood in the town square. Now the last battle had raged through and left the statue in a rubble of broken pieces.

WHATEVER YOUR HAND FINDS TO DO, DO IT WITH YOUR MIGHT.
ECCL. 9:10, RSV.

Restoration proved to be meticulously painstaking and difficult. Finally, the figure was put together again—except for two missing parts. The soldiers had been unable to find or replace them. Nonetheless, the town officials covered the incomplete statue with a silk drape and set the date for the unveiling. When the mayor of the town pulled-the cord and the drape fell away from the statue, people stared. The figure of Christ had been beautifully restored—but He had no hands. At the feet of the figure, the soldiers had placed a sign: "I have no hands. Won't you please lend Me yours?"

During the time of His ministry on earth, no hands were busier than those of Jesus. His were the tanned, sinewy hands of the carpenter, and with them He elevated manual work to the level of a holy act.

His, also, were *clean* hands, unstained by betrayal or bribes. *Friendly* hands upon the head of a child. *Healing* hands reaching out to despairing sufferers. *Guiding* hands to rescue impulsive Peter from drowning. *Strong* hands to lift up those who have fallen. *Beckoning* hands inviting us to peace and rest. And in the end, *sacrificial* hands nailed to a cross.

For the present He has returned to His kingdom—but *we* are still here. Our hands are the ones He wishes to use in service until He returns. True, He can call in 10,000 angels, but His basic design for His world is that we shall busy ourselves doing His work here. Because working creatively with our hands is marvelously therapeutic for body, mind, and spirit, we should be grateful for the assignment.

[*Set before me clearly today, Lord, the tasks You would have me do. I cheerfully dedicate my hands to do Your work.*]

*Adapted from a story by Tony Weitzel, Chicago *Daily News*.

THE HEALING HAND

Blind and deaf from birth, Helen Keller once wrote in her diary: "My dog was rolling in the grass. I wanted to catch a picture of him in my fingers, and I touched him lightly. Lo, his fat body revolved, stiffened, and solidified into an upright position. He pressed close to me as if to crowd himself into my hand. He loved it with his tail, his paw, his tongue. If he could speak, I believe he would say that with me, paradise is attained by touch."

REACH OUT YOUR HAND TO HEAL . . . THROUGH THE NAME OF . . . JESUS.
ACTS 4:30, TEV.

A foremost hand surgeon, orthopedist Virchel Wood, M.D., has given much thought to the health-enhancing effects of touch. He describes four ways hands influence us: 1. The hand of learning enables us to express our feelings and construct our civilizations. 2. The deformed or lost (amputated) hand produces severe emotional problems far beyond physical limitations. 3. The hand of rejection ranges from an obscene gesture to a self-inflicted disability to escape responsibility. 4. While God's hand disciplines, it also preserves. "I have written your name on the palms of my hands" (Isa. 49:16, TEV). How then could He ever forget us?

Current legal threats, combined with our Puritan heritage, suggest (wrongly) that all bodily contact is either sensual or combative. Of course, it's a fine line between sex-linked touching and the gesture of friendship, between slap-on-the-back horseplay and the warm I-really-care-for-you embrace. Consequently, our illiteracy in the art of touching has caused generations of people to suffer from "skin hunger." Remember, a handshake can mend a quarrel. A hug can relieve stress. An arm around the shoulder conveys concern.

Extensive research has shown that a loving touch has more far-reaching results than we ever suspect. It holds true in both animals and people. University tests have shown that mental ability develops as the ability to use the hands increases. Touch magically dissolves emotional barriers—those huge walls we build around ourselves. From birth to death we need touching, for it helps us grow both physically and mentally. Indeed, touch is the first sense we develop, even before birth.

Having programmed us for touching, Jesus demonstrated throughout His ministry the way it works—that simple touch of compassion and healing.

I will touch at least one person today, Lord. Let Your love and power flow from You through me to them.

THE RIGHT AND LEFT HANDS

For centuries the 10 percent of the population who are left-handed have endured powerful prejudices against them. The ominous word *sinister* comes from the Latin for "left." Our word "left" derives from the Anglo-Saxon *lyft,* meaning "weak and useless." For generations, schoolteachers dealing with "southpaw" students considered it their moral duty to change them over. One of them, Benjamin Franklin, wrote: "More than once I have been beaten for being awkward and wanting a graceful manner." And he was not alone. Other lefties can testify to the humiliation and mockery they endured as they sat at their desks, left hands tied behind them, struggling, in tears and despair, to write righthanded at the old wooden desks. Even today, tools, clothes, cars—everything—are planned for the practical convenience of a right-handed world.

Meanwhile, modern research has uncovered much information about the right and left sides of the brain, wired as they are to opposite sides of the body. Lefties seem to be more than average subject to depression, alcoholism, and autoimmune diseases. On the upside, they can be highly intelligent and creative. Because left-handedness is, to some degree, hereditary, the tribe of Benjamin once produced 700 left-handed warriors, each one of whom could "sling a stone at a hair, and not miss" (Judges 20:16, RSV).

Unfortunately, the ancient holy books, including the Bible, all use this divisive symbolism. God's left hand is not the place to be on judgment day. If Jesus *had* accepted James and John, the fiery sons of Zebedee, to sit at His right and left side in His kingdom, He would still have had to deal with trouble. Which one would get the right side—and why? Their mother apparently didn't see as far ahead as that.

This prejudicial religious symbolism notwithstanding, there is good news. Scientists have begun to recommend that we all practice using *both* hands, suggesting that we are equipped to become ambidextrous. To be sure, Christ is—and we need to be also.

THE RIGHT HAND OF THE LORD DOES VALIANTLY, THE RIGHT HAND OF THE LORD IS EXALTED.
PS. 118:15, RSV.

[THEREFORE] HE WILL PLACE THE SHEEP AT HIS RIGHT HAND, BUT THE GOATS AT THE LEFT.
MATT. 25:33, RSV.

[*Christ, in You there is neither east nor west, left nor right. I come to You, for You are reaching for me with both hands.*]

48 ✳ BIOLOGY

THE FINGER OF GOD

On the ceiling of the Sistine Chapel in Rome, Michelangelo depicted the beginning of time and the fall of humanity. In the painting he portrayed the creation of the first man and woman. At the left Adam languidly reaches his left arm out toward Jehovah, index finger extended. On the right, God keeps Eve tucked under His arm while He brings Adam out from the anesthetic that He applied for the rib surgery—that first bone-transplant operation. With Eve watching alertly, God extends His right hand toward Adam. Their two fingers almost touch, but not quite. God's hand is so vigorously alive, and Adam's is so limp. We almost expect to see the spark of life leap from the Creator to His creature in this electrifying moment. Here, indeed, is a portrayal of God's *finger of power*.

> IF I DRIVE OUT DEMONS BY THE FINGER OF GOD, THEN THE KINGDOM OF GOD HAS COME TO YOU.
>
> LUKE 11:20, NIV.

The recording finger of God is also significant. Moses saw it first atop Mount Sinai. After God spoke the Ten Commandments amid thunder and lightning, He called Moses to return to the mountain and receive the written record. "I will give you the tables of stone, with the law . . . which I have written for [Israel's] instruction" (Ex. 24:12, RSV). The same finger appeared on the walls of Belshazzar's palace, pronouncing the doom of Babylon (Dan. 5:24-28). Then Jesus Himself stopped a quarrelsome party of hypocrites by publicly revealing some of their sins: "Jesus bent down and started to write on the ground with his finger" (John 8:6, NIV).

The *finger of faith* provides infinite comfort. The poor woman, whose physicians had given up on her, came to Jesus for healing—He had the power! Reluctant to step forward, and undoubtedly embarrassed by the nature of her illness, she crept up on Him, just touching the hem of His robe. Jesus publicized her touch because He wanted to use the occasion to define the powerful effect of the faith touch.

The recording finger instructs, the finger of power provides, but the finger of faith reaches up to God. Just a touch—that will do it. One day we shall be able to reach out to Jesus with *both hands*. Meanwhile, the light touch of a single finger will see us through.

[*Father, I would like to hold my faith firmly in my hands. But I am often weak. Sometimes I can reach out with just a finger touch. And You understand.*]

THE BLINDFOLDED EYES

Blind people astonish us with their keen perception of their surroundings. They pick up clues like master detectives. Then we have the necessary clinical blindfolding. Disease or surgery often dictate that the eyes receive complete rest—shielded from the smallest ray of light—so that they can heal. But the "blinding" of Jesus involved something else.

> THEY ALSO BLIND-FOLDED HIM AND ASKED HIM, "PROPHESY! WHO WAS IT THAT STRUCK YOU?"
>
> LUKE 22:64, RSV.

To understand the incident, we need to look at the games we played as children (and later). We blindfolded one another—for blindman's buff, pin the tail on the donkey, post office, and so forth. It seems *fun* to watch people forced into doing silly, embarrassing things. True, it is just a game, but the motivations behind it tell us more than we want to know about ourselves.

We stand amazed at the intoxication, the vulgarity, and the triviality of the mob at the trial of Jesus. Their sense of humor comes through as incredibly coarse and childish. They played an absolutely appalling game. "The mob that had pushed itself into the courtroom surged forward and surrounded Jesus. Some spit in His face, others slapped Him, still others shoved Him, hoping to knock Him down" (Matt. 26:67, Clear Word).

While all of this was going on, Peter remained in the courtyard. Tough big fisherman that he was, he too was blindfolded—spiritually. He was so incapable of recognizing his own weakness that he denied Jesus with cursing and swearing. There are so many ways to be blind. Deprivation of physical light is but a small matter compared to the blindness of that ranting, raging mob.

The incident of the blindfold was but a fleeting experience for Christ. In His divinity He could have probed every circumstance of the crowd's spiritual condition. They were an open book to Him. The rag around His head meant nothing. What sorrow He must have felt for His persecutors as they made Him the center of their hatred and sick sense of humor. He was only days away from returning to His Father in heaven. They, on the other hand, were at the same moment sealing the fate of themselves and their nation forever.

[*You, Jesus, who wore the blindfold of mockery for me, lead me forward today. Give me clear insight, or let me wait in the dark for the answer—if that is best for me.*]

THE SEARCHING EYE

Television has now brought current events into our living rooms and dumped everything right into our laps. We are seeing some new things—among them the secret service men. From the president down to the most despicable gangster—all persons of prominence require protection. Public persons have to have their bodyguards as close as their skins—usually half a dozen or more. Often they are husky, intimidating types whom you would not care to tangle with on a dark night. They dress, however, to match the subject of their concern—jogging shorts to go out with the president in the morning, or Italian suits to accompany a beleaguered lawyer in and out of the courthouse.

THE EYES OF THE LORD RUN TO AND FRO THROUGH-OUT THE WHOLE EARTH, TO SHOW HIMSELF STRONG ON BEHALF OF THOSE WHOSE HEART IS LOYAL TO HIM.

2 CHRON. 16:9, NKJV.

One thing will always be the same. Watch their eyes. Like a lizard's, they flick from point to point. Constantly alert, their gaze records every detail in the landscape. Sometimes, even on dark days, they wear sunglasses to disguise what they are doing. But it's all the same—their eyes are constantly roving to spot trouble before it happens.

When we leave home on a trip, we notify neighbors and friends. "Keep an eye on things for me," we say. Possibly we also install an alarm system that in a crisis will alert the police, the doctor, and the fire chief. Truly, we *want* someone watching out for us.

God's eyes "run to and fro in the earth" for the same reason that the "shifty-eyed" secret service personnel crowd around public officials. The Lord, however, never rests from duty. He is constantly aware of all that has passed, all that is now happening, and all that is to come. On the basis of His knowledge He makes His decisions regarding the welfare of His people. No accidents will suddenly overtake them. Whatever happens will be within the range of His plan—no matter how it looks from our mortal perspective.

At the same time, He invites us to bring our anxieties to Him, for "the eyes of the Lord are on the righteous and his ears are attentive to their cry" (Ps. 34:15, NIV).

[*Lord, keep Your protective eye on me always. Let me never try to hide from Your searching gaze.*]

VICTORIOUS FEET

Feet always interest me—probably because my own have proved to be somewhat inadequate, handicapped by two surgeries. For that reason, I watch ballet and folk dancers with the keenest interest. What would it be to have feet like *that*? I see students on campus loping across the green and taking staircases three steps at a time. Some run marathons. Others jog for hours in the hills. Soldiers drill for long periods on the parade ground. They all have functional feet.

> HIS FEET [WERE] LIKE PILLARS OF FIRE. . . . AND HE SET HIS RIGHT FOOT ON THE SEA AND HIS LEFT FOOT ON THE LAND.
>
> REV. 10:1, 2, NKJV.

John the revelator's vision of our triumphant God portrays Him with His fiery feet planted firmly on both the sea and the land. He thus claims the entire earth. The picture is a magnificent one. But notice still one more thing: feet, standing or walking, leave footprints. Most of us, however, have trouble reading such natural messages—unless, perhaps, it's a fossilized print in stone.

I have always respected and admired those who live so close to the outdoors that they can read signs in the sky, in the trees, and in the fabric of the earth itself. Aboriginal trackers in Australia, Native Americans in forests and deserts, and many others as well have skills that utterly baffle technocrats and urban dwellers like most of us. Given the slimmest of evidence, these remarkable people can pretty well tell us who passed our way, when they did it, and how fast they were going. And whether or not they stopped for any reason. They can look at a snake's trail and tell you which direction the reptile was traveling.

On land God's footprints are often visible. We get concrete evidence of His leading. His path, however, often takes us through the turbulence of the sea, and *there* we can see no footprints. "Your path led through the sea, your way through the mighty waters, though your footprints were not seen" (Ps. 77:19, NIV). At this point faith must take over. No other kind of eyesight will suffice. God's victorious feet have gone ahead of us, but we may not see the actual footprints until we emerge on the eternal shore of heaven itself.

[*My God, You have intervened in my life in strong, visible ways that I can sometimes see. But often the floods of sorrow and fear have hidden Your footprints from me. I pray, therefore, for the clear vision of faith.*]

THE FOOTSTOOL OF GOD

HEAVEN IS MY THRONE, AND EARTH IS MY FOOT-STOOL.

ISA. 66:1, NKJV.

The Kek Lok Si pagoda ("Temple of Paradise") is one of the most spectacular showpieces of the lovely island city of Penang, Malaysia. An artistic textbook of Buddhism, the seven-story Pagoda of a Million Buddhas, the temple, and the monastery buildings cover 30 hillside acres. In the Hall of the Devas you see four enormous bronze images representing the guardians of the east, west, north, and south. Each has his huge, brass-shod feet planted firmly on the necks of his victims. It is a vigorous and victorious stance. The sinners the guardians have destroyed are weeping harlots, reckless gamblers, emaciated opium smokers, black-faced murderers, and the like. The placement of the feet indicates more than just the vanquishing of enemies. "Sitting at the feet" and even "kissing the feet" are traditional acts of submission and humility.

Managing one's feet can be a delicate matter. Upon entering the Temple of the Emerald Buddha in Bangkok, Thailand, you not only remove your shoes, but once inside the shrine, you must take great care to be sure that you do not point your toes toward the gilded image. Temple guards line the walls to be sure that such irreverence does not occur.

The footstool adds another powerful symbol. At one time or another, many of us have had to spend some time with our feet elevated. Getting our feet higher than our heads promotes better circulation to the heart, helps prevent thrombosis of the veins, and reduces swelling. Millenniums ago people invented footstools to make sitting more comfortable. (Many a servant has placed footstools at convenient locations for his aristocratic, gout-ridden master.)

When God announces that heaven is His throne and the earth His footstool, He appears not as a vindictive warrior, nor does He ask people to grovel at His feet. The throne and the footstool go together in a unique way and give a new meaning to the positioning of the feet. They are connected by means of the King's own person. Thus the footstool does two things. First, it is the focal point at which we approach the throne. And second, God's earth gives Him comfort and service.

[*Great Jehovah, even as Your natural world gives You pleasure, so would I cheerfully give You my service this day.*]

THE VOICE OF GOD

In my opinion, just about the most thrilling passages of poetry in the Bible appear in Psalm 29. The psalm falls into three distinct parts. First, David invites angels and human beings alike to worship the glorious Master of the tempest (verses 1, 2). In conclusion comes a blessing from the One who sits above the tumult and reigns in majestic peace (verses 10, 11). In between we hear (and see) the glorious "song of the seven thunders" (verses 3-9).

> THE VOICE OF THE LORD IS POWER. THE VOICE OF THE LORD IS MAJESTY.
>
> PS. 29:4, NEB.

Imagine the setting. David stands in a grove of cedar trees on Mount Hermon. To his right lies the Mediterranean, to his left he sees the Wilderness of Kadesh stretching away to the east. The thunder ("the voice of the Lord") begins out over the sea in roiling gray storm clouds. Sweeping landward, the tempest tears into the trees. "The oaks . . . whirl" and the storm "strips the forests bare" (verse 9, RSV). As "the voice of the Lord . . . breaks the cedars of Lebanon," the whole mountain skips "like a calf" (verses 5, 6, RSV). A veritable earthquake! Then the Lord repeatedly "flashes forth flames of fire" (verse 7, RSV). Thunder and lightning roar and burn simultaneously in different parts of the sky. Finally the storm sweeps out into the desert.

Some people don't care for this kind of weather. Others of us, like David, rather enjoy a thunderstorm—seen from a reasonably safe viewpoint, of course. And again like David, we spontaneously cry, "Glory!" (verse 9, RSV).

This magnificent hymn describing God's natural voice of command is not all. He also speaks to us in at least four other ways:

1. **The announcement:** "A voice came out of the cloud, saying, 'This is My beloved Son. Hear Him!'" (Mark 9:7, NKJV).

2. **The invitation:** "Incline your ear, and come to me; hear, that your soul may live" (Isa. 55:3, RSV).

3. **The life word:** "The dead shall hear the voice of the Son of God, all who hear shall come to life" (John 5:25, NEB).

4. **The whisper:** "But the lord was not in the fire; and after the fire a still small voice" (1 Kings 19:12, RSV).

The voice of God addresses us in so many ways. By surprising us, as He does, He keeps us listening.

> *Keep me alert and sensitive, Lord. Not only must I see You in Your creation and in the people around me; I want to identify Your voice coming from whatever source You choose.*

THE LION TRIUMPHANT

C. S. Lewis wrote a fascinating seven-part allegory of the spiritual life. In *The Chronicles of Narnia* he represents the character of Christ by a glorious, golden-maned lion named Aslan. All of the inhabitants of the forest marvel at the royal strength and the peaceful dignity that make him "good and terrible at the same time."

Beaver describes the magnificent creature to Susan, whom he calls Daughter of Eve. " 'Aslan is a lion—*the* Lion, the great Lion.'

" 'Ooh!' said Susan, 'I'd thought he was a man. Is he—quite safe? I shall feel rather nervous about meeting a lion.' . . .

" 'Safe?' said Mr. Beaver. . . . 'Who said anything about safe? 'Course he isn't safe. But he's good. He's the King, I tell you.' "*

Appearing repeatedly in ancient writings, the lion comes with all the trappings of royalty. The reliefs on the walls of Ashurbanipal's palace at Nineveh (650 B.C.) indicate that lion hunting was a favorite pastime of the Assyrian kings. Since only royalty could be worthy of royalty, the king's staff arranged the lion hunt so the king himself would have the personal honor of killing the lion.

The lion has always been a favorite in the heraldry of Europe. Those medieval noblemen sensed the grandeur and boldness, the power and strength, of the "king of beasts." In heraldry we see the figure of the lion *rampant* (erect, standing on one foot), lion *couchant* (resting, with head raised), lion *dormant* (head resting on forepaws), or lion *gardant* (facing the observer). Often the heraldic lion also wears a crown.

When you see the animal in a zoo—often with a broken spirit and moth-eaten hide—the lion may not resemble a king. But beware. In the wild the male still strikes a regal pose while surveying the grasslands.

In this context, then, we see Jesus acclaimed as the "lion of Judah," with all deference and honor due Him. The believer has the splendid, awesome experience of being safely in His presence, for, as Mr. Beaver said, He is "good." Nonetheless, He is still a ruler who will never be conquered.

> "DO NOT WEEP! SEE, THE LION OF THE TRIBE OF JUDAH . . . HAS TRIUMPHED."
>
> REV. 5:5, NIV.

[*The lionlike characteristics of Jehovah! Worshiping in awe and honoring with love—we celebrate Your goodness.*]

---

*Dorothy Minchin-Comm, "Beware of God," *Adventist Review* (Feb. 19, 1987), p. 23.

THE DEVOURING LION

Nowadays we hear little about the devouring-lion aspect of God. A Calvinistic idea, it nevertheless still exists.

Christians have evolved two popular viewpoints on God—both of them partly wrong. The first is a comfortable and relaxing notion that God is a kind of easygoing, good-natured old gentleman who helps one out of tight spots. He benevolently gives out presents, overlooking our shortcomings. God wouldn't for the world see anyone suffer eternal death. The second concept sees Him as an exacting, vindictive judge who has announced that He hates sin. Becoming enraged, he probes every detail in the little lives of His miserable creatures, and then punishes them for every misdeed. It takes a lifetime to understand this paradox fully.

SO I WILL COME UPON THEM LIKE A LION. . . . LIKE A LION I WILL DEVOUR THEM.

HOSEA 13:7, 8, NIV.

The prophet Hosea graphically depicts the dangerous side of the divine character in the images of three wild beasts: the lion, the leopard, and the bear.

Lions were common in Palestine, and the Old Testament mentions them more than 150 times. Records of their fierce predatory habits indicate that although they were a threat to livestock, a human-eating lion was rather exceptional. The Romans, however, imported lions by the hundreds for the brutal purposes of their games in the amphitheaters.

Several of the lion's habits point up the work of God as a "devouring lion." First, David, who had some personal experience with lions in the sheep pastures, said that the wicked man "lurks in secret like a lion in his covert" (Ps. 10:9, RSV). Also, a lion will hunt until it finds food. In leonine terms Jeremiah warned unrepentant Israel of the invader who would carry them into exile: "A lion has gone up from his thicket, a destroyer of nations has set out; he has gone forth from his place to make your land a waste" (Jer. 4:7, RSV). Finally, the lion's voice alone terrorizes. Jeremiah lamented: "My heritage has become to me like a lion in the forest, she has lifted up her voice against me; therefore I hate her" (Jer. 12:8, RSV).

All of these features also apply to Jehovah. While He may not appear to be present, He is always there nonetheless. He will never fail to accomplish His purpose. Although He is patient, when we hear His voice on judgment day, there will be no questions left to ask.

[*I would not worship You, my God, out of fear, for I know You to be love. Yet only in Your role as judge and destroyer will You finally balance the conflict between good and evil.*]

THE LEOPARD

The glamorous cousin of the lion is the leopard. His sleek body speaks to all of the mysteries we sense when we look at the big cats. With their proud independence and inscrutable gaze, all cats have about them a mystique that humans cannot fathom. No wonder the Egyptians worshiped them!

LIKE A LEOPARD I WILL LURK BY THE PATH.

HOSEA 13:7, NIV.

The leopard shares all of the ferocity and aggressive aspects of the lion, but with one notable addition. Although the leopard is an agile climber, it is often pictured in the crotch of a tree, draped over the branches. Moreover, he can strike like lightning, dropping out of the tree on top of an unsuspecting deer. On the short dash he can outrun most of his prey.

The leopard's glossy coat of pale tan decorated with irregular broken circles of black spots gave rise to the proverb: "Can the Ethiopian change his skin or the leopard his spots?" (Jer. 13:23, RSV). One might wonder if the case of the panther (black leopard) could be a sample of "no spots." Even in its smooth dark hair, however, still darker spots will show through.

Some biblical leopard references no doubt refer to the African cheetah, or hunting leopard, that can clock in at 70 mph. Habakkuk's statement that the Chaldeans' horses "are swifter than leopards" takes some poetic privilege, probably exaggerating the horses' actual abilities (Hab. 1:8, RSV). The hunting leopard has for centuries been domesticated and trained to wear a collar like a dog. A cheetah sitting sedately beside the throne or lying meekly by a couch was an exotic furnishing prized in the home of any king or Roman patrician.

Christ in judgment—this is His leopardlike task. He has pleaded and waited. But His day of reckoning *will* come:

"Day of judgment, day of wonders!
Hark the trumpet's awful sound,
Louder than a thousand thunders,
Shakes the vast creation round!"
—John Newton

Even though the divine summons will confound the unready, it will still show that God's administration of His universe is *right!* Perhaps in the final decisiveness and swiftness of God's justice we will see not only the power of the leopard but even some of its awesome beauty as well.

[*Heavenly Judge, reveal to me today the things in my life that I must set in order. Teach me to love Your law.*]

THE BEAR

Hosea's third metaphor of judgment describes the bear. Bears are a prime attraction of national parks. Once when showing some Australian visitors through Canada's Rocky Mountain parks, I feared that the highway system and protective fencing had driven all of the bears out of sight. Mary, however, determined to stake her life upon seeing a bear. Finally, after we'd driven for many miles, we topped a rise and saw down in the dip a half dozen cars, their occupants standing expectantly on the roadside. "Animals at last!" There, not 50 feet away, stood a brown bear, just turning her broad rump toward the spectators and ambling into the brush, her cub at her heels.

LIKE A BEAR ROBBED OF HER CUBS, I WILL ATTACK THEM AND RIP THEM OPEN.

HOSEA 13:8, NIV.

The park rangers' warnings notwithstanding, we are fascinated with live bears. After all, we all grew up with our teddy bears, didn't we? That charming warm fuzziness vanishes before the bear's huge size, murderous claws, and short temper. One blow of a forepaw can brain any victim. The park rangers are right. Don't try anything with the creatures. Unfortunately, their inventiveness in finding food has always brought bears too easily into contact with people—to mutual disadvantage. The bears will rob and possibly maul the people. The people will destroy the bears for their aggressiveness.

The allusion to a she bear robbed of her cubs appears three times in the Old Testament (2 Sam. 17:8; Prov. 17:12; Hosea 13:8). At birth a cub weighs about 10 ounces and requires care for two or three years—ample time for strong bonding. Stealing cubs to train as performing bears began as early as 400 B.C. No wonder that the anger of a deprived mother became proverbial. A bear may lie in wait, but, being partly herbivorous, it is unlikely to eat its prey. The killing, then, is for defense.

Speaking of the inexorable certainty of the day of the Lord, Amos made a colorful comparison:

"Woe to you who long for the day of the Lord! . . .
That day will be darkness, not light.
It will be as though a man fled from a lion only to meet a bear"
(Amos 5:18, 19, NIV).

The "wrath of God" culminates in judgment day. No one can escape it.

[*Jehovah, You have imaged Yourself in wild animals to remind us that You do demand spiritual discipline. Let me not lull myself into thinking that anything goes with You.*]

THE SERPENT

Snakes have a peculiar effect on us, arousing al-most universal fear and loathing. Our uneasy feelings hark back to that terrible time in Eden when Satan chose the snake as his disguise.

Without ever using the loathsome word "snake," Emily Dickinson describes a "narrow fellow in the grass."* We must admire its graceful movements as it divides the grass "as with a comb," rising like "a whip-lash" in the sun. While the snake fascinates us, it evokes a nervous, self-conscious smile as we instinc-tively retreat, for its "notice sudden is."

In Christian tradition the serpent has come to rep-resent undiluted evil, and our response to them reveals a strange truth.

> **AS MOSES LIFTED UP THE SER-PENT IN THE WILDER-NESS, EVEN SO MUST THE SON OF MAN BE LIFTED UP.**
>
> JOHN 3:14, NKJV.

When Moses fashioned the bronze serpent in the wilderness, two great tragedies had just occurred. Distracted by the Israelites' complaining, he had struck the rock to obtain water, and God had denied him entry into the Promised Land. Moreover, his brother, Aaron, had just died and been buried. The timing was simply *too* bad.

So when the Hebrews started murmuring again, God allowed the poi-sonous desert vipers to swarm into the camp and kill them. The venom of this particular snake, however, did not act immediately. It could take up to four days for the massive and fatal internal hemorrhaging to complete its deadly work. During that time Moses was able to mold the bronze serpent and get the message out to the tens of thousands of people that they should come, look, and live (Num. 21:4-9).

But one question remains: How could the symbol of death and evil become a portrait of the living Christ? For one thing, the criticizing, complaining children of Israel needed a reality check. The serpent of pride and incorrigible selfishness had bitten them—indeed, years of internal spiritual bleeding had eaten away at them. Now the denial had to stop. Only in facing the reality of their sin, in re-penting and in reaching out in faith, could they be saved. Just as the harassed Moses created the instrument of their salvation, likewise the often-rejected Christ would provide us with healing and eternal life by going to the cross.

> [*My God, give me strength to face up to what stands between You and me. In faith I too must look and live.*]

---

*Emily Dickinson, "A Narrow Fellow in the Grass," in *Emily Dickinson* (New York: Dell Pub. Co., 1960), p. 96.

THE DEER

Through the centuries the Song of Solomon has had various interpretations, along with arguments as to why it should or should not be included in Scripture. A delightful collection of wedding poems notwithstanding, tradition has read the story as the Shulamite maid being the church (and/or the individual believer) and her lover as Christ.

> MY LOVER . . . [IS] LIKE A GAZELLE OR LIKE A YOUNG STAG ON THE RUGGED HILLS.
>
> S. OF SOL. 2:17, NIV.

The Uinta Mountains of Utah are a choice place for deer watching. There trains of white clouds hang in the intense blue sky while the sun slides down toward the horizon, shading the hills in soft pastel colors. Now's the time to drive out on the country trails. Perhaps you'll see a doe with two fawns leaping over the rocks. Or a small herd standing in the low scrub just staring at you. Or perhaps nothing at all. You know hundreds of them huddle in the cedar and pine clumps watching you, but they won't let you spot them. Stag hunting has been a royal sport from ancient times.

In the Bible several animals, large and small, come under the general classification of "deer"—gazelle, hart, hind, antelope, the red deer, the fallow deer, and the roe deer. Not only were deer acceptable meat to the Israelites, they have been an integral part of the food chain worldwide.

At the same time, no other animal—other than the lamb—evokes more of the gentleness and sweetness inherent in the animal creation. A young stag on alert in the forest, a spotted fawn hiding in the shade waiting for its mother—they depict something special.

"Maker of earth and sea and sky,
   Creation's sovereign Lord and King,
Who hung the starry worlds on high,
   And formed alike the sparrow's wing;
Bless the dumb creatures of Thy care,
   And listen to their voiceless prayer."

Thus the allegorical view of Solomon's Song makes some significant statements about Jesus when the beloved sings, "My lover is like a gazelle" (S. of Sol. 2:9, NIV). Deer are beautiful and clean, watchful and agile, graceful and swift. And when they sacrifice their lives for food, they sustain and nourish the hungry.

[*Dear Guardian of all flocks and herds, make "my feet like hinds' feet, and set me secure on the heights" (Ps. 18:33, RSV).*]

THE HORN

Have you wondered at Thanksgiving time where the symbol of the horn of plenty, overflowing with fruit and flowers, comes from? Or why folklore retains curious stories about the medicinal uses of the horn of the rhinoceros and the powers of the mythic unicorn?

The horn was a familiar metaphor in Bible times. Dependent on their cattle for wealth, ancient peoples reverenced their bulls. Both Egypt and the people of Canaan worshiped bulls. (Aaron's disastrous creation of the golden calf in the wilderness shows how near the problem lay in Israel's heart.) Mosaic law gave specific instruction for the use of bulls in religious rites. We can scarcely imagine the extent of those enormous sacrifices. The priests at the inauguration of Solomon as king slaughtered 1,000 bulls, 1,000 rams, and 1,000 lambs. Afterward the people sat down to eat and drink "before the Lord with great gladness on that day" (1 Chron. 29:22, NKJV).

The fighting strength of all horned animals lies in their horns. Even a superficial knowledge of bullfighting clarifies this point. Hence, warriors traditionally adorned their helmets with horns—the horn being a common metaphor for fierce power. Sometimes the horn indicated personal success: "I lift my head high, like a wild ox tossing its horn" (Ps. 92:10, NEB). Or national power: "The he-goat is the kingdom of the Greeks and the great horn on his forehead is the first king" (Dan. 8:21, NEB). David praised God's divine power in a series of strong metaphors: my strength, my rock, my fortress and deliverer, my shield. The list culminates most grandly with the "horn of my salvation" (Ps. 18:2). He could not have said more. Rabbinic writers used horn imagery to denote Israel's greatest points of strength, including Abraham, Isaac, Moses, the law, the priesthood, the Temple, and so forth.

It remained, however, for Luke's Gospel to identify the greatest horn of all. Zacharias, the father of John the Baptist, sang of Jesus: God "has raised up a horn of salvation for us in the house of His servant David" (Luke 1:69, NKJV). The Saviour took to Himself the massive power, the elemental strength, and the invincibility of the horn. He *fights for us.*

HE HAS RAISED UP A HORN OF SALVATION FOR US IN THE HOUSE OF HIS SERVANT DAVID.

LUKE 1:69, NIV.

[*Lord, alone I cannot protect myself. I can only turn my battles over to the One who can win them for me.*]

THE LAMB OF GOD

Human beings have seen some animals as divine, and men and women have worshiped them for thousands of years. At the other extreme people have hunted and cruelly slaughtered others. Out of these conflicting perspectives derive the animals who have become symbols. They are basic to the visualizing of the Christian faith and appear and reappear in the arts of the church. No symbolic animal, however, came closer to the hearts of Israel than the sheep. The lamb recalls to us those first bleak days after the sin of Adam and Eve, the days when Abel became the first shepherd and provider of sacrificial lambs—until he himself became a sacrifice to his own faithfulness. Then Isaac inquired of his father, Abraham, atop Mount Moriah, "Where is the lamb for a burnt offering?" (Gen. 22:7, NKJV).

"LOOK," HE SAID, "THERE IS THE LAMB OF GOD; IT IS HE WHO TAKES AWAY THE SIN OF THE WORLD."

JOHN 1:29, NEB.

When John the Baptist announced Jesus as the Lamb of God (John 1:29), he indicated that the Person to whom all of the centuries of sacrifice had pointed had at last arrived. Hence, the lamb often appears in paintings of Jesus, John the Baptist, and some of the Christian martyrs. In fact, the associations of gentle purity were so strong that by the eighteenth century aristocrats were even having themselves portrayed as shepherds and shepherdesses surrounded by lambs.

In the voice of a child, the English poet William Blake (1757-1827) captures the wonder and mystery of Christ—not just as the Good Shepherd, but as the Lamb itself:

The symbol of the Lamb runs full cycle through Scripture, moving always from the material to the spiritual. Beginning in the rocky pastures of Palestine, it ends up portraying one of the deepest truths of the Christian faith. From the watering places of the Judean desert, it passed into the most passionate art the Christian church has produced. An understanding of sheep, lambs, and their shepherds opens up to us a new understanding of the total ministry of Jesus.

> *My Lord, I would think upon Jesus as the Lamb of God.*
> *I would learn life lessons from Him who likened Himself*
> *to such a commonplace and dependent member of His creation.*

THE LAMB WITHOUT BLEMISH

I once heard an insightful physician compare cancer and its growth patterns to the way sin works upon our lives. Then he said, "In all of our research the only animals we have found to be completely free of cancer are sheep and goats. Isn't that interesting—that God chose to call Himself a lamb?" Interesting indeed!

By way of emphasis, Scripture often sets the unblemished lamb against its opposite in nature. While traveling last year, I came across an in-flight magazine that delighted me. The top half of the cover showed a gorgeous golden lion standing on a bed of ferns under jungle trees. But what the pool on the lower half of the page reflected was not a lion, but a lamb. What this Canadian artist, Heather Cooper, was trying to say was that in personalities, we find some lamb in the lion, and vice versa.*

> YOU WERE REDEEMED . . . WITH THE PRECIOUS BLOOD OF CHRIST, A LAMB WITHOUT BLEMISH OR DEFECT.
>
> 1 PETER 1:19, NIV.

But one can read an even deeper meaning into this unusual portrait. Once "across the river" into eternity, we shall find that no hostility exists between the lion and lamb. Indeed, Scripture has often paired the lamb with its enemies (lions, wolves, and serpents) in order to emphasize the new order in the peaceable kingdom of heaven. "'The wolf and the lamb shall feed together. The lion shall eat straw like the ox, and dust shall be the serpent's food. They shall not hurt nor destroy in all My holy mountain,' says the Lord" (Isa. 65:25, NKJV).

Fascinated by this interplay of opposites, I have for years collected pictures of lions and lambs together. Many of my friends know this, and every Christmas I get two or three more cards with new treatments of the idea. One of my favorites shows a lion letting out a huge roar of "Peace!" Between his forepaws lies a lamb, round-eyed and startled at the sudden command.

When you begin to look for this pair, you'll find the theme more common than you ever imagined—common, because the lion and lamb *together* say something that the world is desperate to hear. Together they form such a paradox that its richness of meaning quite overwhelms us. It invites our imagination to travel in many directions.

> *Today I will think upon the perfection of the Lamb of God. It stands in perpetual contrast to the many shapes of evil that surround us—never changed, always pure.*

---

*Hemispheres, April 1994, p. 16.

THE SLAIN LAMB

After the fall of humanity, God had to give animals over to Adam and Eve for food and clothing. Then the sacrificial system called for the slaughter of millions of animals. Still, many love nature so profoundly that they find the death of an innocent animal repulsive. Indeed, in the sacrifice of the lambs, that is exactly what God hoped would occur—that people would find the death and dying so repulsive that they would reject the sin that caused it.

The poet captures a tender moment of contemplation of the sacrificial Lamb of God:

"All in the April evening,
April airs were abroad.
The sheep with their little lambs
Passed me by on the road. . . .
All in the April evening
I thought on the Lamb of God.

"The lambs were weary, and crying
With a weak human cry.
I thought of the Lamb of God
Going meekly to die.

"Up in the blue, blue mountains,
Dewy pastures are sweet,
Rest for the little bodies,
Rest for the little feet.

"But for the Lamb, the Lamb of God
Up on a hilltop green,
Only a cross of shame,
Two stark crosses between.

"All in the April evening,
April airs were abroad.
I saw the sheep with the lambs,
And thought of the Lamb of God."
—Katharine Tynan

THE BOOK OF LIFE [BELONGS] TO THE LAMB THAT WAS SLAIN FROM THE CREATION OF THE WORLD.

REV. 13:8, NIV.

[*Dear God, let me never lose sight of the meaning of the slain lamb. It speaks to me of the horror of sin and the mercy of the sacrifice of Your Son.*]

THE LAMB TRIUMPHANT

Whoever coined the expression "gentle as a lamb" simply didn't have all of the facts. As children in New Zealand, my sister and I were delighted when one of the nearby farmers offered us an orphan lamb. Thus Peter became our special charge, and we fell in love with him immediately. Four-year-old Eileen loved to feed him from his big bottle—even when he bowled her over. We'd find her lying on her back, doggedly holding the bottle with Peter boisterously dragging on it. Although our parents were not amused when he harvested all the spinach out of the garden, we thought he had rendered a fine public service. Then we left the country when Peter was about 9 months old. I like to think that the man we gave him to kept his word and did not send our lamb to the slaughterhouse.

I LOOKED
·AND SAW
A VAST
THRONG,
WHICH NO
ONE COULD
COUNT, . . .
STANDING
IN FRONT
OF THE
THRONE
AND BEFORE
THE LAMB.
REV. 7:9, NEB.

The sacrificial lamb meekly going to slaughter is one thing. But there's nothing more robust than a healthy lamb, so in the dramatic scenes of the book of Revelation, Christ appears in His role as the lamb triumphant. First comes the judgment that separates the sheep from the goats. Then with the glorious scenes of the Second Coming, the earth stands in terror of the wrath of the Lamb as unready people call for the rocks and the mountains to hide them. The angelic chorus breaks into song: "Worthy is the Lamb, who was slain, to receive power and wealth and wisdom and strength and honor and glory and praise!" (Rev. 5:12, NIV). Finally, the action transfers into heaven itself. "And I saw no temple in the city, for its temple is the Lord God the Almighty and the Lamb. And the city has no need of sun or moon to shine upon it, for the glory of God is its light, and its lamp is the Lamb" (Rev. 21:23, RSV). Thus enter in those "who are written in the Lamb's book of life" (Rev. 22:27, RSV).

No wonder church art sometimes portrays the Lamb boldly wearing a crown, carrying a banner on His shoulder, and marching as if to a trumpet call. Here, at last, is an invitation to celebration.

[*Dear God, I believe in the Lamb triumphant. I would follow Him beyond the grave, through the gates of the city, to the throne He shares with You, the Father.*]

THE EAGLE

To motivate my writing students to creativity, I sometimes ask them to describe the creature they would choose to be if they had to cease being human. Usually 60 percent or more of them would like to be birds. And of those, more than half will decide to be eagles. What is the strong attraction we feel to the eagle? Obviously, we admire its beauty, and we marvel at its great size. But above all, we crave its freedom, for it points us to two of Christ's most exalted attributes.

[THE EAGLE] SPREADS ITS WINGS TO CATCH THEM AND CARRIES THEM ON ITS PINIONS.

DEUT. 32:11, NIV.

At least eight kinds of eagles live in Palestine—hence the prevalence of eagle imagery in Scripture. First, the eagle exemplifies God's swift decisiveness. The strong, majestic birds have vicious hooked beaks and long curved talons for tearing their prey. The remains of the eagle's kill may be no more than a couple feathers or a few tufts of fur, for the eagle is awesomely efficient. Its enduring strength is breathtaking. "But they who wait for the Lord shall renew their strength, they shall mount up with wings like eagles, they shall run and not be weary, they shall walk and not faint" (Isa. 40:31, RSV).

Second, the eagle's lightning swift strength is augmented by the power of renewal. Realizing that the bird has an unusually long life span, people came to believe that it molted at certain times. (Nowadays we can distinguish between what is real and what is imagined in eagle lore.) Then by some unknown means, the new feathers brought renewed youth. "Bless the Lord, O my soul," sang the psalmist, "[for He] satisfies you with good as long as you live so that your youth is renewed like the eagle's" (Ps. 103:2-5, RSV).

Jesus, however, does not simply "renew our youth" in a temporary forestalling of age and death. With Him it is not just a matter of new feathers. Instead, He opens up the powerful resources of heaven that will enable us to have *perpetually* renewing life. That provision will carry us all the way out into the most vast and distant expanses of eternity. The eagle's wilderness habitat provides a vivid setting for this promise.

[*Today, my Jesus, I claim the two promises of the eagle* *—strength for my tasks and, at last, eternal life itself.*]

THE NEST

The home, mother's arms, the cradle, the nest—all of these comforts belong to young creatures. Without such nurture they would die. All parents, human and otherwise, however, face the decision as to how long is too long to be at home with the nest. The time comes when the young must move on. The eagle breaks up her sparse nest of sticks in order to evict the fledglings.

[HE IS] LIKE AN EAGLE THAT STIRS UP ITS NEST AND HOVERS OVER ITS YOUNG.

DEUT. 32:11, NIV.

Nonetheless, the eagle is a model parent. Because the birds need a large hunting range, they lay few eggs and rear only one or two nestlings. Bigmouthed and demanding, the babies are so ugly that assuredly only a mother could love them. Yet they are so weak that at first they cannot even raise their bald heads. The mother force-feeds them until they can hold their own.

Scripture pictures God's loving care for His people, together with His dramatic methods of delivering enslaved Israel out of Egypt, through one of the eagle's most curious habits. In stirring up the nest, the mother urges her young to try their wings, to become independent. At the same time she watches to see if they are too weak. Perhaps they do falter. Then in a flash of power and a mighty rush of wings, she rescues them. Many believed that she carried her young back to accessible mountain heights.

Built in high places, the eagle's nest is beyond the reach of inquisitive invaders. One Old Testament prophet described its remoteness thus: "Though you soar aloft like the eagle, though your nest is set among the stars, thence I will bring you down, says the Lord" (Obadiah 4, RSV).

Jesus performs both of the eagle's nesting functions. First, He loves and protects us, nurturing us in our weakness and passing over the ugliness of our characters. He prepares us for heavenly mansions, nests "set among the stars," far beyond human grasp. To accomplish this He must break up the nest, for He does not want His children clinging to bare sticks, imprisoned on earth when they can soar in the sky.

Perhaps today, Lord, You will stir my nest. Maybe I need to mature in some ways I don't yet understand. Give me patience to recognize Your leading in these matters.

BIRD TRAINING

The now rare bald eagle has always been a symbol of courage and power. Known worldwide, it appears on the great seal of the United States and is the trademark for hundreds of commercial products. Its discipline and intelligence has long fascinated us.

Bible writers, however, were less interested in scientific facts than they were in making the magnificent bird an illustration of spiritual truth. Occasionally they alluded to the considerable amount of folklore surrounding the eagle. Among several curious beliefs about eagles was the idea that every 10 years the great bird disappeared directly into the sun. When you consider an eagle on a faraway cliff top, silhouetted against the sky, you will not be surprised at such a notion. Then, like the sun, he supposedly dropped down into the sea and arose again refreshed—again, the embodiment of renewal and hope.

"YOU HAVE SEEN WHAT I DID TO THE EGYPTIANS, AND HOW I BORE YOU ON EAGLES' WINGS AND BROUGHT YOU TO MYSELF."

EX. 19:4, RSV.

Also, the eagle reputedly forced her young to look directly into the sun's face—perhaps as preparation for "homing in." Solomon may have referred to this quaint superstition when he warned against the deception of accumulating great wealth: "When your eyes light upon it, it is gone; for suddenly it takes to itself wings, flying like an eagle toward heaven" (Prov. 23:5, RSV).

The directness of the eagle's flight images God's modes of judgment. "The Lord will bring a nation against you from afar, . . . as swift as an eagle flies" (Deut. 28:49, RSV). This is the other side of the coin. On one hand we have His enormous patience and mercy. On the other lies the speed and finality of His judgment.

We may pass through long cloudy tunnels of indecision, depressing spells of inactivity, and patches of "woolly thinking." Still, we need have no doubt about how Jesus will direct our lives—if we allow Him to do so. He would, however, have us clearly see these opposing aspects of His character. When we do, we can face each new day with all the optimism and vigor of the eagle greeting the dawn from its high craggy refuge.

> *In whatever choices I must make today, Lord, help me to approach them with cheerful decisiveness.*

THE DOVE

In London authorities have urged people eating lunch in the courtyard in front of the British Museum not to feed the pigeons. It is a difficult restriction, though, for sharing food with a friendly, bright-eyed bird is a satisfying kind of communion. The sweet murmur of flocks of doves cooing softly to one another attracts us. No wonder the Greeks made the dove sacred to Aphrodite, goddess of love.

HE SAW THE SPIRIT OF GOD DESCENDING LIKE A DOVE AND LIGHTING ON HIM.

MATT. 3:16, NIV.

The dove has other attractive characteristics. Shy and retiring, it hides "in holes in the cliffs or in crannies on the high ledges" (S. of Sol. 2:14, NEB). In sending out His disciples "innocent as doves," Jesus recognized the bird's gentleness (Matt. 10:16, NEB). Finally, at Jesus' baptism the dove wonderfully exemplified the Holy Spirit (Matt. 3:16).

Thus the dove introduces us to a special intimate side of the Holy Spirit's ministry. To domesticate doves, we build dovecotes, multistoried bird houses, to entice them into our gardens. Ambitious owners train homing pigeons to carry messages—a talent perhaps inherited from the dove that carried the olive branch back to Noah's ark, promising peace and safety after the Flood (Gen. 8:8-12).

Our dove picture now has yet another feature. Christ is the resting place, the dovecote, to which we all come home—led by the Spirit. It makes no difference with what wings we fly to Him. We need only to *come*. The young just learning to fly and the old. The weary and lonely who have been long on the way. Those who have kept all the commandments from childhood as well as those who have broken them all. We all have different temperaments—feverish and languid, impetuous and cool, affectionate and shy. Thus we can not expect the finch to sing like the nightingale or the sparrow to fly like the seagull. Nor will the dove arrive on eagle's wings. Instead, we can only come as *ourselves*, imitating no one. Such is the message from the dovecote.

> I pray today for the sweet, gentle ministry of the Holy
> Spirit. It leads us all, whoever we are, home to You.

THE HEN

Since childhood my attitude toward chickens has remained ambivalent. They are serviceable, harmless creatures, and certainly I've never wished them any ill. Indeed, a friend of mine breeds exotic chickens and has a yard full of strutting roosters and plump hens, all in a blaze of technicolor designs, wearing plumed headdresses and fluffy leg coverings and trailing long tail feathers. They are gorgeous, to be sure. On the other hand, chickens have always struck me as singularly stupid and foolish—possibly the most witless of all of God's birds.

As a 4-year-old living on my grandpa's farm in Iowa, I loved visiting the henhouse. The interminable scratching, the vulgar cackling, and the flapping about in the roosts fascinated me. And when I was alone with them, I took great delight in creating little disturbances among those simpleminded birds just for the pleasure of seeing them explode into a panic of feathers and squawks.

Yes, chickens are commonplace. So very ordinary. Thousands of years of using the birds for our domestic purposes have conditioned us to see them in highly practical terms. A broiled pigeon in a peasant's cottage, a roasted peacock on the table of a Roman emperor, fried chicken dinners—we have eaten the birds and gathered their eggs until they have little glory left.

Yet Christ chose a hen to create a picture of Himself. If He hadn't, we might otherwise have overlooked something very beautiful in chickens. Hens have a powerful instinct to shelter their chicks under their wings—a joy denied to incubator chicks. Whether speckled balls of fluff or downy yellow, the little ones find perfect safety hiding under their mothers' wings. Helpless and endowed with little intelligence, the chicks do have a wonderful, life-preserving provision—the mother will defend them to the death. She understands how to give shelter, and her children understand obedience. What more does any creature need?

"O JERUSALEM, JERUSALEM, KILLING THE PROPHETS AND STONING THOSE WHO ARE SENT TO YOU! HOW OFTEN WOULD I HAVE GATHERED YOUR CHILDREN TOGETHER AS A HEN GATHERS HER BROOD UNDER HER WINGS, AND YOU WOULD NOT!"

MATT. 23:37, RSV.

[*Jesus, I am too proud and independent. But then I feel very small and vulnerable. I need the shelter of Your wings.*]

THE SHELTERING WINGS

Fowling has long been a sport, and perhaps in more primitive times, a necessity. The psalmist here describes God's ultimate mother hen protection wherein we are the chicks pursued by the bird catcher and He is the hen, waiting and ready for us to rush to the safety He provides.

Contemplating His world, fallen into evil times, God sent His Son to ransom us, hostages to the archterrorist, Satan. The door of escape opens before us, but we hold back. Perversely, we reject the rescue and turn back toward destruction. Even a fledgling bird, surviving only with its tiny brain and natural instincts, knows better than that! Advising her daughter-in-law on how to approach Boaz, Naomi described Ruth's coming to Israel in terms of the secure, sheltering wings: "May you be richly rewarded by the Lord, the God of Israel, under whose wings you have come to take refuge" (Ruth 2:12, NIV).

At the end of His three-year ministry to His chosen people, Jesus sat on the Mount of Olives and looked down upon Jerusalem, the royal city. Secure in their own traditions and proud of their exclusiveness, the people continued to live unaware of the terror soon to unleash upon their city. Just a few more years, and it would be over for them. So the Master wept for what "might have been."

At this point His mind turned to the humble hen, the lowly bird who understood little else than the care of her little ones, perverse as they might be. One of the few things she could do for their protection was to shake out her feathers and let them creep into the warm hiding place while she alone faced danger for them.

The same loving, yearning care filled Jesus' heart, and He cried out through His tears: "O Jerusalem. How often would I have gathered your children together as a hen gathers her brood under her wings, and you would not!" (Matt. 23:37, RSV). Rejected—after He had come alone to face death and the horrors of sin in our place!

> SURELY HE SHALL DELIVER YOU FROM THE SNARE OF THE FOWLER AND FROM THE PERILOUS PESTILENCE. HE SHALL COVER YOU WITH HIS FEATHERS, AND UNDER HIS WINGS YOU SHALL TAKE REFUGE.
>
> PS. 91:3, 4, NKJV.

[*Jesus, let me never reject the loving provision You offer. May the risk that You took never be lost on me.*]

THE BIRD OF PREY

A bird-watcher's paradise, India boasts many exotic birds—from colorful visitors at your bedroom window to wild peacocks calling in the forests. Most unique are the vultures, sometimes called the sanitary inspectors of the countryside.

FROM THE EAST I SUMMON A BIRD OF PREY . . . , A MAN TO FULFILL MY PURPOSE.

ISA. 46:11, NIV.

Once while on a road in Rajasthan I saw some 50 of them at work. I arrived, camera at the ready, just as a flock of them descended on the carcass of a newly dead cow. Some stood about three feet tall, and all were clad in somber gray feathers. Their gaunt, grotesque faces were something that even their mothers must have had difficulty loving. As they circled the corpse, they uncannily called to mind solemnly suited morticians of the nineteenth century. Then without further ado, the biggest tore into the feast. The middle-sized ones skirted around the edges of the orgy, grabbing a mouthful as they could. The younger, smaller ones had to stand out on the edge of the circle watching. With fearful thoroughness, the eating went on. In lest than 10 minutes they had the bones picked clean. Then the big boys lumbered off to relax. The youngsters searched the skeleton, but scarcely a sniff remained for them.

To be sure, it was not a pretty sight. The single-minded ferocity of the affair brooked no mercy, no charity, not even a mouthful for the children of the family. The vultures' decisiveness and speed was breathtaking, terrifying.

In forecasting the Babylonian captivity, Isaiah speaks of the power from the east that will destroy unrepentant Israel. Commissioned as a bird of prey, the king will carry out Jehovah's judgment. The simile calls up fearful images to the imagination.

We have almost instinctively associated the work of Jesus with the watchcare of the hen, the strength of the eagle, the gentleness of the dove. But there *is* another side to the picture.

At a certain point in human affairs it will be closing time. Enough will finally be enough. God will mete out judgment, and there will be no turning back. Indeed, there will be a time and a place for distributing eternal rewards. "The Lord roars from Zion on high. . . . The Lord brings a charge against the nations" (Jer. 25:30, 31, NEB).

[*Keep me always mindful, my God, of Your precepts.*
Let me never take Your love and mercy for granted.]

THE ROCK OF REDEMPTION

D esert dwellers love rocks. Timeless and virtually indestructible, friendly givers of shade and protection, they answer some of people's deepest needs. The Hebrews had an innate fear of the sea because of suspicion and little experience with it. Consequently, sea imagery in the Bible is always negative, while rock images are consistently positive. For example, Job, in recalling his former affluence, remembered when "the Almighty was still there at my side, . . . while my path flowed with milk, and the rocks streamed oil!" (Job 29:6, NEB).

> "YOU ARE MY FATHER, MY GOD, THE ROCK MY SAVIOR."
>
> PS. 89:26, NIV.

Familiarity with rocks led Semitic peoples to identify locations by certain distinctive rocks. A prince was executed at the rock of Oreb (Judges 7:25; Isa. 10:26). Samson hid in the cave at the rock of Etam (Judges 15:8). The 600 Benjamite survivors fled to the rock of Rimmon (Judges 20:47-21:13). Amasa was murdered at the great rock in Gibeon (2 Sam. 20:8-12). David took cover at the rock in the Desert of Maon (1 Sam. 23:25) and then craved the water of Bethlehem while he sheltered at the rock at the cave of Adullam (1 Chron. 11:15).

Moses, a man who in his long life in the desert had a great deal of experience with rocks, first painted the picture of "God, the Rock of Salvation." His song of blessing on Israel just before his death contains a hymn of praise to the Rock of Israel (Deut. 32:1-43). Perhaps he drew his inspiration from the earlier reference of the patriarch Jacob to "the Shepherd, the Rock of Israel" (Gen. 49:24, NIV). In any case, the metaphor held throughout the rest of Scripture, particularly in the poetry of the prophets.

In claiming his preeminence over all others, Jehovah appropriates the image to Himself: "Is there a God beside Me? Indeed there is no other Rock; I know not one" (Isa. 44:8, NKJV). Repeatedly the psalmists say, "Blessed is my rock" (Ps. 18:46, NEB); "O Lord, my rock and my redeemer" (Ps. 119:14, NEB); "O my Rock, be not deaf to my cry" (Ps. 28:1, NEB).

Instinctively we're drawn to look at things larger than ourselves—sea cliffs, canyon country, the Rockies, the Alps, and the Himalayas. In their presence we suddenly see ourselves in perspective. How much more so when we look to Christ, the Rock of Ages.

> [*Lord, I flee to the Rock that is change-*
> *less. Hide me there where I may be safe.*]

THE NURTURING ROCK

The traveler in Jordan should take time to ascend Mount Nebo. From there one views the Promised Land as Moses did just before his death on the mountaintop. To the left lies the Dead Sea, and straight ahead, in the far distance, the towers of Jerusalem. And to the right, however, you see the "Spring of Moses." Tradition declares that it is the place where Moses struck the rock twice. Be that as it may, it is a green oasis in the dust-brown hills. At the eastern end, under a single enormous tree, still flows a spring of water.

THEY ALL DRANK FROM THE SUPERNATURAL ROCK THAT ACCOMPANIED THEIR TRAVELS— AND THAT ROCK WAS CHRIST.

1 COR. 10:4, NEB.

Palestine's limestone rocks can provide water, when, at unexpected points, the water seeps down through crevices to break out in springs. God showed Moses one such place. Thus, with one blow of his staff, Moses first brought forth water from the rock at Horeb (Ex. 17:1-7), and the complaining Hebrews and their livestock drank their fill! Later, on the final approaches to Canaan, another water crisis occurred. This time, promised that "it will yield its water," God told Moses simply to "*speak* to the rock." Exasperated, however, by more than 40 years of coping with "these rebels," Moses struck it—twice. True, "the water gushed out in abundance and they all drank, men and beasts" (Num. 20:8-12, NEB). But never was water supplied at a higher cost. Because of Moses' impulsive action, God denied him entrance into Canaan.

The nurturing water drawn from the rock remained forever a vivid picture. The Jews never forgot how God "opened a rock" (Ps. 105:41, NEB) so that they did not die from thirst (Isa. 48:21; Neh. 9:15). The idea of "God, the rock of His people" expanded through centuries of religious thought. Finally, the apostle Paul gave the image a mystical application for Christians of all time. "They . . . drank the same spiritual drink; for they drank from the spiritual rock that accompanied them, and that rock was Christ" (1 Cor. 10:4, NIV). Christhe rock that moves and from which flow the pure waters of the gospel.

> O Rock of Ages, quench my thirst this day,
> even as You did long ago in the desert.

THE ROCK OF REFUGE

Rocks provide a place to hide—for the games of children and for lovers. "My dove in the clefts of the rock, in the hiding places on the mountainside, show me your face" (S. of Sol. 2:14, NIV). More seriously, however, the rocks offer safety and refuge.

The ambitious, deluded seer Balaam looked down upon the camp of Israel and realized he could do nothing to threaten them. "Firm is your dwelling place, and your nest is set in the rock" (Num. 24:21, NKJV).

> **THE LORD HAS BEEN MY DEFENSE, AND MY GOD THE ROCK OF MY REFUGE.**
>
> PS. 94:22, NKJV.

In his ongoing efforts to escape the wrath of King Saul, David became the classic refugee, well acquainted with the most practical hideouts available. One was En Gedi, where the king with 3,000 men chased him up into the "Rocks of the Wild Goats" (1 Sam. 24:1, 2, NKJV). En Gedi ("spring of the kid") is a spring issuing from the limestone cliffs above the western shore of the Dead Sea. No part of the Wilderness of Judah is more bleak, for the dark waters of the sea, heavy with minerals, has long since obliterated every form of life. In contrast, the stream above splashes down through the trees in a cool shower. David and his men could have enjoyed safety, even comfort, here for a long time. (In vision Ezekiel saw En Gedi as the "seed" for a restored and enlivened Dead Sea [Eze. 47:10-12].)

Because of such experiences, David and the other psalmists delighted in the picture of the "rock of refuge," using it as a salutation to open many of their songs. The Lord was not just the Rock. He was an entire garrisoned stronghold (Ps. 18:2); a "fortress of defense" (Ps. 31:1, NKJV); the "rock of my strength" (Ps. 62:7, NKJV); the "Rock of our salvation" (Ps. 95:1, NKJV).

In predicting the approaching reign of righteousness, Isaiah beautifully combines the compassionate Rock of nurturing with the powerful Rock of refuge. A time will come—a time of justice—when we can fully trust every human being around us, great and small:

> "Each man will be like a shelter from the wind
> and a refuge from the storm,
> like streams of water in the desert
> and the shadow of a great rock in a thirsty land"
> (Isa. 32:2, NIV).

[*Renewer of Life, I would be that kind of person today. May those around me find in me shelter and peace. May my life nourish and heal them.*]

THE HIGHER ROCK

One of the highlights of my childhood in the Orient was visiting my cousins in Borneo. The Gus Youngbergs had pioneered Christianity in the jungles of Sarawak during the early 1920s, but by the time I came along they were stationed in British North Borneo. The mission—with school, church, and office building—was advantageously situated atop Signal Hill, overlooking the city of Jesselton (now Kota Kinabalu) and the China Sea. Their big, airy bungalow had more windows than walls. The surroundings were a virtual "theme park" for children.

HEAR MY CRY, O GOD. . . . LEAD ME TO THE ROCK THAT IS HIGHER THAN I.

PS. 61:1, 2, NIV.

A precipitous outcropping of rocks beside the house was one of our favorite resorts. From the top we viewed all of Signal Hill, the town, and the sea. Up there we felt a power and self-importance all out of proportion to our real place in the world. Some days, bursting with confidence, we'd grab our tin plates of rice and curry and shinny up onto the rocks to eat our lunch. There we sat like lords, defying any children from any of the neighboring villages to approach except by our invitation.

In one of his most exuberant declarations of faith, David praised God for saving him in the time of trouble: "He will keep me safe and hide me in His Holy Temple." Next came the ultimate restoration: "He will set me high on a rock above my enemies. Then I will be able to hold my head high" (Ps. 27:5, 6, Clear Word).

Thus God calls us to come out of the valley, to rise above ourselves—our foolish pettinesses, our short-sighted vision, our narrow concerns, and our self-importance. He would have us catch a glimpse of our lives from His eternal viewpoint, and that is possible only when our feet are set upon the higher Rock. Healing comes in looking at things larger than ourselves—that is the attraction of desert vistas, meadow landscapes, and seashore views. God designed us for mountaintop experiences, and we have no business groping blindfolded in the dark canyons of discouragement.

[*Dear Lord of the Rocks, lift me out of my smallness and triviality. Set me in a high place where You can show me Your purposes.*]

THE FOUNDATION ROCK

Of all of the dwellers in "rock cities" around the world, surely none have surpassed the achievements of the builders of Petra, in south Jordan. A magnificent mile-long gorge, the *Siq*, serves as the entrance to the ruins of the city, with its Roman amphitheater. The historic ruins occupy an open basin among the mountains. As early as 800 B.C. the Edomites, the children of Esau, discovered this unique spot (which they called Sela). They fought to preserve their unusual stronghold. The passage through the rocky labyrinth is sometimes only 10 feet wide, with walls towering 100 feet above and almost meeting overhead.

> "ON THIS ROCK I WILL BUILD MY CHURCH, AND THE GATES OF HADES WILL NOT OVER-COME IT."
>
> MATT. 16:18, NIV.

Within 300 years the Nabateans, a nomadic Arabian tribe, dispossessed the Edomites. They carved their capital out of the rosy sandstone cliffs—temples, dwellings, and tombs.

While those desert Arabs probably pitched their tents in the open space within the inaccessible gorge, when they came to die they chose to carve their tombs out of the cliffs, always lovely in the changing light, shifting in color from pink to mauve to beige. In death the Nabateans wished to lie in the one place they believed to be permanent—the rocks.

It is virtually a basic human instinct to want to know that we have a solid foundation under our feet. In His parable of the house built with expense and difficulty on the rock, as opposed to the house erected so quickly on the sand, Christ drove home the truth of this necessity (Matt. 7:24, 25). Prophesying against Babylon, Jeremiah described the builder's worst nightmare: "No stone of yours shall be used as a corner-stone, no stone for a foundation" (Jer. 51:26, NEB).

As He set up His church to endure the trials of the early years, Christ fittingly announced that He would establish it firmly upon the Rock, Himself. As he always did, however, David made the application of the foundation rock intensely personal to the believer:

> "He brought me up out of the muddy pit,
> out of the mire and the clay;
> he set my feet on a rock
> and gave me a firm footing" (Ps. 40:2, NEB).

[*Dear Father, guide me in my decisions today. I would not stand on any foundation other than the Rock of Your building.*]

THE GREAT MOUNTAIN

A ny visit to Bali, Indonesia, should include a trip to the "mother temple" in the mountainous interior of the island. Ringed by steamy, greenclad volcanoes, you climb a steep flight of steps to the shrine at the top. There you stand and look up the ascent to the Hindu *gopuram,* a gray-stone pile shaped like a mountain and covered with elaborate carvings. You watch the clouds sailing across the airy blue passageway through the split gate.

> THE MOUN-
> TAIN OF THE
> LORD'S
> HOUSE
> SHALL BE
> ESTABLISHED
> . . . AND ALL
> NATIONS
> SHALL FLOW
> TO IT.
> ISA. 2:2, NKJV.

The "stone mountain" has been sliced in half, the sides pushed to each side. When you walk between the smooth inner walls, you have literally entered into the mountain and into the presence of the god. These symbolic gateways grace not only every temple and family compound but also the entrances to even the humblest home.

Humanity has always conceived of the gods as dwelling on the mountains. The pattern appears in every culture. The great medieval Christian cathedrals evoked the same idea. Worshipers entered those massive buildings through huge portals usually decorated with carvings of God sitting in judgment and saints welcoming the flock into the mystical world of the spirit. Bathed in the cool glow of stained-glass windows, even today's most materialistic tourist cannot enter such awesome "mountains" of architecture without feeling the tug of the sacred at his or her heart.

Our current fascination and pleasure in exotic mountain scenery, however, is a relatively modern and romantic idea. Traditionally, mountains not only provided barriers capable of fortification and suitable for guerrilla warfare; they were of themselves places of mystery and fearful powers. The abode of supernatural forces, they were the distant places of the gods.

Old Testament writers repeatedly invited Israel to Mount Zion to rejoice "in His holy mountain" (Ps. 48:1, NKJV) and to celebrate in the "mountain of the Lord" (Isa. 30:29, NKJV). Daniel's dream about the sequence of human government, however, ended with the catastrophic appearance of the stone that demolished the great image and "became a great mountain and filled the whole earth" (Dan. 2:35, NKJV).

The great mountain of God prevails at last—the stronghold of strength, the refuge of the weak, and the retreat for the weary.

[*Lord, use the majesty of Your everlasting mountains and eternal hills to remind me of Your power over all of life—even in the trivia of my personal affairs.*]

THE EARTHQUAKE

Few happenings terrify us more than major earth movements: "A falling mountain-side is swept away, and a rock is dislodged from its place" (Job 14:18, NEB). True, God often speaks to us in a whisper, but at other times He must get our attention through more massive exhibitions of His power—storm, fire, and earthquake (1 Kings 19:12).

As a teenager in New Zealand I experienced my first earthquake—a noisy but short-lived affair. Back then we just took such things as they came. Nowadays, as a resident of California, I have not only been through many more earthquakes but have also been informed in great detail about preparation for them, their intensity, their appearance on the seismograph, and so forth.

YOU WILL BE PUNISHED BY THE LORD OF HOSTS WITH THUNDER AND EARTH-QUAKE AND GREAT NOISE.

ISA. 29:6, NKJV.

Earthquakes are nothing to trivialize. No matter how often you feel them, you never overcome the feeling of helplessness while your world rocks and rolls about you. Our last major episode in southern California woke me up about 5:00 a.m., rattling me into full wakefulness. So I got up and went to work at my computer. Then just before 8:00 came the second shock, worse than the first. I turned off the computer and waited. The epicenter, however, had to be at some distance because I still had electricity. Therefore, I turned on my machine again and went back to my task. For the rest of the morning, however, the computer would let out a small croak about two seconds before each new little tremor hit. By noon I actually felt ill—from motion sickness.

Scripture presents an impressive sequence of earthquakes, escalating in significance. Apart from scientific explanations, with God earthquakes do mean something. First, several prophets referred to the great quake in the time of Uzziah (Zech. 14:5; Eze. 38:19; Amos 1:1). Next the crucifixion and resurrection of Jesus occurred between two earthquakes (Matt. 27:54; 28:2). Then came the earthquake that opened the prison of Philippi and liberated Paul and Silas to continue their founding of the infant Christian church (Acts 16:26). Finally, the book of Revelation is full of celestial fireworks and earthquakes, culminating in the upheaval that ushers in the end of time (Rev. 16:18-21).

Master of the Elements, I listen for Your whispered messages. But prepare me for the times when I may need to face great disaster.

THE LIVING WATERS OF GRACE

Water is indispensable. Without it no life could exist. Its absence creates famine and deserts in a shockingly short space of time. Moreover, water is one of earth's substances that we use again and again. It is, in fact, indestructible.

That last cold, sparkling glassful with which you quenched your thirst may have been around since the creation of the world. The water you used to wash the dinner dishes may once have been part of King Nebuchadnezzar's bathwater. Or it may have floated the lordly barge of Joseph along the Nile River. Perhaps slaves carried it to serve the palace of Caesar. Again, it might have filtered through the mudflats of the mighty Amazon River. Maybe it was once part of an ice cave in an Arctic glacier. It's probably also had experience as clouds, rain, snow, and steam. Moreover, water is not just a gift for human physical well-being, but for our spiritual life as well.

> "IF ANYONE IS THIRSTY LET HIM COME TO ME; WHOEVER BELIEVES IN ME, LET HIM DRINK."
>
> JOHN 7:37, 38, NEB.

No wonder that God describes His divine blessings in terms of water: "For I will pour out water on the thirsty soil, streams on the dry ground. I will pour my spirit on your descendants, my blessing on your children" (Isa. 44:3, Jerusalem). Likewise, believers who have drunk freely of the water of life themselves become a source of blessing: "Whoever believes in me, as the Scripture has said, streams of living water will flow from within him" (John 7:38, NIV).

Almost the last words in the Bible invite us to drink of this Source. Jesus' final appeal includes everyone: "The [Holy] Spirit and the bride [the church] say, 'Come!' And let him who hears say, 'Come!' Whoever is thirsty, let him come; and whoever wishes, let him take the free gift of the water of life" (Rev. 22:17, NIV).

In our selfishness and pride, however, we've rejected the fresh, flowing waters of God's grace, choosing instead the stagnant water supply we've stored up for ourselves. "My people," the Lord said, "have committed two sins. They have forsaken me, the spring of living water, and have dug their own cisterns, broken cisterns that cannot hold water" (Jer. 2:13, NIV).

Considering the terms of God's invitation, who could delay a moment in accepting it?

[*I see the difference, Lord. Refresh me with the pure flow of Your grace. I don't understand why I've drunk so long from my polluted cistern.*]

WATER: THE WELL

Tropical climates receive regular, ample rainfall. Public works departments keep a steady flow of clean water piped directly into the homes in large, well-engineered cities. As a result, we tend to forget that water is a precious possession. Like King David, we may need to have our memories jogged.

"MY PEOPLE . . . HAVE FORSAKEN ME, THE SPRING OF LIVING WATER."

JER. 2:13, NIV.

Well-digging in Palestine opened up underground water sources, and the ownership of wells was a serious matter (Gen. 21:25; Deut. 6:11). They often had special names. Both Abraham and Isaac had conflicts with their neighbors over wells. The one they dug at Beersheba resulted in the founding of an important city. Tradition says the name "Beersheba" means "the well of swearing seven." There Abraham sacrificed seven lambs and made a peace treaty with Abimelech (Gen. 21:25-34).

When the Philistines occupied David's hometown of Bethlehem, they drove him and his army into guerrilla warfare. Under the stress, he had a nostalgic memory: "Oh, that someone would get me a drink of water from the well near the gate of Bethlehem!" (2 Sam. 23:15, NIV). Immediately, three of his devoted followers broke through the enemy lines, drew the water from the well, and carried it back to their chieftain. Stunned by the risk they had taken, David could not even sip from the cup. Instead, he poured it out on the ground in an act of worship: "Far be it from me, O Lord, to do this!" (verse 17, NIV).

Jesus' most profound discussion of Himself as the water of life occurred at Jacob's Well—a place where today an overheated traveler may still draw a bucket of cold water. To the despised Samaritan woman He said: "Everyone who drinks this water will be thirsty again, but whoever drinks the water I give him will never thirst. Indeed, the water I give him will become in him a spring of water welling up to eternal life" (John 4:14, NIV).

Wells mean life. "With joy you will draw water from the wells of salvation" (Isa. 12:3, NIV). That well is within reach. It is full and will never run dry. But we have *one* requirement to meet. We must let down the bucket of faith and draw up the water from the divine supply.

[Today, Lord, I must drink deep at Your well of grace. Let me never neglect this basic need that I have. My health and my survival depend on it.]

WATER: THE FOUNTAIN

L et no modern observer, lulled by the convenience of having water available in his or her
own house, overlook the significance of water
and its spiritual meaning in the Bible.

THEY HAVE FORSAKEN ME, THE SPRING OF LIVING WATER.

JER. 2:13, NIV.

Though underground water can emerge as springs
in the desert valleys, it was not easily found (2 Kings
2:19). In the first days after the Red Sea experience,
Moses had a great deal of trouble with the water supply for the murmuring tribes of Israel—until they arrived at Elim: "There were twelve springs and seventy
palm trees, and they camped there near the water" (Ex. 15:27, NIV). It must
have been hard for them to move on after camping in such a pleasant oasis.

It comes as no surprise, then, that desert dwellers have a keener eye for
the beauty of flowing water than most of us do. Celebrating the loveliness
of the Baca Valley, the psalmist sang: "They make it a place of springs; the
autumn rains also cover it with pools" (Ps. 84:6, NIV). And again:

> "You care for the land and water it;
> you enrich it abundantly.
> The streams of God are filled with water
> to provide the people with grain,
> for so you have ordained it" (Ps. 65:9, NIV).

The lover in Song of Solomon 4:15 described His bride in a double
water image: as "a garden fountain" and as "a well of flowing water stream-
ing down from Lebanon" (NIV). We love those through whom God's grace
flows, those whose lives are full. Tap them at any level, and you'll never
hear the dull, depressing thud of emptiness.

The living, underground springs never cease sending forth streams. The
fountain symbol points repeatedly to Christ, the springhead of living water,
who can open springs in our hearts. Nothing in the world can pay the price
for *that* kind of water supply. "On that day a fountain will be opened to the
house of David" (Zech. 13:1, NIV). And of Jerusalem, the chosen city, Joel
wrote: "A fountain will flow out of the Lord's house and will water the valley of acacias" (Joel 3:18, NIV).

> "Come, Thou Fount of every blessing,
> Tune my heart to sing Thy grace;
> Streams of mercy, never ceasing,
> Call for songs of loudest praise."
> —Robert Robinson (1758)

WATER; THE RIVER

Most people know about the curious properties of the Dead Sea. Sunken into the Judean wilderness at almost 1,300 feet below sea level, it truly lives up to its name. Taste it and the salt burns your tongue, for it is six times more salty than the ocean. Try to swim and you float on the mineral solids that make up 27 percent of the volume of the dark, brackish water. Yes the Dead Sea is *dead*. The Jordan River feeds it, but it has no outlet, so the hot desert sun simply evaporates the water, concentrating its saltiness.

On its way down from Galilee, however, the river brings life and fertility. The prophet Ezekiel goes to some pains to explain what happens: "Swarms of living creatures will live wherever the river flows. There will be large numbers of fish, because this water flows there and makes the salt water fresh; so where the river flows everything will live" (Eze. 47:9, NIV). If you do swim in the Dead Sea, En Gedi is the place to do it, for there you can bathe afterward in a fresh stream before the sun burns the encrusted salt into your skin. The fertile ravine of En Gedi once sheltered the fugitive David and his men, and they could not have chosen a better hiding place.

It is no accident that all of the civilizations of the ancient world arose along great rivers. Indeed, rivers are the earth's vascular system. A glacier melts into rivers that crisscross a continent, sweeping the landscape clean. Baptism, one of our spiritual rites of passage, employs water symbolism. And how often in our arts have we portrayed death and resurrection as a river crossing?

Meanwhile, sin has created a Dead Sea in our experience, but there *is* a remedy. Issuing from the throne of God, the river of salvation flows through our wasteland. Jesus, on the cross, channeled its flow toward us. So as the gospel spreads over the earth, it enlivens the wilderness and transforms dying people. The river is deep. It is for total immersion, not just for wading.

THEN THE ANGEL SHOWED ME THE RIVER OF THE WATER OF LIFE, AS CLEAR AS CRYSTAL, FLOWING FROM THE THRONE OF GOD.

REV. 22:1, NIV.

[*"Shall we gather at the river where bright angel feet have trod,*
With its crystal tide forever flowing by the throne of God?"]
—Robert Lowry

WATER: THE CISTERN

The island of Grand Cayman today is a prosperous business/resort area, but it was not always so. Seventeenth-century pirates of the Spanish Main used it as a cache for their ill-gotten treasure. The lack of water and the difficulty of growing sufficient food on the sand-covered coral rocks for a long time curbed population growth. The first overseas mission appointment for my husband and me took us to the Cayman Islands in 1954. Having never heard of them before, we had to study a map to locate them, just south of Cuba. The sugar-white beaches and turquoise ocean delighted us. In the matter of water, however (at least for us), things hadn't changed much since the days of the pirates.

> MY PEOPLE . . . HAVE DUG THEIR OWN CISTERNS, BROKEN CISTERNS THAT CANNOT HOLD WATER.
>
> JER. 2:13, NIV.

We lived in a large and ancient house where the walls constantly rattled with hermit crabs and splintered with termites. In the backyard we had a covered, frog-infested cistern, some 10-feet square, that collected rainwater off the eaves. From time to time we scooped out the dead and dying frogs, while the survivors went on singing their cheerful chorus in the dark, dank shadows of the cistern. A 40-gallon drum on the roof had to be filled by a hand-operated pump—our daily morning task. Then, with the law of gravity in our favor, we could bring our frog-flavored water into the house.

Life-giving water cannot always come from a fresh source. Cisterns are simply an emergency device for storing rainfall. Despite the fact that the ancients identified it as the land "flowing with milk and honey," Palestine has always been just a hair's breadth from reverting to the desert, and people had to dig cisterns to provide for any population growth. Such cisterns had to be constructed properly as well as repaired periodically. Yes, cisterns are a necessary and practical device for water storage, but inconvenient as they are, they should never be our first choice. At best they offer only a second-rate water supply.

Israel's rejection of God's fountain of life-giving water led Jeremiah to paint a sad picture: they tried to store stale water in leaking cisterns of their own making. How much better, however, it is to discover God's fresh springs in the desert.

> *I am grateful, Lord, for the emergency water supply You have provided for me. But let me not become independent of it. I seek Your fresh supplies of grace, new every morning.*

WATER: CHANNELS

Nowhere is the power of water more evident than in the ebb and flow of the tides. "Deep calls to deep in the roar of thy cataracts, and all thy waves, all thy breakers, pass over me" (Ps. 42:7, NEB). More than one terrified swimmer has fixed his eye on a landmark on the beach only to find himself caught in the drag of an undertow that he never suspected was there. He struggles to reach safety, only to feel the ocean surge about him, relentlessly pulling him down the shoreline. Or worse still, out into the open sea. If the person panics, he is lost.

EACH MAN WILL BE LIKE . . . STREAMS OF WATER IN THE DESERT.

ISA. 32:2, NIV.

The tides come and go. At one time they toss up seaweed, and at another they sweep the accumulation of debris off the beach. In any case, water can move with irresistible strength. Ancient Roman engineers harnessed the tides for the highly sophisticated sewer system honeycombing the city of Caesarea Maritima, in Palestine (27 B.C.). With the mighty sea power channeled into those large water tunnels, the system completely flushed out with each tide.

Like the force of the spillway of a great dam, the channeling of the water of life has great momentum. And we are the appointed channels! "He who believes in Me . . . out of his heart will flow rivers of living water" (John 7:38, NKJV). God intends for us to transmit this living, flowing water. The call demands activity—no loitering around our old broken cisterns!

Surely no other portrait of Christ is more comprehensive than that of the life-sustaining benefits of water. The refreshment of streams in the desert. The beauty of flowing fountains. The depth of cool wells. The calm of little ponds. The security of big reservoirs and quiet lakes. The energy of foaming rapids. The steady thrust of water turning mill wheels. The mysterious vitality of hidden springs, high in the mountains, where they become the headwaters of thundering waterfalls and the mighty rivers that surge out to the sea. The infinite breadth of the ocean itself.

We can hardly see Jesus in a more lovely or complete way.

[*Dear God, I would not linger by the broken cisterns. I don't want to just wait at the well or stand on the riverbank. Connect me with You so that I may become a channel of blessing to others.*]

WATER IN THE DESERT

Scripture images Jesus in the abundance of life-giving water. In the humid tropics, where even fence posts sometimes recover the spark of life and sprout leaves, we naturally take water for granted. But He is also represented in the *scarcity* of water.

In the desert water takes on an urgent meaning. Deserts, to all intents and purposes, do not have water. The dry heart of Australia, for instance, climaxes in the Nullabor Plain, where the railway line goes straight for 400 miles without a rise, fall, or bend. Water is present, however, though hidden. Artesian wells sustain cattle and scattered settlements. Thus "springs in the desert" create oases, pockets of life in the waste places. Indeed, Jehovah opened one up for the distraught Hagar, abandoned in the Wilderness of Paran (Gen. 21:15-21).

SEE, A KING WILL REIGN IN RIGH-TEOUSNESS. . . . EACH MAN WILL BE LIKE . . . STREAMS OF WATER IN THE DESERT.

ISA. 32:1, 2, NIV.

The desert cities of the American Southwest have cultivated a pattern of resort living that attracts thousands of visitors, many of them "snowbirds" enticed south for the desert winter. The scenery is magnificent. Brown mountain ranges crouch like huge coyotes along the horizon, changing color from pink to beige to pink to lavender. Gilt-edged clouds roll across the valleys under clean, clear skies. The crisp, dry air cools the palm trees on moonlit evenings.

Desert dwellers carefully husband their water to create dramatic contrasts. At one point the white sands blow themselves into drifts around the scraggly sagebrush. Only a cactus here or there bespeaks life. Then suddenly you come upon a lovely compound. Palm trees stand with variegated flower beds flourishing around their feet and ornamental bushes at their knees. Bougainvillea spills over the walls. Turquoise swimming pools glint in the sun. Oleander hedges the broad streets, and finely manicured lawns fill in the spaces in between. But just a few hundred yards away the oasis ends and the wilderness begins all over again. None of this has happened by accident. It is possible only with the diligent use of water.

In the desert people must be conscious of it every moment of their lives. No wonder Christ uses water in the desert as a special illustration of His transforming power.

[*My Lord, I often find my life dry and barren. Thank You for offering me the possibility of finding water in the desert so that growth can occur. Help me plan my life to become a lovely garden of Your design.*]

WATER: THE RIVER OF LIFE

Perhaps the most ancient piece of literature in the world, the Gilgamesh epic (about 2500 B.C.) recounts the adventures of the Akkadian king Gilgamesh, who, among other things, searches for the gift of immortality. After heroic effort, he secures the sacred plant from the bottom of the sea. Then on his way home, while he rests by a river, a serpent slithers out of the water and steals the prize. It's another version of the old Eden story—the snake got it!

The theme reappears in many cultures. That is, access to everlasting life depends on eating or drinking something mystical. Thus what keeps the physical body alive becomes a symbol for the preservation of the life of the spirit. The complex connection evolves into one of the most significant symbols in the Christian life. Jesus' conversation with the woman of Samaria symbolizes the issue: "Whoever drinks of the water that I shall give him will never thirst. . . . [And it] will become in him a fountain of water springing up into everlasting life" (John 4:14, NKJV).

For this reason, God had to evict Adam and Eve from the Garden of Eden. He had to cut them off from the source, the tree of life, and the water sustaining it. Their sin had disqualified them for immortality—and as we already have observed, the snake had done it.

But this is only half of the story. In his thrilling preview of the Holy City, John points out two significant objects. First, the river of life "clear as crystal, proceeding from the throne of God" (Rev. 22:1, NKJV). Then arching over that river and growing from both banks stands the tree of life (verse 2). Here is the end of our quest. Here we reconnect with the source of life, and we eat and drink for eternity.

No wonder the service of Christian Communion has such profound meaning, based as it is on the earthly acts of eating and drinking. And when we partake in faith, we anticipate the elemental source of life itself.

THEN THE ANGEL SHOWED ME THE RIVER OF THE WATER OF LIFE, AS CLEAR AS CRYSTAL, FLOWING FROM THE THRONE OF GOD.

REV. 22:1, NIV.

[*Fill my cup, Lord. I lift it up, Lord!*
Come and quench this thirsting of my soul.]

THE WAVES

Consider the boundary where earth and water meet. Waterbirds strut along the shore, hunting for crabs in the seaweed the ocean has tossed up. They sail over the heaving sea or swoop skyward in graceful flight. Here the ceaseless waves constantly lick at the land and fill the tidal pools, gaining and losing ground in their eternal push and tug.

Some of us grew up near the ocean. Swimming came as naturally as walking, and our beach days are now unforgettable childhood memories. We let the huge surf crash on our heads and smash us down into the sandy bottom. The unmerciful surge twisted and tore at our bodies. Then, giddy and laughing, we'd scramble up for air and wait for the next big one. We respected this enormous primal power and knew just how far out we could go before the lethal undertow could catch us.

> DEEP CALLS TO DEEP IN THE ROAR OF THY CATARACTS, AND ALL THY WAVES, ALL THY BREAKERS, PASS OVER ME.
>
> PS. 42:7, NEB.

Once on a beach on the island of Guam I watched towering breakers thunder in. Sometimes the approaching blue wall of water would contain a shark or barracuda. High drama then ensued as the powerful creature turned and dived back toward open sea just seconds before the high curl of the wave would have pulverized it on the high rocky shore. I can't remember having seen a more spectacular exhibition of sheer force before.

A curious little twelfth-century tale tells of Canute the Dane (994?-1035), a king of England. Despite the chaotic times, he maintained peace and order. The adulation of flattering courtiers had its effect. Sitting down in a chair on the beach, he regally commanded the waves to stop rolling in. Naturally, they kept coming—as if he were no more than a piece of driftwood on the sand. Some say the episode exhibited pride, others humility. Either way, Canute conclusively demonstrated the limits of his kingly power.

Ocean waves do embody relentless, impersonal power. They often roll over us. The overwhelming force within them, however, is still subject to One stronger—the One who created the laws that govern them. Unlike King Canute, King Jesus stands up in a boat on stormy Galilee and says, "Peace, be still." And the waves obey.

[*Master of the Sea, I would learn the lesson of the waves. No temptation can ever be greater than the power You give me to make me victorious.*]

THE TENDER PLANT

Chlorophyll is that green substance that turns earth's moisture and air's carbon dioxide into sugar and becomes the link between sunshine and life. Thus light energy becomes food energy and fuel energy. So basic to our existence, plants feed, clothe, and shelter us. They provide the very oxygen we breathe.

> HE GREW UP BEFORE HIM LIKE A TEN-DER SHOOT, AND LIKE A ROOT OUT OF DRY GROUND.
>
> ISA. 53:2, NIV.

Asia is one of the best places to see chlorophyll at work. Watch the rice seedlings grow their fine-haired little shoots in nursery boxes, waiting to be transferred into the rice paddies. Their color is unlike any other green you've ever seen—brilliant, pure, and intense. Then the rice planters, nearly knee-deep in muddy water, set them out one by one—perhaps to the rhythm of a lilting work song.

With good reason we call the place where we buy plants and supplies for our gardens a "nursery." (The word derives from a Latin term meaning "nourishing.") At the nursery you can purchase seeds to take home to start your own seedlings. Or you can buy young sets of tomatoes, onions, and flowers in tiny boxes, already safely established. And if you're in a hurry, you can buy an adolescent plant in a gallon tin or a late teenager in a five-gallon container. If you have, say, $1,000, you can order a full-grown palm tree brought in and planted in your garden. Most of us, however, have to begin somewhere down near the "childhood" level of the plant. Thus we learn that a plant nursery (not unlike a baby nursery) promotes health and growth, but requires intensive work.

The portrayal of Christ as a "tender green shoot" (Isa. 53:2, TLB) springing out of dry ground is dramatic. One does not expect to find a young healthy plant alone in a parched landscape. Yet in the desert sometimes we're surprised to find a tall succulent plant growing from soil that hasn't a visible drop of moisture in it. That means that its roots have struck down deep to draw their nourishment from a hidden source. A corrupt age made it a harsh "nursery" into which Jesus, the tender plant, arrived. Indeed, humanity itself is a discouraging soil.

[*Sometimes my circumstances seem to have set me in a dry wasteland. Like my Lord, let me push my roots down to reach the living waters below.*]

THE ROOT OF DAVID

In our fractured modern society many people have taken renewed interest in investigating their family histories. Genealogical studies and publications expand by the month, it seems. Death, divorce, or any other disaster can sever us from the bloodline link we have with our past. One must approach genealogy, however, with a neutral mind. Tales of heroism and endurance will show up. But also expect that villains will mix with the saints. Fanatics and geniuses will mingle in our ancestry. The sick and the hearty. Peasants and professionals. Maybe a nobleman or two—even a king! They're all part of your story. As Samuel Johnson once said: "Every man is an omnibus in which all of his ancestors ride, and once in a while one of them looks out the window and embarrasses him."

> I AM THE ROOT AND THE OFF-SPRING OF DAVID.
>
> REV. 22:16, NIV.

One of the most remarkable family sleuths of our time was Alex Haley (1921-1992). An African-American, he pursued his family line back to the slave plantations, to the slave ship, and then beyond to a man named Kunta Kinte, taken into slavery in Gambia in 1767. At the end of 12 years of research he published his Pulitzer Prize-winning book *Roots* (1976). The next year, in its film form, the story became the highest-rated television program up to that time. America began seriously looking at itself.

Several scriptures refer to Christ as the Root of David (Rom. 15:12; Rev. 5:5). Isaiah pictured the Messiah as a fresh sprout from the stump of a tree that has been cut down—that is, the defunct monarchy of David. "Then a shoot shall grow from the stock of Jesse, and a branch shall spring from his roots" (Isa. 11:1, NEB). Jesus came of two royal houses. In His humanity, He was descended from the royal Jewish line. In His divinity He had laid aside his heritage as king of heaven.

It's a paradox—a mystery—of Christ's coming that in His preexistence He was the "root" of David while He was also a "branch," a descendent. Like King David, we too may be rooted in Him: "Live your lives in union with him [Christ]. Be rooted in him; be built in him; be consolidated in the faith" (Col. 2:6, 7, NEB).

[*Jesus, my world is so fractured that rootlessness seems to be the hallmark of my age. Whatever my surrounding circumstances, keep me rooted in You, I pray.*]

THE BRANCH

People who live through the northern winters savor the arrival of spring. Overnight the skeletal tree branches silhouetted in the snow begin to show the faintest fuzz of green as the sap begins to flow. Next come fresh new leaves, followed by blossoms. One admiring Englishman exclaimed: "Each spring sees a *million glorious beginnings*. . . . A sunlit heaven in every opening leaf, warm perfection in every stirring egg, hope and fear and beauty beyond computation in every forest tree."*

IN THAT DAY THE BRANCH OF THE LORD SHALL BE BEAUTIFUL AND GLORIOUS.

ISA. 4:2, NKJV.

This springtime revival brought to the mind of suffering Job the first intimation we have in the Old Testament that a personal resurrection is a possibility. Looking at a tree, he mused, "There is hope for a tree, if it be cut down, that it will sprout again. . . . But man dies, and is laid low" (Job 14:7-10, RSV). But wait! Is not a man more than a tree? "If a man die, shall he live again?" (verse 14, RSV). Finally, he cries exuberantly, "Oh, that my words were written! . . . For I know that my Redeemer lives, and at last he will stand upon the earth; . . . then from my flesh I shall see God" (Job 19:23-26, RSV).

The Bible, however, makes the imagery of the branch double. First, it is Jesus, harbinger of hope, prosperity, and peace (Isa. 11:1; Jer. 23:5; 33:15; Zech. 3:8). Second, it represents us. "The righteous shall flourish as a branch" (Prov. 11:28). Christians, then, can build Christlike beauty in their lives—and in the end, prosperity, too. Such a transformation is possible to believers, for "if the root be holy, so are the branches" (Rom. 11:16).

For us, however, the picture has one important condition—our productivity. Jesus said, "Every barren branch of mine he cuts away; and every fruiting branch he cleans, to make it more fruitful still" (John 15:2, NEB). We *must* remain attached to Him!

[*As You, Lord, are the beautiful and glorious branch, so would I maintain that connection that will make me a fruitful branch for You.*]

---

*H. G. Wells, cited in Rita Snowden, *When the Candle Burns* (London: Epworth Press, 1942), p. 37.

THE CEDAR TREE

Once growing abundantly in Palestine, the cedar tree is mentioned repeatedly in Scripture. Some references may refer to pines in general or to desert junipers. But what Ezekiel had in mind here was clearly the magnificent cedar of Lebanon. Stately with wide-spreading branches, it grew to 100 feet in height and thrived even 6,000 feet above sea level. Like the California redwoods, its rings can show up to 3,500 years of growth. Its pleasant aroma and durability brought it much praise (S. of Sol. 4:11). Because of its strong "flavor," insects leave it alone. Also, it has great resistance to fungus diseases.

No wonder cedar was Solomon's wood of choice for the construction of the Temple, his palace, and his trade ships. For 25 years he sent 10,000 men a month to cut down the trees—accompanied by 3,300 slaves to cart the valuable logs and float them down the coast to Joppa, the port of Jerusalem. It was a busy time, with another 3,300 officers managing the enormous project. But they did it with little thought of conservation—Lebanon was indescribably rich, and Hiram gave cedars away as royal gifts (1 Kings 10:9, 11).

During the rivalry in the divided kingdom, King Jehoash of Israel replied in a sarcastic political fable to an invitation to do battle with Amaziah, king of Judah: "The thistle that was in Lebanon sent to the cedar that was in Lebanon, saying, 'Give your daughter to my son as wife'; and a wild beast that was in Lebanon passed by and trampled the thistle" (2 Kings 14:9, NKJV). Subsequently, Judah suffered defeat. Because kings and other "great ones" traditionally identified themselves with the cedar, the courtship between the magnificent tree and the lowly thistle is both ridiculous and presumptuous.

Jesus as the cedar tree is a powerful image indeed. All kinds of people seek rest in Him—the young and the old, the rich and the poor. They are "birds of every sort." The mighty cedar accommodates them all—forever.

> I WILL PLANT IT; AND IT WILL BRING FORTH BOUGHS . . . AND BE A MAJESTIC CEDAR. UNDER IT WILL DWELL BIRDS OF EVERY SORT; IN THE SHADOW OF ITS BRANCHES THEY WILL DWELL.
>
> EZE. 17:23, NKJV.

[*There are so many of us, Lord. And even my moods change from day to day. Whatever circumstances prevail, I know that You will provide shelter for me. I thank You for that.*]

THE OLIVE TREE

Hosea's picture of Israel restored promised beauty "like the olive" (Hosea 14:6, RSV). Those of us far removed from the practical values of the olive tree, however, may not much appreciate the twisted trunk, the small leaves, the uneven pendulous branches, and the bitter dull-green berries. People of the Mediterranean know otherwise.

> I AM LIKE A GREEN OLIVE TREE IN THE HOUSE OF GOD.
>
> PS. 52:8, NKJV.

Olive oil was one of Palestine's most valuable products. It had religious and cosmetic purposes, as well as medicinal properties and a hundred other daily uses. Even a single tree yields abundant flowers, berries, and oil. By nature, the olive tree is wild. A cutting from a good tree must be grafted into the wild unfruitful one to make it productive. But the Gentiles were wild olives to be grafted into Christianity. Then they could draw on the powerful nutrients of the source into which they had been implanted (Rom. 11:17, 24)—a process that truly "ran contrary to nature."

Today at the Garden of Gethsemane a few of the ancient olive trees remain from within a few years of Jesus' time—truly a sacred place to walk.

To stand as flourishing green olive trees in the Lord's court is our calling. Our wildness may be permanently tamed through what happened there in Gethsemane. Then in the olive garden, if we so choose, the grafting takes place, and we are enabled to bear the fruits of the Spirit.

[*My Master, I choose to share the olive grove experience with You. I would enter the suffering and then come out with the victory.*]

THE HYSSOP

Hyssop is a mintlike herb with tough woody stems and small aromatic leaves. In modern Europe and the United States, physicians once used hyssop leaves to treat pulmonary disorders. A similar plant traces back into the ancient Middle East where it came to have great ceremonial importance.

The humble hyssop rose to biblical prominence at the time of the Exodus. Instructions for the first Passover included dipping the hyssop (sometimes translated "marjoram") in the blood of the sacrificial lamb and smearing it onto the lintel and doorposts of the house (Ex. 12:23).

Hyssop became closely connected to Jewish experience and followed them from Egypt, through the Sinai wilderness, and all the way into Palestine. Mosaic law prescribed the use of hyssop for the ritual cleansing of leprosy (Lev. 14:4, 6, 52) and the defilement of contact with a corpse (Num. 19:18). Later the remarkable range of King Solomon's knowledge of the natural sciences encompassed "all kinds of plant life, from the cedars in the Lebanese Mountains to the hyssop that grows out of the walls" (1 Kings 4:33, Clear Word). Finally, the ceremonial significance of hyssop reached its climax at Jesus' crucifixion. There could have been other ways to get a drink up to Christ on the cross (Matt. 27:48), but the watchers "filled a sponge with sour wine, put it on hyssop, and put it to His mouth" (John 19:29, NKJV).

Paul elaborated the symbolic use of hyssop in describing Hebrew worship: Moses took "a twig with hyssop leaves wrapped in red wool, used it to sprinkle blood on the written law and out toward the people saying, 'This blood symbolizes the blood that will be shed to fulfill the covenant God has commanded you to keep'" (Heb. 9:19, 20, Clear Word).

In this context we must read David's penitential Psalm 51 in which he draws on ancient rituals. The poem grew out of special, painful circumstances in his life—his seduction of Bathsheba and murder of her husband. He was agonizingly conscious of his guilt and felt completely alienated. "Purge me with hyssop," he cries, for his sin disease is worse than leprosy.

> TAKE HYSSOP AND SPRINKLE ME, THAT I MAY BE CLEAN; WASH ME, THAT I MAY BECOME WHITER THAN SNOW.
>
> PS. 51:7, NEB.

[*"Lord Jesus, I long to be perfectly whole; I want Thee forever to live in my soul;*
. . . Now wash me, and I shall be whiter than snow."—James Nicholson]

THE FIG TREE

Growing good figs is a complex matter requiring skill and hard work. Figs are far more than just a luxury dessert, a sweet morsel in a fancy box. They have always been basic to the diet of Mediterranean lands and Asia. The hardy tree may die in freezing temperatures, but new shoots will sprout from its roots.

When the Spanish first introduced figs into the New World, beginning early in the sixteenth century, transplantation revealed another problem. In order to mature, the figs had to be pollinated by small wasps *(blastophaga)* who bred in caprifig trees. They did not live in America, so the European colonists imported caprifig fruits (complete with wasps). In his vision of two baskets of figs, Jeremiah described the disappointment of a failed crop. The King James translators said quaintly: "One basket had very good figs, even like the figs that are first ripe: and the other basket had very naughty figs, which could not be eaten, they were so bad" (Jer. 24:2).

The account of the cursed fig tree near Bethany points up the tree's peculiar way of producing fruit *before* the leaves. Jesus' withering pronouncement over the tree rebuked its false pretensions. It had "advertised itself" ahead of all of the other trees with a great showing of leaves. Consequently, a passerby who had the right to pick a fig or two also had the right to expect ripe fruit. The arrogant Bethany tree was as bare, however, as the other ordinary trees. It had no figs because the right time had not arrived for any of them (Mark 11:13).

Complex as fig culture is, however, humanity has considered it worth the effort since ancient times, when people considered it a sacred fruit. Scripture employs the possession of one's "own vine and fig tree" as an illustration of the godly walk. Commitment to hard work, persistence, intelligence, and honesty leads on to the promise of happiness, hope, permanence, and security.

> JUDAH AND ISRAEL CONTINUED AT PEACE, EVERY MAN UNDER HIS OWN VINE AND FIG-TREE.
>
> 1 KINGS 4:25, NEB.

[*The significance of the fig tree pervades so many cultures. Let it not be lost on me. I would not pretend to be what I am not, Lord.*]

THE APPLE TREE

As a centerpiece on my dining room table I keep a bowl of "fruit": wooden bananas, grapes, and pineapple from the Philippines, agate mangoes from Mexico, and a fanciful painted "ball" from Kashmir. The loveliest piece of all, however, is a hand-blown glass apple from Venice—perfect in size and shape—topped with a single delicate green leaf and stem. It is forever just ripening, the colors of its smooth skin ranging realistically from blush-red to pale green to yellow. The "apple" is universally appealing in many cultures.

LIKE AN APPLE TREE AMONG THE TREES OF THE FOREST IS MY LOVER.

S. OF SOL. 2:3, NIV.

Apples as we know them, however, were not indigenous to Palestine. Several Scripture texts identify features that possibly point to other fruits: "Apples of gold in a setting of silver" (Prov. 25:11, RSV) could refer to the orange that produces fruit and flowers simultaneously—and that also "rejuvenates." "Refresh me with apples" the Shulamite bride sang (S. of Sol. 2:5, RSV). The fragrance of quince might answer to "the scent of your breath [is] like apples" (S. of Sol. 7:8, RSV). The apricot, however, appears to be the most convincing substitute. These "golden apples" of Cyprus also grew in mainland Palestine during Old Testament times. Generously perfumed, richly sweet, and embedded in pale, silvery leaves, apricots grow on large, shady trees.

Some have seen Song of Solomon as comparing Christ to the apple tree. Surprisingly, He is found "among the trees of the wood." One does not expect to find a domesticated fruit tree in the wild. And as such, He surpasses all others around Him. With "great delight" we may sit "in his shadow," breathing in the perfume that emanates from Him. Moreover, His fruit is most delicious to the taste (S. of Sol. 2:3, RSV).

Perhaps no other picture of Jesus the Beloved is more sensuous than this one. Because it is couched in a passionate Eastern love poem, it appeals to us at a very beautiful, very basic level. The fruitfulness and strength, the beauty and sweetness, the leisure and exclusiveness—Jesus would enter into *this* part of our lives also!

[*Lover of my soul, You both calm and energize me. I choose not to rest in any place other than Your presence.*]

THE ALMOND TREE

Remember the story of the budding of Aaron's rod? After Korah's rebellion the test of the 12 rods settled the priesthood on the tribe of Levi. Jehovah's choice was clear when Aaron's staff "sprouted and put forth buds, and produced blossoms, and it bore ripe almonds" (Num. 17:8, RSV)—quite a definitive piece of work in the space of one night!

Native to Palestine, almonds, it is surmised, were introduced to Egypt during Joseph's governorship. Now Aaron's rod, apparently an almond branch, had come *out* of Egypt. In due course, instructions for making the golden seven-branched lampstand for the sanctuary required that almond shaped oil-cups, decorated with "capital and flower," be part of the design (Ex. 25:32-34, RSV).

> THE WORD OF THE LORD CAME TO ME: "WHAT DO YOU SEE, JEREMIAH?" "I SEE THE BRANCH OF AN ALMOND TREE," I REPLIED.
>
> JER. 1:11, NIV.

From early Christian times artists have employed the "mandorla," a sacred almond-shaped space created by the intersection of two spheres representing earth (matter) and heaven (spirit), respectively. Signifying purity, the figure of Christ (and sometimes His mother, Mary) often appeared within the mandorla shape. Thus the Creator stands between death and life, descent and ascent.

In this connection, certain facts about the almond tree clarify these spiritual meanings. The Hebrew word for almond means "wakeful." In fact, the almond is one of the first trees to flower in the spring, as early as January. The sweet, white blossoms appear on the bare branches long before the leaves. This small member of the rose family is, however, delicate and vulnerable, for late frosts can easily destroy its flowers.

In vision God showed Jeremiah an almond rod, reminiscent of Aaron's staff. Using a play on words, He commends the young prophet for his alertness in recognizing the almond branch. "You have seen well, for I am watching over my word to perform it" (Jer. 1:12, RSV). To be sure, Jeremiah needed encouragement as he went out to face the opposition to his ministry.

God never sleeps (Ps. 121:4). What a relief! Like the "wakeful" almond tree, He is watchful, alert to every crisis in human events.

> *Jesus, infuse me with Your divine life. Let my barren branch flower forth with blossoms that beautify and with fruit that nourishes. Let me be always alert to every possibility You set before me.*

THE SHADE

Symbolically, the Lord's shade provides essential rest and renewal. In His shadow we build the strength to return to our labors in the heat of the day (Lam. 4:20). Those who "return and dwell beneath my shadow . . . shall flourish as a garden" (Hosea 14:7, RSV). We seek refuge in the shade of God, our rock and fortress in the desert (Ps. 62:6).

THE LORD IS YOUR SHADE ON YOUR RIGHT HAND. THE SUN SHALL NOT SMITE YOU BY DAY.

PS. 121:5, 6, RSV.

God, however, has taken His provision of life-preserving shade one step further. For the irritable, reluctant prophet Jonah He even altered the laws of nature. Bemoaning his evangelistic success with the Ninevites, Jonah built himself a "booth" so he could sit outside of the city and be sullen. Obviously his shelter was insufficient, so "the Lord God appointed a plant" to grow up and "be a shade over his head, to save him from his discomfort" (Jonah 4:6, RSV). Although Jonah was "exceedingly glad," he had a lesson to learn. The next day a worm attacked the shade plant and it withered. A hot east wind blew up, and the sun "beat upon the head of Jonah," so that he almost fainted (verse 8, RSV).

The Lord's shade "in a weary land" (Isa. 32:2, RSV) is a gift. Never take it for granted.

Provider of rest and renewal, You have created oases of protective shade where I can rest from the heat of my daily affairs. Let me never take Your provision for granted.

THE COVERT

Instinctively, coverts—shelters or hiding places—attract us. Didn't most of us as children make private little places—"houses"—by upending the dining-room chairs and draping blankets over them? In busy households youngsters don't always get much privacy—and everyone, no matter how young, enjoys having a secret or two. At night we cased out our bedroom for "boogeymen" and dived into the warm safety of the bedclothes. And how naturally we took to playing hide-and-seek, a game as old and universal as the history of humanity.

> **THOU HAST BEEN A SHELTER FOR ME. . . . I WILL TRUST IN THE COVERT OF THY WINGS.**
>
> PS. 61:3, 4.

Then again, animals seek safety in their natural habitat. Behemoth, the mighty "hippopotamus" of Job, hides by the riverbank. "Under the lotus plants he lies, in the covert of the reeds and in the marsh. . . . If the river is turbulent he is not frightened" (Job 40:21-23, RSV). Even your dog is likely to hide under a bed during a thunderstorm.

Anyone traversing enemy territory, of course, knows the importance of finding cover. When Abigail's boorish husband, Nabal, offended David, she "came down by the covert of the hill" to negotiate peace with the outlaw prince (1 Sam. 25:20, KJV). Warfare has always fostered the use of coverts—foxholes in the front lines and military bunkers behind barbed wire. Fugitives always risk their lives crossing borders. And many, as the former Berlin Wall witnessed, died in their efforts to run across exposed, open land.

The wise men of the Hebrews always looked forward to a coming age of justice and safety when the rulers would be people of integrity, when kings would exhibit patience and high-mindedness (Prov. 8:15-21), when "the mouths of fools" would no longer "feed on folly" (Prov. 15:14, RSV). In fact, a man could be a "covert" to his fellows. In their better moments some of the kings of Judah did manage to provide protection for their people: "A king will reign in righteousness. . . . [He] will be like a hiding place from the wind, a covert from the tempest" (Isa. 32:1, 2, RSV). The complete understanding of the prophecy, however, can have its fulfillment only in Christ.

Perhaps God built into us a natural need for "coverts" so that it would be easy for us to turn to Him for shelter.

[*Protector and Provider, I do not even know what hazards I will face today. As always, I trust You to supply my needs for the unknown.*]

THE VINE

I AM THE
VINE; YOU
ARE THE
BRANCHES.

JOHN 15:5, NIV.

While participating in an archaeological dig in Israel some years ago, I one day walked up the hill out of the City of David into Jerusalem. I passed some of the most attractive little homes I saw anywhere in Israel. Grape arbors loaded with fruit framed tiny gardens in which women whiled away the hot afternoon hours. In front of one of those ages-old stone cottages a handsome, curly headed lad trimmed the vines while down below a pair of black silky haired goats with brilliant blue eyes ate the leaves. The branches sagged with the weight of huge green grape clusters, heavy enough to have attracted the attention of any one of Moses' 12 spies, for this was an "exceedingly good" land (Num. 14:7, RSV).

We can learn much of the spiritual significance from vineyards. This basic analogy of the vine, however, describes a special relationship. Many metaphors and parables fail to "walk on four legs." That is, they do not correlate completely with reality in every detail. But here we have a very striking connection, though, one very close to the hearts of Jesus' hearers.

This picture tells us three things about the relationship between Christ and His believing people. First, the vine is rooted in rich earth, a reliable source of vitality. Second, any branch that stays connected to the vine will live. There's nothing casual or temporary about the connection. The branch becomes a part of the living vine. Third, fruit-bearing is the natural result of staying connected. From the roots to the branches, the vine communicates the life and strength necessary to productivity. If, however, a branch bears no fruit, the gardener must destroy it, because it saps the strength of the whole plant.

The joy and pleasure of the spiritual Vine comes as the Christian reflects in his or her own life the character of Jesus. As we do so we nourish people around us. Bereft of life, power, and fruit, the detached branch is nothing but dead wood. Although Christians are rightly concerned with bearing the fruits of the Holy Spirit, they can never do so as detached branches. They will inevitably fall away like the pruned leaves the Jerusalem goats ate so enthusiastically.

[*Jesus, You have revealed a lifesaving secret. I know now that, first and foremost, I must stay connected with the true Vine.*]

THE BURNING BUSH

When I first came to southern California I saw a burning bush that taught me a useful lesson. Headed toward Idyllwild in the San Jacinto range, I had just turned out of the valley toward the base of the mountain. In an area covering no more than a couple square yards beside the road, a little bush burned. Unaware and ignorant, I started up the winding way. After a few turns I came upon a van pulled to the side. Beside it a man stood gazing intently down at the fire a hundred feet below him. *Should I stop and take a license number or something? No place to park, however—just one curve after another. No business of mine,* I decided.

> GOD CALLED TO HIM FROM WITHIN THE BUSH, "MOSES! MOSES!"
>
> EX. 3:4, NIV.

How wrong I was! The evening news announced that the brushfire now raged out of control while the police searched for the arsonist. I'd *seen* the man and then done nothing! I hadn't realized that California brushfires are costly annual events. Four days later the fire had devoured thousands of acres and several homes. It took skilled ground crews, helicopters, and planes working together to bring the fire under control. I hadn't paid attention, and I'd let a criminal escape.

Now we shall alter the scene a little. A burning bush in the desert *is* always important. Naturally, it would spread with the winds and destroy everything in its path. The burning bush to which God called Moses, however, was different. Jehovah became an arsonist in order to deliver an urgent message. Blazing with blinding brilliance in one spot, God's fire affected nothing around it. As expected, the desert shepherd turned aside to "see this great sight" (Ex. 3:3, NKJV). In a short time Moses and Aaron were on their way back to Egypt to work on the deliverance of the Hebrews.

Unlike human arsonists, God knows how to focus and control His fires. When He sets a fire in your life, it may startle you at first. Like Moses, however, you will find the encounter an occasion for divine guidance (verses 4-22).

Responsible Christians will always turn aside to examine burning bushes. Somehow or other, they will find a place to park. They will pay attention. If they don't, the results will be enormously destructive to themselves and to others.

> *There will be obvious times in my life when You particularly want to get my attention, Lord. I don't want to miss any one of them.*

THE ORCHARDIST

Spring Park is in the district of Upper Swan, 30 minutes northeast of Perth, Western Australia. It is an old farm, dating back to the beginnings of the pioneer settlement of Swan River Colony. Nearby is a tiny church, the first to be built in the colony in 1839. In that churchyard lie the graves of many of my ancestors. Although the sturdy brick farm buildings of my great-grandfather still stand, his mud-brick homestead house on the riverbank "returned to the dust" a few years ago.

Grandfather Alfred, however, must have been a knowledgeable horticulturist. One of his fruit trees still remains, bearing fruit as it has been doing for more than 150 years. Extraordinary in another way, it's a large, colorful "orange-lemon" tree, the product of very skillful grafting. At present, developers are turning part of Spring Park into what they describe as an "exclusive rural retreat," a secluded, high-quality housing development. I can only hope that someone in charge will preserve the old orange-lemon tree. It doesn't deserve the death sentence.

> IF THEY [THE BROKEN BRANCHES] DO NOT PERSIST IN UNBELIEF, THEY WILL BE GRAFTED IN, FOR GOD IS ABLE TO GRAFT THEM IN AGAIN.
>
> ROM. 11:23, NIV.

Meanwhile, I've just planted a little "three-apple tree" in my own backyard. Since I am neither a gifted gardener nor an orchardist, I can only believe the nurseryman when he says that I shall eventually harvest three kinds of apples. Already it's putting forth brave little blossoms.

Successful grafting is no task for beginners. The "stock" is the supporting plant. The "scion" is the twig, stem, or bud that the horticulturalist joins to the stock. Grafting offers several advantages. A scion known to produce good fruit may be grafted into a stronger tree that of itself has less-desirable fruit. Also, grafting propagates seedless fruits, such as certain oranges and grapes. The wound opened up in the process is sealed with grafting wax and perhaps also tape.

God as divine orchardist designs all believers to be grafted into the sturdy stock of Christ. Not only can fresh young shoots join in but also unlikely scions such as dry "broken branches." If they will but believe again, life-giving sap will enliven them as they are joined to the divine stock and sealed with love and mercy.

[*Dear Lord of the orchard, preserve me from becoming a broken branch that will be cast out. Keep me grafted into Your Son.*]

THE GREEN TREE

A small encounter took place at Jesus' crucifixion, just after Simon of Cyrene picked up the cross and before He reached Calvary. We generally overlook this exchange, standing, as it does, between Pilate's judgment hall and the scene at the cross.

"Many women" joined the crowds surging through the Jerusalem streets to the place of execution that day. They "mourned and lamented over him" (verse 27, NEB). We don't know exactly who they were, but they doubtless represented a cross section of those who had followed Him through His three years of ministry. While many curiosity seekers went to executions, no doubt the women were there for other reasons. The brutality of the event notwithstanding, some had probably been recipients of His miracles, and they now came to be with Him. Most, no doubt, had listened to His teaching and believed. His departure signaled the loss of their dearest earthly friend. Some were no doubt merciful women who brought soothing herbs and drugs to ease the final hours of the condemned ones. Apparently, the Roman authorities allowed the women to render such services. In any case, Luke the physician is the only one of the Gospel writers who mentions Jesus' conversation with the women.

Although preoccupied with what lay ahead of Him, Jesus still responded to their cries of distress about Him. He did not solicit sympathy for Himself—nor does He now. His suffering is past, and He invites us to be joined to Him. "Daughters of Jerusalem, do not weep for me," He told the women. "Weep for yourselves and your children" (verse 28, NEB). Christ knew what they could not yet understand. His death would seal the fate of their nation. Conditions would worsen until fiery destruction overtook Jerusalem just a few decades later.

He framed His message in an apt metaphor. "See what the Romans and the Jewish administrators are doing to Me, the living tree? I am always fruitful, always green. I have undying divinity."

What then will come to those who are "dry" (verse 31, NEB)—those who lack life-giving righteousness, who are withered away with sin? They can never endure the fires to come.

FOR IF THESE THINGS ARE DONE WHEN THE WOOD IS GREEN, WHAT WILL HAPPEN WHEN IT IS DRY?

LUKE 23:31, NEB.

[*Comforter in trouble, let me not dry out from neglect and guilt. Let my tears be shed for the right reasons.*]

THE TREE OF LIFE

In his allegory *The Great Divorce,* C. S. Lewis describes a fantastic bus ride from hell to heaven. Upon experiencing the density and staggering *reality* of heaven, however, most of the frail ghosts aboard the bus decide to make it a round trip and return to hell. Life there is very like earth—as near as possible to "nothing," and with plenty of room for disbelief and cynicism. Hell's borders are limitless, because everyone hates everyone else, and people don't want to live near one another.

ON EACH SIDE OF THE RIVER STOOD THE TREE OF LIFE.

REV. 22:2, NIV.

A few choose to stay in heaven, where they'll mingle with the "solid people" and be taught by the "bright people" (the angels). They will eat of the tree of life—but they must learn how to approach it. So that they can walk on the grass without cutting their feet they must intensify their unsubstantial bodies. In addition, they must become strong enough to pick the incredibly heavy fruit from the tree. Lewis describes the glorious tree:

"Where the [waterfall] plunged into the lake there grew a tree. Wet with the spray, half-veiled in foam-bows, flashing with the bright, innumerable birds that flew among its branches, it rose in many shapes of billowy foliage. . . . From every point, apples of gold gleamed through the leaves. . . . Round the tree grew a belt of lilies."

Attempting to seize the golden apples, one pitiful ghost couldn't even get past the lilies. "[He] might as well have tried to tread down an anti-tank trap as to walk on them." Finally he managed to pick up the smallest apple under the tree and stagger back toward the bus. A voice from the waterfall thundered, "Fool, . . . put it down. You cannot take it back. There is not room for it in Hell. Stay here and learn to eat such apples."*

The tree of life, once lost out of the Garden of Eden, is our only means of maintaining immortality. Eating from it will be a daily meal for the saints. But, as Lewis so vividly demonstrates, heaven will not be a place of living joy for those who have not prepared beforehand for its lifestyle. Indeed, having made their choices, it will be a mercy that God excludes the unsaved from Paradise.

Putting aside lightweight pursuits that I consider so important in my daily life, I determine to begin training to cope with the "heavy" obligations of heaven.

*C. S. Lewis, *The Great Divorce* (New York: Macmillan Co., 1946), pp. 48-52.

THE LIVING LEAF

Apart from the Genesis story, the Babylonian *Epic of Gilgamesh* (2000 B.C.) is perhaps one of the oldest pieces of literature that we have. The hero, Gilgamesh, is the legendary king of Erech (now Warka, Iraq). He determines to discover the secret of eternal life by seeking out the wise man Utnapishtim (the Babylonian Noah), the only mortal ever to have escaped death. From him Gilgamesh learns that the secret is exclusively a gift of the gods. A sacred herb growing at the bottom of the sea produces eternal youth. After many adventures, the courageous Gilgamesh secures the plant and heads home to Erech. He stops at a spring to bathe and rest, and while he is thus preoccupied, a snake steals the plant of immortality and makes off with it. Bitterly disappointed, the king realizes that no human can escape old age and death. Discouraged, he returns to his homeland to share the fate of all humanity, and there he dies.

> **AND THE LEAVES OF THE TREE ARE FOR THE HEALING OF THE NATIONS.**
> REV. 22:2, NIV.

Human experience has shown us that we maintain life by means of the food we eat. (And *fresh* food is more highly recommended than ever.) We must "fuel" our bodies just as any machine must have an energy supply in order to function. But there's more! No matter how much anatomy and physiology we learn, the wonder remains—a mystery for which we lack an explanation. How does a piece of bread become an intention to keep an appointment we've made? How does a bowl of rice transfer into an act of kindness? Precisely what is the connection between a green salad and our ability to affirm that God exists?

Leaves provide us with life and health. They need light for photosynthesis—the process that produces food and life-giving oxygen. Interestingly enough, the two colors of the light spectrum used by the leaf are red and blue. Symbolically, red and blue stand for forgiveness and obedience, respectively. Keep the leaf in darkness, however, and the whole action stops. Without leaves, earth lapses into a lifeless desert.

Honored in so many cultures, the tree of life is heaven's most practical feature. The leaves of the tree plus the light of God (Ps. 119:105) together ensure eternal life. At last we shall recover what the snake stole from us so long ago!

[*I long today, Lord, for the light and glory of Your kingdom. I pray that You will bring us home soon.*]

THE HEDGE

Accusing God of favoritism, Satan here declares that Job is righteous only because of the material benefits his obedience buys. The comment about God's protective care being like a hedge is correct, however, even if the picture did originate with Satan.

The English landscape portrays the hedge picturesquely:

1. **A hedge defines boundaries.** Ancient hedges crisscross the meadows, dividing pasture lands. They separate cottage gardens from one another.

2. **A hedge protects** against outside intrusions and ensures seclusion. Living plants have overgrown earth mounds and old stone walls, creating barriers more dense and decisive than any single masonry wall.

3. **A hedge is beautiful.** The "great houses" of England are a study in a lavish lifestyle. Their gardens are works of art. The topiary experts trim hedges of green and golden yew or box into fanciful shapes, perhaps a geometric maze, high bushy walls, or an expanse of hedged "rooms." Little manicured hedges enclose colorful knot gardens. Or they shape yew trees into cylinders, pyramids, spirals, bells, fanciful birds and animals—even chess pieces.

4. **A hedge is alive.** The centuries-old hedgerows engulfing narrow country lanes have been habitat to generations of field animals. In his charming fantasy of the English countryside, *The Wind in the Willows* (1908), Kenneth Grahame brings hedgerow society to life in the characters of Rat, Mole, and Mr. Toad.

In accordance with Satan's initial complaint, the hedge around Job effectively kept Satan out. God had laid down property lines over which evil could not pass. Even when God permitted Satan to carry out his experiment, one hedge still remained: "All that he has is in your hands," God said. "Only Job himself you must not touch" (Job 1:12, NEB). Then sick and stripped of all he had, Job had nothing left but pain, sorrow, and ugliness. Now we realize how very beautiful God's hedge really is. Yet we're not prisoners. Growing to meet every need and teeming with life, God's hedge surrounds us with joy.

> "HAS NOT JOB GOOD REASON TO BE GOD-FEARING? HAVE YOU NOT HEDGED HIM ROUND ON EVERY SIDE WITH YOUR PRO-TECTION?"
>
> JOB 1:10, NEB.

[
Let me learn to rejoice, Jesus, in the
freedom that Your hedge gives to me.
]

THE ROSE OF SHARON

Although wildflowers abound in Palestine, Scripture has given us—surprisingly—few passages about flowers. Both of the primary ones, those referring to the rose and the lily, are associated with Christ. Although they were ordinary wildflowers, both were beautiful and fragrant. In his Messianic portrayal of spiritual prosperity, Isaiah said: "The desert shall rejoice and blossom as the rose" (Isa. 35:1, NKJV).

"I AM A ROSE OF SHARON."

S. OF SOL. 2:1, NIV.

There are several varieties of Palestinian "roses"—the mountain tulip, the rock rose, and the Phoenician rose (crocus). The rose of Sharon, however, was possibly the "bunch-flowered" *Narcissus tazetta*. (The Martha Washington and Primrose Beauty are but two modern descendants of *tazetta*.) After a rainfall these hardy flowers—almost overnight—could cover the desert with clouds of heather-like bloom.

The rose that we know today, however, is a flashy immigrant from Persia, born at the horticultural center at the Elamite city of Susa. (There Scripture records King Ahasuerus as having a splendid garden party lasting 180 days [Esther 1:4].) Since it is related to the cabbage, people first valued this fragrant flower as a food upon its arrival in Europe!

In Western tradition the red rose became a symbol of love, forgiveness, and martyrdom, while white roses exemplified purity and pain. Wild or cultivated, the rose has become to us a popular symbol of elegance, love, and perfection. It appears in our architecture and music and has inspired poets and painters.

In associating the rose with Christ, the church fathers no doubt had the Persian delight in mind. (Legend had it that the rose acquired its thorns after the fall of humanity and thus reminded us of sin and foreshadowed the crown of thorns Christ would wear at the cross.)

[*It is well that all the world loves roses. May it help us all to think upon You, the matchless rose of Sharon.*]

THE LILY OF THE VALLEY

The figures of speech employing flowers between the lovers in Song of Solomon give rise to the most romantic poetry in Scripture. The bride says, as they sit together among the wildflowers, "I am a lily of the valleys." Modestly she compares herself to the ordinary field lilies. Jesus later chose those everyday flowers to illustrate perfect trust. Beautiful but wild, they neither "toil nor spin." "See," He said, "how they grow?" Easily, freely! (Matt. 6:28; Luke 12:27).

"I AM . . . A LILY OF THE VALLEYS."
S. OF SOL. 2:1, NIV.

Her royal lover, however, gracefully turns the Shulamite's words into a compliment by contrasting the lily with the thistle: "Like a lily among thorns is my darling among the maidens," he replies (S. of Sol. 2:2, NIV). In contrast, he seems to be referring to something more dramatic, perhaps the *anemone* coronaria. That wild and prolific scarlet-purple flower could certainly have surpassed "Solomon in all his glory." Or was it the tall Madonna lily *(Lilium candidum),* a majestic flower that did not reach Europe until the Crusades? In any case, the king regarded his beloved more lavishly than she did herself.

Scripture mentions lilies 15 times, and their sweet loveliness has long shadowed forth the preciousness of Christ to His church. Medieval artists repeatedly pictured Mary and the virgin saints with the Madonna lily or the fragrant hyacinth that in the spring turned the hillsides of Galilee blue. The French kings adopted the fleur-de-lis as a national emblem.

No doubt the word *shoshan,* meaning "lily" and "whiteness," was—like the rose—connected with Shushan, the garden palace of Ahasuerus. There all kinds of lilies, including water lilies, were beloved. Since then, in both East and West, lilies have stood for cleanness and grace. Greek and Roman bridal wreaths of lilies and wheat symbolized purity and perfection, fertility and excellence. Christian legend traces the Arum lily back to the Garden of Eden, representing the tears of the penitent Eve.

This rich imagery points to Christ's church, which has been a "lily among thorns" many times through the ages. Large and elegant in form, vigorous in its strength, gorgeous in its coloring, the lily lends deep spiritual meaning to our faith.

> *Lord, Your lilies are lovely. They tell me that true repentance is the true beginning of beauty.*

THE WREATH

In presenting Himself to Israel as a "beautiful wreath," God struck a high note of encouragement. Isaiah's message came to "the remnant"—people who had been hunted and slaughtered, impoverished and exiled. It was a marvelous symbol of love, honor, and protection!

The idea of the old Anglo-Saxon word "wreath" has been with us for a long time. Any child who has not sat in the spring grass weaving a chain of daisies or crocuses has missed something. The Orient offers such a variety of richly fragrant flowers that wreaths of orchids, magnolias, or "temple flowers" are almost the norm. A Hawaiian lei welcomes a tourist. Necklaces of *sampaguita* flowers hang on the windshields of Philippine jeepneys. Wreath-making speaks to something deep inside of us all.

The wreath is significant in two ways. The "laurel wreath," so prized by the sports-loving ancient Greeks, came from the evergreen bay tree and served both as a mark of honor and as a defense against pestilence. Twisted circles of leaves, flowers, or fabric may hang on the door or in the window to mark occasions of either joy or sorrow. We leave them on the graves of loved ones or mount them on the walls of public buildings. They portray honor and celebration, grief and remembrance—along with the whole range of feelings lying in between.

Also, flower wreaths spell out love, gladness, and trust. Flowers "teach you that you are not placed on earth merely to delve for self, to dig and build, to toil and spin, but to make life bright and joyous and beautiful with the love of Christ . . . , to gladden other lives by the ministry of love."*

We learn to hold up our heads and wear the wreath of God before a scornful world, for heaven has given it for joy and reward. Moreover, like the ancient Greeks with their medicinal crowns of bay leaves, the Lord, our wreath, preserves us from the loss of our souls. We may wear it in peace and contentment.

IN THAT DAY THE LORD ALMIGHTY WILL BE . . . A BEAUTIFUL WREATH FOR THE REMNANT OF HIS PEOPLE.

ISA. 28:5, NIV.

[*The picture of the wreath, my Jesus, combines all that is lovely, joyful, and victorious in Your creation. Worn either for life or death, the wreath is triumphant and everlasting.*]

*Ellen White, *Thoughts From the Mount of Blessing,* p. 145.

[PART TWO]

Social
Relationships

THE FAMILY

THE COMMUNITY

POLITICS

RELIGION

OTHER SIGNIFICANT RELATIONSHIPS

THE SON OF GOD

From the pharaohs of Egypt to the emperors of Japan, the claim to divine parentage has had great political and psychological power. To account for its beginnings, almost every culture tells of a first king with supernatural origins. Establishing such a connection conferred many privileges upon the kings and their dynasties. First, it created a divine-human hierarchy in which the king could do no wrong. Second, it suggested that to rebel against him was to affront the gods and undermine the divine order of the whole universe. Altogether, the system worked admirably to control people and to prevent rebellions. Since "all power corrupts and absolute power corrupts absolutely," more often than not, kings have abused their positions. Their devious deeds fill the pages of history.

> GOD LOVED THE WORLD SO MUCH THAT HE GAVE HIS ONLY SON.
>
> JOHN 3:16, NEB.

The most vital part of the multifaceted Sonship of Jesus was His claim to be the Son of God. Because He didn't look or act like a king with "divine rights," and because not even the disciples could grasp the nature of His promised kingdom, the issue provoked controversy to the very end of His earthly ministry. First, God claimed Him as "my beloved Son" (Matt. 3:17; 17:5). Then Satan inquired, "If thou be the Son of God . . ." (Matt. 4:3). Unclean spirits found themselves forced to cry out, "You are the Son of God" (Mark 3:11, NEB).

Jesus explained the relationship clearly: "No one knows the Father but the Son and those to whom the Son may choose to reveal him" (Matt. 11:27, NEB). Indeed, He asked no disciple a more significant question than the one He put to Peter: "Who do you say I am?"

With characteristic zeal Peter replied, "You are the Messiah, the Son of the living God" (Matt. 16:15, 16, NEB).

When it was all over, it took the pagan Roman centurion in charge of Christ's crucifixion to speak for everyone: "Surely he was the Son of God!" (Matt. 27:54, NIV).

Now we, 20 centuries later, must also settle this issue clearly in our minds. Either Jesus *is* the Son of God or nothing else we say or do in our religious profession makes any difference.

> *Dear Father, You sent Your Son to live among us. Please let me never lose sight of the precious meaning of that Gift.*

THE SON OF DAVID

As a special research assignment in English classes, I have occasionally asked students to investigate their ancestry by creating a genealogical tree and collecting pictures and recording the traditions of their family circles. The students almost invariably do well because it gives them roots in a fractured society. Ultimately, bloodlines supersede separations, even death and divorce. Moreover, old relatives dearly love to be asked to tell stories. Indeed, when they die they take with them generations of information forever lost to their descendants.

"CAN THIS BE THE SON OF DAVID?"
MATT. 12:23, NEB.

Jesus' role as Messiah had political significance to the Jews, who conceived of Him as a champion of their cause against the Roman occupation. Therefore, certifying His royal descent from David was not only obligatory, it also established His humanity.

The patriarchal birthright blessing from Abraham evolved into a kingly line with David. Eldest sons automatically inherited a double portion of property as well as the spiritual leadership of the clan. Esau, however, surrendered his privilege to his younger brother, Jacob (Gen. 25:29-34). In the next generation Reuben lost it for a serious moral offense (Gen. 35:22). Then the birthright bypassed the next two brothers, Simeon and Levi, for their murderous attack on the incapacitated men of Shechem (Gen. 34:1-31). That made Judah the next in line. Matthew tracks the 42 generations from Abraham through David to Joseph, the "husband of Mary" (Matt. 1:1-17).

Despite all this legal concern with the genealogy of Jesus, His lifestyle and teachings puzzled the people of His time. Trying to seize upon the thread of royalty, they, like the two blind men on the road to Jericho, hailed Him as "son of David" (Matt. 20:29-34). Not surprisingly, He made His triumphal entry into Jerusalem under the title "son of David" (Matt. 21:9).

Christ's miracle-working often called for exclamations of joyful recognition. "Can this be the son of David? Is the Messiah really here?" Fearfully, Jewish legislators hastened to tear down the idea of Jesus' royalty before it could take root.

Christian believers have a much clearer view of their lineage. Yes, Jesus' human genealogy *is* distinguished. But His true royalty (and through Him, ours) derives from the kingdom of heaven.

[*Heavenly King who took the name of the Son of David, I cherish the grace with which You identified with humanity—me included.*]

THE SON OF MARY

Today we take our surnames for granted. They are part of what holds a family together. Still, they are relatively new inventions. William the Conqueror, a wily politician, imposed surnames on the English for his convenience in keeping the tax records of the Domesday Book. The most ancient formula for identification, however, was that of relationship—"the son of," "the wife of," "the father of."

"ISN'T THIS THE CARPENTER? ISN'T THIS MARY'S SON . . . ?"

MARK 6:3, NIV.

For Jesus His human relationships were tenuous. In the Nazareth synagogue Jesus' encounter with the hostile citizens revealed an undercurrent of suspicion. "Isn't this the carpenter?" Not the "carpenter's son." So why was He not, as the eldest son, at work in the family business? Therefore, we must assume that Mary was now a widow. "Isn't this *Mary's* son? . . ." (Mark 6:3, NIV). The town gossips had been working on that story for the past 30 years. Mary's son indeed! A teenage girl goes out of town and then comes back with a story about being pregnant because of the visit of an angel? Really!

Let us recapture that electric moment when Gabriel and Mary met. For the announcing angel, his mission had no precedent in all of eternity. He stood at the crossroads of time, literally joining heaven to earth. Oblivious to the workaday world just outside the window, the two face each other:

"The angel and the girl are met . . .
See, they have come together, see, . . .
Each reflects the other's face
Till heaven in hers and earth in his
Shine steady there. He's come to her
From far beyond the farthest star,
Feathered through time. Immediacy
Of strangest strangeness is the bliss
That from their limbs all movement takes.
Yet the increasing rapture brings
So great a wonder that it makes
Each feather tremble on his wings."
—Edwin Muir (1887-1958)*

[*Jesus, as Mary's Son, we find You
sympathetic to our family concerns.*]

*Donald Davie, ed., *The New Oxford Book of Christian Verse* (Oxford, England: Oxford University Press, 1988), p. 264.

THE SON OF MAN

Master storyteller David Kossoff's *The Book of Witnesses** imaginatively expands the circle of people who knew Jesus during His sojourn with humanity as the "Son of man." The life of one of the New Testament's most unlikely characters curiously portrays the meaning of this title. According to Kossoff, Barabbas had a wife. Lydia was one of the 11 witnesses to the last week of Christ's life. A strong, serious woman from a respectable family, she served Pilate's wife, Claudia, as a maid. At the trial of Jesus she first saw the Zealot Barabbas, a handsome "gutter boy" who had risked his life for the Jewish independence cause. Afterward, they married, for he had become less opinionated, a truly gentle man.

> "THE SON OF MAN WILL BE BETRAYED TO THE CHIEF PRIESTS AND TEACHERS OF THE LAW."
>
> MARK 10:33, NIV.

Ten years after the Crucifixion, Lydia recalls, "If Jesus hadn't died, I wouldn't have my Barabbas . . . [He] and I were at the Crucifixion. How could we not be? It changed Barabbas. Me too." Kossoff decides that Barabbas must have become a Christian. How could he not?

Interestingly, the name "Barabbas" means simply "the son of a father." Any human father. This fact points up the enormous contrast in Pilate's question to the raving mob: "Which would you like me to release to you—Jesus Bar-Abbas, or Jesus called Messiah [the Anointed One]?" (Matt. 27:17, NEB). Thus the liberated prisoner Barabbas became the "generic man"—all of *us!* His career is ours. The headstrong pursuit of sins of every shape and color. The defiance. The riotous living, either high or low. The brush with the law, imprisonment, and the waiting on death row. Then comes the encounter with the Man, Jesus—followed by the choice for life. Yes, Kossoff must be right. Barabbas *had* to have become a changed man.

In assuming the title "Son of man" Jesus took on our humanity at its most humble, ordinary level. It bespeaks all the miserable frustration, the tedious "dailyness" of our lives, and our inability to escape that. Divinity's encounter with humanity, however, directs us to the possibility of change, of healing.

[*Son of man, I often feel very ordinary. Be with me in my tasks today. Thank You for adding humanity to Your divinity in such a practical way.*]

---

*David Kossoff, *The Book of Witnesses* (Glasgow: William Collins, 1971). As a Jewish character actor, Kosoff first presented these stories of Jesus' contempararies in radio broadcasts on the BBC in London, England.

THE FIRSTBORN

Psychologists have now described the effects of birth order on our personalities and careers. In my family I was the firstborn—and for eight years thereafter, the only child. In reviewing this circumstance, I have considered the meaning of being firstborn. I have discovered some reasons I think Jesus chose this relationship to reveal more of Himself to us.

WHEN GOD BRINGS HIS FIRSTBORN INTO THE WORLD, HE SAYS, "LET ALL GOD'S ANGELS WORSHIP HIM."

HEB. 1:6, NIV.

To begin with, the first offspring comes under considerable pressure to be the perfect child. New at their job, parents are usually determined to do everything right. Later, being rather tired, they tend to relax more with the second child. (I recall several liberties denied to me that somehow became available to my little sister.) As firstborn, however, you are the object of your parents' marvelous new understanding of the mystery of love. They have experienced the wonder of bringing home that first baby! With the second child, of course, there may be more sleep, less pacing of the floor, more crying, more spilled food, and fewer photographs taken.

Because the firstborn becomes a model for those who follow, expectations usually run high. The career decisions of the eldest can shape the family's entire future course. The birthright ensures that the property, if there is any, will come into his/her hands first. Along with such privileges goes the responsibility for spiritual leadership in the family. The eldest should be a strong anchor point in all the affairs of the clan. Many of us, unfortunately, have fallen short of some—even all—of these ideals.

With God's Firstborn, however, it is otherwise. Jesus has failed in none of His responsibilities. He gave up His heavenly birthright to become a wayfarer among us. Although He was already perfect, throughout His earthly life He daily risked the loss of that perfection by putting it to the most rigid testing. Thus He gave us an infallible model by which to shape our characters.

Finally, He did something absolutely unique to Himself. "Jesus Christ . . . the faithful witness, [is] the firstborn from the dead" (Rev. 1:5, NIV). In one bold stroke, He shattered the tomb and set before us the open door to resurrection and everlasting life.

[*I pray not to fail in my responsibilities as the firstborn. Because others always look to us as models, I know that we all are firstborn.*]

THE SECOND ADAM

The word "Adam" stirs our imaginations with all that is fresh and pristine. He stood at the beginning of things, at the dawn of a golden age. Perhaps that is why the name is enjoying a revival in our times as a good name for small boys. Since America's "rebirth" of arts and self-identity in the nineteenth century, the American dream has beckoned millions of immigrants to the New World. The endless possibilities of the vast continent made it a new Garden of Eden—and the pioneers who opened it up hoped to be like Adam in Paradise. Even though the dream has tarnished and rather diminished over the past 100 years, many hopes and aspirations can still find fulfillment—for the new "American Adams" willing to work and sacrifice.

"THE FIRST MAN ADAM BECAME A LIVING BEING," THE LAST ADAM, A LIFE-GIVING SPIRIT.

1 COR. 15:45, NIV.

The origins of the idea lie in the most ancient recorded past. The Old Testament opens with God producing the human race in His own image. Scripture calls both the man and woman "Adam"—that is, "man" or "earthly"—closely associated with the ground (Gen. 1:27; 5:2). In fact, Eve does not even receive a personal name until after the Fall (Gen. 3:20). After the end of the Eden story, although Scripture mentions Adam hundreds of times, his name becomes almost a common noun—a reference to humanity.

Adam was not of divine birth, with autocratic rights. Rather he was a special creation, standing on the border between God and His created world. He was of the earth but also made spiritually in God's image and destined to be in communion with Him.

When Paul presents Christ as the "Second Adam" he emphasizes this important comparison. *Both* Adams are heads of our human race. Our physical heritage comes from the first. Because of him we enjoy the earth, we make new beginnings, we adventure and follow after our material dreams. In one act of sin, however, Adam lost Paradise, committing us to judgment, condemnation, and death. And we are *all* involved in his sin. Then Jesus came to minister to the eternal needs of our souls. Thus in one act of righteousness, the Second Adam ensured the plan of salvation and regained heaven for us.

[*Dear God, I thank You humbly that You placed the destiny of us, Your creatures, in the hands of the Second Adam and did not leave it with the first.*]

THE ELDER BROTHER

The great houses of England are fabulously beautiful, but they suffer from heavy taxation and costly upkeep. Consequently, they have become burdensome to their owners—many of whom have survived financially only by opening the gorgeous rooms and gardens to the public, and by adding zoos, camping facilities, and amusement parks to help pay the bills. A guide in the home of the marquis of Bath, Longleat, told us that the present marquis lives in a modern house in town and that his younger brother works in business. And his daughter, when she's home from university, serves ice cream out in the pavilion. No one knows who she is, of course.

WE ARE CHILDREN OF GOD. . . . WHEN HE APPEARS, WE SHALL BE LIKE HIM.

1 JOHN 3:1, 2, NIV.

The wealth and encumbrances carried by the eldest son once made sense, of course. After all, we cannot subdivide property indefinitely. But not all elder brothers have done well. Having age, property, loyalty, and influence in their favor, they have sometimes seriously lost their way. The infamous elder brother in the story of the prodigal son is a case in point. He had lived by all of the "elder brother" rules. But now he felt the father's behavior was intolerable. Not only did the prodigal receive all the benefits of home *again,* but more besides. Nothing like grace or forgiveness entered into the elder brother's reckoning.

Jesus, on the other hand, has presented Himself as our Elder Brother. Addressing the Gentiles, Luke makes the genealogical case universal by carrying the line back to Adam (Luke 3:23-38). (Matthew's line opens with Abraham, progenitor of the Hebrew nation.) And at the end we read the most vital phrase of all. Adam is the "son of God" (verse 38).

That means two things: every human being is related to every other human being. Therefore, in this context, John wrote, "He has given us this command: Whoever loves God must also love his brother" (1 John 4:21, NIV). And Jesus, as Son of God, becomes our Elder Brother. From Him we shall have justice, generosity, and compassion—assured.

[*Dear Father, I praise You for giving Your Son to be my Elder Brother—to guide, comfort, and love me. And I thank You for my earthly brothers and sisters You have given me to teach me Your grace.*]

THE HEIR

Since money has long been one of our major motivations, our preoccupation with material property is endless. Who knows what percentage of the population aspires to game shows or plays the lottery. The traditional scenario of the rich uncle reappearing after decades of absence to dispense his wealth among his grasping quarreling relatives is a standard comic situation. Real life, however, is not that funny. Rich legacies have often shredded family relations as an equally acquisitive lawyer conducts the reading of the will.

Old Testament times had no such thing as a "last will and testament." The head of the house, as he felt death approaching, gave verbal instructions about the distribution of his property. Mosaic laws summarized certain guidelines. The eldest son succeeded to the headship of the family (Deut. 21:17). Daughters did not inherit property unless there were no male heirs—and even then they might well have to fight for it. Women married out of the family, so society saw no point letting them take property with them. The same went for widows, who, if they had no grown-up children, found themselves sent back to their father's house.

In the New Testament the word "heirs" usually referred to the relationship of the Christian to the promises made to Abraham. The hope of salvation was not restricted to his physical descendants. Rather anyone could become a spiritual descendant, an "heir," by having the *faith* of Abraham. That is, by being adopted.

Legally adopted children may have good, bad, or average experiences, depending on the stability of the home into which they go. One thing they all have in common, however, is their legal rights. When it comes to the final court hearing, the adoptive parents have to sign a contract agreeing that the adopted child's inheritance will be equal to that of any other children already in the family or yet to be born, that there will be no kind of favoritism.

Jesus' coming threw open the door to all the world. The terms of the adoption contract entitled them to every privilege ever promised to Abraham.

> GOD SENT HIS SON, BORN OF A WOMAN . . . TO REDEEM THOSE UNDER LAW, THAT WE MIGHT RECEIVE THE FULL RIGHTS OF SONS [BY ADOPTION].
>
> GAL. 4:5, NIV.

> [*Heavenly Father, Your adoption plan leaves none of us out,*
> *except by our own choice. As a member of Your family,*
> *I pray that I will do nothing to dishonor the family name.*]

THE LOVER

Love is a much overworked word. We live and move through an extremely complicated network of loves—some essential, some contrived, and some silly. They crisscross the fabric of life endlessly—the love of God and human beings, human and human, parent and child, brother and sister, friend and friend, person and possessions. Paul's definition (1 Cor. 13) offers a checklist to evaluate love, one applicable to any love relationship—divine or human.

1. Love is patient and kind, putting wrongs in perspective so that we can forgive.

2. Love is not jealous and boastful, thus freely allowing people to be themselves.

3. Love is not arrogant and rude, but healing, reuniting, and delighting in service.

4. Love does not insist on its own way, therefore freeing us from enslavement to self.

5. Love is not irritable and resentful, but communicates between people and shields us from a loveless world outside.

6. Love rejoices in the right, basing itself on truth and honesty.

7. Love bears and believes all things, often calling for sacrifice and suffering.

8. Love hopes all things, sharing dreams and enriching our future.

9. Love endures all things, is never erratic, and always builds us up.

10. Love never ends, outlasting human life and conquering death, all the way into eternity.

Being a true lover is the highest possible calling. Therefore, Jesus chose to be the "lover of our souls," to speak to us in the most touching and sensitive human terms. As the perfect lover, He never fails us in a single point. He never imposes Himself upon us. However, day by day He attends to the thousand little needs that make up our security, comfort, and happiness.

Then, like a faithful earthly lover, He waits for us to come to keep our meetings with Him. "Whoever lives in love lives in God, and God in him" (1 John 4:16, NIV). At such times He gives us a foretaste of eternity, in which He will share with us all of love's joys and mysteries forever—love with Him and love with one another.

THIS IS MY LOVER, THIS IS MY FRIEND.

S. OF SOL. 5:16, NIV.

GOD IS LOVE. WHOEVER LIVES IN LOVE LIVES IN GOD, AND GOD IN HIM.

1 JOHN 4:16, NIV.

> [
> *"Jesus, lover of my soul, let me to Thy bosom fly,*
> *While the billows near me roll, while the tempest still is high"*
>]
> —Charles Wesley (1740)

THE SUITOR

Those in love have the privilege to believe that the one they adore is beautiful—even if he or she is not. We've all seen happy, long-married couples and wondered, "He's as homely as a splintered fence post. Whatever does she see in him?" Or "She's so dowdy that I'd think he'd be ashamed to be seen with her in daylight." Herein lies the uniqueness of being in love. Whenever, however it happens, the chemistry of love remains an inexplicable mystery.

In their often flamboyant mating rituals, even birds and animals are perfectly oblivious to the plainness of the female. She, on the other hand, accepts the vanity of the male in good grace. Indeed, courtship creates a strange world of its own.

> MY BELOVED IS ALL RADIANT AND RUDDY, DISTINGUISHED AMONG TEN THOUSAND.
>
> S. OF SOL. 5:10, RSV.

God created human beings, however, to love one another in a far more profound way. He uses this same avenue Himself to reach our hearts. For us the awakening to the love experience goes far beyond outward appearance. God programmed us to love on three levels—the spiritual, the intellectual, as well as the physical. Thus courtship is a delicious time between the first attraction and the making of binding promises. We become acquainted with one another's assets as well as disabilities. Courtship needs plenty of space and time so that we can make these discoveries. Our heavenly Suitor persistently seeks our love. At first He enjoyed the simple companionship of Adam and Eve in Eden. After the coming of sin, however, He became our relentless suitor, planning, providing, and pleading to win back our love and loyalty. Like the Shulamite maid adoring the king, He wants us to find Him. To know again that He is "altogether lovely," the "chief among ten thousand."

Jesus knows the very worst about us—all of that and more. Nothing can surprise Him. Still, He will never willingly give us up. No lover has ever sought his or her beloved with greater devotion than this. God's love makes us beautiful—in spite of ourselves.

If the engagement is broken, it will be our choice, not His.

[*Dearest Friend, thank You for always loving me,*
even at those times when I know I am very unlovely.]

THE BRIDEGROOM

In the Western world today both fashion and finance tend to focus on the bride and her family. Bridal showers and wedding gifts now replace the old bride price, making up somewhat for the lack of a negotiated dowry. Basically, our bridegroom just has to show up at the church on time. If he takes a more active role in the arrangements, it is usually by invitation or by his own insistence. Onlookers generally say "*Here* comes the bride" and "*There* goes the groom."

"HERE'S THE BRIDE-GROOM! COME OUT TO MEET HIM!"

MATT. 25:6, NIV.

In the East, on the other hand, the bridegroom is completely in charge. The marriage of Boaz and Ruth offers an exquisite example not only of ancient Eastern custom but also of Christ's special relationship to the believer. The marriage partakes of both purchase and love.

Following the instruction of her dispossessed mother-in-law, Naomi, the young widow, Ruth, claimed her rights with the wealthy landowner, Boaz. Because there existed someone with a closer relationship, however, Boaz had to negotiate with the elders at the city gate. "When property was redeemed or exchanged, it was the custom for a man to pull off his sandal and give it to the other party" (Ruth 4:7, NEB). Having received his kinsman's shoe, Boaz announced triumphantly: "I have purchased Ruth . . . to be my wife" (verse 10, TLB).

Upon hearing reports of Jesus' opening ministry, John the Baptist caught the excitement of the "wedding day," the bonding between Christ and His believers. Indeed, he described himself as the "best man." "It is the bridegroom to whom the bride belongs. The bridegroom's friend, who stands by and listens to him, is overjoyed at hearing the bridegroom's voice. This joy, this perfect joy, is now mine" (John 3:29, 30, NEB).

Jesus has purchased us at a high price—His own life. He has won back our patrimony—our right to the earth. Also, He is our Lord, for He has received the shoe, a symbol of dominion and authority.

We do not meet the Bridegroom at some intermediary place. He completed the arrangements long ago. Now He has only to come to our house to take us, in bridal procession, to His house. Our sole responsibility, then, is to be dressed and ready to go. Preparations for the homecoming have all been His.

[*Jesus, I thank You for the many ways that You are ever coming to me. Today I am as eager as You are to come and share the marriage celebration You have prepared.*]

THE HUSBAND

We've now had a couple generations wherein romantically involved couples have had open "live-in" arrangements in their desire to bypass the risks and legalities of marriage. "More than half of marriages end in divorce, so why bother?" they say. "Weddings spoil good friendships." Most of the older generation still disapprove, while the younger make airy remarks such as, "Everyone's entitled to a trial marriage" and "Get real! We're entering the twenty-first century." By refusing to take the responsibility, however, they miss a profoundly deep element in their relationship.

> "[THE HOUSE OF JUDAH] BROKE MY COVENANT, THOUGH I WAS A HUSBAND TO THEM."
>
> JER. 31:32, NIV.

The position of husband may sometimes seem mundane—paying bills, mowing the lawn, servicing the car, carrying out the garbage. Indeed, the Old English form of the word indicated that the husband manages his house, is "bonded" to it. Notwithstanding, God still designed this role to be the climax, the crowning achievement, of the "love sequence" with which He identifies: the lover, the suitor, the bridegroom, and the husband.

Avoiding marriage vows depletes the spiritual elements of trust and faith in the relationship. It is tantamount to saying "I can't promise to remain faithful to you alone" and/or "I don't believe that you are going to see this union through to the end."

Assuming the formal titles of husband and wife has important implications. In fact, the case may be made whether the marriage involves the monogamous Christian union or the polygamous connections of more ancient cultures. In either situation, the husband binds himself to certain responsibilities. He vows to be responsible for the mother of his children, for their daily support, for their future security. The entire social and spiritual well-being of the family depends on his success. Of course, women and children do survive—often courageously—in other contexts, without husbands and fathers. Nonetheless, a conscientious and loving husband still represents the ideal—the force binding all together.

Because of these solemn commitments, God cast Himself in this final and ultimately demanding role. He wanted us to be united by His love and protected by His strength.

> *Lord, I am deeply moved by Your promise to be with me for "better or for worse." I pledge You my life and my love.*

THE FRIEND

During early spring I regularly find, mixed in with the graduation announcements, a number of wedding invitations. In recent years I have regarded it as an encouraging step forward when brides and grooms use "Today I shall marry my friend." Considering that a great many people who are *not* friends have still decided to marry one another, I like to see young people announcing themselves as "friends" before they arrive at the marriage altar.

"YOU ARE MY FRIENDS. . . . I CALL YOU SERVANTS NO LONGER."

JOHN 15:14, 15, NEB.

As we have seen, Scripture uses a variety of family metaphors to portray our relationship with God: father, son, brother, and others. Although helpful pictures, they can be frustrating to one coming out of a dysfunctional family. Because none of us can choose our family, such images may not provide a good framework in which to find God. Our friends, on the other hand, are purely a matter of choice. Anyone who has even one good friend can understand the relationship.

"Friendship with God" suggests a number of basics. First of all, He has made the first move. We don't have to seek out His friendship. He's already offered it to us. Second, friendship provides safety, a haven of rest. Third, we have the comfort of a sympathetic ear when we need it. Sharing every experience, we may say, "I am happy for you. You have done so well." We're also free to say, "I think you're making the wrong decision. Let's talk about it."

A colleague of mine, Dan Smith, is currently pastor of the La Sierra University church. He has spent much time in his ministry seeking to define what it means when God calls us friends. In a recent sermon he presented a wonderful fourth conclusion about divine-human friendship. What an exciting possibility is the *delight* that the friendship brings to every believer. While God loves every one, He *delights* in his own (Zech. 3:17). God is the sum of all the best times you've had with all of your friends. And in Christ that delight is permanent and unchanging.

Indeed, no matter what we do, He will not reject us. The delight of knowing Him can always be recovered and preserved.

[*Dear God, though I gladly am Your servant, I delight in Your invitation to be my friend. I would forever be faithful to my commitment to You.*]

THE COMPANION

The quaint tale of *The Velveteen Rabbit** has, with good reason, enjoyed a recent revival. Set in a traditional English nursery, it concerns the destiny of a stuffed bunny. Mocked by the other toys, the rabbit worries about his immobile hind legs that "are made all of one piece." Therefore, he wants to become "real" so that he can run and jump like real rabbits. "Real isn't how you are made," says the old Skin Horse, who befriends him. "It's a thing that happens to you." The magic of becoming "real" occurs when someone loves you. It takes a lifetime, but once you're real "you can't become unreal again. It lasts for always."

OUR LORD JESUS CHRIST . . . DIED FOR US, THAT WHETHER WE WAKE OR SLEEP, WE SHOULD LIVE TOGETHER WITH HIM.

1 THESS. 5:10, NKJV.

The rabbit goes everywhere with his boy and stays with him through a bout of scarlet fever "because the boy needs me." The toy rabbit becomes old and shabby, but the boy's love has made him "real." After the fever, however, all of the child's toys, including the Velveteen Rabbit, are collected to be destroyed and replaced by new ones. At this climactic point the rabbit is "resurrected" among the truly real rabbits of rabbit land.

Years ago I coined the phrase "real people" to describe those few companions who are forever nearest to us. Eventually, I wrote an article on the subject,[†] exploring the various types of "friends" who pass through our lives. Our general acquaintances may deteriorate into opportunists, exploiters, and seducers—very "unreal people." On the other hand, they may ascend to the ranks of friends, fellow workers, and colleagues, and finally into that small select circle of our "bosom friends," our "soul mates." These "real people" are those loyal companions whose strength enables us to survive the vicissitudes of being human.

In another but even more vital picture of reality, Jesus offers Himself as our constant companion, "whether we wake or sleep." His persistent loyalty and endless love are what can truly make us "real." We, in turn, must devote ourselves unreservedly to living in His presence and to allowing Him to free us from our earthly limitations. Only in partaking of that divine bonding can we become "real" enough for heaven.

[*Dear Jesus, I accept Your transforming love and companionship. Make me real, both to my friends and to You.*]

---

*Margery Williams, *The Velveteen Rabit* (Philadelphia: Courage Books, 1984).
[†]"About Real People—Do You Know Who Your Friends Are?" *These Times,* July 1, 1978, pp. 2-6.

THE HELPER

Within the development of Buddhism lies one of the great common denominators of humanity—the need for help.

Prince Siddhartha Gautama of India (c. 563-c. 483 B.C.) rejected his royal heritage to go out and understand the suffering in the world beyond his palace walls. After fasting and meditation, he became the "Enlightened One" (the Buddha). He then defined the "Eightfold Path." When one has mastered these eight precepts (right action, right thinking, right effort, and so forth) he or she has conquered desire and attained Nirvana. People of any religious persuasion, even Christians, would have to agree that such virtues represent a righteous life. The Buddha simply advised his followers to live accordingly.

"THE LORD IS MY HELPER, I WILL NOT FEAR; WHAT CAN MAN DO TO ME?"

HEB. 13:6, NEB.

As Buddhism drifted east, however, the more practical Chinese made an important addition to the creed. People, they found, need *help* to walk the path toward salvation. So they invented *bodhisattvas*. Righteous persons who have qualified to enter Nirvana, they have, however, made a voluntary sacrifice, choosing to remain behind to help others on their way to heaven. Thus salvation would become possible for others.

God did not, however, wait for us to discover that we needed help. He made the provision in the far reaches of eternity. It did not begin at Bethlehem or Calvary, but predates the Garden of Eden and the fall of Adam and Eve. Do we dare to look back into the immensity of eternity and realize that our Helper prepared for us back *there*? He says, "I have loved thee with an *everlasting* love" (Jer. 31:3). Because the fountain of God's love arose in eternity, it cannot be exhausted by time.

Asking for help is not something that comes easily to most of us. Remember the last time you tried to get your husband to ask directions when you'd driven off the map and become lost? How often have you fumbled with a supposedly simple task only to have to go back finally and read the directions?

No matter how often we have disappointed, disregarded, or resisted Him, our Source of help remains constant. God doesn't just tolerate us— He *loves* us. No wonder the believer can proclaim: "I will not fear . . . What can others do to me?"

> *Dear God, help me conquer my pride and selfishness so that the life of Your Son may fill mine.*

THE SUSTAINER

I wish you could know Father Jose as I did while in physical therapy last summer. We used to meet early in the morning in the big swimming pool and had innumerable fascinating conversations out there under the desert palms.

> HE IS BE-
> FORE ALL
> THINGS,
> AND IN HIM
> ALL THINGS
> HOLD
> TOGETHER.
> COL. 1:17, NIV.

For the past 45 years the elderly priest has ministered to Hispanic people in South America, Mexico, and now southern California. His lean face is gentle, kindly—not a gift of birth, but the accomplishment of a lifetime of loving service. Actually, he looks like a figure out of a medieval tapestry. Although he is of Polish descent, Father Jose took the Spanish name in order to identify more closely with his parishioners. "I just love their culture," he said. "And do you know what every Mexican wants most? He can do without anything else except that."

A relative newcomer to the American Southwest, I didn't know.

"He must have a *friend*." Then he went on to explain that after that a Hispanic will relate to family, then school, followed by church and other kinds of social organizations. Finally, surrounded by such support, he or she will strive for success.

I liked the formula. Then I thought of how completely many of us have turned the sequence upside down. Consider the people who doggedly strive first for success at any cost. Then they look around to see which church, club, charity, or other enterprise might augment their success. Perhaps they remember their families. Sometimes they find that they can hold them together. Sometimes not. Finally, up there on the lonely, dangerous summit of success, they look around to see whether or not they have one true friend. It is a pathetic picture of chaos, a total inversion of the divine plan.

The friend must come first. Most particularly, Jesus invites us to find a friend in Him. When we choose Him as our friend, we get a great deal more than we can comprehend. With Him our circles of social relationships widen and deepen. Then out on the growing edges of our experience we begin to reach our goals—the ones we set within His design for our lives. Thus He sustains us in an ordered and satisfying life pattern.

> [*Lord, be the friend who will sustain me in all things. I would order my life according to Your long-range plan for me.*]

THE SLAVE

One of the unique features of the Christian church has always been that when the slave or servant bows in worship before God, he or she becomes the equal of an earthly master and of every other person in the congregation.

"Whatever is, is right."* Until about 250 years ago this bold phrase summed up the comfortable climate of "enlightened" Western society. God, the philosophers said, had ordered His universe in a perfect, systematic way. His angels ranked in nine orders. Within the human range, the chain of command passed from king down to slave, from father to the least member of his household. You were born at the station to which God had appointed you, and you had no right to think of climbing higher. Such a convenient arrangement secured the power of the strong and the submission of the weak, and discouraged rebellions. In a word, once a slave, always a slave.

> HIS STATE WAS DIVINE, . . . BUT [HE] EMPTIED HIMSELF TO ASSUME THE CONDITION OF A SLAVE.
>
> PHIL. 2:6, 7,
> JERUSALEM

Then the English Quakers and the German Moravians raised a new, provocative question: "Could it be possible—just possible—that there might be something wrong with slavery?" That idea set off a pitched battle. The "West India question" raged through Britain's Parliament and in churches, in pubs, and on the streets. "But," the merchants protested, "the Bible says nothing against owning slaves." Christian principles when carried to their logical conclusion, however, dictate freedom for every individual. It took 80 years of controversy to abolish slavery. By English emancipation day in 1833, America had begun to face up to her own slave problem, an issue that climaxed in the Civil War.

Paul advised slaves to learn to live within the present social framework (Eph. 6:5-9). *Christian* slaves, however, became unusual persons in that their witness could "make the teaching about God our Savior attractive" (Titus 2:10, NIV). Sold like cattle in the marketplace, slaves could be abused, even killed. Sometimes they received kind treatment, becoming a part of their master's family. Even so, the basic wrong remained. They had lost their God-given gift of free choice. Yet Jesus chose to place Himself in this context—as a slave but also as a rebel. For Him "whatever is" is *not* always right.

[*You portrayed Yourself as a slave, Lord! I am so glad for what this unusual picture teaches about Your view of freedom and freewill.*]

---

*Alexander Pope, "An Essay on Man," I, 294.

THE SUFFERING SERVANT

The life of a servant, not surprisingly, comes cheaper than that of his employer. The questionable honor of being the king's taster is a case in point. Beset by bloodthirsty rebels and ambitious rivals, kings have always been potential victims of poisoning. For a large enough bribe, the cooks in the castle kitchen might themselves lace the king's food with arsenic. Therefore, the king had to employ another servant—one whom he could implicitly trust and who was willing to lay life on the line at least three times a day. The taster sampled each dish before it went to the royal table. If someone *had* attempted poisoning, let the servant, not the master, die!

SO SHALL HE, MY SERVANT, VINDICATE MANY, HIMSELF BEARING THE PENALTY OF THEIR GUILT.

ISA. 53:11, NEB.

The institution of human servantship is highly complex, having both good and bad features. A servant may be unfaithful, as many of Christ's parables illustrate. Or they could be loyal. A bondservant either served as punishment for a crime or in payment of a debt. Or he or she might take employment purely by choice, as did many of those who came to the colonies in the new world.

Because Jesus freely and lovingly offered His life in payment for the wages of our sin, He chose to be a servant—and to our everlasting shame, an abused servant at that. In His earthly ministry He lived constantly at the poverty level. Even worse, we have often scorned the Suffering Servant. The terrible reality of His pain must always be before us. "Many were astonished at him—his appearance was so marred, beyond human semblance, and his form beyond that of the sons of men" (Isa. 52:14, RSV).

As Servant, Jesus has tasted the poison for us. He has also demonstrated two components of Christian service—the humility to submit and to serve, and the willingness to risk harsh treatment.

[*Deliver me, Lord, from the pride that prevents my accepting the needful position of servant. You have shown me the way.*]

THE EXALTED SERVANT

The laws of life dictate that the suffering comes first and the exaltation afterward. In a time when we are overconscious of promotions and flood the job market with our résumés, we do well to remember that humility—perhaps even suffering—occurs before success. Nowadays, however, an amazing number of young people desire to start near the top rather than at the bottom in the job market. They don't even want to *hear* about their grandparents homesteading on the frontier or their parents working for 10 cents a day during the Depression. Swept along with bright, high-tech ambitions, sometimes they do bypass the servant-class obligations.

BEHOLD, MY SERVANT SHALL PROSPER, HE SHALL BE EXALTED AND LIFTED UP, AND SHALL BE VERY HIGH.

ISA. 52:13, RSV.

Still, we blush for the man who went to the wedding feast, took the seat of honor, and then found himself asked to step down for a guest more distinguished than himself (Luke 14:7-11). By starting at the bottom, one may, like Mordecai, who displaced the haughty Haman, receive an invitation to higher honors.

Servants come in two types—good and bad. A servant may be clumsy and abysmally stupid, a constant vexation to his overseer, but still ambitious. Again, a servant's intelligence, efficiency, and self-reliance may bring prosperity to his employer. As lord of a vast household, King Solomon observed: "Like the cold of snow in time of harvest is a faithful messenger to those who send him, he refreshes the spirit of his masters" (Prov. 25:13, RSV).

The full culmination of the servant image, however, is not yet come. Isaiah's prophecy looks ahead. The gift having been given, we now see the Messiah, the divine servant, rising from His self-chosen bondage and ascending in a blaze of glory to His heavenly throne. "Even far-off foreign nations and their kings . . . shall stand dumbfounded" (Isa. 52:15, TLB).

Jesus had to fulfill the duties of His human servanthood before He could be exalted. In looking to the finale of our "Christian servitude," should we expect to do less?

[*With You, Jesus, I am looking forward to that day when servitude brings its eternal rewards.*]

THE EXCLUDED ONE

Probably we all have too-vivid memories of our first day at school. Or perhaps it was kindergarten or day care. In any case, at a time when we had few resources for coping with major traumas, we found ourselves thrust out of the security of home in which we knew we belonged into a strange place in which we were sure we did *not* belong.

When I was 9 years old, a difficult sequence of events occurred when the careers of my missionary parents mixed with the exigencies of war and health problems. As a result, I had the questionable privilege of attending seven different schools in seven different countries in seven consecutive years. I feel, therefore, that I am something of an expert in understanding what it means to be an excluded one—forever the new kid on the block.

Probably every one of us can recall those epic battles in the school yard at recess time. Of being that one lone child surrounded by a ring of terrorists, all calling names and shouting, "Yeah-yeah-ya-yeah-ya." The mockery and the infernal rhythm of that wicked little school-yard taunt is in any time or any place absolutely infuriating. One has just two choices—retiring ignominiously from the battlefield or confronting one's tormentors head-on in a pitched battle. The pain of being excluded from a group is often one of the first forms of suffering a youngster experiences. Being pushed out of the circle is sheer agony.

But think of the pain of exclusion Jesus felt. It embodied all of the misery that all the adults and all the children of all ages have collectively endured. His incredible sacrifice in leaving heaven and entering into the sordid, selfish society of the creatures He had created and then to have them exclude Him from their lives defies all comprehension!

It is well worth remembering that whenever we say or do anything that *excludes* Christ, we are literally speaking the words and doing the acts of the devils themselves. The ones who through the voices of the Gadarene demoniacs shouted, "You son of God . . . what do you want with us?" (Matt. 8:29, NEB).

> HE . . . [WAS] A MAN OF SORROWS AND ACQUAINTED WITH GRIEF.
>
> ISA. 53:3, NKJV.

[*Let nothing today build a wall of prejudice around me. I would not hide myself from any responsibility, however painful it may be.*]

THE REJECTED ONE

An interesting collage by Alfred Gescheidt.* interprets the symbolic presence of Christ among us. It is a composite photograph of an American city street in the 1930s. At the center some 20 people walk under the steel girders of an overpass. The structure casts a strong pattern of shadows on the brick pavement below. In the open street beyond, half a dozen square-topped automobiles date the picture.

HE IS DESPISED AND REJECTED BY MEN.

ISA. 53:3, NKJV.

In the lower foreground, facing the reader, we see the pensive figure of Christ, clad in a light tunic and sandals. He moves through a design of light and dark like the spokes of a wheel, trolley lines criss-crossing around Him. He is alone, however, because all the other pedestrians have already passed by Him on the other side. Although the figures are dark, we can make out the silhouette of businessmen in bowler hats. Newsboys and a couple women break stride and walk into the heavy shadows on the right. And there go some workmen, perhaps headed for a soup kitchen.

Almost all have turned their backs on Christ. One is even climbing the steps to the overhead bridge, thus avoiding any possibility of contact with the Man on the street below. The cars all drive away too. Those facing us in the distance appear to be parked. Of the few figures traveling in Jesus' direction, one is so far behind that he has not yet even reached the overpass. Three more pass at the far left in deep shadow. And the one nearest to Jesus' path simply stands still, looking across the street, his back to us, arms folded.

A powerful parable without words, the photograph mercilessly interprets our rejection of Christ. The "real Jesus" walks among us, on the very streets where we live. He could replace prostitution, drunkenness, and political corruption with faith, simplicity, and honesty. Jesus would sympathize with our most commonplace concerns.

But what have we done? We have chosen to walk through the shadows alone, as far away from Him as possible. Or we've lagged far behind, hoping, perhaps, that He won't find us. And some of us have walked right out of the picture altogether.

[*Jesus, I would not walk in the shadows alone today. Keep me close by Your side so that I cannot turn my back on You.*]

---

*In Patrick Allitt, "The American Christ," *American Heritage*, November 1988, p. 129.

THE VICTIM

A professional colleague of mine once helped me understand the limits of victimhood. He was about 10 years old when his parents became charter members of the Seventh-day Adventist church in a small western Canadian town. In keeping with their decision, his mother instructed George not to fight with anyone at school, no matter what they said or did. Since the family had become "peculiar people" in the community, the lad quickly began to endure painful persecution. Arriving and leaving school, as well as the lunch and recess periods in between, became absolute horror. He passively took daily beatings from the bullies.

HE WAS AFFLICTED, HE SUBMITTED TO BE STRUCK DOWN AND DID NOT OPEN HIS MOUTH.

ISA. 53:7, NEB.

Finally he had to confide his misery in his father. A strong German farmer with a keen sense of justice, he said, "Son, it's enough. Fight." Then he added, "Don't tell your mother."

The next day at recess when the taunting resumed, George, small and swift on his feet, plowed into the big boys, fists flying. Completely taken by surprise by the wiry little fury on the attack, the enemy retired in confusion. Even some blood flowed. From that point on no one raised a finger or said a word against George Shankel.

While I did not engage in physical combat in the open field, I often went home in tears because someone had taken my pencil or broken my pen nibs. Because I have always loved peace, I had the makings of an ideal victim.

Jesus, of course, became the victim above all others as He endured injustice. From the inception of Christianity we have dwelled largely upon His suffering, His meekness, His patience. And so we should.

At the same time, however, we need to remember that this same persecuted Man was the One who drove the money changers out of the Temple with a scourge. Even victimhood has a limit.

We all have the misfortune to know some "professional" victim—someone who absorbs endless quantities of loving concern, who must constantly be propped up, who never lays down the "cross," who really enjoys poor health. Granted, such things are an inevitable part of the Christian walk. Still, Christ, our exemplar, made it very clear that being a victim has a statute of limitations. His coming kingdom will settle all accounts.

[*Dear Saviour, gentle and wise, please help me to discover the fine line between suffering and fighting the enemy.*]

THE BENEVOLENT MASTER

A master is one who has control, authority, and power over others. The word derives from a Latin term meaning "great." We must live in submission to whatever master we have chosen. Lord Acton said that "power tends to corrupt" and "absolute power corrupts absolutely." It was a rather dismal observation! Unfortunately, though, we do have the full range of masters from good to bad. Few manage to handle power with grace and humility.

> "THE MASTER IS HERE; HE IS ASKING FOR YOU."
>
> JOHN 11:28, NEB.

Recently we have seen the owner of one large American company doing unusual things. Though a giant of commerce, he appears to have none of the usual executive detachment or the arrogant presumption of many in his position. He goes down to the assembly line and mixes with his employees. Putting on his bathrobe, he makes his own TV commercials to advertise his product. Instructing his managers to travel economy class, he reminds them that "the back end of the plane arrives at the same time as the front end." This "common touch," he has discovered, is simply good business. And he has brought his company from bankruptcy to prosperity in a surprisingly short time.

Stop to think of it. If you want something done, ask a busy person. Truly important people often prove to be more gracious and accessible than their administrative staffs. A Ph.D. is quite likely to be more casual about his or her education and expertise than a 14-year-old graduating from grade 8.

Many of Jesus' contemporaries addressed Him as the Master. And so He was. Yet He never allowed either title or position to put a distance between Him and the people He served. When Lazarus died, He was surprisingly slow in heeding the pained cry of Martha and Mary for their brother. When He did arrive, Martha saw Him first. Running to find her sister, she cried, "The Teacher has come and is calling for you" (NKJV). In the hour of grief, in the stress of the moment, the Master called for the girl—and then wept with her.

As the kindly Master, Jesus comes down to the assembly lines where we all work. We talk to Him. Although all-powerful, He still makes Himself totally accessible to us. What more could we ask?

"O Master, let me walk with Thee in lowly paths of service free;
Tell me Thy secret; help me bear the strain of toil, the fret of care."
—Washington Gladden

THE GOOD MASTER

Dishonesty used to be fairly straightforward—burglary and theft, embezzlement, cheating in examinations, forgery, and so on. Most of the time you thought that you knew how to defend yourself. The repertoire of the con artists today, however, has increased in proportion to available technology.

If you are a woman alone, watch out if you buy a car by yourself or when you take your car in for servicing. If you are elderly, you are, by that fact alone, a prime target for exploitation. Keep your hand on your wallet and hope that no one discovers your credit card numbers. Unnecessary medical attention can impoverish you. Anyone might be carrying a gun, so you don't open the door to strangers. Sometimes you wonder if you should lock yourself inside your house and never go out again. But no, that wouldn't help. You now hesitate to pick up the telephone for fear of falling into the clutches of yet another fraudulent, fast-talking salesperson. Although you try not to be rude, in the end declining the offer usually provokes the caller to wrath. Must you get an unlisted phone number after all?

Is there anyone out there whom you can trust? Is anyone truly *good?*

In addition to being the humane and sympathetic Master, Jesus earned the title of "Good Master." When an employee or other inferior calls his or her master "good," that is a true index to character. In this case, Christ received the title from a surprising source—a rich young ruler, himself a master. The encounter of the two men is fascinating. They may well have been about the same age. To all outward appearances the aristocrat was superior to Jesus in rank and birth and, most certainly, in wealth. And yet the youthful inquirer called him Master—more than that, a "good" Master. In other words, he acknowledged a person whom he could trust. He perceived Jesus' integrity and knew that he could accept His counsel without question.

The fact that the young ruler failed the test makes the case all the sadder. Recognizing and trusting the Good Master is one thing. Obeying His Word and following it is something more.

> "GOOD MASTER, WHAT MUST I DO TO WIN ETERNAL LIFE?"
>
> MARK 10:17, NEB.

[*Give me the holy desires of the rich young ruler. Then endow me with the willingness to follow and not to turn away.*]

THE UNEXPECTED GUEST

So many restrictions govern hospitality. With whom one eats and drinks matters. The house one sleeps in makes a social statement. We may feel too proud, too inferior, or too busy to entertain a guest. Jesus, however, will enter anywhere He is invited. It's that simple!

No wonder little Zacchaeus "made haste and came down" when the Master announced that He would be his guest (Luke 19:6, NKJV). The man rushed to accept the unprecedented offer. Zacchaeus was not poor. No, the head of the tax and customs organization in Jericho would be rich enough. The problem would have been his job and the friends he kept. No Jew who cared for his or her reputation would have been seen in the company of a *publicanus*—the man who collected money for the Roman government.

An unknown Victorian woman has described her preparation for the heavenly Guest in this quaint poem.

> "IF ANYONE HEARS MY VOICE AND OPENS THE DOOR, I WILL COME IN AND SIT DOWN TO SUPPER WITH HIM AND HE WITH ME."
> REV. 3:20, NEB.

Homely Work

Homely work is mine today—
Floors to sweep, and fires to lay;
Plates to wash, and clothes to mend,
Work which never seems to end.

Yet I pray,
"Jesus, be my guest today,
Not as one to dwell apart
In the spare room of my heart,
But as one to whom my prayer
May confide the smallest care.

Thus I pray,
"Lord, be Thou my guest today."
He reproves me if I fret
Over work unfinished yet,
Or some work He does not ask.
My dear Guest
Wishes me to work and rest.
At the closing of the day,
When once more my heart shall say,
In this busy life of mine—
"All the glory, Lord, is Thine."

"Christ," I pray,
"Be the guest of every day."

Receiving guests into our homes does require time, energy, and expense, but the rewards are more than worth the effort. We convert strangers into friends. And while we are at it, may we always have room reserved for Christ, the guest of every day.

[*Christ, become so much a part of my every day that You will always be present and never again unexpected.*]

THE FAMILIAR GUEST

In the National Art Gallery in Berlin, Germany, there hangs the original of an insightful turn-of-the-century painting. The work of Fritz von Uhde (1848-1911), it is entitled *Christ the Welcome Guest.** In the very plain all-purpose room of a peasant cottage we see the table set for supper, with soup plates and spoons only. No tablecloth. No rugs, no pictures on the wall. At the right, the smiling *hausfrau* is just setting the bowl of soup in the middle of the table. At the left, her toilworn husband bows and indicates a place at the table. He is dressed in his work clothes and wooden shoes. Farther in the background, at the right, we see the four children—three waiting respectfully by their chairs and baby with his round face just visible over the edge of the table. Still farther back are the grandparents, just about to take their seats. Every eye is fixed on the tall Guest in the foreground who has just stepped into the room, leaving the door ajar. (Every eye except that of the dog crawling under the sideboard.)

> "HE HAS GONE IN . . . TO BE THE GUEST OF A SINNER."
> LUKE 19:7, NEB.

Despite the poverty and meager furnishings of the home, every person in Uhde's picture is in an attitude of respectful welcome. Not one member of the three-generation family appears surprised. Making one more place at the table for a stranger is obviously a habit with them. But Christ clearly is not a stranger here. We get a strong sense that this has happened many times before. The artist has captured here so much of the blessings of work and the integrity of simple living in his picture. No wonder Mark observed that "the common people heard Him [Jesus] gladly" (Mark 12:37, NKJV).

Alistair Maclean has said that Christ "enters by a secret stair into every individual." Are those steps worn from frequent visits? And does our heavenly Guest find all of our doors forever open when He arrives?

[*Thank You, Lord, for making it possible for You and me to have a constant, ongoing friendship, and for not ever being far away from me.*]

*In Cynthia Maus, *Christ and the Fine Arts* (New York: Harper Brothers, 1959), pp. 205, 206.

THE HOST

Near Shannon, Ireland, you may go back centuries in time when you attend a medieval feast in Bunratty Castle. You leave our contemporary climate of impersonal motels and faceless resorts, where everyone lives in self-sufficient independence and privacy (often to the point of bleakest loneliness), and enter a world in which hospitality to strangers is the sacred duty of all persons, rich and poor.

> THE LORD HAS PREPARED A SACRIFICE AND HAS HALLOWED HIS GUESTS.
>
> ZEPH. 1:7, NEB.

Then, as now, however, opening your door to whoever asked for entrance poses a risk. Therefore, when you enter Bunratty Castle, two liveried servants holding a crude wooden platter heaped with broken pieces of bread meet you at the door. In the middle of the platter is a pile of salt. You are required to take one piece of bread, dip it into the salt, and eat it in the presence of the doorkeepers. Having partaken of this elemental food provided by your host, you have pledged yourself to peace and goodwill. You will not now, on your honor, enter the lord's feasting hall and kill anyone. Nor will you create a disturbance of any kind, because you have, by these to kens, pledged yourself to loyalty. If you cannot commit yourself to your host in this manner, then do not think of asking for hospitality.

Once inside, you are guest to a bountiful banquet, to much music, to lively fellowship with others, and to the personal attentions of the host—all because you ate the bread and salt and because you have submitted to the conditions which the lord of the castle has laid down.

As the Lord of heaven, Jesus has given an open invitation to all humanity to share forever in His hospitality. This prospect is the ultimate hope of every Christian. Because it involves a risk, however, God must lay down certain entry rules. They are really quite simple—just a pledge of loyalty. A promise of commitment to the requirements of heaven that will prevent anyone from entering to cause another "sin disturbance" in the universe. The tokens of our submission are not just those of the Communion service. They encompass the whole intent of our daily living, of our allowing our Host to "hallow" us, His would-be guests.

[*Dear heavenly Host, I gladly commit myself to the requirements for entry into Your eternal home, acknowledging Your every claim on my life.*]

THE ROYAL HOST

All aristocrats have special exclusive powers. Although few monarchs still rule among us today, the remaining royalty retain a certain social distance from their subjects. The media, for instance, understand that they are not supposed to photograph kings and queens at table eating and drinking, or smoking, or doing many other commonplace public acts that the rest of the world takes for granted.

> "THE HALL WAS PACKED WITH GUESTS. . . . [AND] THE KING CAME IN TO SEE THE COMPANY AT TABLE."
>
> MATT. 22:10, 11, NEB.

In ancient times absolute kings and lords would not, of course, eat with commoners. The very act of dining together represents a certain equality and cordiality. When Joseph, incognito, first entertained his 11 brothers at dinner in Egypt, the protocol became complicated. Joseph sat alone because he was the prime minister. The brothers sat separately, arranged (much to their astonishment) in order of their ages. The Egyptians who would ordinarily have eaten with Joseph had to dine by themselves because for them to "eat food with the Hebrews" was an "abomination" (Gen. 43:32, 33, NKJV). Certainly an irony not to be lost on Joseph!

Not accidentally, the most prestigious place for dinner aboard a ship is at the captain's table. In an effort to make the hierarchy a little more democratic, the legends of King Arthur conceived of a *round* table where all guests would be equal—except, perhaps, for those chosen to sit at the king's right hand—or left.

Jesus' parables of kings hosting banquets retain a similar kind of organization. It mattered greatly who sat in the "high" seats and who in the "low." While kings might extend invitations clear out into the highways and byways, once they arrived, guests had to sit in the right place and be dressed in the right clothes. The royal host would come in to see that everything was in order, and then the feast could begin.

Jesus hosted the Last Supper as an itinerant healer, a soon-to-be-arrested prisoner. At that time, nonetheless, He spoke of the most significant social event of all eternity—the forthcoming welcome-home banquet for the redeemed from earth. Our kingly Host has promised that He will not drink wine again until "that day when I drink it new with you in My Father's kingdom" (Matt. 26:29, NKJV).

> [*Gracious Lord, I accept Your royal invitation to attend that homecoming banquet. This is my RSVP. Look for me to be in my place at the table.*]

THE KING

Over the years I have collected cartoons—for use on those days when life needs a little lightening up. One of my favorites shows two portly bearded figures striding along side by side, deep in conversation. Both are wearing crowns. The caption reads: "It took me a while to accept it, to truly accept it, but once I realized that I, as king, could do no wrong, I was able to give up therapy."

> "BEHOLD, A KING SHALL REIGN IN RIGHTEOUS-NESS AND HIS RULERS RULE WITH JUSTICE."
>
> ISA. 32:1, NEB.

Today it is hard for us to re-create the climate of ancient and medieval times, when all kings ruled by "divine right." They had power of life and death over the entire population from the highest nobleman on down to the last peasant. Kings did exactly as they pleased, and they did it when and where they wanted to. While citizens may have had their own opinions, they either kept them to themselves or voiced them only secretly.

History is strewn with the wreckage caused by kings who abused their privileges and permitted unspeakable injustices. In 1215 a courageous group of English barons discussed their grievances and decided to protect themselves and the general population from the encroachments of royal authority. On June 15 they confronted King John in the meadows of Runnymede and forced him to sign the Magna Carta. The document guaranteed feudal rights, defined relationships, and regularized the judicial system, thus becoming the foundation of all future democratic systems. Though not a complete cure, the Magna Carta was a wonderful antidote for the detestable theory that "the king can do no wrong."

In all fairness, kings and politicians have, more often than not, taken up their duties with honorable intentions. But human fallibility renders them hopelessly vulnerable, and they lapse into corruption almost as a matter of course. Moreover, a little power in the hands of any one of us is a potential trap. We *all* sin.

Isaiah points to the coming of the King whose government is *wholly just*. It is a splendid prospect as we struggle wearily under governments tainted with inconsistency, favoritism, and greed. Our only hope rests in the coming of a truly righteous King who does no wrong.

> [*King of righteousness, You alone deserve loyalty and trust.*
> *I give You my complete allegiance, without reservation.*]

THE CROWNED KING

Some years ago in one of my writing classes I had a Romanian girl—a new Christian, fresh out of Communism, and new to America. Those of us present won't forget an essay Mari wrote and then read to the class.

"I HAVE
ENTHRONED
MY KING
ON ZION
MY HOLY
MOUNTAIN."

PS. 2:6, NEB.

Like many others, she was fascinated with the glory of pageantry. Although Communism had purposefully dulled much of the mystique of royalty, Mari's childish imagination provided her with vivid pictures. From her village below, she would look up to the castle on the hill above. Peopling it with kings and queens, knights and ladies, she convinced herself that she belonged up there—that she was, in fact, a princess.

Conditions in Eastern Europe at the time were such that people did not discuss any possible aristocratic connections. The girl could not prove that she belonged to the royal line. Yet no one could certify that she did *not* have a regal heritage. So she dreamed on in her workaday world, always looking wistfully to the castle on the hill. Then, in a bold move, she escaped first into Germany and finally to America. There Christ found her. "Now I know for sure that I *am* a princess, the daughter of the King," Mari declared in triumph. "It doesn't matter anymore whether I belong to the castle on the hill or not—not when I know that my Father is the king of heaven."

The coronation of a king or queen is a truly spectacular event. The inauguration of a president or the installation of a city mayor may be grand, but it pales beside the ceremony that invests a monarch with both spiritual and civil powers. The ritual legalizes the new reign and ensures the succession of the royal line.

Jehovah, the psalmist assures us, has enthroned His Son in Zion. The coronation has already occurred. Now it remains only for us, His children, to discover that we do indeed have a royal lineage. We need not stay in the valley, fantasizing about a castle on the hill, wondering whether or not we belong to it. Instead, we may be certified descendants of the royal line. When the King comes for us, He will be in royal procession, crowned and ready to merge the earthly portion of His kingdom with the heavenly.

[*My Lord and King, what relief I feel in the certain knowledge that my royal lineage is assured! I accept my heritage with gratitude and humility.*]

THE DIADEM

Heads and the hair upon them have always had symbolic importance. Most of us, in our toddler days, probably gave ourselves a haircut or treated one of our siblings to a new "hairstyle." It was something that we *had* to do, almost instinctively. Hair may be curled or straightened, colored or spiked, augmented or transplanted, cut or shaved, teased or greased. Headdresses feature precious stones, gold chains, feathers, and wreaths of leaves and flowers. Whatever we do with our hair or put on our heads, we're trying to make a statement—about honor, dignity, power, rank, rebellion, or whatever.

> "ON THAT DAY THE LORD OF HOSTS SHALL BE . . . A BEAUTIFUL DIADEM FOR THE REMNANT OF HIS PEOPLE."
>
> ISA. 28:5, NEB.

Unlike a hat, which has a basic, functional purpose, the crown is strictly symbolic. It surmounts the top of the body, adding height. Thus it signifies preeminence. During coronation ceremonies a priest or some religious functionary presides over the moment of the placing of the crown on the monarch's head. The king or queen thus acknowledges allegiance to God, a connection that once guaranteed them their "divine rights."

A diadem is a special kind of crown—sometimes a plain white fillet (band) but often a richly ornamented headband. Favored by the ancient Persians, the regal symbol was adopted by the ambitious Alexander the Great (356-323 B.C.) for himself and for his Greek successors. Scholars have also translated Isaiah's metaphor of the "diadem" as a "wreath of splendor," a miter, or a turban. In any case, the entire East recognized the diadem as a symbol of honor and royal dignity. Instead of sitting on top of the head, the diadem securely bound the forehead and hair. It would not easily be lost or dislodged, even in the heat of battle.

Jesus has presented Himself not only as the king but also as the high priest authorized to crown kings. Finally, we discover that He Himself is the crown—not just another crown, but a *diadem*. Because He binds His church together, Christians should wear their faith with pride and dignity. Since Christians on their knees can see farther than an atheist atop a ladder, we have nothing of which to be ashamed—not when Jesus confers the honors of heaven itself upon us. He is our *beautiful* diadem.

[*Jesus, my days are long and ordinary. I have little claim to distinction. But I have accepted You, and You crown my life with beauty and peace.*]

THE PRINCE OF PRINCES

The savage story of Gideon tells us something about expectations of princeliness. Gideon had defeated the nomadic Midianites with his 300 warriors, but the kingly right of capturing the two Midianite kings, Zebah and Zalmunna, was his alone. They hid on the other side of Jordan.

"HE SHALL EVEN RISE AGAINST THE PRINCE OF PRINCES."
DAN. 8:25, NKJV.

When political matters had been settled, the Israelite commander turned to his obligation to personal revenge. Earlier some of Gideon's brothers (all sons of "the same mother") had perished at the hands of the Midianites. Now he asked the two captive kings, "Where are the men whom you slew at Tabor?"

"As you are," the kings replied, "so were they, every one of them, they resembled the sons of a king" (Judges 8:18, RSV). In effect, one can identify a prince just by looking at him.

When Gideon ordered his eldest son to slay them, the youth shrank from the bloody task. Knowing desert protocol, however, Zebah and Zalmunna told Gideon to do it himself "like a man." Traditionally, peasants killed peasants and servants killed servants, but kings could be slain honorably only by those of equal rank—and Gideon had become Israel's king equivalent.

The old story indicates a deep-seated human expectation that princes should stand out in a crowd—even as Saul did (1 Sam. 9:2). We should be able to identify royalty by behavior. Having aristocratic manners and living apart from commoners, they will stoop to nothing servile. Unquestionably their dress and lifestyle must proclaim their rank.

Few monarchies have survived to the beginning of the twenty-first century. Of those that have, modern media has told us more about them than anyone cares or needs to know. Consequently, the shining image of kings and princes is rather tarnished for us.

As the Prince above all princes, however, Jesus gathers to Himself all the richest elements of ancient royalty. Nobles of whatever rank acknowledge His authority. Yet He administers justice with compassion, discipline with love. Only He is fit to confront the sometime "king of this world," Satan. Although Jesus sojourned among us as a Prince in disguise, He frequently spoke of the royal court of heaven. He has set the door ajar, to let a little of the light of His kingdom stream across our way today.

[*Prince of all princes, Your promises fire up my imagination. I respond to Your royal appeal to peace, beauty, and holiness.*]

THE PRINCE OF LIFE

The ancient Greeks touched upon a universal truth in the myth of Aurora and Tithonus. As the story goes, the goddess fell in love with the handsome human, Tithonus. Knowing that in the course of events she must lose him, she went to the god Zeus and begged him to give Tithonus immortality. The request granted, the couple lived together happily for many years. Then Aurora's mistake became obvious. (For a goddess, she *should* have been wiser.) Tithonus began to suffer the ravages of age. He became older and older, incredibly ancient, until he longed to die. Pitying him, Aurora pleaded with Zeus to let him go. But the gifts of the gods once given cannot be taken back. The best Zeus could do was to turn the man into a grasshopper—which he had rather begun to resemble, anyway. The Greeks were right. Immortality in the human context is a disaster.

> "BUT YOU . . . KILLED THE PRINCE OF LIFE, WHOM GOD RAISED FROM THE DEAD."
>
> ACTS 3:14, 15, NKJV.

Nonetheless, God has programmed us with the desire, the hope, the utter human *need* to find eternal life. At Creation God set it within our reach, but we lost it through sin.

Just after Pentecost, Peter stood on Solomon's Porch in Herod's Temple to address the crowds at the Temple gate. He reminded them that they had rejected the Holy One in preference to a murderer. The apostle's accusation has a fine irony. "[You] killed the Prince of life. But," he hastens to add, "God raised [Him] from the dead."

How could Christ as Prince of life be killed? The Creator, He had given life to all—even to the serpent. How then could He die? It could be, of course, only in a first and human death. Peter insisted upon this point, opening up to his audience the amazing fact that what they had seen at Calvary a few weeks earlier was not at all what they thought it was—the death of an itinerant teacher. Rather, it was an event that split human history in half. The crucifixion and resurrection of the Prince of life was exactly what it had taken to make death temporary and life eternal and once more to put immortality within our grasp.

[*Prince of life, You planted within me the desire for everlasting life. But I ask for it only on Your terms—not with my pitiful human limitations.*]

THE PEACEMAKER

As a small but intense book-loving youngster, I remember studying a picture of English prime minister Neville Chamberlain holding up a piece of paper that he had just persuaded Adolf Hitler to sign and saying, "I believe it is peace for our time." The old gentleman had done his best, but in a matter of weeks World War II broke out.

In the quaint language of the seventeenth century, the English Prayer Book contains a collect for peace: "O God, who art the author of peace and lover of concord . . . defend us thy humble servants in all assaults of our enemies." A fine and comforting prayer, to be sure. Moreover, peace was the watchword of the angels' birth message to the Bethlehem shepherds: "On earth peace among men" (Luke 2:14, RSV). It was also Jesus' own legacy to us: "Peace I leave with you" (John 14:27, RSV).

> HE HIMSELF IS OUR PEACE, WHO HAS MADE BOTH ONE, AND HAS BROKEN DOWN THE MIDDLE WALL OF SEPARATION BETWEEN US.
>
> EPH. 2:14, NKJV.

There is more here, however, than meets the eye. Peace does not just "happen." It is *made*. People have to work at it. God reserves a distinct blessing for those who do: "Blessed are the peacemakers, for they will be called sons of God" (Matt. 5:9, NIV).

We must do something active about peace. "*Love* truth and peace" (Zech. 8:19, NEB); "*Be* at peace with one another" (Mark 9:50, NEB); "*Follow* after all things which make for peace" (Rom. 14:19). Counseling his patients on stress management, one wise physician said, "It's your thoughts. . . . Peace is a choice, and it has nothing to do with what other people do or think."*

Some philosophers have declared that a state of war is natural to humanity—that peace is the exception. Debilitated by millennia of sin, we have little strength or talent left for peacemaking. As the Prince of Peace (Isa. 9:6), however, Jesus not only promised peace to His followers, He became the maker of that peace. Through Him we can break down "the middle walls of separation" among us. Spiritual peace constantly eases our lifetime pilgrimage. Finally, it enables the Christian to endure incredible suffering and still die in hope and faith: "The end of that [upright] man is peace" (Ps. 37:37).

[*My Prince of Peace, I thank You for Your promised gift. Now work with me all of this day to make peace in my portion of Your world.*]

---

*Gerald G. Jampolsky, M.D., in *Pace* magazine (Pace Communications, Inc.).

THE LORD

Being a compulsive dog person, I recently brought home a new toy Pomeranian puppy. The color of chocolate and butterscotch, Schatzi weighs in at less than five pounds, soaking wet. Her playmate is Ladybird, a handsome 80-pound mix of German shepherd and Doberman. To watch the two of them at their fun and games is pure relaxation. Nonetheless, they have a very clear understanding between them.

> "YOU CALL ME 'MASTER' AND 'LORD,' AND RIGHTLY SO, FOR THAT IS WHAT I AM."
>
> JOHN 13:13, NEB.

During the first few hours that Schatzi was in the house, considerable uneasiness prevailed. Though gentle and patient, Ladybird skulked about with a worried look on her face. Then suddenly the puppy rolled over on her back and lay like a little zoology specimen, pinned flat to the floor. She allowed Bird to sniff over her tummy all the way from chin to tail. Ever since, Bird has been the acknowledged "top dog," and we have no problems—even though the puppy teases her mercilessly. Several times a day, however, Schatzi lets Ladybird reexamine her underside—it's just a way for the two girls to keep their relationship in balance. Although they are the dearest of friends, the little one is wholly submissive to the big one.

Brought up in a culture that fiercely defends independence and personal freedoms, most of us have trouble submitting to authority. While much can be said for the courageous fighting spirit, the confident self-image, and the healthy ego, we still face times when we *must* submit. Nowhere is this more true than in the specialized circumstances of our relationship to God. No one, however, becomes a doormat. Submission actually enables us to face the world with *more* self-worth than ever before—all because of the price that God paid for us.

God is our Lord and Master, and He wants us always to keep this fact in mind. Considering His omnipotence and omniscience, we should not find it hard to do. We are the creatures of His making, and whatever we have and whatever we do is simply what He endows us with. Even so, most of us have to work every day of our lives to learn to submit and to trust Him.

[*My dear Lord and patient Friend, I acknowledge Your authority in my life. Let me never persist in having my own way.*]

THE LORD OF THE SABBATH

While visiting friends in Germany, I joined them after church for a spartan lunch—just a bowl of soup, one bun, and a banana. "For us," our host explained, "to eat such a meal is part of our Sabbath blessing." No overeating at a lavish church potluck or at home. At the end of the afternoon, however, they had a magnificent German Black Forest cake, followed by a delicious dinner over which we lingered far into the evening.

> **"THE SON OF MAN IS LORD OF THE SABBATH."**
> MATT. 12:8, NIV.

Sabbath observance among Adventists raises many questions. You might take a walk in the woods but not swim. Some will remember compromising with wading. Then, how deep could you wade? What happened if you "accidentally" fell into the water? On the other hand, others freely spend Sabbath in their swimming pools or at the beach. Some will sleep, others will visit the neighbors. Historically the old "Continental Sunday" contrasted markedly with the "Puritan Sunday," for the customs of Sabbathkeeping have varied greatly from culture to culture.

As the Lord of the Sabbath, however, God has the last word on the subject. He has basically just one statement to make: "The Sabbath was made for man, not man for the Sabbath" (Mark 2:27, NIV). He set this block of time aside for *us* as a gift! Not only does it give us pleasure, it's also good for us. Sad, then, when we too often wear the obligations of Sabbathkeeping like an old horse chafing under the weight of a heavy saddle.

Scientific studies on fatigue (physical and mental) show that for our efficiency rest *must* follow periods of exertion. When Hitler's bombers blitzed Britain during World War II, the very survival of the nation was at stake. Although factory workers making bomber parts willingly agreed to work 74 hours a week, absenteeism, illness, high tempers, and low morale soon scuttled the plan. When management cut shifts back to 48 hours a week, productivity increased by almost 20 percent.*

So much for the mental and physical health. In order to add the all-important spiritual component to human lives, the Creator introduced the seventh day of rest for His children. Custom-designed to fit our needs, it is not a straitjacket into which we must force ourselves.

[*Father, You have given me the gift of Sabbath rest for my well-being, both now and in eternity. Let me never regard it as a burden.*]

---

*Mervyn G. Hardinge, M.D., "Fatigue," in *A Philosophy of Health* (Loma Linda: Loma Linda University School of Health, 1980), pp. 15-19.

THE OVERSEER

Overseeing is a demanding, unenviable, second-level management position. Above you is the CEO and those who have big expense accounts and who are frequently absent. Below are the laborers you supervise. For relatively modest pay, overseers must constantly be on the job—organizing, implementing, keeping time, writing reports. They discipline, hear complaints, and anticipate disputes.

The taskmasters of Egypt have had—with justification—a good deal of bad press concerning their management of the Israelite slaves (Ex. 5:10-14). Additionally, Joseph's appointment as overseer of the household of Potiphar so involved him in the details of that family that he almost lost his life (Gen. 39:2-23). Concerned to see his vast building projects done perfectly, King Solomon appointed 3,600 overseers to supervise 80,000 quarry workers and 70,000 burden-bearers (2 Chron. 2:2, 18)—that is, one overseer for approximately every 40 workers. A rather large responsibility. The overseer must be on the job every instant of the workday.

In more recent history we have the overseers in the slave colonies. The planters themselves tended to be often absent from their estates. As "second-class Whites," the overseers took the risks, endured the criticism, and did the tedious, dangerous work of the plantations. They made few, if any, trips home to Britain or Europe. In real life, masters sometimes died in slave rebellions. But in most cases slaying an overseer satisfied the need for revenge. After all, *their* life was expendable.

In Acts we learn that the Holy Spirit appointed "overseers" of the early Christian church. Their responsibility required the same meticulous, but often unglamorous, attention to duty. They not only had to "care for the church of God" but also guard against the "fierce wolves" who would attempt to attack it (Acts 20:28, 29, RSV).

In announcing Himself as an overseer, Jesus wants us to understand that He is not an absentee landlord. Paying attention to everything necessary to our spiritual safety and ultimate salvation, He is with us, on the job, every day. He listens to complaints, guides, provides—yes, and writes reports, too.

FOR YOU WERE LIKE SHEEP GOING ASTRAY, BUT NOW YOU HAVE RETURNED TO THE . . . OVERSEER OF YOUR SOULS.

1 PETER 2:25, NIV.

[*Overseer of my soul, I thank You for stooping to take this care for my well-being. As Lord of all creation, You did not have to do this for me.*]

THE ELECT

To be "chosen" is a wonderful experience. Remember at recess time how you used to wait to be selected for the ball team? If you weren't distinguished in sports, perhaps you got tapped for the spelling bee. When you began to notice boys—or girls (as the case might be)—you waited to be chosen for skating, for Saturday night dates, maybe even to be a steady boy/girlfriend. Later on, if you were a good student, your classmates wanted to study with you. (Even though you occasionally came away with the uneasy feeling that they had benefited more than you had, they had at least complimented you.) Then one day perhaps someone asked you to marry him or her. What a thrilling selection *that* was! All such "elections" have enormously deep significance to us.

> "BEHOLD! . . . MY ELECT ONE IN WHOM MY SOUL DELIGHTS! I HAVE PUT MY SPIRIT UPON HIM."
>
> ISA. 42:1, NKJV.

Even though the uproar of party conventions and the slippery morals of certain politicians leave us disillusioned, democracy has much to be said for it. We try to remember that the voting, the choosing itself, is a great privilege. Elected officers, decorated heroes, Olympic winners, successful students, chosen friends, lovers—they all take pride in their *elected* status. Having worked hard for election, they continue to do so to maintain it. To be "diselected" is always a huge disappointment and a disgrace.

Isaiah's prophecy of Christ indicates the delight of the Father in His Son—"My Elect One," chosen to accomplish the task of salvation for humanity. Throughout His lifetime here, Jesus celebrated His privileged connection with God and reminded the Jews of their responsibility as the chosen ones. Amid the horror of the Crucifixion, however, the mob turned the title against Him in a fit of bitter mockery. "The people stood watching . . . [and] they said, 'He saved others; let him save himself if he is the Christ of God, the Chosen One'" (Luke 23:35, NIV).

While the possibility of Jesus' election caused Him joy, the responsibility was incredibly heavy, involving scorn and death. To be chosen is no light matter.

We, in turn, have been given a vote. We can choose or reject the Chosen One. Will we add to the scorn or will we increase His joy by choosing Him for ourselves?

> *My Jesus, You were chosen for me.*
> *Without reserve I now choose You.*

THE ADMINISTRATOR

One disease of the personality, as far as I know, has never been defined in medical literature—the "executive syndrome." Still, we've all seen it. Visible "busyness," running to committees, rushing to planes, dictating instructions on the cellular phone. Intimidating secretaries, meeting important contacts at "power" lunches, wearing importantly "correct" clothes, rejecting cars that do not make a good enough statement. Those having the syndrome must fly only first class. It takes limitless expense accounts, of course, to support such administration. Sadly, the executive syndrome is an occupational hazard for those working in positions of authority.

Such overfed egos appear at every level of administration. As often as not, the less leadership talent they have, the more ostentatious the symptoms of the illness they exhibit. It would no doubt come as a surprise to them to know that the literal meaning of the word "administrator" is "to serve."

"TO US A CHILD IS BORN, . . . AND THE GOVERNMENT WILL BE UPON HIS SHOULDER. . . . OF THE INCREASE OF HIS GOVERNMENT AND OF PEACE THERE WILL BE NO END."

ISA. 9:6, 7, RSV.

The story of the centurion reveals a man who properly understood how good administration works. Influential as he might be, he was aware of his place in the chain of command. "I am a man under authority, with soldiers under me." Efficient and effective, he not only received respect, he also knew the impact of a single word of command. "I say to one, 'Go,' and he goes, and to another, 'Come,' and he comes, and to my slave, 'Do this,' and he does it" (Matt. 8:9, RSV).

But the Roman officer had another side to his character. His heart ached for his servant who lay "in terrible distress," suffering, apparently, from a stroke. In Christ, the centurion sensed One who knew how to handle authority. Even from a distance he believed that Jesus could speak the word and his servant would be healed.

By every imaginable scheme and promise we have sought to create the perfect government. We will find it only under the ultimate administration of God. There, and only there, justice and mercy, strength and compassion will finally blend.

Father, with love and executive skill You manage the entire universe. Preserve me, I pray, from the folly of pride as I work among my colleagues today. Whatever authority I have received, let me carry it lightly and humbly.

THE SUPERVISOR

Setting aside the theology of faith and works, we shall assume here that we have committed our-selves to Christ, that we have a deep concern for doing His mission in the world, and that we have a desire—yes, a cheerful desire—to "do good works." With this attitude, doing good works ought to be easy, right? Wrong!

Most of us can remember being subservient to an autocratic, insensitive work supervisor. We know about being the proverbial square peg in the round hole. Or someone has manipulated us with a heavy assignment of *ought to's*. The result has been a stagger-ing load of guilt—either because we failed altogether in our performance or because the work became so distasteful and out of character for us that we could endure it no longer. The wise supervisor always knows how to match the worker to the task.

WE ARE GOD'S WORKMAN-SHIP, CRE-ATED IN CHRIST JESUS TO DO GOOD WORKS, WHICH GOD PREPARED IN ADVANCE FOR US TO DO.

EPH. 2:10, NIV.

Workmanship implies God's creativity that makes it possible for us to fulfill our purpose. The machine, so to speak, has been painstakingly crafted to fulfill its function. Then the task itself has been pre-arranged, custom-tailored for each of us. A wide range of good works lies before us: healing, welfare, visitation, administration, finance, technology, counseling, teaching, and so forth.

Not every "good work," however, fits every Christian. Too often we sup-pose that every consecrated believer should be able and willing to do every conceivable task. God implanted our personal gifts and limitations, however, in us even before birth. (I know that one of the best things that happened to the medical profession in recent times occurred when I did *not* enter it.) Moreover, our choices in education and work opportunities affect—for a life-time—the quality of our work and the enjoyment we have in doing it.

How infinitely comforting to know that for each of us our heavenly Supervisor has "prepared in advance" a specific task for us! Therefore, we must, with patience and tolerance, make space for one another, so that we *all* may do the precise work "for which God has designed us" (Eph. 2:10, NEB). Only thus can we blend into the body of Christ as complementary members.

[*Lord, You have given me such wonderful possibilities. I have complete freedom of choice, but I also have a custom-made plan You've made for my life. What a marvelous arrangement!*]

THE LEADER

Not once but probably several times in our lives we've observed the application of the Peter Principle. That is, "in a hierarchy every employee tends to rise to his or her level of incompetence." Furthermore, "in time, every post tends to be occupied by an employee who is incompetent to carry out its duties."* Perpetually, things go wrong. We ask, "How did *he* get that job?" Or "Who voted *her* into office?" In despair we wring our hands and cry, "O Lord, how long?"

HIS SUFFER-ING MADE JESUS A PERFECT LEADER, ONE FIT TO BRING THEM INTO THEIR SALVATION.

HEB. 2:10, TLB.

Leadership, however, we must always have. Leaders come and go among us. Some are above us, others are beside us, and some below. Maybe most of them have good intentions when they begin, but as often as not, they fail the trust their followers have placed in them. Innately we feel that we could do better if we were in their place. Disappointment and loss of faith in leadership embitter us. Our material lives get turned upside down and the vitality drains out of our spiritual experience.

Following a bad leader is servility. Committing oneself to a good leader is obedience. What then can we expect in good leaders? Here are a few defining characteristics. They will:

Inspire rather than drive those under them.

Abide by the law of love and mercy.

Earn goodwill rather than demand it from a position of authority.

Base policy on practical experience, not as another means of climbing the ladder.

Arouse enthusiasm rather than fear.

Not expect tasks of others they are not willing to do themselves.

Say "we" instead of "I."

Be humble and approachable.

Have no fear of being investigated, because their internal life matches their external.

Jesus answers every good leadership qualification to perfection. He keeps telling us a thousand different ways that love, not fear, is the basic principle of His kingdom.

> "Father, lead me day by day, ever in Thine own sweet way;
> Teach me to be pure and true; show me what I ought to do."
> —John P. Hopps

*Laurence J. Peter, *The Peter Principle* (New York: William Morrow and Co., 1969), pp. 25, 27.

THE SUPPORT STAFF

History is one dismal trail of failed alliances, treachery, and broken promises. Ezekiel points up a case in point. His "sevenfold doom of Egypt" (Eze. 29-32) predicts that never again will Israel trust Egypt. The latter betrayed her against Babylon. Judah will repent of turning to Egypt for leadership, will receive a "new spirit," and will return to God. They will realize that the one true God is better than a whole nation of military experts. A vast, bureaucratic "support staff" is both dangerous and unnecessary.

Several years ago, Victor Kiam, president of the Remington Company in Connecticut, had an interview on television. "How," the host of *60 Minutes* asked, "did you manage to make such a success of a dying business?" Kiam's reply was interesting. First of all, he did his own TV ads, announcing on them in various languages, "I bought the company." Next he fired 70 executives (the entire "support staff") and hired back only one of them. Then he took time to go into the factory and talk with the workers himself. He flew commercial airlines and not first-class. All in all, Kiam made Remington successful and has even been able to tackle Japan with his American-made products.

"Busyholics" find themselves corrupted and inflated by the support staffs that surround them. Thus we come across bizarre stories such as that of a man who worked for some 30 years in a large federal government office. He went off into retirement in good form, having labored well for his fellow human beings and having received an appropriate salary. Or so it seemed. When he died, however, it was discovered that in all those years he had literally done *nothing*. Indeed, he used his office and staff to operate a private business of his own. It's a dangerous thing to confuse movement with action. Being surrounded by agitated groups of supporters does not necessarily mean that anything is being accomplished.

In the light of many scriptural warnings, it's a good idea to let God organize our support staffs.

> "THE SUPPORT THAT YOU [EGYPT] GAVE TO THE ISRAELITES WAS NO BETTER THAN A REED. . . . WHEN THEY LEANED UPON YOU, YOU SNAPPED AND THEIR LIMBS GAVE WAY."
>
> EZE. 29:6, 7, NEB.

[*I am grateful, Lord, for the support staff of the loving friends You have given me. But I always want to keep You as my first line of defense. Protect me from those who would divert my focus.*]

THE DISCIPLINARIAN

Years ago one of my small cousins attended office worship with his parents one day. The morning speaker enlarged upon the sufferings of the apostle Paul, who said, "Three times I have been beaten with rods" (2 Cor. 11:25, RSV). Posing what he thought to be a purely rhetorical question, the preacher asked, "Now none of you have ever had to suffer like that, have you?"

A loud voice came from the front row: "I have." Young Jimmie still smarted from a disciplinary encounter with his mother at breakfast. His big brown eyes burned with conviction. "I was beaten with rods *today*."

> "WOE TO THE WICKED! . . . FOR THE REWARD OF HIS HANDS SHALL BE GIVEN HIM."
>
> ISA. 3:11, NKJV.

Discipline, of course, is a central issue in every part of human life. But how do you walk the thin line between discipline and abuse? How can we give just punishment in a spirit of love? Can God be a loving Saviour and a strict judge at the same time? Law and grace—how do we get them in proportion? Old Testament Jehovah and New Testament Jesus—how do They relate?

The impact of God the disciplinarian has often overpowered us. "Thou dost beset me behind and before, and layest thy hand upon me" (Ps. 139:5, RSV). He seems chronically exacting and vengeful. And in moments of self-recognition, we know that we deserve punishment.

God is absolute goodness, while sin is absolute evil. Light vanishes darkness. Blazing fire eliminates cold. Antiseptic destroys germs. These things do not happen because of some furious temper or a passionate spirit of vengeance, but because of their basic natures.

Divine discipline, then, arises naturally out of God's nature. God is not easygoing, nor is He vindictive. But He *can* be dangerous, for His presence means death to every form of evil. "Brought forth in iniquity" (Ps. 51:5, RSV), however, we are all infected with evil. But because God has made us for Himself, we have implanted in us a desire for the splendid experience of living in His presence. How do we fulfill it?

Simple. Jesus said, "I am the way . . . no one comes to the Father, but by me" (John 14:6, RSV). Herein lies perfect peace, perfect safety.

> [*Father, teach me to accept Your loving hand of correction, knowing that You have guaranteed the way by which I may come to live with You.*]

THE REWARDER

In 1766 Oliver Goldsmith wrote *The Vicar of Wakefield*. He modeled the unworldly, kindly Dr. Charles Primrose on the character of his own father, a poor clergyman living in Ireland. The family undergoes a series of Joblike disasters, and the generous vicar himself ends up in debtor's prison. Still faithful to his calling, however, Dr. Primrose preaches a powerful sermon to his fellow prisoners. He consoles them by urging them to look beyond their suffering to heaven, for "death is the only friend of the wretched." They are, indeed, the best equipped to savor the raptures of heaven. Primrose speaks with the quaint deliberation of his age:

> "REJOICE AND BE EXCEEDINGLY GLAD, FOR GREAT IS YOUR REWARD IN HEAVEN."
>
> MATT. 5:12, NKJV.

"To [the happy] in eternity but a single blessing, since at most it but increases what they already possess. To [the miserable] it is a double advantage; for it diminishes their pain here, and rewards them with heavenly bliss hereafter. . . . Providence has given the wretched two advantages over the happy in this life—greater felicity in dying, and in heaven all that superiority of pleasure which arises from contrasted enjoyment."*

The story reaches a Joblike conclusion. With typical eighteenth-century optimism and wisdom, love makes the reckless youth honorable, those who deserve wealth get it (a great deal of it), and all the suitable people get sorted out so that they can marry each other. All's right again with the vicar's world.

That's how life's *supposed* to be. The entire book of Job, however, is a refutation of the wisdom theory (a theme reiterated throughout the Old Testament). The wise men had long tried to establish an absolute connection between moral behavior and prosperity. They wanted to guarantee that the righteous will prosper and the wicked suffer. Job found himself to be a grievously misunderstood exception. While his friends hounded him to repent of his sins, he cried, "I have *not* denied the words of the Holy One" (Job:6:10, RSV).

We see that life's distribution of rewards may not be instantaneous. So then Goldsmith's vicar was right when he directed the wretched prisoners to look to their heavenly reward.

[*Give me patience to accept what circumstances—and perhaps my own lack of judgment—have brought to me. I trust You for my just reward in Your own time.*]

---

*Oliver Goldsmith, *The Vicar of Wakefield* (London: W. Suttaby, 1808), pp. 172-177.

THE ALIEN

Being a foreigner can be an extremely disabling condition. Nobody was really at fault, I suppose, but between the ages of 11 and 18 I lived as a perpetual stranger. (During those years my parents lived in seven different countries.) How desperately I wanted familiar surroundings. Instead, I lived forever on the front line, always hunting for new friends, craving new connections. Not that my schoolmates were malicious—not exactly. It's just that it took so much effort just "to belong."

> "I WAS A STRANGER AND YOU WELCOMED ME."
>
> MATT. 25:35, RSV.

During those years of travel (and after), I had occasion to watch immigration and customs officials at work. Too often noncitizens suffer humiliation and unnecessary trauma. I am *still* amazed at the fragile excuses we use to exert authority over one another. Prejudice and elitism can instantly raise their ugly heads.

While Mosaic law required that God's people show kindness to aliens, they still had many social limitations and legal restrictions. Even today one's passport and/or green card (alien registration in the United States) are treasured possessions. They give us, if not always acceptance, at least a secure identity.

Jesus took on the humblest human form. Indeed, since He was an itinerant teacher, those in high places often questioned His presence. His discourse on the great judgment day to come, however, revealed some vital facts about Himself.

Great compassionate teacher that He is, He has told us beforehand exactly what the examination questions will be. Paradoxically, God uses an unexpected basis of judgment. He warns those who think that because they are serving God in an obvious and direct way it will ensure salvation. Instead, we find that the determining factor lies in the manner we treat others. Compassion is a major indicator of the fact that the "Christ spirit" lives within us. Christians must be known by the way they love one another. Jesus lived His earthly life as a stranger in order to demonstrate this point.

[*My door stands open to You, my heavenly Stranger. Help me to turn away no one today, no matter how incomprehensible or unlovely they may seem.*]

THE GENTLEMAN

Royalty is an "aristocracy of birth." Being a gentleman is, however, a matter of good breeding. In our loud, profane, rough-and-tumble world of sheer survival, a few "gentlefolk" in every society float to the top and assume the title of "gentleman." Thus, with their education, refined manners, and good breeding, the gentry have become "genteel"—even qualified to attend royalty. In his rollicking social satire, the English writer P. G. Wodehouse created the character of Jeeves, the impeccable "gentleman's gentleman" who serves his idle, inept employer, Bertie Wooster, through a series of social crises.

"I AM GENTLE . . . AND YOU WILL FIND REST FOR YOUR SOULS."

MATT. 11:29, RSV.

The word "gentry" has now become rather corrupted. We have even replaced the labels of "gentlemen" and "ladies" on public restroom doors with "men" and "women," as if we were embarrassed to be thought high-class. "Gentlefolk" has come to imply snobbishness, ineffectuality, artificiality, and laziness—not an attractive picture.

In understanding Jesus' claims to "gentleness," however, we must return to the original meaning of the word. Presenting Himself as the complete "gentle Man," Christ makes gentleness a requirement for all of His followers. It is, indeed, one of the Christian's five major duties: "Clothe yourselves with compassion, kindness, humility, gentleness and patience" (Col. 3:12, NIV). Now here are the marks of a truly gentle person—and they are wonderful qualities of "unfading beauty" (1 Peter 3:4, NIV).

Elsewhere Paul describes his own ministry: "We were gentle among you" (1 Thess. 2:7). He counsels church leaders not to be "violent" or "quarrelsome" (1 Tim. 3:3, RSV). The apostle invites the believers to put on the "meekness and gentleness of Christ" (2 Cor. 10:1, NIV), to cultivate "gentleness [and] self-control" (Gal. 5:23, RSV) and to have a "gentle spirit" (1 Cor. 4:21, NIV), and to let their "gentleness be evident to all" (Phil. 4:5, NIV).

The Christian, Peter tells us, should not even declare his or her faith stridently. We should speak of our hope only "with gentleness and reverence" (1 Peter 3:15, RSV). Thus our gentility will put to shame those who would scorn or even abuse us (verse 16).

Best of all, Jesus gives His promises based upon His honor. They are the unfailing word of a perfect Gentleman.

> *Gentle Christ, no matter how strong my convictions are, do not let me forget that I am among the gentlefolk who bear Your name. Help me not, under any circumstance, to deny You by my anger or loss of self-control.*

THE MESSIAH

In ancient Mexico Quetzalcoatl, the Plumed Serpent, was the god and legendary ruler of both the Toltec and Aztec Indians. Symbol of death and resurrection, he was exiled by the opposing deity, Tezcatlipoca (god of the night sky). According to prophecies, however, the god (described as light-skinned and bearded) would return to earth. Therefore, when the Spanish conqueror Hernando Cortés appeared in 1519, the Aztec king, Montezuma II, let himself be easily persuaded that the promised god had returned. The point is, as long as people have suffered oppression—and that's from the beginning of time—they've needed liberators, or "messiahs."

> "MESSIAH SHALL BE CUT OFF, BUT NOT FOR HIM-SELF; AND THE PEOPLE OF THE PRINCE WHO IS TO COME."
>
> DAN. 9:26, NKJV.

Scripture traces the coming of Messiah Christ in detail.

1. The Messiah was *promised*. The Hebrew name for the promised deliverer of humanity is "Messiah," or the "Anointed One." Thus consecrated—the purpose of anointing—to his office, the Messiah would have priestly powers (Ex. 28:41) and would be dedicated as a prophet (1 Kings 19:16). He would also embody the ideal king, in the manner of David. The Jews, unfortunately, tended to overlook a fourth characteristic—the Messiah would *also* be a suffering servant (Isa. 53).

2. The Messiah was *expected*. The promise of the grand Messianic event followed immediately upon the fall of humanity (Gen. 3:15), with the promises growing brighter and more specific as the time approached. For the Jews He would fulfill all of their needs. They kept the expectation alive generation after generation.

3. The Messiah was *anointed*. John preached "how God anointed Jesus of Nazareth with the Holy Spirit and with power" (Acts 10:38, NKJV).

In His ministry Jesus qualified as priest and prophet. He approached the suffering of crucifixion as the suffering Servant. Then His mocking persecutors cried, "Let the Messiah, the king of Israel, come down now from the cross" (Mark 15:32, NEB). They said more than they knew, for with His death and resurrection His messiahship became complete reality.

> "Come, thou long expected Jesus!
> Born to set thy people free,
> From our fears and sins release us,
> Let us find our rest in thee."
> —Charles Wesley (1707-1788)

THE CHRIST

eter's confession came just after the death of John the Baptist. Immediately afterward the faith-confirming experience of the Transfiguration occurred. In between Jesus took His disciples to Caesarea Philippi. The terraced heights of the city overlooked the gushing source of the Jordan that flows down through quiet, palm-encircled pools. Above everything stands snow-crowned Mount Hermon.

SIMON PETER . . . SAID, "YOU ARE THE CHRIST, THE SON OF THE LIVING GOD."

MATT. 16:16, NKJV.

In this extraordinarily beautiful setting Jesus raised a question: "Who do men say that the Son of man is?" (Matt. 16:13, RSV). Acknowledgments of Jesus as merely a prophet were insufficient. He pressed the crucial question: "But who do *you* say that I am?" (verse 15). With characteristic zeal, Peter spoke for them all. "You are the Christ" (verse 16). Some of the others, perhaps, would have hesitated to make such a bold, all-encompassing declaration. Peter's vehement loyalty, however, arose from sheer faith. As another Passover season approached, Jesus knew what Peter could not foresee—the proclamation of the Christ in Jerusalem would mean certain death.

In the single word "Christ" Peter said it all—the "anointed Messiah." While the Jews had long looked for the Messiah to come, when actually He arrived He gave them much more than they expected or were prepared for. He was the Holy One, of the very substance of the living God, having the essence of life within Himself.

Of the many names of Jesus, "the Christ" has been most influential. "Christology" is the study of the person and work of Jesus Christ and His relationship to us. We presumptuously speak of "Christian nations." The early church, however, was reluctant to take up the name of "Christian." They called themselves "brethren," "saints," or "believers." The Greco-Roman world applied the term to them. Luke records that "a large company of people" in Antioch "were for the first time called Christians" (Acts 11:26, RSV). Later Peter advised the believers not to be "ashamed" to suffer "as a Christian" but to glorify God "under that name" (1 Peter 4:16, RSV).

In taking the name of Christ we acknowledge His divinity and the power of His Messiahship. If we lack faith to say this much, then we cannot rightfully assume the name of Christian.

[*Jesus Christ, I believe that You are the Son of God. I would always bear Your name faithfully—and with pride.*]

THE SIN-BEARER

S hould you happen to be in the Philippines during Easter, you would see that religious festival celebrated more elaborately than you might have imagined possible—the chanting of the "Pasyon," the dramatization of the legend Longinus, the seclusion of Black Friday—and the flagellantes. Most of us conceive of the "bearing of sin" as a troubled conscience or the harboring of an unspeakable secret. Devout Filipinos, however, demonstrate this interior condition in a highly visible, physical way. Almost every season one or two people will carry their crucifixion or flagellation a little too far and die.

> [CHRIST] HIMSELF BORE OUR SINS IN HIS OWN BODY ON THE TREE.
>
> 1 PETER 2:24, NKJV.

Amid the fiesta mood of the *barrio*, the flagellantes will prepare for their ordeal. To open a blood flow, they slash their bare backs and chests with razor blades and broken glass. Then they beat themselves with sharp bamboo scourges and chains. Usually they have at least a mile to walk to the church. Friends alternate between beating the flagellantes with sticks and offering them drinks and raw eggs to sustain them on their terrible journey. Some will prostrate themselves in the dust every three paces. They take the last 500 yards to the church on elbows and knees. At the entrance comes one final whipping. Inside, the cement floor is so slick with blood that the now almost senseless penitents virtually slide into the altar at which they cry out their prayers for mercy. Any blood spattered on spectators (and there is much of it) supposedly transfers the flagellante's sins to the bystanders. The older participants who have made this journey annually for 30 or 40 years have a strong spiritual commitment, keeping their vows with, as they say, "pure hearts."

While we recoil from the horror of such self-abuse, we too often flagellate our minds and spirit. We inflict grievous, useless wounds of guilt upon ourselves. But we need to remember that our Sin-bearer "on himself . . . bore our sufferings, our torments he endured" (Isa. 53:4, NEB). Here is true horror. In going to the cross, however, He provided us with a double blessing—spiritual peace now and physical safety hereafter.

Sin will *always* remain a horror—whoever is carrying it.

> [*My Saviour, help me give up my guilt. You have borne the sin burden for me and left me free. I choose this day not to carry it any longer.*]

THE PROPHET

The word "prophet" has come, nowadays, primarily to mean someone who foretells future events. The profession of prophet, however, was far more comprehensive than that. The prophet had to be a "forth-teller," one who spoke in behalf of another—usually God. Our current practice of preaching has evolved from the ancient gift of prophesying. The prophet/preacher, most important, was and is commissioned to maintain moral standards and to reprove the sins of the nation.

Most prophets, both true and false, had several things in common. They fell into trances, had visions, predicted the future, and had important political influence. Pagan prophets also required gifts. Their messages were often ambiguous and came upon request (after payment of the fees).

The true prophet-preachers of Scripture, on the other hand, often spoke urgently and unbidden, sometimes to the great discomfiture of their listeners. God had some, such as Ezekiel, Hosea, and Jeremiah, perform symbolic public acts to visualize their messages. Such incidents often looked ridiculous and were often personally inconvenient to the prophet. Because of hardship and little material gain, a *true* prophet often took up the task only reluctantly.

As prophet and preacher, Jesus used just two methods in His itinerant earthly ministry. First, He preached—that is, He proclaimed publicly. Anyone, anywhere, was welcome to hear. Second, He focused intensely on "the gospel of the kingdom." That is, the "good news" about salvation—the only topic worth preaching about. All of those who preach, whether on a large or small scale, do well to keep their messages swift and lean, like those of the Master Preacher Himself.

> **"A GREAT PROPHET HAS APPEARED AMONG US,"** THEY SAID. **"GOD HAS COME TO HELP HIS PEOPLE."**
> LUKE 7:16, NIV.
> **JESUS WENT ABOUT . . . PREACHING THE GOSPEL OF THE KINGDOM.**
> MATT. 9:35, RSV.

[*Lord, help me always to discover the eternal essentials of Your gospel. Let me not be distracted by empty, dramatic "effects."*]

THE HIGH PRIEST

S ince sin fractured our relationship with God, no one has ever been able by themselves to cross the gulf between earth and heaven. Pagans also sense their separation from the divine—a need that they've supplied with priests and magicians.

For Israel, however, God appointed a unique priesthood involving divine revelation. Those anointed to this special office came from the tribe of Levi (Ex. 25-40). Deprived of the birthright (along with Simeon) after the treacherous massacre of the men of Shechem, Levi had no land allotment. The tribe's later decisive moral energy, however, restored the Levites when, at Sinai, they emerged as courageous and intelligent spiritual leaders.

Descending the mountain and discovering the religious orgy around the golden calf, Moses went to the gate of the camp and thundered, "Who is on the Lord's side? Come to me." The shouting and dancing trailed off into ominous silence. Here and there a movement appeared in the camp. One by one all of the sons of Levi separated themselves from the rest, taking up positions by their leaders, Moses and Aaron. Then, from the midst of his company of Levites, Moses gave the command to destroy. Within the hour 3,000 men died (Ex. 32:25-28).

"Today," Moses announced, "you have ordained yourselves for the service of the Lord, each one at the cost of his son and of his brother" (verse 29, RSV).

A visible reminder of God's righteous requirements, the priestly hierarchy of the Levites had three parts. First, the high priest represented all of the people before God, in purity and in honor. Then the ordinary priests ministered at the altars, burned sacrifices, and managed worship. Last, the rest of the Levites cared for the sanctuary and its services and taught religious law.

The many references to Christ as "our high priest" in the New Testament elicited many rich associations for both Jewish and Gentile converts to Christianity (Heb. 5:14; 10:21, 22). Only through Him, acting on our behalf, can we come into God's presence without fear.

> SEEING THEN THAT WE HAVE A GREAT HIGH PRIEST WHO HAS PASSED THROUGH THE HEAVENS, JESUS THE SON OF GOD, LET US HOLD FAST OUR CONFESSION.
>
> HEB. 4:14, NKJV.

[*You, Jesus, are the perfect high priest. I need no other to bridge the chasm between earth and heaven.*]

THE SYMPATHETIC HIGH PRIEST

If you're sick, you see a physician. Should you struggle with mental distress, you go to a psychologist. And if you want to find God, you need a priest.

A high priest, however, can be a rather forbidding personality. By the time of the Protestant Reformation the Christian priesthood had become fearfully remote. Physical separation between the congregation and the activities at the church altar combined with services in the now little-known language of Latin. While one might encounter a friar on the road or poor parish priest in the village, speaking to a "high priest" was not something that most people expected ever to do in their lifetime.

Jesus, on the other hand, is qualified in three ways to be our High Priest.

1. He is everlasting. Christ is a priest "according to the order of Melchizedek" (Heb. 7:17, NKJV)—Melchizedek, that mysterious, shadowy figure (without "beginning or end") to whom Abraham paid tithes. From the tribe of Judah and not Levi, Jesus went beyond the Levitical code. He was not bound to "regular channels."

2. He is sinlessness. Aaron and all who have followed him were mortal, fallen human beings. They offered sacrifices endlessly for centuries. Then Jesus appeared, the perfect sinless High Priest. First He came to us to relieve us of the horrors of sin. Now He stands for us before the Father's throne (Heb. 8:1, 2; 9:24).

3. He is approachable. Not only has He included us in His own household, He's bonded Himself to us and us to one another in a series of images of family relationship. This family thrives on love, equality, and unity. As He represents us before God's throne, He wears the names of everyone who has accepted Him—wears them as did the Hebrew high priest who bore the names of each of the 12 tribes engraved on his ephod (Ex. 28:11, 12, 21).

Christ is a priest of eternal and universal availability, perfection, and accessibility! Could we ask for more in a high priest as we contemplate facing judgment day?

> HE HAD TO BE MADE LIKE THESE BROTHERS OF HIS IN EVERY WAY, SO THAT HE MIGHT BE MERCIFUL AND FAITHFUL AS THEIR HIGH PRIEST BEFORE GOD.
>
> HEB. 2:17, NEB.

[*I bring only myself to You, Lord, knowing that Your intercession is sufficient for all my needs.*]

THE SACRIFICE

The sacrificial system required the giving up of some personal possession in order to feed the gods (as the pagans believed), to give thanks, to make requests, and/or to repent of sin.

For the Hebrews it began with every man performing his own ritual, such as Cain and Abel (Gen. 4). Then the responsibility went to the head of the family, who celebrated the ritual, as in the case of Noah (Gen. 8:20) and Abraham (Gen. 12:7). Ultimately, it became a town or national event, with the high priest managing the complex procedures of sacrifice. Classical and biblical literatures abound with descriptions of enormous sacrifices for special occasions, involving many *hecatombs* (groups of 100 perfectly matched animals). In cases of extreme importance, humans have replaced animals. Usually, a society employed "replaceable" victims—captives; slaves; those with disabilities; children; and virgins. Like public execution, the scene of such a public sacrifice became an unforgettable experience for every spectator.

While the sacraments of the church have preserved some of the powerful atmosphere of the sacrificial system, we have lost much of the "presence," the immediacy of ritual, that the entire ancient world knew.

When God offered His only begotten Son as a sacrifice, He gave up what was His own. In providing *Himself* as the perfect sacrifice, Jesus presented the ultimate gift—His life. Thus heaven disrupted itself for sinning humanity. And that sacrifice forever erased the human race's debt. Jesus Himself said so from the cross, just after He tasted the sour wine: "It is finished" (John 19:30). We need make no further payments on the sin debt. Our credit is ensured.

> CHRIST OFFERED FOR ALL TIME ONE SACRIFICE FOR SINS, AND TOOK HIS SEAT AT THE RIGHT HAND OF GOD. . . . FOR BY ONE OFFERING HE HAS PERFECTED FOR ALL TIME THOSE WHO ARE THUS CONSECRATED.
>
> HEB. 10:12-14, NEB.

[*Let me take nothing for granted. Let me remember every day of my life that moment when Jesus Himself became our sacrifice.*]

THE PASSOVER

The Passover combines the sacrificial lamb with the feast of unleavened bread, offerings of both flock and field. Jehovah appropriated familiar symbols to mark Israel's destiny. We note three important features of Passover:

CHRIST, OUR PASSOVER LAMB, HAS BEEN SACRIFICED.

1 COR. 5:7, NIV.

1. Freedom and deliverance. Yahweh brought Israel out of Egypt with "a strong hand and outstretched arm" (Deut. 26:8, NEB). The exodus from Egypt had only a limited goal, realized more than 40 years later in Canaan. Jesus, however, did what Moses could never have accomplished. He extended the great deliverance to include *true* freedom—freedom from sin. Thus Jews and Christians alike honor the theme of deliverance.

2. Commemorative ordinances. A frequent refrain in the writings of all of the prophets, God's deliverance was to be remembered in all Hebrew households. "This day shall be to you a memorial; and you shall keep it as a feast to the Lord throughout your generations. You shall keep it as . . . an everlasting ordinance" (Ex. 12:14, NKJV).

Jesus' institution of the Lord's Supper went one step further. The solemn breaking of bread and drinking of wine previewed the way the Christian church would perpetuate the Passover theme in a new context. Also, the timing of Jesus' death wasn't accidental. John has Jesus' activities as Messiah climax in the events of His last Passover, dying on the first day of the Passover, the seven-day Feast of Unleavened Bread (John 19:14).

3. The Covenant. The overarching theme of Passover and the Last Supper, however, is more than sacrifice and deliverance, bread and wine. It reaffirms the covenant between God and His people. In his picture of the new Passover, Paul made this point by combining three strong imageries of Christ: the sacrifice, the Lamb, and the deliverer from death. Moreover, he uses a present tense form of the verb. The sacrifice is now. We don't wait for the future. "Indeed our Passover *has begun;* the sacrifice *is offered*—Christ himself" (1 Cor. 5:7, NEB).

In keeping with the nineteenth-century emphasis on sacrificial blood, an old song we used to sing declares:

> "'I will pass over you when I see the blood';
> I will pass over you—'tis a saving flood. . . .
> The precious blood of Jesus."*

---

*F. E. Belden, "The Passover," *Christ in Song,* No. 38.

THE TRANSFORMER

We've come a long way with transformers in the past generation. Most of the time we take their service for granted—the delivery of electricity through power generating stations to our homes and businesses and the reproduction of fine sound in our high-fidelity music systems and televisions.

The traveler, however, is the one who's likely to have unpleasant episodes with electricity in strange places. Our lives would be simpler if every nation in the world had decided to use either 110 volts or 220 volts. Additionally, electricians have not gotten together on a universally accepted electrical outlet design. But since no one agrees even on major life-and-death issues, complaining about such inconveniences now is futile. In any case, when you carry electrical equipment on a journey—anything from a slide projector to a hair dryer—you'd better be extra-careful about how you connect it to the source of power.

Most of us can remember those heavy old transformers, the size of car batteries. Then they began to shrink, until finally all we had to carry was a little unit weighing a few ounces. Next came those clever appliances with built-in "double" transformers. You just changed from 110 volts to 220 volts with a flick of the switch. For forgetful people in a hurry, however, it was still a high-risk device. If you forgot to activate the transformer, you had a flash of sparks, a fiery hiss, and a puff of smoke. And there, inert in your hands, lay your appliance, burned out and dead, with no hope of revival. Finally, however, technology has caught up with *my* needs. My new notebook computer thinks for me. I can plug into current anywhere in the world, and the computer accepts whatever it gets. State-of-the-art electronics.

The cross of Christ is our mighty spiritual transformer. Our humanity is extremely low voltage compared to heaven's high frequencies and massive power. Without this Transformer, we can never connect. Or if, through perversity or negligence, we attempt to use some other connecting device, we shall burn out—forever. In the realm of the Spirit, from the beginning of time Jesus has been our perfect transformer.

> GOD FORBID THAT I SHOULD BOAST OF ANYTHING BUT THE CROSS OF OUR LORD JESUS CHRIST, THROUGH WHICH THE WORLD IS CRUCIFIED TO ME AND I TO THE WORLD!
>
> GAL. 6:14, NEB.

[*I recognize the risk, Lord, in dealing with the powerful issues of the Spirit. Stand always between me and them so that my life may be fitted for Your kingdom.*]

THE RESURRECTION

No matter what our personal desires might be, the gift of immortality within a human context would be nothing short of a disaster. In a previous reading we looked at the ancient Greek myth of Tithonus and Aurora, in which the goddess of the dawn fell passionately in love with the handsome youth Tithonus. Knowing that she would ultimately lose him, she went to Zeus, pleading for immortality for the man she loved. But when Tithonus began to age and finally grew to be extremely feeble, the goddess saw her mistake. How could she have been so shortsighted, asking for immortality *without* youth and health to go with it?

"I AM THE RESURRECTION AND THE LIFE. HE WHO BELIEVES IN ME WILL LIVE, EVEN THOUGH HE DIES."

JOHN 11:25, NIV.

Outliving one's generation coupled with the ravages of old age is pure tragedy. Christ worked a great variety of miracles. Conquering every kind of disease, He also healed sick minds and hearts and brought the dead back to life. But never once did He reverse the aging process. He never made anyone young again. Though He might easily have done so, He never thus removed anyone from their social context.

That is not to say, however, that He had no alternative plans. He did! And it is not turning us into grasshoppers, as Zeus did of Tithonus! What God has always had in mind is the resurrection—that moment when we undergo a complete body transplant. The believer moves from time-bound earth to where there is *no* time. Jesus' reference to the possibility of a person living "even though he dies" proves that the death we know here has nothing to do with life as God has planned it hereafter. It serves only as the threshold to immortality.

[*Lord, sometimes the lengthening days of my life also weary body and mind. Help me always to fix my eyes on the gift of life that You have reserved for me.*]

THE SAVIOUR

In my house at the moment we are searching for some important papers that are lost—and have been lost for quite a while. Unfortunately, we're responsible to someone else for them and have long been promising, "Yes, we're looking. And we're going to find them." As usual, they have been put in a place so safe that no one can remember where it is. Now we are taking the house and garage apart drawer by drawer, shelf by shelf, file by file, box by box.

Along the way we have discovered many other long-lost treasures—plus an overwhelming amount of junk. Sometimes a fire, an earthquake, or some other catastrophe removes all need for saving anything. We, however, now have the obligation of looking at everything we own and making a decision—to save or throw it out.

The salvation equation has four parts. First, someone or something has been lost. Danger and disaster have struck, and things have gone terribly wrong. Usually, we cannot set them right alone. What is lost must be moved from peril to safety, from hazard to security. Good must replace evil. Second, there has to be a savior. The person must be able to recognize the problem of "lostness" and must have the power to save the situation, to perform the act of *saving*.

Third, the savior must decide whether or not the work of salvation is worthwhile. Whatever or whoever is lost—is it expedient to expend the necessary effort to save it? Finally, the lost one must not resist the savior's efforts to rescue him or her.

Now, my lost papers are lying hidden somewhere awaiting discovery. They can do nothing to help me in my search. Lost people, on the other hand, are already in a known place—and God knows exactly where they are and what they need. Quite likely they are aware of their condition, at least to some extent.

While we have saviors in all kinds of circumstances, only one Saviour exists. It is one of Christ's most significant titles. We have only to be willing for the Saviour to do His work in us. He's already shown us that He accounts us worthy of His salvation.

> WHEN THE KINDNESS AND LOVE OF GOD OUR SAVIOR APPEARED, HE SAVED US, NOT BECAUSE OF RIGHTEOUS THINGS WE HAD DONE, BUT BECAUSE OF HIS MERCY.
>
> TITUS 3:4, NIV.

[*Thank You, dear Saviour, for finding me where I am. Now work out the salvation that You planned for me from eternity.*]

THE BURDEN-BEARER

A best-seller for centuries, *The Pilgrim's Progress,* by John Bunyan (1628-1688), allegorizes our spiritual journey. A man named Christian sets out from his City of Destruction for the Celestial City hampered by an enormous burden of sin on his back. When he bows in repentance at the foot of the cross— an early way station on his road—the bundle miraculously falls off and rolls down the hill. Free, he rises to face the coming trials without any encumbrances.

"COME TO ME, ALL YOU WHO ARE WEARY AND BURDENED, AND I WILL GIVE YOU REST."
MATT. 11:28, NIV.

In his short story "The Celestial Railroad," Nathaniel Hawthorne (1804-1864) parodies Bunyan's Pilgrim, mocking the theology of Hawthorne's time. Hawthorne's pilgrims ride on a train powered by fire-breathing Apollyon. Along the way they have no awareness of their burdens. They've brought everything with them, and their luggage rides conveniently in the baggage car. They bypass all the difficulties along the way—except for one. The rail line does *not* cross the River of Death to the heavenly shore. Instead, a devilish ferryboat carries the people downstream.

Those of us in technologically developed countries really don't know much about carrying a burden. We do little walking, and whatever we have to transport we put into the car. At the most, we'll carry our luggage from the car to the check-in counter at the airport—where conveyor belts take it to the plane. Life's easy—at least physically.

Other times and places, however, have been different. Boys exiled from Zion "staggered under loads of wood" (Lam. 5:13, NKJV). The psalmists reviewed the "burdens" of Israel in slavery in Egypt. Egyptian tomb paintings show slaves working on the construction of Pharaoh's cities. Men, strong and stubborn as donkeys, carried baskets of clay and bricks on their shoulders and had to steady them with their hands. Jehovah, however, changes all of that. "I removed his shoulder from the burden; his hands were freed from the baskets. You called in trouble, and I delivered you" (Ps. 81:6, 7, NKJV).

With our invisible burdens of the mind and heart, however, many of us drag heavier loads than ever did a slave, donkey, or camel. We cannot haul guilt, hatred, and greed in a basket or check them in at an airline counter. They are forever with us—until we allow the Burden-Bearer to do as He has promised—remove our burdens from us.

[*Christ, I carry heavy burdens. I keep setting them down and then picking them up again. Give me trust to leave them with You.*]

THE SUBSTITUTE

Four million died in the extermination camp at Auschwitz, Poland, between 1939 and 1945. Among them, one man was unique.

An exceptional student, Raymond "Maximilian" Kolbe (1894-1941) became a Franciscan priest and earned two doctorates. He went as a missionary to Japan and later founded a monastery in Poland. For his refusal to collaborate with the Nazi regime the Germans arrested him early in 1941.

THE LIFE I NOW LIVE IS NOT MY LIFE, BUT THE LIFE WHICH CHRIST LIVES IN ME.
GAL. 2:20, NEB.

As Number 16670, Father Maximilian entered Auschwitz in May. In August a prisoner from Block 14 escaped and eluded capture. At roll call the next morning the guards detained the inmates of Block 14 in the quadrangle. They stood there all day, 10 ranks of living skeletons. Retribution came at 6:00 p.m. The *lagerführer* (camp commandant) Fritsch randomly chose 10 prisoners to be sent to the death bunker in Block 13.

When called, Polish Sgt. Francis Gajowniczek cried, "My God! My wife! My poor children!" Before the doomed men could be marched off, however, Prisoner 16670 stepped forward before the stunned company. "I'm alone. That man has a family to live for . . . Please."

Stunned, the commandant barked, "Who are *you?*"

"A priest." Serene eyes looked out of a wasted face. "I want to take his place."

"Ach! Another priest pig!" As Fritsch turned away, however, he muttered, "Accepted."

The doomed men lay in the dank dungeon day after day, without food or water, Father Kolbe ministering to them. They sang, they prayed, and one by one they died in the priest's arms. At the end of two weeks only Father Maximilian and three others remained alive. Impatient for the end, the commandant ordered lethal injections. The last to die, the priest held out his arm for the needle, smiling and whispering, "Ave Maria."

At the end of the war Gajowniczek returned to Warsaw to find his two sons slaughtered but his wife alive. Together they began a new life in a small village. From then on they told and retold the story of Father Maximilian's sacrifice and redemption.

What then of the Man who has substituted His death for ours? His eternal life for ours?

> *My Jesus, let me never neglect to tell the marvelous story of Your offer to live and die as substitute for me.*

THE RESTORER

I have an antique rolltop desk that I value highly. Before a favorite aunt bequeathed it to me she had it "restored." She told me that it had been in very poor condition when she found it in a secondhand shop and bought it for $20. Today, however, it stands before my study window, fully restored, looking as good as when it was new some 130 or more years ago and with a potential value of several thousand dollars.

I always admire people who restore things—even when I don't fully understand how or why they do it. The individual who spends tens of thousands of dollars to revive an antique car. The couple who study every available book and magazine so that they can turn their house into the Victorian mansion it once was. The wallpaper, the furniture, the bathtub, the mirrors—everything has to be correct. They may have to remove layers of paint to reach the original surfaces. Some architectural features will have to be custom-made. What looks like a flat black table may turn out to have a gorgeous grain or inlay work—after you have removed a half dozen coats of varnish and stain.

The word "restoration" implies that something has been damaged or perhaps altogether lost. The time in English history known as the Restoration refers to the return of King Charles II to the throne in 1660, following the Puritan interlude of Oliver Cromwell. Restoration involves more than a coat of paint or a bit of Scotch tape. *That* is only makeshift repair. Complete restoration means "good as new." Sometimes it is even better!

When David cried, "Restore to me the joy of Your salvation," he spoke more than he knew (Ps. 51:12, NKJV). God's restoration is complete! Long ago, at the beginning of our sin problem, we spoiled God's creation. All of it—physical, moral, everything. The good news of the book of Revelation, however, is that the Divine Restorer is going to give it all back to us. "Then he who sat on the throne said, 'Behold! I am making all things new!'" (Rev. 21:5, NEB). Eternity will even restore to us the time we have lost!

"I WILL RESTORE TO YOU THE YEARS THAT THE SWARMING LOCUST HAS EATEN."

JOEL 2:25, NKJV.

[*Heavenly Craftsman, I can never be content with a patch-up repair to my life. Restore Your life in me—completely. At any cost.*]

THE CARETAKER

Years ago, when we lived in Jamaica, our favorite—virtually only—recreation was swimming, snorkeling, diving, and building what remains to the present time to be a fairly impressive collection of Caribbean shells. One day, along with friends, we decided to spend the afternoon at Black River. Somehow the black sands of the beach there produced exotic driftwood and colorful shells. We parked our cars in front of a tiny fishing village. Every inhabitant, I believe, came out to watch us take out our snorkels, fins, and food. A large, impressive man watched me locking our car. "Not to bodder, missus. No one steal." He drew himself up proudly. "Me the in-charge heah." The "in-charge" was as good as his word. We returned to find our cars perfectly intact.

> CAST ALL YOUR CARES ON HIM, FOR YOU ARE HIS CHARGE.
>
> 1 PETER 5:7, NEB.

The business of a caretaker is always to be in charge. In older, less democratic days, the caretaker (or steward) was the one who managed the servants and who kept the great house always in order. At whatever time the master returned, the household, down to the least detail, had to be ready to receive him and his retinue. People with holiday homes, with houses to rent, with any property to which they cannot give personal and continuous supervision, need a caretaker.

Then there is the matter of taking care of people. The modern solution in the Western world frequently comes as a shock to people in developing countries. We speak of "convalescent hospitals," knowing full well that few if any of the patients ever come out alive. Those who still see the care of the sick and the elderly as the responsibility of families regard such hospitals and nursing homes with contempt. The greater life expectancy given us by modern medicine today has resulted in old people taking care of still older people—at great emotional as well as physical expense.

We cannot resolve the all-comprehensive problem of caretaking here, of course. But we can note the prime requisites of a good caretaker: responsibility, loyalty, decisiveness, and energy, for a start. To this *must* be added love. The basic functions of caretaking *can* be performed without love—at least temporarily. Without love, though, the one cared for will surely decline.

With God in charge we can relax. He qualifies on every possible point.

> *Lord, take my life in hand today. Preserve the good.*
> *Eradicate the evil. Fill my whole house with Your love.*

THE GUIDE

The dictionary defines a maze as "a network of intercommunicating paths, arranged in bewildering complexity, so that without guidance it is difficult to find one's way through the labyrinth." Without a guide, the challenge of a maze can be terrifying.

An art form in gardening and stonework, mazes date back some 4,000 years. Ancient cultures used them for ritual dances and processions. To ensure a safe voyage and a good catch, fishermen in old Europe walked through stone mazes to the shore. Medieval Christians borrowed the pagan maze for enacting pilgrimages to the Holy Land. In the fourteenth century maze herb gardens graced almost every aristocrat's garden. By the nineteenth century the Victorians had perfected the puzzle maze. Today's entertaining "maze craze" has prompted us to use patterned plantings of dwarfed yew and box hedges in both private gardens and public parks.

For 34 years the Reverend Harry Cheales served as rector of the parish church in Wyck Rissington, Gloucestershire, England. He created a uniquely spiritual maze in the church yard. Signboards symbolized the Christian life and pointed to the destination of the maze, heaven. Those intricate, winding paths led people through the gospel story, from Jesus' birth to resurrection, ending at a magnificent, giant, century-old Sequoia tree. Today not a trace remains of Reverend Cheales's mystical object lesson. When he retired in 1980, he had the maze destroyed. He would not allow it to fall into secular hands or to become a curiosity for tourists.

Considering the "a-mazing" mysteries of Christ's life, we understand why Christendom's most beloved song is "Amazing Grace." That grace, however, calls forth none of the negative old meanings of the word. Rather it relates to the loved, carefully tended garden, the place where we may sometimes be bewildered, but where we always find a Guide. Because the Divine Guide stands above the maze, He can direct each of us through the individual trails to which life calls us.

Although the way is well signposted, and while we may consult the opinions of fellow travelers, we dare not rely upon our own understanding. Our Guide is indispensable.

> **"DO NOT LET YOUR HEARTS BE TROUBLED. . . . YOU KNOW THE WAY TO THE PLACE WHERE I AM GOING."**
>
> JOHN 14:1-4, NIV.

[*"Guide me, O Thou Great Jehovah, pilgrim through this barren land; I am weak, but Thou art mighty; hold me with Thy powerful hand."*]

THE SUSTAINER

With typical juvenile compulsiveness, my Australian cousins and I used to set ourselves to a real challenge. We decided that when we went on the electric train down to the city, we would try to hold our breath all the way across Sydney Harbor Bridge. We devoted ourselves whole-heartedly to the task.

> HE IS BEFORE ALL THINGS, AND IN HIM ALL THINGS HOLD TOGETHER.
>
> COL. 1:17, NIV.

As the train shot onto the bridge, we'd all look at one another, draw a huge breath, and then settle back, eyes popping. About three quarters of the way across, we'd begin to feel dizzy and faint. But we'd hang in there until we were about to turn blue and collapse in the aisle. Then, one by one, we'd have to give up and breathe again. Although none of us ever made it to the far end of the bridge, we did come close. Close enough so that we never stopped trying. Now probably a physically fit adult could have achieved the goal. But a bunch of crazy little kids? Not likely. In any case, an adult wouldn't see any point in attempting such a silly stunt, so we'll probably never know.

Nonetheless, we children learned how to fix our energies on a goal (however unworthy it might be) and gave it all we had. But our best was never enough. We just didn't have the lung capacity to sustain us all the way across the bridge.

Christ the Sustainer works with us in three ways. First, He's the One who gives us the ambition and drive to set a goal. Then He provides us the stamina to carry on. Our journey across the bridge of life can be discouraging. It seems that we will never reach the end. Still, we keep our eyes focused on the end.

No matter how hard we work, however, it's never enough. Under our own power we will never arrive. It's simply too far. Then our Sustainer steps in. "My child," He says, "let Me do it. I'll take you through to the end."

Unless we're able to allow the all-sufficient Jesus to take over and manage our journey, we'll never finish. One by one we will turn blue and collapse. We simply don't have the capacity to succeed alone.

[*Giver and sustainer of all life, I realize that my best efforts have failed. Please take me the rest of the way to eternity with You.*]

THE STRENGTHENER

When I was a child, we had a strange woman in our church. I realize now that she was mentally disturbed and should have been on medication and/or taken into some kind of custody. Back then, though, things looked different. Almost every Sabbath she'd start an uproar in church. I and every other bored youngster in the congregation looked forward to seeing the deacons march forward in a body and carry her out the door. Once she showed up at our house to lecture my mother on idol worship. She turned every picture to the wall. Smitten with curiosity, I somehow got in her way. When she grabbed my arm, I squealed with pain, realizing then why my mother was letting her have her way with our pictures. At 8 years of age I already stood taller than the woman. Thin as a spider and quick as a cricket, she had a grip that broke bones. Unbelievable!

> I HAVE STRENGTH FOR ANYTHING THROUGH HIM WHO GIVES ME POWER.
>
> PHIL. 4:13, NEB.

In His design of the human body, God planted within us a wonderful "strengthening" device. Our vital adrenal glands, situated one atop each kidney, secrete special hormones. In times of emotional stress and the excitement of danger, an adrenaline rush instantaneously equips us with sometimes superhuman physical strength. (Old Mrs. H_____ had a constant flow!) Instantaneously our entire body mobilizes for physical exertion—our blood pressure rises, energy-giving sugar pours into the system, and the body's message system declares, "All systems go!"

With this charge of power, one little woman dragged her husband, twice her size, away from an accident scene. Another lifted a tractor to free a victim caught beneath it. During fires others have lugged great pieces of furniture out of the house, heavy as themselves. One way or another we've all had some experience with such emergency physical strength.

When Paul wrote to his friends in Philippi, however, he pushed the metaphor far beyond the simple realm of natural physical strength. He declared that through the infinite power of Jesus Christ, he had "strength for anything." *Anything* must also include every kind of moral strength. He hit upon an electrifying idea. After commitment to God, we may expect a "rush" of spiritual adrenaline to see us through every temptation we face.

> *Dear Provider of every good thing for my welfare, I thank You for the promise that You will strengthen my mind for temptation just as You do my body for physical needs.*

THE UPLIFTER

Several years ago a student passed my way—a pretty little blond with smiling blue eyes. Almost every time we talked, Lynn's parting words were, "Be encouraged!" as she walked off, head high, to her next task. To this day she signs her notes at Christmastime in the same way. The words have remained her hallmark—and her body language also spoke volumes.

> BUT YOU, O LORD, ARE . . . MY GLORY AND THE ONE WHO LIFTS UP MY HEAD.
>
> PS. 3:3, NKJV.

The bowed head, the hunched shoulders, the downcast eyes, the aimless walk—we recognize them as symptoms of depression. Conversely, the uplifted head stands figuratively for all that prospers the human soul. In Scripture, "lifting up the head" has at least four interpretations.

First, Joseph interpreted the dream of the imprisoned chief butler: "Within three days Pharaoh will lift up your head and restore you to your place" (Gen. 40:13, NKJV). That is, one receives again former dignity and honor.

Second, Gideon so powerfully defeated the Midianites in battle that "they could no longer hold up their heads" (Judges 8:28, NEB). After long oppression, Israel once again recovered her former strength.

Third, in declaring his adoration of his God, whose company drives out fear, David wrote: "Now I can raise my head high above the enemy all about me; . . . and sing a psalm of praise to the Lord" (Ps. 27:6, NEB). With such confidence, he knew he would have complete and lasting victory over the many difficulties troubling his life.

Finally, in describing the signs of the end of time, Jesus said, "When these things begin to take place, stand up and lift up your heads, because your redemption is drawing near" (Luke 21:28, NIV). Here is a magnificent cause for fresh hope and great rejoicing!

David's announcement of the coming of the Lord climaxes in the promise "He shall lift up the head" (Ps. 110:7, NKJV). Jesus *does* "lift up our heads" in every possible way. He restores what sin has lost for us. In Him we have power to defeat our enemies and claim victory. Finally, He sets before us our eternal hope.

[*Dear Lord, I praise You for the many reasons You have given me to want to live, both now and later. When my head does droop, lift it once more.*]

THE CONSOLER

We have intense, personal seasons in our lives that we cannot endure alone, times when we need a comforter. As a 10-year-old I remember falling off my new bicycle and virtually tearing my left kneecap off. In the midst of the gushing blood and the incredible pain, I just lay in Mom's arms and cried until no more tears would come—it hurt so much. Much later, when my father died suddenly while on a trip to eastern Asia, I sat numb and cold in my bedroom that early Sunday morning after the telephone call came. Numb until one of my dearest friends arrived with a box of Kleenex under her arm. We just sat together and hung on to each other while we wept. She knew and loved him too.

> AS CHRIST'S CUP OF SUFFERING OVERFLOWS, AND WE SUFFER WITH HIM, SO ALSO THROUGH CHRIST OUR CONSOLATION OVERFLOWS.
>
> 2 COR. 1:5, NEB.

How often God the consoler reaches one human heart through *another* human heart. Often, too, He does not remove us from our trouble. Rather, as He did with the three Hebrews, He enters into the furnace of affliction *with* us. Besides, however many our misfortunes may be, Jesus has passed over the road ahead of us. "The Lord is close to those whose courage is broken, and he saves those whose spirit is crushed" (Ps. 34:18, NEB).

What broke your heart? Unkindness in a friend? Betrayal by someone you trusted? Thwarted ambition—you had to give up a dream? Physical problems? Whatever the cause, the heartstrings snap. You droop. Just then the great Comforter comes. In fact, our very brokenness *attracts* God.

> "God hath not promised skies always blue,
> Flower-strewn pathways all our lives through;
> God hath not promised sun without rain,
> Joy without sorrow, peace without pain.
> But God hath promised strength for the day,
> Rest for the labor, light for the way,
> Grace for the trials, help from above,
> Unfailing sympathy, undying love."
> —Annie Johnson Flint

His promise is as sure today as when He made it to Israel: "You shall lie down to sleep with no one to terrify you" (Lev. 26:6, NEB).

[*Great Comforter, dispel the fear. I count wholly upon Your faithfulness. Show me that my enemies are not as strong as they seem.*]

THE EXEMPLAR

You know how everyone expects an older child to be a good example to all the younger kids. I have just one sister. When I was 16 and she was 8, her persistence in following me around and wanting to do everything I did was a great nuisance. I had little patience with her tagging after me, pretending to be a "big kid."

A little later, however, it began to dawn on me that I, willing or not, had always been an example to her. She watched *me*, shy and bookish as I was. And if she was copying me, then probably some other youngsters were too. Suddenly I saw myself in a new light, a sobering, even frightening role—that of the exemplar.

Remember how it was when you were a child? As a boy you probably fell in love with your kindergarten teacher and idolized some cool high school basketball hero. You tried to develop brawn and muscle as fast as you could. Or as a girl you fixed your affection upon some young married woman—and you wanted to be *just* like her. At the same time you also adored the handsome young bachelor who taught seventh-grade English. That's how you looked through the open door into maturity.

Then almost overnight you somehow crossed that subtle boundary. Instead of being the kid, you now found yourself the object of some other youngster's worship—his or her ideal. You could do no wrong. Even amid the ordinariness of your workaday world you became "heroic." This new sense of responsibility is, doubtless, our most natural path into parenthood and future leadership tasks.

But we are so fallible. At any time of life, the knowledge that someone—anyone—is watching us, learning from us, and admiring us accentuates our inadequacies. Most of the time we despair of ever measuring up.

To be our exemplar was, however, the whole purpose of Christ's assumption of humanity. Certainly He was our example in suffering. But with the same openness, He invites us to examine every part of His life and to learn all His ways. He has modeled the whole of life for us. And He has done so with 100 percent reliability.

> CHRIST SUFFERED FOR YOU, LEAVING YOU AN EXAMPLE, THAT YOU SHOULD FOLLOW IN HIS STEPS.
>
> 1 PETER 2:21, NIV.

[*Lord Jesus, purify my life. I would stand freely before those who have chosen to take me as an example, and I would have them see only Your life in mine.*]

THE REFRESHER*

P icture the prisoner leaning against the cold wall, staring listlessly at the mold-stained stones and idly fingering his grizzled gray beard. His chains lie in a heap by the floor bolts, scarcely needed to restrain him. The man is under the death sentence. "It would be nice to be able to do something for the poor old fellow," the guard muses. But he can think of nothing that would help.

Suddenly the sentry hears a knocking at the gate that opens up to the sunny world above, to freedom and life. A cheerful, familiar face peers through the grate. "Good morning, sir! I've come to see Brother Paul." The hearty voice electrifies the whole dungeon. "May I come down?"

The prisoner sits forward eagerly at the sound of the voice, straining his tired old eyes to catch the first possible glimpse of his visitor. A striking pair they are—the old man awaiting execution and the younger one turning aside from his busy life to bring cheer into the house of death.

Later, when Onesiphorus is gone, the guard looks into Paul's cell again. Now even the little oil lamp seems to burn brighter. Elasticity in his step, the prisoner paces up and down, as far as the length of his short chains will allow. What did the young man say to Paul? We don't know. But the apostle gained new courage. Moreover, it was not just one visit. Paul wrote to Timothy that Onesiphorus "often refreshed me, and was not ashamed of my chain" (2 Tim. 1:16, NKJV). We know little else about this man who risked visiting a political prisoner in Rome.

In choosing the lovely vocation of Onesiphorus, refreshment, we are indeed doing Christ's own work. Because nagging thirst is even worse than gnawing hunger, Christ offered Himself as refreshment to the thirsty. The all-too-common picture of somber Christians doggedly going about their tasks of doing good, of relieving fatigue and depression, however, is incongruous. Refreshment is *a joyous* occupation—open to everyone. Like Onesiphorus, most of us are not highly distinguished in our fields of endeavor, but here we can all shine.

> "IF ANY ONE THIRST, LET HIM COME TO ME AND DRINK. . . . 'OUT OF HIS HEART SHALL FLOW RIVERS OF LIVING WATER.'"
>
> JOHN 7:37, RSV.

[*Jesus, I would drink daily of the refreshment You offer. Then help me make the work of being an "encourager" a habit of life.*]

*Based on Dorothy M. Comm, "On Refreshment," *Adventist Review*, June 26, 1975, p. 12.

THE GIFT

Ideally, a gift is something you do not ask for. It usually comes as a surprise, but if expected, at least the content will be a novelty. Someone who loves you or who wants to honor you in some way provides it. Probably you will not know its price.

Unfortunately, some use a gift as a way of putting another person under obligation. The giver expects something in return. Perhaps it is an outright bribe. Also, the giver may spend beyond his or her resources. (Christmas shopping, if done carelessly, can bankrupt a family in a single season.) Also, advertising fills our mailboxes with fakery, offering technicolor promises of "gifts" from faceless promoters. *Real gifts—gifts that mean something—just don't come to us that way.

Receiving a gift graciously takes as much talent as making and giving one—perhaps even more. I know one individual who is so driven to make sure that the books are always balanced that one can hardly do anything for her. She matches and reciprocates on every gift, so the whole matter of generosity and love virtually degenerates into an exercise in bookkeeping. It is rather like our annual decision about who should and who should not stay on the Christmas card list. Did we hear from them last year? Do they care? Should we take this opportunity to drop their names and relieve them of further responsibility for communication?

God's generosity takes somewhat different forms. The best gifts He has to offer are *free,* but because we know Him, we know the price He paid. We never need concern ourselves with who deserves what or what secret motivation may lie behind His presents. Second, His gifts must be *asked for*—and we are not accustomed to doing this. In fact, it embarrasses us. Prayer, however, is the link between our human hearts and the divine hand that waits to supply our needs. Finally, like the woman at the well of Samaria, we simply do not understand God's gift-giving. If we comprehended our need, and if we could estimate even a fraction of heaven's bounties, we would surely ask Him for more.

> "IF YOU KNEW THE GIFT OF GOD AND WHO IT IS THAT ASKS YOU FOR A DRINK, YOU WOULD HAVE ASKED HIM AND HE WOULD HAVE GIVEN YOU LIVING WATER."
>
> JOHN 4:10, NIV.

[*Sometimes in the complicated human arena of gift-giving I become confused.*
Let me always remember the utter simplicity of Your eternal gifts, Lord.]

THE FORGIVER

A grudge is one of the most painful possessions we can ever acquire. We may pick it up anywhere, at any time of life. Perhaps from a father/husband who never praised but always criticized. A mother/wife who was unfaithful and irresponsible. A teacher who played favorites. A committee that bypassed us when we were due a promotion. A boss who fired us in order to make room for a favorite. A church riddled with hypocrisy. The list has no end. Thus feeling powerless, we cling to that bitterness that hardens the inner core of our being. But the results are lethal.

"IF YOU FORGIVE OTHERS THE WRONGS THEY HAVE DONE, YOUR HEAVENLY FATHER WILL ALSO FORGIVE YOU."

MATT. 6:14, NEB.

The unforgiving spirit flares up in a rage that craves revenge. We confront our opponents in bitter denunciation. Or even worse, we brood over the injustice, plotting the vicious words we *wish* we had said. Our very blood boils for justice! But to accept what happened, to forgive, seems like giving in, of submitting and capitulation.

But that is not the case at all! In fact, usually the person(s) we refuse to forgive are oblivious to our attitude. They may not be aware of our anguish. Perhaps they don't even realize they hurt us. Therefore, they won't even know that we've forgiven them (unless we tell them). Hence, the act of forgiveness is for *us*. The words "I forgive you" pack an enormous amount of power. By them we unhandcuff ourselves from the people who hurt us.

Forgiving releases the wounded spirit, opening channels of peace up to God and out to our world. The Master of forgiveness designs that this gift should flow from Himself, through us, and on to those living in bondage to their anger. No wonder Jesus set forgiveness right in the middle of the model prayer He taught His disciples.

> *"Forgive us our debts, as we forgive our debtors" (Matt. 6:12, NKJV).*

THE FARMER

I n our high-tech, urbanized world we tend to forget that agriculture demands *hard work*—all day, every day, all year, every year. Generations of children have now grown up believing that milk comes in a carton, eggs in a box, and bread in a bag. Synthetic yarns have made it hard for any of us to remember that sheep ever gave us anything or that cotton came from the hard-labor-driven cotton plantations.

> **SEE HOW THE FARMER WAITS FOR THE PRECIOUS FRUIT OF THE EARTH.**
>
> JAMES 5:7, NKJV.

In the ancient world, however, life centered wholly on the land, and religious rituals marked each of the seasons. Virtually everything the people did related to rain and drought, planting and harvesting—followed by celebrations of thanksgiving for survival. Their absorption in the labors of the land became real to me when I married a son of western Canada pioneers. Only then did I understand the realities of life on the farm. I marveled at tractor tires taller than I was and surveyed the huge combines, almost complex enough to require a degree in engineering to cope with them. I admired the endless fields of grain—green and growing, golden when ripe, and lying in wide swaths with even lines and long curves. I watched trucks unloading grain at the elevators that mark every small western Canada town.

In between visits to the farm we received many family letters. Invariably they reported on the weather and the crops. Especially the weather. For me, weather has always been just something that happens. Hurricane or drought—you take what you get. But on the farm it matters intensely. Indeed, life revolves around the weather.

The Hebrews were first and foremost people of the land. Only after they went into exile did they develop the other skills for which they have since become famous. Not surprisingly, then, Jesus drew many pictures of Himself based on agricultural pursuits. No farmer has ever dealt with his responsibilities more diligently than Christ did in His cultivation of His people. Hard work? To be sure! "The Lord worked with [the disciples] and confirmed their words by the miracles that followed" (Mark 16:20, NEB).

[*God of the land, I thank You for Your persistent care.*
Today, let me grow, whether it be in sunshine or in rain.]

THE LORD OF THE HARVEST

M y most vivid memories of farm visits in the Canadian north relate to the harvest season. The short growing season pressures everyone to panic point. Neighbors help one another, and extra hands hire on. Women provide wonderful meals, younger ones drive tractors and trucks, and young men fill the granaries. Children run errands, watch babies, and wash dishes. Meanwhile, the machinery roars around the clock, with the men taking turns catching a few hours of sleep.

"THEREFORE PRAY THE LORD OF THE HARVEST TO SEND OUT LABORERS INTO HIS HARVEST."

MATT. 9:38, NKJV.

Imagine standing out in a field under a full moon—the harvest moon. It rises huge and icy yellow, whitening the fields and enlarging the dividing rows of trees with shadow. Cold winds bite through your jacket. Is it going to snow tonight already—when the work isn't even half done? The trucks and combines ceaselessly rumble back and forth like great insects with shiny eyes. The women bring more hot drink and sandwiches. Obviously, in this urgent time, someone must be in charge. Such a great undertaking calls for wise management.

Of the many farming roles Christ has taken to Himself, that of "Lord of the harvest" is one of the most powerful. The wealthy Boaz of Bethlehem exemplifies the role perfectly. Daily he walked among his workers and knew exactly who was on his property—both his own employees and the poor gleaners. He took special note of Ruth, a foreigner, who might easily have been exploited. Besides eating and drinking with them all, near the end of the harvest, he slept with them on the threshing floor. Then after Ruth's memorable request, he promptly went to work on the case the very next morning (Ruth 2, 3).

We can count on Jesus, as Lord of the harvest, to know every detail concerning each of His workers—in fact, of anyone who enters His field. All through the busy season of harvest He will be personally and constantly with them. Moreover, having vast resources, He can arrange anything He wishes in their behalf—and that He will do in a prompt businesslike way.

The workers in His fields have only to trust and obey.

[*I go to do Your work today, Lord. I can do so in confidence because I can trust Your divine management.*]

THE SEED

The parable of the mustard seed is a tiny analogy with a huge meaning. "The kingdom of heaven is like a grain of mustard seed . . . ; it is the smallest of all seeds, but when it has grown it is the greatest of shrubs and becomes a tree, so that the birds of the air come and make nests in its branches" (Matt. 13:31, 32, RSV).

Almost every elementary classroom has some kind of windowsill garden to induct children into the mysteries of a sprouting seed and, thence, the wonders of life itself. Notice three things about seeds. First, a seed—any seed—is small and plain. Nothing about it looks exciting except its latent promise. If you believe with "faith as a grain of mustard seed, . . . nothing will be impossible to you," Jesus said (Matt. 17:20, RSV). Second, as the center of life and according to its kind, a seed (or egg, the animal counterpart) is capable of producing a carrot, an apple, a tree, a snail, a dolphin, a giraffe, a skylark—or a child. Finally, because of such properties a seed always represents potential and hope.

God first promised the Saviour of the world to Adam and Eve as just a seed (Gen. 3:15). So great was their faith and anticipation that Eve even thought her first child could possibly be the promised Seed. "I have given birth to a man! Maybe he is the One who will break the power of sin and death" (Gen. 4:1, Clear Word). Later when Abraham fretted about his lack of an heir, Jehovah intervened with a miraculous seed-management measure in his behalf, resulting in both material and spiritual prosperity (Gal. 3:16).

Within the humble figure of the seed lies the whole of the conflict between good (the Seed, Christ) and evil (the seed of Satan). And the mustard seed, the smallest of them all, contains the whole promise of Christ's kingdom. It not only grows to be a mighty tree, but it offers "shade" for the weary and safe nesting for the "birds." Even the slenderest thread of faith can move us toward this great hope.

"I WILL PUT ENMITY BETWEEN YOU AND THE WOMAN, AND BETWEEN YOUR SEED AND HER SEED."

GEN. 3:15, NKJV.

[*Whatever challenges face me this day, let me have enough faith, my God, to see hope and promise in even the most discouraging circumstances.*]

THE SOWER

On my first visit to Petersfield, England, the Hampshire town from which my ancestors emigrated to Australia, I went immediately to the village church. (Those in quest of family roots all know that the parish church is the place where one must begin.) Long a market town, Petersfield boasts a handsome church surrounded by neatly clipped lawns. Too neat. I found that, for the convenience of power mowers, all of the tombstones had been taken up. Some of them had been used for retaining walls and some for pavement. Still others leaned disconsolately against the church, as if awaiting further assignment. "But why?" I asked the sexton. "How can I find anyone?"

"HE WHO SOWS THE GOOD SEED IS THE SON OF MAN."

MATT. 13:37, NKJV.

"Ah well, they've been a fair while, you know. And who's to look after all of those graves? No other way to keep it tidy."

Disappointed, I gazed over the churchyard, tidy to be sure, but the ancestors were now truly beyond identification. All for the sake of a lawn mower!

Modern technology and mass production have robbed us of more than this. No valiant hand-to-hand combat—we press a button and drop a bomb. Few family gatherings at a death bed—everything's taken care of with remote sterility in a hospital. Little handicraft—we can get almost anything we need off an assembly line. Few personal, thoughtfully worded letters anymore—we would rather make a phone call, buy a commercial greeting card, or computerize a letter for the fax machine. In the same vein, modern farm machinery has made the lone figure of the sower almost obsolete.

The individual whom Jesus chose to image Himself through, however, took no shortcuts. He walked over every inch of the field himself, carrying the seed. (And anything as potent as a seed deserves the most studious care.) He planted as close as possible to the edge of his field so that any receptive soil, no matter where, could be seeded. Even when the seed fell on hopelessly infertile soil, the sower still has given the opportunity for growth.

The divine Sower knows, however, that He also has good soil. It will produce abundantly, "a hundred, sixty or thirty times what was sown" (Matt. 13:8, Clear Word).

[*I'm glad, Lord, that You have taken such care with Your spiritual plantings. I want my life to be a fertile garden plot.*]

THE VIGNERON

My grandfather was, as the French would have it, a *vigneron*. He kept a fine vineyard in Caversham, just north of the Swan River in Western Australia. The temperate climate, the easy balance between sunshine and rain, and the thin soil bordering the river made it an ideal place for growing grapes.

Hard times, however, prevailed in Australia at the turn of the century. Therefore, Grandfather and the older sons managed the vineyard and garden, while Grandmother, the girls, and the younger children kept a grocery in Cottesloe, a suburb of present-day Perth. Each weekend Grandfather hauled a wagonload of produce into town for sale. The family specialty seems to have been raisins, and the shop built up a reputation not only for excellent produce but also for congenial company.

Today his grapevines still thrive, now under the auspices of a winery. Their wine cellar and tasting room rest on the foundation of Grandfather's house. His raisin-drying stands and at least one of his grape arbors remain.

The pleasures of wine, sweet or otherwise, have been universal. And people have long appreciated raisins as a portable, tasty source of strength, a high-energy food (S. of Sol. 2:5). For these reasons, men and women have not shied away from the unremitting toil required to keep a successful vineyard. Probably no other crop requires more constant attention. The ongoing process of pruning and the monitoring of growth and dormant periods call for an expert, a professional *vigneron*.

Jesus compared Himself to both the vine and to wine. His "parable of the kingdom," however, points to the work of maintenance. Heaven invests enormous energy in the keeping of the church, the earthly vineyard. The Vigneron knows exactly which branches need to be cut away, being irretrievably dead, and which believers need pruning in order to be even more productive in reproducing His own character.

"I AM THE TRUE VINE, AND MY FATHER IS THE VINE-DRESSER. EVERY BRANCH IN ME THAT DOES NOT BEAR FRUIT HE TAKES AWAY; AND EVERY BRANCH THAT BEARS FRUIT HE PRUNES, THAT IT MAY BEAR MORE FRUIT."

JOHN 15:1, 2, NKJV.

[*I stand ready, my divine Vinedresser, for whatever corrections You find necessary in me.*]

THE FIRSTFRUITS

Scripture has a good deal to say about "first-fruits"—all of which were held sacred to the Lord. They included the firstborn of men and cattle (Ex. 22:29) as well as the first production of the fields, orchards, and vineyards, including oil, wine, and wool (Deut. 18:4). When we examine the offerings of Cain and Abel, we note an interesting contrast. Not only did Cain disobey as to the type of offering, but he didn't even bring the first of his fruit! "Cain brought *some* of the fruits of the soil. . . . But Abel brought fat portions from some of the *firstborn* of his flock" (Gen. 4:3, 4, NIV). Eventually, in the Hebrew context, this original consecration of people and the products of the land came to include money (tithe) and even clothing. The firstfruits principle of offerings to Jehovah carried with it a strong promise of prosperity (Prov. 3:9, 10).

CHRIST WAS RAISED TO LIFE—THE FIRSTFRUITS OF THE HARVEST OF THE DEAD.

1 COR. 15:20, 21, NEB.

Soon the literal applications took on symbolic meaning. Jeremiah declared Israel to be "the firstfruits of [the Lord's] harvest" (Jer. 2:3, NIV). For James, Christians stand in this special position: "He chose to give us birth through the word of truth, that we might be a kind of firstfruits of all he created" (James 1:18, NIV).

Paul, however, is the one who touches upon the most thrilling application of the symbol: "But Christ has indeed been raised from the dead, the firstfruits of those who have fallen asleep. . . . For as in Adam all die, so in Christ all will be made alive" (1 Cor. 15:20-22, NIV). Then, he adds, "We . . . who have the firstfruits of the [Holy] Spirit" can taste of wonderful things to come (Rom. 8:23, NIV). Jesus went *first!* Since He "experimented" with the resurrection, we can now follow.

[*I reserve the firstfruits of every part of my life for You, Jesus. Let me never give second-best either to You or to others.*]

THE LANDSCAPE ARTIST

Of the many enchantments inviting the traveler to the Old World, gardens rate near the top of the list. In Europe the windows of the great houses—and the small—look out upon manicured lawns and geometrically designed flower beds. Summer brings hanging baskets and sidewalk containers, all ablaze with blossoms. The spacious houses of the Tyrol wear bright window boxes on their dark faces. For centuries the Arabs have cultivated elegant gardens, walled in for privacy from the aridity of the desert beyond. Having no more than two square yards of space between his front door and the street, a Japanese will still transform it into a miniature natural garden. When all else fails, most of us nourish at least a flowerpot or two in the house. Indeed, our impulse to tame the wilderness, to make it beautiful, and to bring it close to ourselves is deep-seated and occupies uncounted hours of loving labor around the world.

THEY WILL BE CALLED OAKS OF RIGHTEOUSNESS, A PLANTING OF THE LORD FOR THE DISPLAY OF HIS SPLENDOR.

ISA. 61:3, NIV.

Perfect as His newly created world was, God established within it a garden for Adam and Eve. A garden for nurturing, for tranquillity and spiritual renewal, for the love of beauty. No wonder we shall always be homesick for Eden until we return to it.

As we consider this powerful image of the church, we must assume four basic premises. First, a garden materially is exactly like the wilderness outside. The same laws of planting and growing apply in both places. Second, landscape artists will select and position the plants according to *their* plan. Third, they must do a great deal of cutting and pruning, an operation requiring a great deal of time. Finally, the horticulturist will establish a maintenance program to keep the garden alive.

[*I invite You, the heavenly Gardener, to help me tend my life-garden today. Show me the design You have in mind for me.*]

THE OWNER OF A GARDEN

Spring Park is in the district of Upper Swan, 30 minutes northeast of Perth, Western Australia. An old farm, it dates back to the beginnings of the pioneer settlement of Swan River Colony. Nearby is the first church to be built in the colony in 1839. Its church-yard contains the graves of many of my ancestors.

MY BELOVED HAS GONE DOWN TO HIS GARDEN.

S. OF SOL. 6:2, NEB.

My great-grandfather planted many fruit trees, some grafted specimens still living after more than 150 years. I have relatives who carry on his tradition in their flourishing gardens. I try, because I do love a gar-den. Since I am neither a gifted gardener nor an orchardist, however, I can only believe what nurserymen tell me and envy my friends who seem to command healthy plants to spring out of the ground. It's a matter of priori-ties. I just forget.

When we plant such trees we are only echoing God's own love for a garden. He is continually trying to cultivate us. "The Lord will guide you al-ways. . . . You will be like a well-watered garden" (Isa. 58:11, NIV). He began with the Garden of Eden (Gen. 2:15). and will end with the recon-struction of a new earth (Rev. 21) During His life on earth Jesus prayed in the Garden of Gethsemane.

Naturally, the Lord knows all about tree-grafting. Paul employs the grafting of olive trees as a symbol of Christian relationships. Like God Himself, He has commissioned us also to plant, tend, and water—to turn wastelands into gardens.

> "The kiss of the sun for pardon,
> The song of the birds for mirth.
> One is nearer God's heart in a garden
> Than any place else on earth."

[*Dear God, don't let my spiritual garden become a reflection of my failure with physical gardens. Please help me to remember to care for it.*]

THE MOWER

Having grown up in the tropics and being ac- customed to jungle growth, I was a teenager before I saw the work of a true landscape artist in the gardens at Niagara Falls, Canada. Squares of exquisite lawn lay amid rainbow-hued flower beds. I had never seen anything like that short, dense grass. Later I learned that one can obtain such fine emerald lawns only through repeated mowings.

> **AS FOR MAN, HIS DAYS ARE LIKE GRASS; HE FLOUR- ISHES LIKE A FLOWER OF THE FIELD.**
>
> PS. 103:15, RSV.

In vision Amos described "the latter growth after the king's mowings" (Amos 7:1, RSV). The first growth would have gone as taxes to the king, while the Hebrew farmer waited for the regrowth that oc- curred after the mowing.

God will mow the grass of our inner lives many times over. Although today grass mowing implies power mowers and loud noise, the picture here is of the human mower silently wielding his scythe in the sunny fields. Perhaps by listening carefully we may even hear the sound of Jesus' whet- stone on the blade. He has different instruments to tend His lawns—the scythes of pain and disappointment or sometimes even the sickle of death.

And mowing does mean death. The scythe may bring us adversity that robs us of health, friends, and money. But the mower must tend to the weeds in our lawn. Some of them may be dandelions and daisies or tall, flowering grasses, of which we may be rather proud. But if they remain, they coarsen all the grass, and we will never have fine, pure growth. So the mower cuts them down, and those frail weedy flowers of our complacency and selfishness die in the cut swathes. Then the landscape artist will gather and throw them away, leaving behind healthy grass that now thrives.

God's grace is "like rain that falls on the mown grass" (Ps. 72:6, RSV). The mowing comes first, and then the rain. And how we savor that deli- cious scent of damp, freshly mown grass that forecasts the beginning of new growth. With new and stronger roots of love and prayer, we grow into greater beauty and better service. Even through repeated mowings, the Christian should enjoy perfect peace following the use of the King's scythe.

[*Lord, don't spare me any of the mowings that You see are necessary for shaping my character.*]

THE GOOD SHEPHERD

All of my life I've seen lovely pictures of sheep grazing. We all have. We can't even remember the first time we studied that familiar picture of Jesus with the lamb in His arms. And most of us can recite verbatim that infinitely comforting shepherd's psalm (Ps. 23). Deeply we love the idea of the rich pastures, the still waters, the loving and attentive care of the Shepherd. The concept has become unspeakably beautiful to us.

THE LORD IS MY SHEPHERD, I SHALL NOT BE IN WANT. HE MAKES ME LIE DOWN IN GREEN PASTURES.

PS. 23:1, 2, NIV.

Our longtime fascination with sheep and shepherds is, indeed, deeply ingrained in us. We forever busy people, who live in vast housing developments, drive fast cars, and spend our working years imprisoned in high-tech offices and factories, crave country life. Centuries before Christ, the Greeks—disquieted by the stressful ways of urban life—invented "pastoral poetry." With its celebration of love and leisure, beauty and music, and the pleasures of shepherding, pastoralism fed the yearnings of city-bound people throughout the ancient world. Indeed, the charms of country living have followed us, in one form or another, all the way into the twenty-first century. Thus we too can feel the drawing power of the ancient practices of shepherding.

Centuries of sacred art have thus kept this picture constantly before us. When the artistic and wealthy new converts from the Graeco-Roman world accepted Christianity, they brought marble statuary and their elaborate tomb art with them. What had first been a picture of a shepherd boy carrying a lamb on his shoulder or perhaps a representation of Apollo, the god of pastoralism tending his flocks, suddenly changed. In those classically perfect marble figures the new Christians now saw the Good Shepherd, the Son of God. It was a wonderfully rich and familiar symbol! To be sure, no other picture of Jesus was more beloved in the early church as the Christians faced impoverishment and persecution.

Our awareness of the loving care of the divine Shepherd should bring us the same comfort and security that it did those early believers.

> "Gentle Shepherd, come and lead us,
> For we need You to help us find our way.
> Gentle Shepherd, come and feed us,
> For we need Your strength from day to day."

THE GOOD SHEPHERD: A PERSONAL FRIEND

On an early spring day I walked through the paddocks at my cousin Allan's new sheep ranch in Western Australia. The Arthur River cutting through his lands was at full flood, and ghostly gray-and-green eucalyptus trees mirrored themselves in the pools that the overflow had formed in the meadows. Scattered as far as anyone could see, the merinos grazed under the trees and by the water. They appeared to have been painted into the landscape by a master artist, and the scene seemed storybook perfect.

HE LEADS ME BESIDE QUIET WATERS, HE RESTORES MY SOUL.

PS. 23:3, NIV.

But not quite. Here and there, under bushes and in the grassy hollows, lay dozens of dead sheep. Their dense wool matted and muddy, they lay in heaps, their sightless eyes staring at the broad sunny bend in the river where they would never drink again.

Allan sensed my surprise and concern. "I'm sorry. I just didn't have time to pick them up before you came." He answered my unspoken question. "The move down here from the ranch up north was hard on them. I've lost almost a hundred."

But why, I wanted to know. "Whatever happened?"

"Sheep simply give up and die. They don't even try." He looked at the flock with a practiced, clinical eye. "Believe me, they just aren't too bright."

Fittingly enough, Scripture compares us Christians to flocks in the care of the divine Shepherd. In assuming this relationship we admit to a potentially fatal weakness in ourselves. While we would like to think of ourselves as intelligent and self-sufficient, we're so easily deceived. Like Allan's sheep, we can, virtually without warning, irrationally plunge ourselves into despair and discouragement. How quickly we find ourselves led into temptation! Gullible in the face of deception, we're just *not* too bright.

At times when we simply cannot know the answers, we must have our Shepherd-Friend to guide us. To help us make the right choices. To calm our fears. To point us not just toward survival, but on to inexpressible peace and contentment, no matter what our surrounding circumstances. What folly then—no, what a *tragedy*—to lie down in the meadow and die simply because we have wandered and not kept our Shepherd in view.

[*Good Shepherd, preserve me from my all-too-human tendencies to depression, fear, and despair.*]

THE GOOD SHEPHERD: A PROVIDER

On another sheep ranch in Western Australia, with yet another cousin in her old jeep, I jounced over the rutted roads that skirted the pastures. On our way back to the house we spotted a fat old ewe lying up against the fence. "Ah-hah!" Alice exclaimed as she brought the jeep to an abrupt stop. "I'll lose that one if I don't look smart."

THE LORD IS MY SHEPHERD, I SHALL NOT WANT.

PS. 23:1.

Out of the car and across the road in a flash, she unlatched the gate. We both tromped in, ankle-deep in the mud. Together we dragged the lethargic animal up onto her feet. Then we steadied her until she ambled off toward the rest of the flock and started grazing again. "If she'd stayed there in the mud," Alice remarked as we climbed back into the jeep, "she'd never have stood up again."

Though lovely and picturesque and forever attractive to us, the ideals of pastoralism completely overlook the fact that shepherding is, in reality, a cruelly difficult work, and that sheep are smelly, dirty, and abysmally stupid. No other domestic animal, apart from pampered household pets, receives such individualized, perpetual care. More than other farmers, shepherds have a high risk of loss. They often live like doctors on 24-hour-a-day call, with no days off. This fact must tell us something, then, about the nature of sheep. In other words, about the nature of us, the perverse, fatalistic people whom Jesus committed Himself to saving. It is an appalling thought to realize how vulnerable we are.

Jesus declared, "I am the good shepherd; I know my own sheep and my sheep know me" (John 10:14, NEB). It is His commitment to us, His assurance that He understands and will supply our every need. He lays this claim on us because He would not have us victimized by the unfaithful hireling, attacked by the thief, or deceived by the stranger (verses 1-3). He goes, as He plainly states, "before [the sheep] and [they] follow him, for they know his voice" (verse 4, NKJV).

Thus it is only our willing response to the nurturing of the Shepherd, wherever He finds us, that puts us on our feet again.

> *Shepherd of souls, sometimes my ignorance shocks even me. Please don't let me be stupid again today.*

THE GOOD SHEPHERD: A DEFENDER

Several years ago a young English family, recently emigrated to New Zealand, were visiting the famous thermal region of Rotorua. As they walked among the boiling mud pots and steaming hot pools, their little dog fell into one of the pits. Almost automatically, the father leaped forward to rescue the pet. In so doing, he lost his own life.

"I AM THE GOOD SHEPHERD. THE GOOD SHEPHERD LAYS DOWN HIS LIFE FOR THE SHEEP."

JOHN 10:11, RSV.

Jesus offers His life for His sheep. Sheep being what they are, of course—helpless and slow-brained—it stands to reason that they exist on the very edge of destruction. They need a constant defender, and without one, few could survive to adulthood. Since sheep were the foundation of Israel's economy, they were worth some risk.

David, of course, is the prototype of all shepherd boys. He was "called to his kingdom" from Bethlehem, where he tended his father's sheep (1 Sam. 16:11). Later, when requesting King Saul to allow him to fight Goliath, David appeared a handsome but unlikely opponent to face the Philistine giant. His qualifications that persuaded the king, however, were his bare-handed encounters with both lions and bears as he guarded the sheep. Indeed, he had rescued lambs alive out of the mouths of such predators (1 Sam. 17:34-36). In doing so, he had obviously put his own life on the line.

Jesus reemphasized the shepherd's commitment. "If one of you has a hundred sheep and loses one of them, does he not leave the ninety-nine in the open pasture and go after the missing one until he has found it?" (Luke 15:4, NEB).

> "Even though I walk through the valley of the shadow of death,
>> I fear no evil;
> for thou art with me;
>> thy rod and thy staff,
>> they comfort me" (Ps. 23:4, RSV).

The rod of discipline and the staff of protection go together.

From our perspective the idea of dying for the sake of an animal may be incomprehensible. But love is part of the equation too. Saving a puppy from the volcanic geysers? The King of heaven dying for a sheep? Like us? Yes, love overrides all.

[*Lord, I stand amazed at the risk You took for me.*
It's Your grace alone—and I am very grateful.]

THE GOOD SHEPHERD: A DOOR

In the first five verses of John 10 we learn something of Eastern ways of shepherding. A large fold accommodates a great number of sheep belonging to various shepherds. Each one could not afford to build his own fold separately and employ a doorkeeper. The shepherds themselves could take turns guarding the fold at night. In the morning they separated the various flocks as each sheep recognized and followed the voice of his or her own shepherd.

Jesus' listeners, however, did not understand His first allegory of the sheep, so He *"again* said to them, 'Truly, truly, I say to you, I am the door of the sheep'" (verse 7, RSV). He could not have been more clear about His special kind of shepherd duty. A poet of another generation paints a word picture of the task:

"I Am the Door" *

"A traveler once, when skies were rose and gold
With Syrian sunset, paused beside the fold
Where an Arabian shepherd housed his flock;
Only a circling wall of rough, gray rock—
No door, no gate, but just an opening wide
Enough for snowy, huddling sheep to come inside.
'So,' questioned he, 'then no wild beasts you dread?'
'Ah yes, the wolf is near,' the shepherd said.
'But'—strange and sweet the words Divine of yore
Fell on his startled ear, *I am the door!*
When skies are sown with stars, and I may trace
The velvet shadows in this narrow space,
I lay me down. No silly sheep may go
Without the fold but I, the shepherd, know.
Nor need my cherished flock, close-sheltered, warm,
Fear ravening wolf, save o'er my prostrate form.'
O word of Christ—illumined evermore
For us His timid sheep—'I am the door!'"

"I AM THE DOOR OF THE SHEEPFOLD. . . . ANYONE WHO COMES INTO THE FOLD THROUGH ME SHALL BE SAFE. HE SHALL GO IN AND OUT AND SHALL FIND PASTURAGE."
JOHN 10:7-9, NEB.

[*Jesus, I am safe with You, the Door. Guard all the entrances and exits of my life.*]

---

*Cynthia Pearl Maus, *Christ and the Fine Arts* (New York: Harper and Brothers, 1959), pp. 221, 222.

THE CHIEF SHEPHERD

The final coming of the "Head Shepherd" is, to be sure, the culmination of all the pastoral pictures in Scripture. We know a great deal about the excellence and reliability of Jesus the Chief Shepherd Himself, but what do we really know of *ourselves?*

When He announced Himself as the Good Shepherd, Jesus spoke to people who lived close to the land, people who understood the full implications of shepherding. Sheep are dumb and lazy. If not guided constantly, they will follow one another to destruction. They get lost and have to be found.

Sheep, as we might expect, have an extremely limited understanding of the world around them. In a dozen lines of verse written for Christmas recently, my friend Hugh McKellar, of Toronto, Canada, fancifully described the First Advent from the viewpoint of one of those dim-witted Bethlehem sheep:

> "What business had they to disturb my sleep
> And violate the dreams of decent sheep?
> A foreign flock assailed our field tonight,
> Most strangely woolly, though past question white.
> Lambs lost or hungry I can understand,
> But not the bleating of that noisy band!
> At last they left; and then, first thing I knew,
> Away had scampered all our shepherds too,
> Whom duty bids close by our side to stay;
> Now wolves are free to spring and lambs to stray.
> Mankind perhaps this night in mind may keep;
> But how am I supposed to get my sleep?"

Have sleep and comfort dulled our vision? Are the meadows where we graze too lush? Have our lives evolved into a mindless routine that we pursue day after day without question? Are we too preoccupied with following the rest of the flock? Worse still, have we wandered out of earshot of the Shepherd's voice?

We might fail, then, to hear that final call of the Chief Shepherd—His last invitation before He leads us into His heavenly pastures.

Father, how I long to go home to Your heavenly pastures. We've all been in the wilderness a long time.

WHEN THE HEAD SHEPHERD APPEARS, YOU WILL RECEIVE FOR YOUR OWN THE UNFADING GARLAND OF GLORY.

1 PETER 5:4, NEB.

THE RED HEIFER

Jean-Francois Millet painted rural scenes that celebrated the innocence and nobility of French peasant
life. His "Birth of a Calf" shows two men carrying a
straw litter on which the newborn calf lies. As they
reverently approach the stone gateway, the mother
cow follows, licking her baby. Upon seeing this picture, Van Gogh caught the significance of Millet's
farmyard processional. "It was so powerful as to make
me tremble," the Dutch artist exclaimed. With the calf
destined for slaughter, just as the Man Jesus had been
born for sacrifice, Millet endowed this ordinary scene
with deep spiritual overtones. He visualized the "doc-
trine of Christ," not just portrayed His image.

TELL THE ISRAELITES TO BRING YOU A RED COW WITHOUT BLEMISH OR DEFECT, WHICH HAS NEVER BORNE THE YOKE.

NUM. 19:2, NEB.

As we have already noted, priests often slaughtered sheep and oxen, traditional sacrificial animals in
the ancient world, by *hecatombs* (groups of 100 per-
fectly matched animals). The red heifer, however, was different. First, the
complex Mosaic laws called for elaborate (and often costly) programs of
sacrifice. The offering of the young cow had its own unique regulations.
Indeed, its death did not even appear to *be* a sacrifice at first. Second, instructions concerning this special rite apparently came during the early days
of the wilderness wandering, a time of despair for a doomed generation of
Israel. Third, the offering was designed to be simple and cheap. Just one red
cow (a common color for cattle). Yet, she was to be "without spot." Jewish
regulations later insisted that if she had even two white or black hairs in
any one place on her body, it would disqualify her. Fourth, because the
bearing of a yoke was universally regarded as confining and degrading, she
was never to have been harnessed for work. Finally, unlike most sacrificial
animals who were male, this young offering was to be female.

This exceptional symbol of the red heifer foreshadowed the one
Sacrifice that would ultimately rescue deathbound humanity. Just one offering was required, and He would be common enough to be accessible to
anyone who desired Him. At the same time He would be spotlessly perfect. He would also have that gentle tenderness usually associated with the
feminine personality. And He would embody freedom forever. Neither rejection nor suffering nor the grave itself could hold Him.

[*I stand in awe, Lord, of Your magnificent offering—single, perfect, and complete.*]

THE HOUSEWIFE

One day in India I saw a family passing through a village. Obviously it was a total house move from one location to another. At the head of the procession marched the father, a staff in his hand, and the eldest son carrying nothing. Next came a large flock of goats followed by a couple donkeys laden with household goods. At the end followed the mother—as thin as a stick under the huge bundle of kindling she balanced on her head. On her back were two large bundles. With one arm she held a baby and with the other a collection of pots and pans. Four or five small children clustered around her legs, at least two of them clutching at the skirt of her sari.

No further commentary is necessary regarding the status of women in that place. Until relatively recent times, however, one could observe the same scene anywhere in the world, with little variation. Given the Jewish community into which Jesus came, it should not surprise us to see Him identify Himself with women. In the next 16 pictures we find Him imaged in objects taken strictly from the world of women's concerns. Yes, one *can* find God in the most unexpected places!

Jesus Himself told the parable of the lost coin, in which He is the anxious housewife searching for part of her dowry set. The clay floors of the house were periodically strewn with rushes as a "carpet." Spring-cleaning time simply meant throwing fresh rushes down on top of the old ones, year after year. Naturally, the silver coins—and much else besides—could fall into the straw. To "sweep out the house" required much work.

Christ's life and death would seal the marriage contract between us and God. Each believer is one of the silver coins He is determined to take with Him. He spares no effort in searching for us. Sadly, it is possible for us to hide in the old rushes and refuse to be found. Then we shall have to be swept out with the rubbish.

> "IF A WOMAN HAS TEN SILVER PIECES AND LOSES ONE OF THEM, DOES SHE NOT LIGHT THE LAMP, SWEEP OUT THE HOUSE, AND LOOK IN EVERY CORNER TILL SHE HAS FOUND IT?"
>
> LUKE 15:8, NEB.

[*Dear Lord of household affairs, never stop searching for me, and make my tarnished silver shine.*]

THE GOOD NEIGHBOR

We have now had at least two generations grow up who know nothing about good neighboring. How could they? We have burglar alarms on our houses and cars and bars on the windows and chains on the doors. Most of our friends live on the other side of town or on the other side of the country. If we want to see them, we get into the car and go, or we chat on the telephone. Senseless violence and crime have made us cautious to the point of paralysis. We will make that 911 call for help only if we're sure we won't get hurt. As for the people next door or down the street, we probably don't even know their names unless they appear on the mailboxes. As for needing to borrow a cup of sugar and gossip for a while, who does that? Hardly anyone is baking at home anymore. Either we don't know when anyone is coming home for a meal or we're going out to eat anyway.

"AND WHEN SHE HAS FOUND [THE LOST COIN], SHE CALLS HER FRIENDS AND NEIGHBORS TOGETHER, SAYING, 'REJOICE WITH ME.'"

LUKE 15:9, NKJV.

Even in the slower-paced, less-fractured setting of Bible times, the question about loving one's neighbor came up. Jesus made it clear that it was a primary obligation for those seeking eternal life (Luke 10:25-28). Then, in answer to the next vital question, "Who is my neighbor?" He told one of His best parables (Luke 10:30-37). Our neighbor, we discover, is anyone who needs care and kindness.

The parable of the housewife, however, is a little jewel, for it carries the idea of neighboring one step further. She didn't ask her neighbors to help her clean the house—though she might have done so. Instead, she calls them in to rejoice with her over finding her silver coin. It's a party!

In case the crowd missed the point (as they often did), Jesus made the application Himself: "There is joy among the angels of God over one sinner who repents" (Luke 15:10, NEB). Then, as if to drive the point home even harder, Jesus went on directly to the story of the prodigal son—which ends with *another* party with the neighbors. Joy unshared soon fades.

[*Dear God, lonely people wait behind almost every door out there. Help me find one today—not just that I may fill a need, but that I may share a joy also.*]

FULLERS' SOAP

Soap as we know it did not exist in ancient times. Instead, a cleanser made of olive oil and the ashes of certain plants worked as an alkaline bleach and was called "fullers' soap." The fuller's art is an ancient one. Their business was to clean, shrink, and thicken newly shorn wool. Before the raw fibers could be used for making clothing, they had to be "fulled." After the soaping, the fuller washed the fabric through many changes of clean water, sometimes employing small boys to tread it into the stony bottom of a running stream. Or they might hammer it out with mallets at a fountain. Then the fuller laid the material in the sun to dry and bleach. Because the process of fulling (or "making white") caused bad odors, the fuller's shop was usually located outside of the city. Isaiah refers twice to the Fuller's Field and its pool by the western highway out of Jerusalem (Isa. 7:3; 36:2).

"BUT WHO CAN ENDURE THE DAY OF HIS COMING? . . . FOR HE IS . . . LIKE FULLERS' SOAP."

MAL. 3:2, 3, RSV.

Mark tells us that when Jesus was transfigured on the mountaintop, the disciples marvelled for "his garments became glistening, intensely white."— white "as no fuller on earth could bleach them" (Mark 9:3, RSV). A short while later, when his Master tried to wash Peter's feet at the time of the Last Supper, the poor man recognized for the first time that he really could *not* keep himself clean. "Lord," he cried, "not my feet only but also [wash] my hands and my head" (John 13:9, RSV).

When Malachi writes that the Lord of Hosts is "like fullers' soap," he indicates that Jesus is the solution to the sin problem. Only He can cleanse us from the stains of evil that none of our human detergents can reach. He will be extremely thorough in washing out sin—sometimes gently, sometimes pounding it away.

But He promises us: "Though your sins are like scarlet, they shall be as white as snow; though they are red like crimson, they shall become like wool" (Isa. 1:18, RSV). He washes the impurities out of our lives and whitens them. And then, like the fuller, He makes our experience full with His rich blessings.

[*God, whatever it takes to make me clean, do it.*]

FRAGRANCE

When we rank our five senses, we tend to put vision and hearing at the top of the list. Touch, taste, and smell take subordinate places. If we had to give up one of our faculties, most of us assume that we would not miss smelling. Indeed, if we are to believe anything the advertising copywriters tell us, we might suppose that a completely deodorized and sanitized world would be ideal! We could *not* be more wrong.

CHRIST . . . GAVE HIMSELF UP FOR US AS A FRAGRANT OFFERING AND SACRIFICE TO GOD.

EPH. 5:2, NIV.

While our modern cosmetic industry offers everything from cheap chemical perfumes to extremely expensive natural fragrances, the Middle East still has the edge on us. We know nothing to match the dazzling bridal procession of Solomon who came "up from the desert . . . perfumed with myrrh and incense" to receive his Shulamite bride (S. of Sol. 3:6, NIV). The making of perfume was never a casual occupation in Israel. Moses commissioned a gifted craftsman, Bezalel, to prepare sweet oils and fragrances ("pure [and] compounded by the perfumer's art") to fill the wilderness sanctuary (Ex. 37:29, NEB).

From the most ancient times people have used perfumes and cosmetics to attract admiration and to give pleasure. "Oil and perfume bring joy to the heart," the wise man said (Prov. 27:9, NEB). Evil-smelling substances, on the other hand, repel and embarrass. Our sensitivity to odors is a necessary but fragile gift. Any smell, either good or bad, fades away in a matter of seconds as our noses register the first powerful impression and then dismiss it into memory. Fragrance messages are delicate, profound, and transient.

The gorgeous, sensual, and holy scene imaged in the bridal procession of Solomon is, however, often perverted. The prophets frequently denounced harlots and their seductive uses of cosmetics (Isa. 57:9; Prov. 7:17, NEB). Furthermore, sin registers with God as a bad odor. Besides being unable to tolerate filth, slovenliness, and unfaithfulness, He rejects the incense of the hypocrite, with its scent of pride, selfishness, and disobedience. Christ accepts only the "sweet savor" of a repentant sinner's prayers.

Our heavenly Bridegroom shows us the sweet loveliness of the life He would have us live. His sacrifice is refreshing and beautiful to us as He makes Himself our "fragrant offering."

[*As I go about my work today, Lord, let me be totally enveloped in the fragrance of Your grace.*]

THE LAMP

One of my prize possessions from India is an antique bronze lamp that hangs suspended by a chain by my front door. Placing oil in its central bowl and wicks in its seven peripheral "lips," I light it so that I am saying, in the Indian tradition, "Welcome to life, joy, and peace in this house." I love the way the six little tongues of flame shine so courageously on a moonless night. No wonder seeing the Lord as a lamp to light our lives is such a rich symbol—for we find it impossible to function in any kind of darkness. Our original lighting system was, of course, all natural—sun and moon. Then came the darkness—both physical and moral. Lamps for the house and torches for night journeys helped.

> "YOU ARE MY LAMP, O LORD; THE LORD TURNS MY DARKNESS INTO LIGHT."
>
> 2 SAM. 22:29, NIV.

Ancient pottery lamps dating back to 3300 B.C. began as open bowls containing oil and a wick. For sanctuary use the priests combined seven lamps into the menorah that became a symbol of the divine light of God's presence.

We need lamps for three reasons. First, darkness frightens us. But it comforts us when we can see familiar faces and surroundings. Second, we need a lamp to guide us in places where we have never been before. Third, given the limitations of our human condition, we can never seem to complete our day's work by daylight. More often than not, our tasks carry on into the night—perhaps far into the night. And we need the steady light of a lamp to enable us to continue our work.

Using a lamp, however, is not like opening the door to the morning sunlight. It requires effort. The domestic lamp could hold enough oil to last through the night. The wick, however, had to be adjusted every few hours as it burned down. Hence, the virtuous housewife "never puts out her lamp at night." She needs the flame to light her fire in the morning, so she rises to trim her lamp several times during the night (Prov. 31:18, NEB).

Jesus is a lamp for our dark way. He will never leave us in darkness, but we cannot take Him for granted.

[*Lord, You have provided a lamp for my journey through darkness. I desire to be diligent in caring for this light so that I shall not lose it. Preserve me from the tragedy of the extinguished lamp.*]

THE OIL OF GLADNESS

If you know the right place to shop in Jerusalem, you can buy a "tear bottle," a tiny glass vessel to collect tears. Thus you could prove to your neighbors how great your grieving has been. David alluded to the custom when he wrote: "You number my wanderings; put my tears into Your bottle" (Ps. 56:8, NKJV; the Hebrew word translated "bottle" is that for a wineskin). In cultures in which loud mourning is a competitive profession, such evidence would be useful.

HE [GOD] HAS SENT ME . . . TO GIVE THEM . . . [THE] OIL OF GLADNESS INSTEAD OF MOURNER'S TEARS.

ISA. 61:1-3, NEB.

Scripture sets the "oil of gladness" in opposition to the mourner's tears. The origin of the uses of oil are lost in antiquity. In the ancient Near East, however, olive oil was a necessity of life—for food, illumination, commerce, and religious purposes. It also protected the skin from the desert heat. In describing Canaan as a "land of olives [and] oil," Moses could not have offered a better recommendation for it (Deut. 8:8, NEB). (Even today olive oil has emerged as among the more healthful fats and oils!)

The benefits of oil were so great that it was withheld only in times of mourning and fasting. It came to signify affluence and a high standard of living. The tribe of Asher is a case in point. His father, Jacob, predicted that he would "have rich food as daily fare, and provide dishes fit for a king" (Gen. 49:20, NEB). Centuries later Asher's taste for living well persisted. Moses said, "Asher is most blest of sons, may he be the favourite among his brothers and bathe his feet in oil" (Deut. 33:24, NEB). In other words, he would have wealth and plenty to spare. Not just oil for anointing, but for bathing!

The roll call of Deborah and Barak, however, points up one temptation for people like Asher. When the summons came to fight the Canaanites, he "lingered by the sea-shore" rather than joining the fighting (Judges 5:17, NEB). Asher's lucrative commerce with the Philistines and other sea peoples had blunted the edge of his zeal for fighting the Lord's battles.

God does not deny us the "oil of gladness." He is the one who provides us with life's pleasures and comforts. Indeed, His church has always had affluent believers to bear the burdens for the poor members who have nothing.

[*Dear Father, I thank You for the "oil of gladness" that You dispense daily. Give me just as much of it as I can safely handle without losing sight of You.*]

THE OIL OF HEALING

As we've seen, olives and olive oil have been among the most valued products of the Near East. Oil healed in two ways—physical and spiritual. Ancient peoples connected both magic and medicine to religion. The natural and supernatural touched in the symbol of oil.

The prophet described the erring kingdom of Judah in clinical terms: "From the sole of your foot to the top of your head there is no soundness—only wounds and welts and open sores, not cleansed or bandaged or soothed with oil" (Isa. 1:6, NIV).

Not surprisingly, we find oil in the good Samaritan's travel kit. When he found the victim of the bandits on the Jericho Road, he had the necessaries for first aid—oil and wine. Undoubtedly, the priest and the Levite carried the same provisions on their journeys, but they chose not to waste them on an unknown Jew beside the road. Moreover, should he already be dead, touching a corpse would defile them and interrupt their service at the Temple.

In the desert heat the Samaritan's application of oil relieved the bruises and abrasions, restoring the tone of the torn, parched skin. The alcohol in the wine cleansed the deeper wounds.

The despicable Herod died of a devouring disease. Josephus spares no grotesque detail, from the "intolerable itching" to the "dropsical tumors" in his feet—and much else besides. His physicians ordered the old king to immerse himself in a large vessel of warm oil—a measure that seems only to have hastened his wretched end.*

The founders of the early Christian church, however, remembered that Jesus' disciples had gone about preaching first repentance and then anointing the sick with oil and healing them (Mark 6:13). "Is anyone among you sick? Let him call for the elders of the church, and let them pray over him, anointing him with oil in the name of the Lord" (James 5:14, NKJV). Such anointing with "holy oil" has had deep spiritual meaning ever since. It augments our most intense prayers of faith.

> "HE [A SAMARITAN] WENT UP AND BANDAGED HIS WOUNDS, BATHING THEM WITH OIL AND WINE."
>
> LUKE 10:33, 34, NEB.

[*Great Healer of body and spirit, I would pray the "prayer of faith" for healing, remembering always that the result rests in Your hands. Should physical healing be denied, I gratefully accept the far more necessary heart-healing.*]

*Wars of the Jews, I, 33.5, in Josephus: Complete Works, trans. by William Whiston (Grand Rapids: Kregel Publications, 1974), p. 469.

THE OIL OF REPROOF

My high school mates in Canada will remember Miss Louise Dedeker, our French teacher. Because she was a proper, incredibly forceful little woman, not one of us dared approach her except under extreme necessity. Legend had it that she had become "that way" after her fiancé died in World War I. Be that as it may, I discovered her as a warm, gracious friend only when I was on the same faculty with her during my first year of teaching, five years later.

LET HIM REPROVE ME; IT SHALL BE EXCELLENT OIL; LET MY HEAD NOT REFUSE IT.

PS. 141:5, NKJV.

But back in that grade 11 classroom we sat terrorized. We could write our quizzes only on one certain kind of yellow scratch pad (available in the school bookstore). Any other size or color she sifted out and dropped into the wastebasket, something she demonstrated before the class so that everyone understood. She insisted absolutely on a period firmly set down at the end of every sentence. Nothing hasty or haphazard for her. "People will be kept out of heaven," she declared, "for just one small sin." And with that, the whole sentence, whatever other virtues it might have had, was marked wrong.

Albeit under considerable stress, we all did learn French that year—we couldn't help it. Although I took another two years of French in college, I actually learned nothing new. I had invested so much in my high school French that it has lasted me for life.

It must be some similar experience that led the psalmist to speak of reproof and discipline as "excellent oil." What saved Miss Dedeker from being merely a ruthless dictator was the fact that she made her regulations perfectly clear. From that point on she was absolutely fair and just. Even the most giddy, noncommitted student in the class had to admit that much.

Such is God's discipline. His requirements are quite explicit—and then He applies them consistently. Having the tendency to be irregular and erratic, however, we often find the reproof extremely painful. Then where does the "excellent oil" come in? The protection and the healing? That is when we discover that in the end it was all for our own good and that we've gained eternal benefits. Dear old Miss Dedeker! Bless her heart!

[*My heavenly Schoolmaster, I would learn from You today. Let me endure whatever reproofs You have for me, until I can see that they are "excellent oil."*]

THE LIVING WINE

Wine making goes back to earliest recorded times. Shortly after the Flood Noah planted a vineyard, made wine, and got drunk (Gen. 9:20, 21). The beloved Greek wine god, Dionysus, appears in one ancient painting alone in a boat, surrounded by sporting dolphins. The mast has turned into a grapevine, providing him with a perpetual supply of wine. Because the body so easily absorbs grape juice, wine became associated from earliest times with blood, sacrifice, and healing. Wine also signified youth and eternal life. Ancient poets extolled the "divine intoxication" that could, fleetingly and blissfully, seem to transport humans into the realm of the gods.

> "THIS IS MY BLOOD OF THE COVENANT, WHICH IS POURED OUT FOR MANY FOR THE FORGIVENESS OF SINS."
>
> MATT. 26:28, NIV.

We usually associate Jesus with the wine of Communion. And this, to be sure, is an important connection. But when, in this context, He announced Himself as the "living wine" He also uncovered another important facet of the picture. When His disciples became too sour and solemn, He inquired, "Can the wedding guests fast while the bridegroom is with them?" (Mark 2:19, RSV).

All of which brings us to Cana. At the wedding there Mary left her catering of the feast to approach her Son. "They have no wine," she whispered (John 2:3, RSV). No wine? Impossible! Who would plan a wedding reception and not have enough wine on hand? Wine meant celebration, relaxation, friendship, hospitality, good cheer, and much more. Sweet in the mouth and warm in the heart.

Jesus' miraculous transformation of water into wine defines a bright association for us. The people who have no spiritual wine are surely to be pitied. Like the interrupted wedding feast at Cana, their lives collapse. All the zest and sparkle is gone. Their work becomes drudgery, and living itself turns dull and gray. In their anxiety not to be accused of drunkenness, they have lost most of that divine exhilaration that is also a proper part of the Christian life.

Awash with all of their problems and responsibilities, even the Christians attending the wedding feast with the festive Christ sometimes forget. Freedom and joy have gone out of their lives. "We have no wine!" they cry.

Not so! Jesus is here. He says, "I am the living wine, My friends. Drink!"

[*I would not be dull and insensitive. Even when I'm busy with other things, I would praise You every hour of the day.*]

THE SIFTER

"I . . . WILL
SIFT THE
HOUSE OF
ISRAEL
AMONG ALL
NATIONS,
AS GRAIN
IS SIFTED
IN A SIEVE."

AMOS 9:9, NKJV.

As a teenager I had little more than a lethargic interest in kitchen chores. I never worked up a passion for cooking and baking. One recipe instruction pertained to sifting flour. I would look at the flour carefully. "It looks OK. Why do I have to sift it? Too much bother." So I would dump it into the mix as it was. Presently flour came labeled "presifted." *Good!* I thought. *No more worries.*

Later service in remote tropical mission stations, however, taught me the virtues of sifting. I sifted not only flour, but everything else smaller than marbles.

Then I served on an archaeological team at Caesarea Maritima, Israel. Again I had to take sifting seriously—this time in reverse. Our dig square that summer went down through a Muslim cemetery, followed by some ancient Christian burials. Finally, at the bottom we reached the Roman city of Pilate, complete with mosaic floors, fountains, and drains. People then, as now, tended to lose their rings in the drains. So virtually every *gufa* of dirt that we took out had to be sifted to save jewelry and bits of Roman glass.

Sifting serves a double purpose. First, it eliminates what we don't want. We save the siftings and throw out the contents of the sieve. Second, it enables us to isolate precious things from the residue—and we save what remains in the sieve.

Both functions have spiritual application, but Amos refers to a third use—the scattering of the Jews, the chosen people. In one sense it was punishment, of course. But in another, however, it carried the word about God throughout the world.

This third use of sifting applies also to Christians. Rather than confine ourselves to tight little communities where all the people tend to resemble us, we should venture out, as we sometimes say, into the "world." Out there waits a world that desperately needs Christianity sifted through its dark texture. It's something like the old-fashioned way of decorating a chocolate cake by sifting confectioners sugar through a doily, beautifying it with a white, lacy pattern on its surface.

[*Father, sift me all three ways. Remove what is harmful. Preserve what You can use. Then scatter my influence so I can be of service to You this day.*]

THE YEAST

Some time between 3000 and 2000 B.C. the Egyptians discovered yeast and invented ovens. They turned breadmaking into an art, creating round, cubical, braided, and animal-shaped loaves in more than 50 varieties. Upon leaving Egypt, the Hebrews carried such bread secrets with them and enshrined unleavened bread in their wilderness sanctuary. By the time of Christ all the cities of Palestine had commercial bakeries.

> "THE KINGDOM OF HEAVEN IS LIKE YEAST."
>
> MATT. 13:33, NEB.

My first serious encounter with yeast was much less artful than Egyptian breadmaking. A bride of just four weeks, I was living in a remote town in Newfoundland, Canada. As minimal as my knowledge of cooking was at that time, I should never have attempted making anything as exotic as Vegex. The lively salt flavor of this yeast spread is an acquired taste, but those of us who grew up on Marmite or Vegex on toast love its dark pungency.

Since my mother's recipe for homemade Vegex had served our family well through the years, I thought nothing of stirring up a batch. The hostile old oil stove in our bleak little apartment glowed an angry red as I set the saucepan on it. Without warning the yeast brew welled up and over —and it kept coming and coming and coming! Frantically I tried to catch the heaving tide of would-have-been Vegex, seizing upon every kettle and dishpan I owned. I even resorted to the wash tub. The steady power and relentless "lava flow" of Vegex was appalling. Whoever would have thought that simple yeast could virtually bury my entire kitchen!

Paul inquired of the Corinthians, "Don't you know that a little yeast works through the whole batch of dough?" (1 Cor. 5:6, NIV). Had the apostle seen me cleaning up my kitchen, he might have put the case to them even more strongly. I was not dealing with a little leavening in bread dough, I was contending with *quantities* of pure yeast!

In its many uses yeast exemplifies the characteristics of Christ's kingdom. Medicinally it provides vitamins and processes antibiotics and hormones. Nutritionally it augments both human and animal food. And finally there is that inexorable *power* it has to leaven bread.

Yet yeast *can* become inactive. Through delay and neglect, the powerful principles of the kingdom can also vanish from our minds and no longer activate our lives.

[*God of kitchen craft, work through my life. Let there be no end to Your influence and power in my little world today.*]

THE LIVING BREAD

Just the previous day Christ had multiplied the loaves and fishes to feed 5,000 people. Now the crowd had caught up with Him again in the Capernaum synagogue. Having had one free meal, they hoped that He might somehow become a long-term provider. But they had completely missed the spiritual significance of the previous day's miracle. Remembering the manna that God had supplied for 40 years in the wilderness, they asked themselves whether Jesus might do something like that for them now.

Before we criticize their blind materialism, however, we should remember that they were chronically poor people, always wondering where their next meal would come from. And so they pressed about Him: "Sir, give us this bread now and always."

Christ's magnificent reply is one of the classic pronouncements of all Scripture: "I am the bread of life. Whoever comes to me shall never be hungry."

We all know about bread. It synthesizes all the aspects of food—both physical and spiritual. And when Jesus takes the symbol to Himself, something from everyday life suddenly gets elevated to divine dimensions. This miracle happens when we accept Jesus Himself as the holy bread that feeds our souls.

Therefore, He gave us the Communion service to remind us of His special relationship with His people. He knew that bread and wine and eating together would speak of our deepest needs, and that they would satisfy hungers that we didn't even realize we had. Also, He recognized that strong bonds of loyalty and friendship develop at dining tables. With these things in mind, He instituted that Christian service that looks forward to the glorious heavenly supper He is preparing for us.

And so in those marvelous beginning days of eternity we shall sit down together at His table and share the immortal fruits of heaven. Then for the first time we shall really begin to understand how wonderful it was to have fed upon the bread of life. Like the hungry multitudes on the shores of Galilee, we too shall cry: "Lord, give us this bread now and always!"

> **"JESUS SAID TO THEM, 'I AM THE BREAD OF LIFE. WHOEVER COMES TO ME SHALL NEVER BE HUNGRY.'"**
>
> JOHN 6:35, NEB.

[*Christ, how I long for that first day in eternity to begin, the day when You will satisfy all our hungers.*]

THE ESSENTIAL BREAD

The concept of food creates for us a powerful cluster of feelings. As human beings we're never more relaxed, more civilized, or more open to benevolent impulses than when we sit down together to eat. We exchange dinner invitations with friends and acquaintances. Birthday and anniversary celebrations call for food. The bridal couple's first act after the wedding ceremony is to entertain their guests at a reception. The funeral feast gathers the mourners together after the burial. In a word, the significance of food goes far beyond its physical function of sustaining life. That Judas could sit with the other disciples at the Last Supper, be Christ's guest at the table, and then go out to collect the silver shekels for his Lord's betrayal—this ironic blend of symbols emphasizes the enormity of his sin.

> "MAN CANNOT LIVE ON BREAD ALONE; HE LIVES ON EVERY WORD THAT GOD UTTERS."
>
> MATT. 4:4, NEB.

Above all other foods, bread is a symbol so universal, so basic to human experience, and so powerful that people of any age, in any place, and at any time can grasp its meaning. The breads of the world, indeed, declare cultural uniqueness as clearly as do the national flags. Mexican tortillas, Indian chapatis, English muffins, Scottish scones, Irish soda bread, Persian lavash, Middle Eastern pitas, Jewish challah, Chinese rice cakes, Russian black rye, American cornbread, French croissants, German pumpernickel, Italian grissini, and Australian damper.

In taking bread as a representation of His life and ministry, Jesus reached straight into the heart of our human experience. Nowadays people consume a lot of junk food—a feeble substitute for plain, wholesome bread. "Why spend money on what is not bread?" the prophet reasoned. "Listen to me, and eat what is good, and your soul will delight in the richest of fare" (Isa. 55:2, 3, NIV).

The current rush on bread-making machines has once again filled Western homes with the fragrance of good, fresh bread—just when we feared that the pace of modern life had robbed us of that homespun joy. "Bread" is a generic term, and the goodness of homemade bread has both material and spiritual meanings.

> *"Break Thou the bread of life, dear Lord to me,*
> *As Thou didst break the loaves beside the sea."*
> —Mary A. Lathbury

THE BREAD OF GOD

I n all its marvelous variety, bread is a vital part of life. Both in reality and in symbol it speaks to some of our deepest needs. A golden-crusted loaf coming from the oven breathes a fragrance that stirs our most ancient hungers. Signifying all things necessary to life, it promises sustenance and security.

The Lord's Prayer depicts both our physical and spiritual survival by bread: "Give us this day our daily bread" (Matt. 6:11). Bread amplifies the daily and the ordinary to the level of a profound truth. Jesus took great care that we should not miss the lesson.

In John 6 He gave His disciples a painstaking discourse on bread, concerned that they grasp the vital meaning of the symbol. "If any one eats of this bread," He concluded, "he will live forever. This bread is my flesh, which I will give for the life of the world" (John 6:51, NIV). It is, perhaps, not pressing the analogy too far to say that Christ, as the living bread, was "baked" in the fires of affliction, leavened in the tomb, and rose at last to the mystical banquet table of heaven.

In his poem "The Everlasting Mercy," John Masefield beautifully celebrates the elevation of bread from the material to the mystical. The character Saul Kane has found Christ in the night, and he now anticipates feeding on the Bread come down from heaven. In the early clear morning, he leans on the farm gate and watches the plowman at work in the field:

> "O Christ who holds the open gate,
> O Christ who drives the furrow straight, . . .
> Lo, all my heart's field red and torn.
> And Thou will bring the young green corn, . . .
> And when the field is fresh and fair
> Thy blessed feet shall glitter there.
> And we will walk the weeded field
> And tell the golden harvest's yield.
> The corn that makes the holy bread,
> By which the soul of man is fed,
> The holy bread, the food unpriced,
> Thy everlasting mercy, Christ."

> "THE BREAD THAT GOD GIVES COMES DOWN FROM HEAVEN AND BRINGS LIFE TO THE WORLD."
> JOHN 6:33, NEB.

Now, my Lord, I understand! What we call "conversion" is simply finding the holy food that satisfies our soul hunger.

SPICE

Europeans were never the same after they discovered that spices not only preserved food but that they also added delightful flavors heretofore unknown in the West. Soldiers of fortune took dangerous voyages, fought battles, and died in quest of spices. Indeed, America was accidentally "discovered" by European adventurers hunting for a passage to the Spice Islands.

"Piquancy" is an old word we don't use much anymore. It indicates a flavor or odor that has a surprising (but not disagreeable) sting—a stimulating taste or a sharp smell. Onions are a case in point. Many have praised them for their piquancy. Long used for relish, food, and medicine, they've enjoyed little honor. Has anyone ever written a poem in praise of onions? Or sung a song?

> WHAT IS THAT COMING UP FROM THE WILDERNESS . . . PERFUMED . . . WITH ALL THE FRAGRANT POWDERS OF THE MERCHANT?
>
> S. OF SOL. 3:6, RSV.

Yet how could anything so strong, so piquant, be overlooked! When the murmuring Israelites in the wilderness found their heaven-sent manna tedious and demanded meat, they recalled something else too: "We remember," they wailed before Moses, "the leeks, the onions, and the garlic" (Num. 11:5, RSV).

Onions, of course, must be used judiciously. Mixing onions and honey would not be a success, we know. Moreover, we don't *live* on onions, chiles, or nutmeg—even though the desire for spices and pungent flavors and odors is universal among humanity. Addiction to sharp flavors will eventually ruin our taste for delicate foods—like manna.

Piquant foods never adapt well to dilution. By the same token, Christianity is a bold and distinctive belief. Because we insist on its being pure and unadulterated, its effects on our lives are often startling. The "spice of life" is not an idle phrase. With good reason, interpreters of the Song of Solomon connect Christ here with a wide and rich range of sensory experiences: sweetness of frankincense and myrrh, the preserving powers of nard, the refreshment of exotic fruits. Our faith in Christ has also been associated with salt and the tasty shock of mustard. With such lively relief for bland diets, how can spirituality ever be boring?

[*Thank You, God, for paying attention to my small human needs. You care that my friendship with You should give pleasure, taste good, and be interesting.*]

HONEY

Given my childhood in the tropics, I can't re-member ever having tasted honey until we went to live in New Zealand in 1944. We lived in a plain little square house surrounded on three sides by lush green sheep paddocks (pastures). Actually, everything about our lives was pretty plain. Since we had only one tiny coal fireplace, I recall being very cold all winter. And as wartime privation still prevailed, our food was also extremely plain.

SWEETER ALSO [ARE THEY] THAN HONEY AND DRIPPINGS OF THE HONEY-COMB.

PS. 19:10, RSV.

But with one exception. Somewhere, somehow, my parents had acquired a square five-gallon tin of hard white honey. Having no refrigerator, we kept it in the cold storage room—though any room in the house might have served the purpose equally well. One of our nursery rhyme songs featured the queen "sitting in the counting house eating bread and honey," and my sister and I knew how clever the queen was. So like her we demanded bread and honey three times a day. Almost every day I would go in just to look at the big container of honey. And I offered what I thought was a prayer of gratitude for such a great blessing in our poor little house.

In Old Testament times the Hebrews had only two ways of sweetening food. The word "honey" may refer to wild bee honey and honeycombs or to syrups derived from dates, apricots, or grapes. By the time of Hezekiah, however, we find evidence of domestic hives. The "firstfruits" offerings to the Levites included honey along with wine, grain, and oil (2 Chron. 31:5).

Artists eventually employed three Christian symbols: honey (Christ), the bee (the Christian), and the hive (the community). Moreover, the "honeyed words" of the gospel bespoke eloquence in spiritual things. Reputed never to sleep, the industrious bee became a model for the zealous believer. The bee-hive stood for the pious, unified, and well-ordered religious community.

Anyone can appreciate Christ and His teachings as honey—especially when you consider how rare the flavor has been. In fact, I can recall that New Zealand winter so vividly that even today, eating white, whipped clover honey is for me almost a sacrament.

[*Lord Jesus, I would always, even on my darkest days, find Your Person and Your teachings as sweet as rare honey.*]

THE CUP

The useful and commonplace cup has come to signify our eternal destiny. The most primitive cups were small shallow bowls before they acquired a handle or two. Drinking vessels might be made of pottery, bronze, silver, or gold. Royal wine cups often had extravagant decoration. In the figurative language of the Bible, however, the contents were of more concern than the vessel itself. The spiritual drink is either sweet or bitter.

WHEN WE BLESS "THE CUP OF BLESSING," IS IT NOT A MEANS OF SHARING IN THE BLOOD OF CHRIST?

1 COR. 10:16, NEB.

The psalmists introduce us to the two cups from which we have to choose. The first stands for earthly prosperity and material blessings. Beyond that lie the rewards of heaven. "Thou anointest my head with oil, my cup overflows" (Ps. 23:5, RSV). In this picture, the believer receives an abundant portion of blessings, as a guest would the wine cup of hospitality from his host.

Conversely, when the wicked offend God, they receive a cup of punishment. And since all have sinned, to drink of the latter cup is the obligation of every one of us: "The Lord holds a cup in his hand, and the wine foams in it, hot with spice; he offers it to every man for drink, and all the wicked on earth must drain it to the dregs" (Ps. 75:8, NEB).

We have but one alternative. Our only escape from drinking the bitter draft is to accept Jesus. In so doing, we acknowledge that He drank the terrible potion of wrath for us. He once questioned His disciples: "Can you drink the cup that I am to drink?"

Having no idea what they were talking about, they replied confidently, "We can" (Matt. 20:22, NEB).

Later in Gethsemane, of course, He had to drink alone. "My Father, if it is not possible for this cup to pass me by without my drinking it, thy will be done" (Matt. 26:42, NEB).

The Communion "cup of blessing" referred to by Paul stands in mute testimony against the alternative cup of wrath apportioned to all sinners. No wonder the cup and the sacrament of Communion have remained so essential a rite of Christian faith. We dare not lose sight of the "two cups." We must drink of *one* of them—we have no other choice.

[*Dear Father, I claim my Saviour's part in drinking the terrible cup for me. Now I ask for the sweet cup of blessings that He has promised.*]

THE ROBE

Graduation day on college campuses represents a major event. It contains grand music, the processional, elegant speeches, the conferring of degrees, and a high-minded charge to the students going out into the real world. In particular, all of the participants have put on academic robes. We've inherited them from a time when learning and religion existed much more closely together than they do today. Both professors and students wore the robes daily, and taking a degree permitted the addition of the university colors. Improvements have continued, and the higher the degree the more colorful the satin-lined hood becomes (no longer just a device for covering the head). Then we have bands of velvet, cords, and insignia. On ceremonial campus occasions the otherwise rather dull-looking faculty now blossom forth like a veritable flower garden.

FOR HE HAS CLOTHED ME WITH GARMENTS OF SALVATION AND ARRAYED ME IN A ROBE OF RIGHTEOUSNESS.

ISA. 61:10, NIV.

The numerous biblical references to robes indicate that they were then, as now, worn for special meanings and effects. Donned by royalty, priests, and high-ranking officials, the long, loose outer garment was rich in texture, color, ornamentation, and style. Jacob elevated Joseph's position in the family by giving him "a long, sleeved robe" (Gen. 37:3, NEB). David's act of cutting off part of Saul's royal robe in the cave at EnGedi was as close as he could come to defiance without actually killing the king. Moses prescribed in detail the priestly robes for Aaron and his sons (Ex. 28:4, 31). Surrounded daily by the Jewish scholars who trailed Him about, Jesus—clad in a simple tunic—remarked: "Beware of the scribes, who desire to go around in long robes, love greetings in the marketplaces, the best seats in the synagogues, and the best places at feasts" (Mark 12:38, 39, NKJV). The only rich garment Jesus ever wore was the royal purple one put on him in mockery at His crucifixion (John 19:2).

Robes for the spirit are, however, quite another matter. Not only do they display social rank, they also cover up whatever is underneath. We sinners have a great deal to hide. Indeed, without the robe of Christ's righteousness—and no other—we can never be presented to heavenly society. Whatever their appearance, such robes will all be alike and will serve the same purpose—to make us pure.

> *Dear Jesus, I would lay aside any other robes I have acquired for the privilege of wearing the one You offer me.*

THE LAWGIVER

Most children spend more than half their childhood looking forward to the day when they shall be free of parental supervision. The task of "lawgiving" at any level is a heavy responsibility, neither easy nor pleasant. For whatever reason, I set my sights on the day I would become 18. Then I would have total liberty. I would go in and out as I pleased. I would (I imagined) have my own car. No one would discuss bedtime, meals, clothes, entertainment, or any other activity with me. Not that I was planning any kind of massive rebellion. I just didn't want anyone telling me what to do. The prospect of liberty was so delicious I could almost taste it.

THERE IS ONE LAWGIVER, WHO IS ABLE TO SAVE AND TO DESTROY. WHO ARE YOU TO JUDGE ANOTHER?

JAMES 4:12, NKJV.

Well, as most of us found out, about the time we turned 18 we began to have a glimmer of the truth about freedom. You have it only when you abide by certain basic laws, otherwise it simply doesn't work. Then as we moved on into professions, marriage, and family, we found that if we wanted to survive, we ourselves had to become "lawgivers." (As for the car, I couldn't afford it. I got it only by marrying a man who already had one!)

In praising the leadership of the tribe of Gad, Moses said: "He carried out the Lord's righteous will, and his judgments concerning Israel" (Deut. 33:21, NIV). He was a "lawgiver," transmitting God's will to the people. John, in turn, gave the title to Moses: "The Law was given through Moses" (John 1:17, NEB). Such authority, of course, is safe only in the hands of a just leader.

By the time of Christ, however, Old Testament law, the Torah, had acquired such a complicated maze of added do's and don'ts that no one, without considerable assistance, could hope to get everything right. Therefore, Jesus Himself, as lawgiver, inquired of the scholars, "Did not Moses give you the law, and yet none of you keeps the law?" (John 7:19, NKJV). Then He wrote the legal "bottom line": "Love the Lord your God with all your heart. . . . Love your neighbour as yourself" (Mark 12:29-31, NEB). Love, carried to its full extent, would cover *all* regulations.

[*My True Lawgiver, let me not chafe and complain at Your leading. And in my own little area of lawgiving may I model my instructions on You.*]

THE INTERPRETER OF THE LAW

T im was a general nuisance in the public high school at which I worked one year. Like most of the other teachers, I preferred to see him going rather than coming. That is, until the day when we read the story of the prodigal son out of the grade 10 English reader. For Tim and many others, it was simply another story. To see how well they understood the meaning, I made a writing assignment: "Rewrite the story keeping the same characters and theme, but put it in a twentieth-century setting."

Most enjoyed the challenging homework. Only Tim hung around at the end of class after the others were gone. "I just don't understand the story."

"What part is difficult for you?"

"About the father." Tim thrust his hands into his jacket pockets and stared at me with troubled blue eyes. "Why, if I did something like that, my father would kill me! He would. I could *never* go home."

> "DO NOT THINK THAT I CAME TO DESTROY THE LAW, OR THE PROPHETS: I AM NOT COME TO DESTROY, BUT TO FULFILL."
>
> MATT. 5:17.

Knowing that the boy had little in his disordered home life to help him, I tried to explain that it was a picture of *God*. That He *is* that kind of father. Poor Tim. The interpretation of the word "father" that he had from his parent made the whole story of the prodigal incomprehensible.

An interpreter is supposed to render a correct concept of an original. He may be dealing with language. Or an idea. Or perhaps he describes an event or setting of 3,000 years ago in contemporary terms. We can safely undertake the delicate work of interpreting the mind of God only with the guidance of the Holy Spirit.

Ezra was the founder of the scribes, who for 400 years handled the interpretation of the law. Because of so much unwarranted "interpretation," the original simple rules often became complex. The scribes were, obviously, the ones who gave Jesus the most opposition. Although Christ made many references to the Old Testament, when it came to an interpretation of the law, He simply said, "I am here. Listen to Me. Look at My life. This is how the law works." No scribe or Pharisee could have said as much!

> [*Jesus, help me today to interpret the mind of God for those around me. May they read You clearly in the smallest detail of my life.*]

THE SURETY

S ir Walter Scott (1771-1832) was a Scottish lawyer who found time to write. He made his mark as a poet, biographer, editor, critic, translator, and historical novelist. Today you can visit his lovely home, Abbotsford. As you look at his collection of weapons from the battle of Waterloo, the gardens, the fine dining room, his gracious library, you may think, *This man had it all.* But that's only part of the story.

STAND SURETY FOR THE WELFARE OF THY SERVANT; LET NOT THE PROUD OPPRESS ME.

PS. 119:122, NEB.

At age 55 he became entangled in the failure of two publishing houses for which he had stood "surety." Rather than take the easy recourse of bankruptcy, Scott struggled heroically for the rest of his life to repay the debt of more than £120,000. After he died in 1832, the sale of the copyrights on his last writings settled all of the debts —but it took 15 years. Could you ask advice from this upright man, he would probably tell you, "Never stand surety for anyone, not even your best friend."

In biblical law, the "surety" is the person who, when the debt is due, "intervenes" in order to help the insolvent debtor. He must assume responsibility for the payment of the debt either by taking it over or by substituting himself for the debtor. The act of intervening was symbolized by "striking hands" (or shaking hands). Cosigning, going surety for anyone, is a high-risk venture. The wise men had a good deal to say on the subject. They regarded both friends and strangers as equally hazardous: "My son, if you become surety for your friend, if you have shaken hands in pledge for a stranger, you are snared by the words of your own mouth" (Prov. 6:1, 2, NKJV). Such a person is "devoid of understanding" (Prov. 17:18, NKJV). Indeed, "one who hates being surety is secure" (Prov. 11:15, NKJV).

In his meditation on the law (Ps. 119), the poet makes an outrageous request. He asks God to "stand surety" for him (verse 122, NEB). In considering this wonderful possibility, the author of Hebrews exclaimed, "How far superior must the covenant also be of which Jesus is the guarantor!" (Heb. 7:22, NEB).

Jesus *took* that risk. Even when all the wise men said it couldn't work, He still pledged Himself to pay our debt.

[*God, what a chance You took on us. You became eternal guarantor for us when not even our friends would stand a small surety for us.*]

THE SENTENCING JUDGE

Several years ago the O. J. Simpson case was tried right in our living rooms. We all learned more than we ever wanted to know about courtroom affairs and marveled at high-tech forensic evidence. Some of us thought that if the evidence concerned the case it would be heard. Not so. Others thought that a witness under oath would not tell lies. Wrong again. Then the jury, which we couldn't see, proved restless, and we certainly heard about them. And in the middle of it all was Judge Ito. No one, indeed, would have wanted to change places with him.

YOU, SIR, WHY DO YOU PASS JUDGEMENT ON YOUR BROTHER? . . . WHY DO YOU HOLD YOUR BROTHER IN CONTEMPT? WE SHALL ALL STAND BEFORE GOD'S TRIBUNAL.

ROM. 14:10, NEB.

By definition, a judge is one who governs, protects, and dispenses justice. In such a role, even though he or she may be a pagan or an atheist, a judge is a representative of God, a solemn calling indeed. Significantly, the first mention of a judge in Scripture refers to God Himself. Arguing with his two angelic visitors about the fate of Sodom, Abraham cried, "Shall not the Judge of all the earth do right?" (Gen. 18:25, NKJV).

The patriarchs exercised judicial authority over their families. The Hebrews appointed "judges and officers" in the wilderness to assist Moses in settling disputes (Ex. 18:13-27). By the time Israel had conquered Canaan, judges had taken a major leadership role in the nation, beginning with Othniel (Judges 3:9) and ending with Samuel (1 Sam. 7:15). The Hebrew monarchy that followed would prove to be more corrupt than even the worst of the judges had been.

Jesus pointed out that judging is a serious hazard for individuals who cannot possibly have all of the facts. And even if they did, who would dare face the risk? "Judge not, that you be not judged. For with what judgment you judge, you will be judged; and with the same measure you use, it will be measured back to you" (Matt. 7:1, 2, NKJV). Ironically, in this same connection, earth's final judgment day rests in the hands of One who was grossly misjudged by human beings (Matt. 25:31-46).

[*God of justice, let me be willing always to refrain from judging my neighbors. Whatever the circumstances, I leave them safely in Your hands.*]

THE BENEVOLENT JUDGE

One of best things about obedience to the law is that it can become a natural part of our lives, preventing stress. You don't get into your car and drive off to work thinking *Now I'm going to obey all of the traffic rules this morning. I'll stop at every stop sign, and I'll not run any red lights.* Nor do you enter the market saying "I'll pay for everything I take out of the store. I won't shoplift." You don't decide "I'm not going to cheat once at school today." Because you already know all the rules, you enjoy perfect freedom in obeying them.

Only the *breaking* of law brings pain. If you've customarily run stop signs, been light fingered at the market, or cheated on exams, you have a problem. Obedience now becomes an entirely different matter. These issues stare you right in the face because you must make conscious decisions. "I wonder if I can get away with it, if I try again." Or "I really want to stop. I don't want to do it again."

> AND NOW THE PRIZE AWAITS ME, THE GARLAND OF RIGHTEOUSNESS WHICH THE LORD, THE ALL-JUST JUDGE, WILL AWARD ME ON THAT GREAT DAY.
>
> 2 TIM. 4:8, NEB.

Only those who have been arrested, handcuffed, and taken off to jail can know what that feels like. The rest of us can only imagine. For law-abiding citizens, jails, courts, lawyers, and even the police themselves are part of a system out there that doesn't seem to be a direct part of our lives. This, I realize, is idealistic, because since our world often operates on a base of suspicion and evil, anything can happen to anyone at any time.

The point is that the eternal Judge of heaven is a sentencing judge. The guilty will pay their accounts in full. This same Person, however, is also the benevolent judge. Those who have taken Christ's righteousness as their own can, with Paul, look forward to the "prize . . . the garland of righteousness" that the Judge will give them at the judgment bar. In this light, one need not fear death whenever it comes. Judgment day is nothing to fear. Jesus' second coming can happen tonight or tomorrow. Whoever has his or her case heard before the benevolent Judge can be at perfect peace.

[*Lord and Giver of rewards, I shall not come before You in my own righteousness— only in Christ's. Therefore, I ask for my hearing before the benevolent Judge.*]

THE COUNSELOR

We have recovery groups for every kind of personal disaster—divorce, grief, and abuse. Groups to help us out of addictions and groups to assist the sexually disoriented to find their identity. Groups for caregivers in all kinds of diseases and groups for those seeking spiritual enlightenment. "Spiritual nudist camps!" mutters one of my old doctor friends darkly. "That's what they are."

HIS NAME WILL BE CALLED . . . COUNSELOR.

ISA. 9:6, NKJV.

By no means are all of these organizations useless—counseling is a necessary profession. Whoever tends to think that if you're a committed Christian, then you shouldn't need any help should think again. Every person, Christian or otherwise, at some time or other, may receive much benefit from talking to a sympathetic listener. Our support group or counselor may offer only commonsense advice. In great distress, however, it's sometimes difficult to summon common sense, to say nothing of courage. And when we hear ourselves talking we might even discover the solution ourselves. Whereas we've long referred to "my doctor," "my dentist," "my teacher," and "my pastor," we may now add to our list "my therapist."

Where does the wisdom of the counselor come from? In the biblical context counseling derives from "assembly," a sitting together. (Here may be the precursor of "group therapy.") Kings had their councils (2 Kings 25:19). By New Testament times the council had evolved into the Sanhedrin, the high court of the Jews. Lesser councils also existed. "Beware of men," Jesus said, forecasting persecutions, "for they will deliver you up to councils and scourge you in their synagogues" (Matt. 10:17, NKJV). Just because a "council" of people said so doesn't, however, make it right.

Counseling may be either healing and helpful or mortally destructive. We should choose a counselor only on the basis of his or her *source* of wisdom and advice. Does it rest on commercial or political considerations? Is it wholly secular and trendy? Or is the counsel linked to the omniscient Counsel of heaven? Scripture often describes God and Christ as being in a council with the host of heaven (Job 15:8; Ps. 89:7). *That* has to be our most excellent source for guidance.

[*Dear Lord, I need the support system of having wise and caring friends about me. Let us together draw from Your sacred counsels.*]

THE WITNESS

Someone has said, "When you hear more than one eyewitness account of an accident, then you begin to worry about history." A witness is a person who saw something happen, who can give a firsthand account of it. Witnesses testify under oath in court. They will also be present at the signing of documents and will attest to the event by attaching their signatures. Naturally we want to know that the witness is true and honest.

> JESUS CHRIST [IS] THE FAITHFUL WITNESS.
>
> REV. 1:5, NKJV.

The problem of false witnesses, however, seems to go back to the beginning of time. Otherwise, why would the ninth commandment read "You shall not bear false witness against your neighbor" (Ex. 20:16, NKJV)? The Deuteronomic code had specific and severe instructions for dealing with perjury (Deut. 19:15-21). As most of us can testify, bearing false witness has been an ongoing problem of the human race.

The wise men of the Bible had to speak of perjury: "The Lord hates . . . a false witness who pours out lies" (Prov. 6:16-19, NIV). "A false witness will not go unpunished" (Prov. 19:9, NIV). "A false witness will perish, and whoever listens to him will be destroyed forever" (Prov. 21:28, NIV). And whoever "by falsehood [denies] justice to the righteous . . . shall be exterminated" (Isa. 29:21, NEB). Strong words these. In addition, we need to add all the false prophets and diviners who fabricated messages, visions, and dreams to delude believers.

Jesus listed perjury in the horrific list of sins that "proceed from the heart . . . [and] defile a man" (Matt. 15:19, NEB). False witnesses participated in His trial (Matt. 26:60). The same people paid for and "set up false witnesses" against Stephen, the first Christian martyr (Acts 6:13, NKJV).

To become a "malicious witness," an instrument of evildoers, is risky (Ex. 23:1, NIV). Paul makes the chilling observation that deceivers will have a "strong delusion, that they should believe the lie" (2 Thess. 2:11, NKJV). They will, in fact, reach a point where they can't know whether they are telling the truth or not.

A wise man put it simply: "A truthful witness saves lives" (Prov. 14:25, NIV). Christ Himself is the supreme true witness.

> [Jesus, in You I find the perfect and faithful witness. Give me patience to endure those times when others have spoken falsely against me.]

THE UMPIRE

In ancient Arabia a "righteous man" named Job became the subject of a dramatic cosmic test between God and Satan. First, the man lost his property, then his servants, his children, and finally his health— all within a terrifyingly short space of time (Job 1, 2). Rejected because of his loathsome disease, he sat in the town dump outside the city walls while his "comforting" friends argued that the righteous prosper and the wicked suffer (Job 4).

> THERE IS NO UMPIRE BETWEEN US, WHO MIGHT LAY HIS HAND UPON US BOTH.
>
> JOB 9:33, RSV.

Unable to think of any unconfessed sin, Job hotly defended his integrity. In his pain and frustration he longed to talk to God as an equal, to understand the meaning of his trials, to debate his problems and protest his suffering, to have a third person intervene in the dispute. But he recognized his limitations—he had no umpire (Job 9:33). The King James Version uses the word "daysman." This old-fashioned word shows that the work of referees or umpires goes back a long way, that the role they perform has been necessary since the beginning of time. Because we have always had violent disagreements with one another over an endless variety of issues, we always need the objective, neutral "daysman" to mediate between contending parties.

Job is, in fact, the first man recorded in Scripture as having laid hold of the idea that there could be—that indeed there *was*—a mediator for him in heaven. In a glorious flash of recognition, he exclaimed, "Even now, behold, my witness is in heaven, and he that vouches for me is on high" (Job 16:19, RSV).

Not a day passes in which we do not, like Job, recognize that we are here and that God is "over there." The controversy between God and us rages constantly. As our law-breaking fuels the fire, we alternate between despair and rebellion, knowing that we too *need* an Umpire—One to stand between the God of goodness and sinful humanity.

Jesus precisely fills the requirement. He is that umpire, the great daysman, who stands between God and us. He's the one who lays His hand both upon His Father's divinity and upon our sinful humanity and gives us peace and reconciliation with God.

[*God of justice and mercy, how thankful I am that I do not stand alone. My daysman is always at my side.*]

THE MEDIATOR

Once in Jamaica a young friend of mine had a classic experience in mediation. A woman doctor, she was driving from Mandeville in the mountains down to Kingston by the sea on her way to the hospital. The narrow roads were squeezed by even narrower bridges. She came to a huge backup of traffic with no way to turn aside. Getting out and walking to see what was the matter, she came to a single-file bridge where two old cars stood nose to nose. Beside them the two drivers debated the crisis in thunderous voices. An interested crowd from the stalled cars at both ends had gathered around to see the show. Each of the two drivers vowed that he would not move—not until judgment day, if need be.

The woman stepped forward. "I am a doctor, and it is very necessary for me to get to Kingston, where I have many patients waiting. Would one of you please move so that the traffic can pass?"

THERE IS . . . ONE MEDIATOR BETWEEN GOD AND MEN, CHRIST JESUS, HIMSELF MAN, WHO SACRIFICED HIMSELF TO WIN FREEDOM FOR ALL MANKIND.

1 TIM. 2:5, NEB.

One of them looked at the woman (who was extremely attractive). "For him," one man shouted, glowering at his adversary, "I would never move my car. No, not until I die. But for you, madam, I will move it. For you and no one else!"

Mediation means intervention between two polarized groups. Employees and management. Ballplayers and team owners. Flight attendants and the airlines. Husbands and wives heading for divorce. Usually the contending parties get locked into a strike. The mediator, a neutral third party, steps in. Everyone concerned is eager to get the matter over with, but sometimes the discussion can last for weeks before everybody can settle on terms.

God is pure goodness, and, tainted with sin as we are, we are barred from His presence. No two groups could be more polarized than the hosts of heaven and the human race. Consider the thought of standing before the tribunal of heaven—whether you are a heinous criminal or a saint with only one sin. It's best not even to *be* there. Let Christ stand up before the judge and say, "Look at Me—not him. Not her. I have satisfied the law for them."

We must have a Mediator to open up the channels of communication. And He's always there.

[*Dear Jesus, You have already settled the dispute with the evil one. Now help me keep my own path to the Father open and clear.*]

THE MEDIATOR OF THE NEW COVENANT

A covenant is a legally binding agreement. While it is possible to sell a house, transfer title, and so forth by ourselves, it is worth the cost to have a real estate agent manage the transaction. Frequently we need to get documents notarized—just to be sure. Some intrepid persons prepare their own tax returns. Realizing the changeability and inscrutability of tax laws, many others hire certified tax consultants to handle the job—just to be safe. Such mediators, we trust, will prevent us from making costly mistakes.

YOU STAND BEFORE . . . JESUS THE MEDIATOR OF A NEW COVENANT.

HEB. 12:22-24, NEB.

Which brings us to the specialized mediatorial work of Christ. Throughout the Old Testament Israel went through a series of covenants vowing exclusive allegiance to God. Human promises didn't hold, and God's people broke the treaty—repeatedly. It was a long, sorry story. The "new covenant," on the other hand, had its basis on what God would do. Here, at last, was an arrangement that could cover human deficiencies. Jesus would take care of the requirement of "works" by giving His life for humanity. At every point at which the sinner failed, He would "make it up"—provided that that sinner had accepted His mediation.

Jesus' responsibilities as a mediator of the new covenant involved much more than just opening up the lines of communication between heaven and earth. Jeremiah pleaded, "Let the Lord be a true and faithful witness between us" (Jer. 42:5, NKJV). The mediating witness! How many rich images that calls to mind.

Jesus brings three qualifications to His task as the new covenant mediator. First, He comes as prophet. He spoke the words of God, but He was Himself "the word of God." Second, He is a priest. In that capacity He made offerings—while He was Himself the offering. Last, He is a king by every divine right, ruling in power and authority. At the same time He is the "suffering servant." He will be a king who rules by serving.

The new covenant, foreordained before the foundation of the world to be manifested in "these last times" (1 Peter 1:20, NKJV), is infinitely older than all of the old ones that preceded it. And it is the only one that can remain unbroken—simply because even our sincerest word cannot be depended on. But God's can.

[*Divine Mediator, I am weary of my fallibility—to say nothing of the people around me. I willingly leave the entire management of my life in Your hands.*]

THE INTERCESSOR

Remember when you were too scared to ask for what you wanted? You approached Dad to ask Mom if you could go to a house party and stay out late. Mom told Dad for you that you really needed a little extra allowance money this week. A classmate interceded with the teacher for extra time to finish an assignment you had. Or you waited until someone else talked to the boss about overtime pay before you said anything yourself. More often than most of us would like to admit, we prefer to stay in the background while someone else "breaks the ice." When it comes to matters that are really important to us, we instinctively want an intercessor. Unfortunately, our requests are usually selfish.

> [JESUS] IS ALSO ABLE TO SAVE ABSOLUTELY THOSE WHO APPROACH GOD THROUGH HIM; HE IS ALWAYS LIVING TO PLEAD ON THEIR BEHALF.
>
> HEB. 7:25, NEB.

Intercession is popularly thought of as some kind of prayer. But it would be a mistake to imagine that Christ is somehow standing before the Father's throne saying prayers for us. After all, God is not going to change. The Lamb was "slain from the foundation of the world" (Rev. 13:8, KJV), and the Godhead made arrangements for dealing with sin long before Adam and Eve fell to the wiles of the serpent. Then God Himself set up the mediatorial system and invited us to use it. Why? He simply wants us to keep the cross of Christ before us. God desires that we remember every hour of our lives that it is our entitlement to heaven.

Jesus prayed on behalf of others rather than for Himself. John 17 records His model prayer of intercession. He prayed for three things: a revelation of His Father's glory, the strengthening of the faith of His disciples, and the unity of future Christians. Only in passing, in verse 5, did He refer to His own need.

Now He continues intercession in heaven, but He left us His prayer to show us how intercession works. And it does work. It assures us of salvation. Christ's intercession takes care of everything. Indeed, we have here "grace guaranteed."

> [O Christ, I thank You for the rich supply of grace You have made available. May I, in turn, serve the needs of others about me.]

THE RECONCILER

Reconciliation is a highly specialized form of mediation. Instead of just opening up the channels of communication and letting people talk, the reconciler goes further. He or she takes an active part in mending the quarrel, making ideas or accounts consistent with one another, establishing peace between warring parties, and then leaving them contented.

"Equality" has been the battle cry of revolutions and democratic endeavors for more than 300 years. It came as a reaction to the hard class lines of the ancient hierarchical systems. So far, so good. The only problem is that people are *not* equal—our best efforts notwithstanding. They're different in thousands of ways, just as Paul pointed out in the "enmity" between the Jews and the Gentiles.

In his celebrated political allegory *Animal Farm,* George Orwell makes an ironic but painfully correct statement. The pigs (Bolsheviks) have taken over the farmhouse and have begun to imitate the lifestyle of the capitalist farmer, whom they have evicted. The rest of the farm animals are illiterate, but they accept the reading that Molly the mule (the only one who can read) gives to the notice the pigs have posted on the side of the barn: "All Animals Are Equal." In time, however, the appearance of the sign changes as the pigs gain more power. The animals want to know what the sign says now. Unwillingly, the discouraged Molly reads it for them: "All Animals Are Equal, but Some Are More Equal Than Others."

There is, in fact, only one way in which all human beings can ever be equal, and that is when they stand in God's presence. This principle enabled slaves and their masters to worship together in the early Christian church. Later, of course, the clergy subdivided themselves into ranks, and the peasants ended up standing outside of the altar rail listening to a service in a language they eventually couldn't understand.

Repeatedly we have to reemphasize our equality before God. The church can so easily splinter. Jesus calls us to Himself as the reconciler. Only before Him can we find peace with one another.

> [CHRIST] IN HIS OWN BODY OF FLESH AND BLOOD HAS BROKEN DOWN THE ENMITY WHICH STOOD LIKE A DIVIDING WALL BETWEEN [GENTILES AND JEWS].
>
> EPH. 2:14-16, NEB.

[*Lord, if I have any unresolved dispute with anyone, help me to make reconciliation today so that we may both stand before You as equals.*]

THE ADVOCATE

Most of us enter into prison and courtroom affairs only by imagination—imagination fed, however, by graphic trial scenes relayed to us by the media. We are obsessed, apparently, with seeing how the witnesses hold up under cross-examination, how the lawyers make their cases, how the police handle the investigation, how the prisoner reacts to all the revelations, and how the jury, finally, brings in the verdict. Then the sentencing.

IF ANYONE SINS, WE HAVE AN ADVOCATE WITH THE FATHER, JESUS CHRIST THE RIGHTEOUS [ONE].

1 JOHN 2:1, NKJV.

Most of us, to be sure, have had no direct connection with judicial proceedings. Nonetheless, we all personally face a tribunal of inestimable significance. The outcome is not imprisonment with or without bail. It is not a sentence with or without parole. The sentence confers on us absolutely either eternal life or eternal death.

The apostle John presents the situation almost theoretically—"If anyone sins . . ." Born in sin, we have sinned, are sinning, and will sin again. What then shall we do? The prospect is terrifying. Before God we must stand in a courtroom that measures sin neither by quantity nor quality. Have we broken every law on earth and in heaven? Have we continued doing so for a lifetime? Or have we "done pretty well," having only a lingering sin or two left on the record? Have we told only "white" lies instead of "black" ones? It doesn't matter. The Judge's sentence for any sin will be the same—eternal death.

Who can ever cope alone with such an event? We *must* have legal representation. John goes on: "If any one sins, we have an Advocate with the Father, Jesus Christ." "Advocate" comes from a Latin word meaning "to voice." The word now means "one called in" or "counsel." Ironically, at His own earthly trial Jesus had no advocate, nor did He say one word in His own behalf.

Yet when He takes up the task of advocate to plead our cause, He fulfills one of His most important roles. When Jesus speaks up on our behalf, it's almost as if we sinners were not even there. He will, in effect, tell the Father, "Don't look at him or her. Look at Me. I have paid the account with My blood."

> *Dear God, we cannot stand in court alone. We choose*
> *Christ to represent our case daily before Your throne.*

THE WARDEN

In ancient and medieval times people rarely received imprisonment as a penalty. Prisoners of war were usually slain or sold into slavery. In general, society did not consider such people "worth their keep." Then came sentencing to the galleys, followed by transportation to the colonies. Until the late eighteenth century, prisons primarily lodged people awaiting trial. The "house of correction" came with early prison reforms, born of the idea that prisoners should be punished and then rehabilitated.

I, PAUL, [AM] THE PRISONER OF JESUS CHRIST.

EPH. 3:1, NKJV.

This notion called for the building of large prisons to hold multitudes of criminals. Penitentiaries were supposed to induce penance and reform among the inmates. At the same time prisoners lived under the "separate and silent system"—single cells with no communication. Later came the "congregate and silent system"—that is, communal work but no conversation. Only in the past 60 years has the silent treatment largely vanished.

The management of the prisons lay in the hands of the warden. The condition of the prison and its inmates has always reflected his policies. The warden supervises three separate staffs. First, the custodial officers (guards). Then the industrial managers who operate prison factories and kitchens. Finally come the professional caretakers—the physicians, chaplains, teachers, psychiatrists, and social workers. The warden has authority over all of them and is responsible for maintaining order, for promoting rehabilitation, and for preventing escapes.

When Paul announced himself a "prisoner of Jesus Christ," he put himself in a unique position. He voluntarily gave himself up to the administration of the heavenly Warden, trading his personal liberty for the exclusive supervision of the Warden. His work might be solitary or among many people. But agreeing to live under any conditions given to him, he would trust his life to the care of guardian angels. He would suffer, if called to do so. At the same time, being a member of the divine system, he would enjoy the ministering services of Christian caretakers.

Above all, Paul *wanted* to be preserved from any temptation to escape the imprisonment of Christ, the confinement to which he had voluntarily given himself. Outside, he knew, lay only destruction.

[*O heavenly Warden, we give ourselves up wholly to be prisoners of Your love. Direct our lives precisely as You see fit.*]

OUR KEEPER

The task of a keeper is not the same as that of a warden. The word "keeper" refers to several biblical occupations, but they all have the same characteristics. A keeper was the one who observed, guarded, and saw to the comfort of those put in his charge.

Abel was a "keeper of sheep" (Gen. 4:2, NKJV). Even David once "left the sheep with a keeper" (1 Sam. 17:20, NKJV). Then came keepers of vineyards (S. of Sol. 1:6); keepers of the watch, the walls, and gates (2 Kings 11:5, 6); and keepers of the fields (Jer. 4:17). In Philippi, at the release of Paul and Silas by means of the great earthquake, "the keeper of the prison, awaking from sleep and seeing the prison doors open, supposing the prisoners had fled, drew his sword and was about to kill himself" (Acts 16:27, NKJV). The keepers of women had desirable court positions (Esther 2:3), as did the keeper of the wardrobe (2 Kings 22:14). The custom of the times dictated that women be "keepers at home" (Titus 2:5, KJV). The guards at Jesus' tomb could not "keep" the grave closed against the Resurrection (Matt. 28:4). The "temple hymn," Psalm 121, is an entire song in praise of "the Keeper" for His demanding task.

When Cain asked insolently "Am I my brother's keeper?" he tried to side-step the responsibility of "keeping" (Gen. 4:9, NKJV). Not so with Christ. When we are saved we are also secure. The "whole spirit, soul, and body [will] be preserved blameless at the coming of our Lord Jesus Christ" (1 Thess. 5:23, NKJV). "He who has been born of God keeps himself, and the wicked one does not touch him" (1 John 5:18, NKJV). No prayer of Jesus was more beautiful than that for His disciples: "Those whom You gave Me I have kept" (John 17:12, NKJV).

Even naughty children want to know that they are "kept." So much so that at times they virtually ask to be disciplined. We *all* have a deep desire to be kept, to have someone who would care very much if we were not there.

> "WHEN I WAS WITH THEM [THE DISCIPLES], I PROTECTED BY THE POWER OF THY NAME THOSE WHOM THOU HAST GIVEN ME, AND KEPT THEM SAFE."
>
> JOHN 17:12, NEB.

[*Keeper of minds and spirits, I wish to be wholly in Your keeping. Let Your guardianship enter every phase of my life.*]

THE PRISONER

A famous castle stands on the shore of Lake Geneva, in Switzerland. The upper rooms, furnished for the nobility, give no hint of the dungeons carved out of the huge rock upon which the chateau stands. Although it is picturesque, what has made the castle of Chillon internationally famous is the spirit of one prisoner.

> "THE CHASTISEMENT FOR OUR PEACE WAS UPON HIM, AND BY HIS STRIPES WE ARE HEALED."
>
> ISA. 53:5, NKJV.

In 1816 the poet Lord Byron became fascinated with the story of the Swiss patriot, Francois de Bonivard, who spent seven years in the dungeon of Chillon, chained to one of the seven Gothic pillars that crop out of the rock-hewn floor. The man's faith forbade suicide, even after his father and five brothers had perished there beside him. By the time he was finally set free in 1536, his glazed eyes could scarcely acknowledge the glorious scenery about him. Body broken, mind dulled, and spirit crushed, he said, in the words of the poet:

> "I learn'd to love despair. . . .
> My very chains and I grew friends,
> So much a long communion tends
> To make us what we are—even I
> Regain'd my freedom with a sigh."

And that, in summary, is the tragedy of being a prisoner. It is not just the physical deprivation. Not even the possibility of death at the end. Rather it's the destruction of the human spirit, the loss of hope. Programmed by God for His divine gift of freedom, we find ourselves quickly and severely scarred by the loss of liberty.

The shame and despair that goes with imprisonment is excruciating for the guilty. But how much more so for the innocent! It takes great courage and patience to rise above the degradation. Although the minds and spirits of some have remained at liberty, many more, however, like the prisoner of Chillon, have broken under the strain.

To provide us with salvation, Christ became a prisoner for us. He entered into the reeking, loathsome prison house that our sin had built. Then He endured the trial and death of a common felon—crucifixion. Pain, yes! But His Spirit remained unbroken throughout His ordeal. He showed us how to survive!

> [*Dear Jesus, I thank You for giving hope to us,*
> *crushed as we are in the prison house of sin.*]

THE THIEF

Jesus a thief? Since He has repeatedly portrayed Himself as a keeper of the peace, this startling image has a touch of ironic humor. Early Christians understood it well. Thieves lurked outside every house every night. "You know perfectly well," Paul said, "that the Day of the Lord comes like a thief in the night" (1 Thess. 5:2, NEB). Usually we have used it to indicate a surprise element of Christ's coming. But really focusing directly on our need for constant preparedness, it is a matter of eternal importance. And we can learn still more from the imagery.

As we examine the thief picture more closely we must set aside the ethical issue. Instead, we shall consider the chief character traits of successful burglars. First, they must be intelligent. Naturally, they know the benefits of surprise and of working under cover of darkness. "If the household had known at what time of night the burglar was coming," Jesus reasoned with His disciples, "he would have kept awake and not have let his house be broken into" (Matt. 24:43, NEB).

Second, thieves make careful plans. They learn the habits of their victims and choose their methods accordingly. Also, they have perfect control of themselves at all times. Thieves must think on their feet and make decisions in the heat of action. Finally, they will be constantly alert to anyone who might stop them.

Preyed upon by evildoers, we spend millions of dollars on the multitude of safety devices available on the market as we seek to protect ourselves and our property. We want more police patrolling the streets. Sometimes our efforts against crime succeed. Other times they don't.

No question, however, can exist about the triumph of Jesus' operations as a "thief." His goal is to save His fallen creatures (sometimes almost in spite of themselves). Long ago He formulated His plan for their salvation. None of Satan's maneuverings can take Him by surprise. He *will* come, and nothing can stop Him. Alert and thoroughly in control, His "raid" on Planet Earth will be no clumsy encounter. His coming is absolutely certain.

"IF YOU DO NOT WAKE UP, I SHALL COME UPON YOU LIKE A THIEF, AND YOU WILL NOT KNOW THE MOMENT OF MY COMING."

REV. 3:3, NEB.

> *I'm amazed, Lord. We're slow learners, but You are ready and able to save us in spite of ourselves.*

A CITY OF REFUGE

Professionals tell us that when we get an "adrenalin rush" from sudden crises, our bodies gear up either to fight or to flee. Our brains shift into automatic and dictate which it shall be, depending on the strength of our adversary. Apparently the fear-or-flight reaction is a basic human instinct.

The idea of places of refuge has a long history among Semitic peoples. Usually they were religious shrines where felons could seek safety and avoid arrest. They afforded relief from the immutable law of retribution and revenge: "Whoever kills any man shall surely be put to death" (Lev. 24:17, NKJV). A corollary to this law was the duty of a relative of the victim to kill the murderer. Ancient retribution made no consideration as to whether the act was deliberate or accidental. Moses specified, however, that a deliberate murderer could *not* find sanctuary at the altar (Ex. 21:14).

> **"THESE SIX CITIES SHALL BE FOR REFUGE FOR THE PEOPLE OF ISRAEL, AND FOR THE STRANGER AND FOR THE SO-JOURNER AMONG THEM."**
>
> NUM. 35:9-15, RSV.

Upon the conquest of Canaan, Joshua humanely named six cities of the Levites as "cities of refuge" (Joshua 20:7, 8), conveniently spaced around the country and on both sides of the Jordan.* In them a killer had respite until a court could investigate the case and act on it. The person could flee to the nearest city and live there permanently, if he or she chose. In the case of accidental killing, the individual either ran to the city himself or was delivered there by the elders of his or her congregation who recognized that the death was not premeditated. God provided specific instructions regarding the use of these cities. They required that the people keep all roads leading to them in good repair (Deut. 19:1-13). Curiously, though the cities must have had considerable use, the Old Testament gives us no stories to demonstrate how the system functioned.

God's spiritual city of refuge utilizes a degree of grace not found anywhere else. Not only does He pardon sins of ignorance, even the most flagrant, He can also erase premeditated crime if we truly repent—with all that that word means.

> [*Our Refuge in the time of trouble, how little we know of ourselves! But You stand at the gate to receive us, however, whenever we flee to You.*]

---

*The cities of refuge were Kedesh, Shechem, Hebron, Bezer, Ramoth, and Golan.

THE DIVINE AVENGER

Remember those schoolyard battles during recess time? Most of us had a personal enemy with whom we exchanged insults on a daily basis. In our fierce determination to survive, our earliest, savage instincts told us that when wrong was done, someone had to *pay*. So we struck back for ourselves.

Vengeance, however, is more than simply getting even. The Hebrew *go'el,* or avenger, was a dark figure in the systems of primitive justice. As the nearest relative of a victim, the *go'el* had the right—indeed, the legal duty—to exact payment for wrongs done. In the case of murder, he vindicated the right of a person to live. His vengeance cleansed the land of the stain of killings without cause. He reclaimed lost family property and took vengeance *on behalf* of someone. Even today the outrage people feel when they perceive that a jury has given the wrong verdict in a trial may cause some to revert to the ancient role of avenger and take punishment into their own hands.

Although the laws of Moses included the widely accepted idea of individual "blood vengeance," it was carefully regulated. Old Testament justice distinguished between accidental and deliberate homicide, and in the settlement of Canaan the cities of refuge protected fugitives from vengeance.

The ground rules of biblical wisdom taught that God rewards right conduct with material prosperity and that He punishes wrongdoers. Here lay the issue between Job (certified righteous by God Himself) and his friends. The evidence, they declared, pointed to sin in Job's life. He stoutly defended his innocence. Jeremiah detected the same difficulty of exceptions to the rules: "O Lord, I will dispute with thee. . . . Why do the wicked prosper and traitors live at ease?" (Jer. 12:1, 2, NEB). (Obviously we can't pass judgment on our neighbor's character by the good or ill fortune that befalls him or her.)

So we return to those schoolyard battles. *How* and *when* do the wrongdoers get punished? "O Lord, how long?" The Divine Avenger has His time and His plan. As *Go'el* He will redress the wrongs done to His perfect creation. He will vindicate our right to eternal life. Satan cannot escape.

"HOW LONG, SOVEREIGN LORD, HOLY AND TRUE, MUST IT BE BEFORE THOU WILT VINDICATE US?"

REV. 6:10, NEB.

[*Dear Champion of my cause, help me let go. Somehow make me willing to leave the settling of accounts in Your hands.*]

THE TAX PAYMENT

I have just written a check to R. Wayne Watts for $590.70. Watts is the tax collector for Riverside County, where I live. Six months from now I'll have to send him another one for the same amount. And I won't feel any happier then than I do now. Knowing that the average American works *five* months of every year just to pay taxes is a depressing thought.

Now, if in return for this kind of expense we were getting a perfectly efficient and honest government, we'd be less frustrated. Instead, we resign ourselves to knowing that such a thing can never happen in this life. Our tax payments will continue to cause hardship and provoke us to anger.

Because taxpayers must direct their checks to R. Wayne Watts personally, he suffers waves of prejudice, certain times of the year being worse than others, I imagine. In fact, a colleague of mine who actually knows Watts affirms that people really do hate him. Moreover, he declares that Watts is a perfect gentleman—a very nice person, just doing the job he was hired to do. Nonetheless, no tax collector we've ever heard of has been respected, much less loved. Jesus Himself faced scorn for even socializing with "tax-gatherers and sinners" (Matt. 9:11, NEB).

In reply to Peter's question about paying dues to Caesar, Jesus performed the miracle of providing a silver coin for the tax payment. Thus He demonstrated two principles. First, taxes to secular governments cannot and ought not to be avoided, no matter how vexing.

Second, He—again miraculously—has provided Himself as a necessary divine tax payment. Since the coming of sin, Satan has regarded himself as the ruler of the earth. He has established a kingdom of death in which our property taxes are mortally high. For millennia he has been exacting payments from us.

Jesus, however, has already offered Himself as the necessary tax payment to settle our sin account. It only remains for Him, at the end of time, to call Satan to the final settlement. After that the devil can levy no more taxes on the earth, and the title will be deeded back to us, forever tax-free.

> "TAKE THE FIRST FISH THAT COMES TO THE HOOK, OPEN ITS MOUTH, AND YOU WILL FIND A SILVER COIN . . . IT WILL MEET THE TAX FOR US BOTH."
>
> MATT. 17:27, NEB.

[*Lord, paying taxes is hard. I don't like it. But You carried the costs of sin for all of us. I thank You.*]

THE BANKER

anks have been available to us for millennia. Money-management matters began in pagan sanctuaries—which accounts for the fact that the architects designed the traditional bank building along the lines of a Greek temple. Today it seems a little odd to think that banking and religion were ever companions. Nonetheless, religious connections or not, people today frequently call the integrity of banks into question. (Some wary persons *still* keep their cash at home under the mattress.) Increasingly, banks are subject to robberies, embezzlement, and corruption of all kinds. Or they may simply fail under the weight of their own large and overly adventurous operations. What to do with our cash and valuables nowadays requires expert advice. The banking principles of heaven, however, are clear enough.

FOR I KNOW WHOM I HAVE BELIEVED AND AM PERSUADED THAT HE IS ABLE TO KEEP WHAT I HAVE COMMITTED TO HIM UNTIL THAT DAY.

2 TIM. 1:12, NKJV.

The commands of King Artaxerxes to the Hebrew exiles teach us something about responsible stewardship. Accompanied by an escort of soldiers, they were to bear the valuable Temple vessels across the desert from Babylon to Jerusalem and to deposit them safely for priestly use. The king insisted upon their absolute honesty and commitment (Ezra 7:19, 26).

When we deal with the bank of heaven, we engage in two kinds of transactions. First, we deposit ourselves and our treasure with God. We can entrust ourselves to Him because we can know assuredly that He will honor our confidence and hold our deposit secure. From long experience with this Banker, we know absolutely that "He is able."

The second part of the arrangement has no real contemporary counterpart. While our banks today are eager enough to have our money to use, the interest they pay has, over the past few years, dwindled to less than 5 percent. Not so with Jesus. He has put a magnificent deposit of heavenly treasure into our hands—His honor and His gospel, His Father's glory and His holy day, and the affairs of His church.

And what joy when our wilderness journey ends, when we shall reach our destination, weigh out the deposit, and then hear the Banker say, "Well done!"

[*I give over my money management to You, Lord. Your banking corporation is one which I can trust fully.*]

THE GAMBLER

While certain kinds of adventure attract me, I find financial risk-taking absolutely appalling. Possibly it is a genetic disability inherited from my father. Having weathered the privations of the Great Depression, he could scarcely enjoy even owning a house. Although he behaved in a normal fiscal manner throughout his life, Dad's natural instinct would have prompted him to hide his money under the mattress. Consequently, the affairs of the stock market terrify me. Most of the *Wall Street Journal* reads like Egyptian hieroglyphics. I refuse to risk even the price of postage on the mass of sweepstakes mail that daily floods the mailbox. Occasionally I have looked in the door of a casino just to study the faces of those throngs of addicted people riveted to the gambling machines. No temptation there for me.

HE HUMBLED HIMSELF, AND IN OBEDIENCE ACCEPTED EVEN DEATH.

PHIL. 2:8, NEB.

Gambling, however, is an essential spiritual activity. By the time Jesus reached the cross, we often assume the plan of salvation was so well in hand that all He had left to do was to "get through it"—the pain, the rejection. Not so. By going to a human death He put His place in heaven at an incomprehensible risk. And all for us! His victorious confrontation with Satan in the wilderness temptations had been but the prologue. The showdown at Calvary eternally resolved the great controversy between good and evil. There Christ abandoned caution and went all the way. And how magnificently it paid off.

It should come as no surprise, then, that our own Christian walk involves some risk-taking. How often we find ourselves, as it were, sitting opposite Satan at the gaming table. In those tense moments we must know that Jesus is at our elbow, ready to consult with us on the right moves to make. With Him, we are certain to win the game.

[*Today I put it all in Your hands, Father. Heaven has already taken all the risks for me. How can I hold back?*]

THE LOST COIN

One of these days I am going to have to decide what to do with my coin collection that resides now in three quart jars. My Midwestern American grandfather (who never left the continental United States) started me on it when I was 4 years old. While spending months abed after an episode of chicken pox, I would listen to his stories. We would take imaginary journeys around the world—geography, history, and excitement, all in one glorious package. For me it became so real that I expected us to leave on the trip tomorrow—if not that night. Ironically, my later life encompassed a great part of that itinerary that Grandpa laid out for me long ago.

"IF [A WOMAN] LOSES ONE COIN DOES [SHE NOT] SEEK DILIGENTLY UNTIL SHE FINDS IT?"

LUKE 15:8, RSV.

I look at my coins and remember. Some coins represent political change. My old British pounds, shillings, pence, ha'pennies, and farthings disappeared into the metric system. Canadian copper pennies from the 1880s are matched by as many contemporary pennies labeled "Newfoundland." Some exotic coins with square centers come from nineteenth-century China, and then a silver dollar from Hong Kong. Lightweight metals from poor countries pale in comparison to the old silver and copper. In 1918, my square two anna India coin tells me, the English monarch reigned as emperor of India. Then my tiny Indian coppers, barely a quarter of an inch in diameter, remind me how poor those people have been—it takes 12 of them to make just *one penny*. One coin from the Sultanate of Brunei bears Islamic characters and dating: 1304. The plumed serpent from Mexico, a harp from Ireland, kangaroos and platypuses from Australia, a combination of Portuguese and Chinese symbols from Macao, the mythic Garuda bird from Thailand—they're all here. Also, travel tokens promising me a full-fare trip in Honolulu in 1924 and city tours of Washington, D.C., and New York City. The square pennies from the Straits Settlements used to buy me a sugared ice ball at school when I was a youngster in Singapore.

Yes, Grandpa taught me good things. If I lost a few of my coins, I probably wouldn't miss most of them. I dare not, however, take *that* chance with my heavenly coinage. The woman in Jesus' parable didn't just lose her small change from the market. Those coins were her marriage dowry, and she knew exactly what she had. The set had to be complete.

[*Keeper of my resources, never let me undervalue them. Therein lies the story of my salvation!*]

THE FISHERMAN

Honolulu, Hawaii, has one of the most fascinating restaurants in the world. A series of walkways and little tea rooms extend over a large, shallow pool. You sit at your table watching hundreds (maybe thousands) of big Japanese carp swimming almost under your feet. The variety and the colors in that fish show never end.

"COME WITH ME, AND I WILL MAKE YOU FISHERS OF MEN."

MATT. 4:19, NEB.

People seem to have strong feelings about fishing as a sport, and many of them sense a spiritual component in the experience. In 1653 the English iron-monger Isaak Walton wrote *The Compleat Angler, or, the Contemplative Man's Recreation*. He waxed lyrical on the excellences of fishing—and perhaps *all* fishermen must embellish their stories when they come home from their adventures. Such accounts (along with the big carp in Honolulu), however, accentuate only recreational pursuits.

The business of real fishing is actually a matter of life and death, a staple part of the diet. Palestinian fishermen formed a distinct class, people who lived together in communities both around Galilee (which abounded in fish) and near the Fish Gate in Jerusalem (Neh. 3:3; 12:39). Exposed to all weathers, the hardy men did strenuous physical work (Luke 5:2). Sometimes they had crude manners and rough speech (Luke 9:49, 54). Yet they—including the volatile Peter—could also be surprisingly patient (Luke 5:5).

Because so many of Jesus' first disciples were fishermen, He delivered some of His mightiest messages from a fishing boat. When He invited His followers to become "fishers of men"—to take sinners in the gospel net—the disciples' earthly occupation became a parable of their divine vocation.

Quite naturally, then, from the beginning fish became associated with Christianity. The Greek word for fish, *ichthys,* served as an anagram of the name of Jesus in Greek: "Jesus/Christ/of God/the Son/Saviour." Thus the sign of the fish became a secret code among Christians. When Tertullian (c. A.D. 160-c. 230) linked the fish as an early symbol of baptism, the believers came to be called *pisciculi* (little fishes) out of the waters of the font or *piscina* (fishpond).

Within this early Christian symbol we find a double meaning. Not only are we the fish, saved clean and alive, but we are also the fishermen, understudies in God's program for calling people into His kingdom.

[*My Jesus, You loved the fish-filled Lake of Galilee more than any other place in Your earthly journey. Now I too would be a fisher in Your crew.*]

THE MERCHANT

The Hebrew word for "merchant" comes from a root meaning "to migrate," "to travel about." As a case in point, Abraham threaded his caravans back and forth across the ancient Arabian trade routes between his first business capital, Haran, and Egypt. Their story includes allusions to a number of business deals he made within the range of his "sales territory." They included control of pasturelands (Gen. 13:8-11), arguing with Abimelech over rights he had to the well of Beersheba (Gen. 21:30), and recovering tribal assets from other predatory merchant princes of the desert (Gen. 14:15, 16). Once he negotiated with God Himself over preserving the prosperous trade cities of Sodom and Gomorrah (Gen. 19).

By Solomon's reign the essentially agricultural Hebrews had entered international trade on a vast scale (1 Kings 9:26), involving cattle, foodstuffs, textiles, luxury items, and so forth. The apostle Paul established the early Christian churches in major commercial centers —Antioch, Thessalonica, Corinth, and Ephesus. Then because of medieval restrictions on Jews owning property, they entered the mercantile world, in which they have prospered ever since. They came by their expertise through long talent and practice.

In his tribute to the capable woman, one of the poets of Proverbs honors her business astuteness. Her business goes well and she never puts out her lamp at night. She looks for good land and buys it, and knows how to market her merchandise wisely. Operating like the ships of the merchant, she explores investments on all sides (Prov. 31:10-31). Nowhere else in Scripture do women get a higher rating.

We note that Jesus' merchant in the parable makes his fortune on pearls, a product of the sea. The Hebrews had comparatively little experience with sea trade, preferring the more mundane services of desert caravans. Our experienced merchant, however, makes his choice based on long experience in the marketplace. Thus he concludes that the kingdom of heaven, when judged against other claims, is clearly the best value for him.

> "A MERCHANT LOOKING OUT FOR FINE PEARLS FOUND ONE OF VERY SPECIAL VALUE; SO HE WENT AND SOLD EVERYTHING HE HAD, AND BOUGHT IT."
>
> MATT. 13:45, 46, NEB.

[Lord, teach me the methods of true spiritual merchandising. Let me not weary of the effort. May I make my decisions wholly on the principles of Your kingdom.]

THE HIDDEN TREASURE

During World War II the Japanese occupational army made the old Manila campus of Philippine Union College one of its command headquarters. Stories of torture and starvation still remain from that time. They include the tale that the Japanese left a golden Buddha and other treasure buried somewhere on the grounds. Pirates' maps abound, as do directions to miners' treasure troves in the mountains. Also, we have information on recovering bullion from sunken ships. We forever thrive on romantic legends of buried treasure, even when we have little to go on but wishful thinking.

Unlike the merchant who bought the pearl as part of his lifetime quest, this man who discovers the treasure does so quite by accident. He grabs the opportunity, however, with total, unquestioning commitment, thinking of nothing except what possessing the treasure can do for him.

In this parable the finder is not a businessman. He had no pirate's map, didn't even buy a lottery ticket, and wasn't looking for anything. Instead, he was just digging in a field when he found the treasure. We call such an unexpected discovery "serendipitous."

Now, at this point his personality changes dramatically. Single-minded in his determination to possess the treasure, he becomes secretive. One can't help wondering that if he'd lived 2,000 years later, the owner of the field would have sued him. Ethically, one struggles a little here, and we have to give up on making the parable walk evenly "on four legs."

The point is, the finding of the treasure changes the man's life forever. He will never turn back. Having bought the whole field, he will stop at nothing.

Some of us arrive at the kingdom after a painstaking search through the spiritual marketplace. Hunting for pearls, we wait until we find the right one. Others stumble upon the treasure by accident, but recognize its value and without a moment's hesitation give all that it takes to secure the prize for themselves. A little childish maybe? No matter. As Master Trader Himself, Jesus is waiting for us, whichever way we come.

> "AGAIN, THE KINGDOM OF HEAVEN IS LIKE TREASURE HIDDEN IN A FIELD, WHICH A MAN FOUND AND HID; AND FOR JOY OVER IT HE GOES AND SELLS ALL THAT HE HAS AND BUYS THAT FIELD."
>
> MATT. 14:44, NKJV.

[*Teach me, Master, to recognize the values of the kingdom. Let me not lose the treasure because I didn't know what it was when I found it.*]

THE AUDITOR

Given human ethics and morals, the question of stewardship is frequently a sticky one. Is a particular financial picture exactly what it appears to be, we ask? Or is there a hidden agenda? For this reason, the occupation of auditor of accounts is a useful—indeed a very necessary—profession. Money and property can so distort judgment that it is absolutely mandatory to have someone wholly impartial to look at the records, do the arithmetic, and offer an opinion.

My good friend Bien has worked for many years in Africa with her husband, who is a mission auditor. Indeed, she herself has strayed from her original job of English teaching to help him in his work. In an engaging little essay* she gave me recently she discusses the case of "Client Z," Zacchaeus, who was as "short on the cash counts . . . [as he was] short of stature." He lived off government revenue, and his books never balanced. Cash would be missing, and some cash receipts never got recorded. Knowing his habits, people labeled him thief, embezzler, cheat, and a variety of other epithets. "Then one day the Auditor came to town. He was just passing through, so this was an unannounced, unscheduled visit. Client Z had made no plans, no preparations for this event. But when the news spread everywhere . . . something stirred within him. He wanted to see the Auditor. *See* Him, mind you. Not talk with or visit with him."

We all know the rest of the story about Client Z. How he and the Guest even did lunch together, and how things changed after the Auditor made His recommendations. Like Zacchaeus, we also need to have our accounts looked at. Our systems of internal control require regular adjustment. Some of our business practices may have strayed far out of line—especially if they have not been recently audited.

Any devoted Christian, high or low, to whom God has committed responsibility should be able to anticipate his or her heavenly audit with joy, not panic. Such is the policy of the company that the Auditor will ultimately examine *everyone's* accounts—and the implications are eternal.

> "THEREFORE, THE KINGDOM OF HEAVEN IS LIKE A KING WHO WANTED TO SETTLE ACCOUNTS WITH HIS SERVANTS."
> MATT. 18:23, NIV.

[*I will not postpone my appointment with You, my Lord. Please examine my accounts today and advise me.*]

*Bienvisa Ladion-Nebres, "The Day the Auditor Came."

THE KINSMAN-REDEEMER

We usually read the story of Ruth and Boaz as a beautiful love story—and it *is* that. Before the love scenes could play themselves out, however, the business of the "kinsman-redeemer" had to be taken care of. And business it was, as laid down in Mosaic law. "If one of your brethren becomes poor, and has sold some of his possession, and if his kinsman-redeemer comes to redeem it, then he may redeem what his brother sold" (Lev. 25:25, NKJV). To redeem means "to buy back, to pay off [a mortgage]." As a blood relative, Boaz brought the matter up in the city gate, offering to make right the misfortunes Naomi's family had suffered and to seal the transaction by marrying Ruth.

"THE REDEEMER WILL COME TO ZION."

ISA. 59:20, NKJV.

The idea of the kinsman-redeemer has always been strong in the East, where our modern law system could never meet the needs of the nomadic desert tribes. Job also applied for this kind of justice. Alone under the influence of the Holy Spirit, he made one of the most thrilling discoveries recorded in the Old Testament. While sitting on the ash heap, the idea slowly grew in his mind. There *ought* to be someone to represent his case before Jehovah, someone to redeem the massive losses he had suffered. Then in a brilliant flash of recognition, Job exclaimed, "I know that my Redeemer lives, and He shall stand at last on the earth" (Job 19:25, NKJV). His kinsman *would* come to right his wrongs! Perhaps not immediately, but certainly later—and Job was content to leave the case with Him. And the arrangement would even include redemption from the power of the grave!

This ancient practice relating to persons and lands illustrates Christ's work. First, as the Son of man, Jesus is our elder brother. He is close to us, near enough to be our kinsman-redeemer. Thus He gives Himself for us "that He might redeem us from every lawless deed" (Titus 2:14, NKJV) and deliver us out of *all* adversity (2 Sam. 4:9). After we've sold ourselves out cheap—for nothing but misery—He redeems us. Finally, He has redeemed our inheritance—the title to Paradise that Adam and Eve lost for us.

[*Father, I'm in over my head with problems and am ready to give my case over to You. I'm sorry I've waited so long.*]

THE RANSOMER

The whole wretched system of kidnapping and taking hostages and then demanding a ransom depends on one unalterable fact. Because we belong to the "chain of humanity," we do not live or die as individuals. We belong to networks of people who *care* about what happens to us. Rarely do we find a person so deprived that there doesn't exist someone somewhere to whom his or her death would make a difference. For this reason, taking hostages and then demanding ransom for their release has succeeded since early times. Bargaining with a human life has profound emotional and material elements that move us deeply.

THE MAN CHRIST JESUS . . . GAVE HIMSELF AS A RANSOM FOR ALL.

1 TIM. 2:6, RSV.

In 1932 the kidnapping and murder of the first child of Charles Lindbergh and his wife, Anne, attracted world attention. It came just five years after the aviator's much-publicized first solo flight across the Atlantic. That celebrated case forecast what has by now become an international pastime: kidnapping and holding hostages in exchange for some political, economic, or military purpose.

Satan is the archterrorist. He has taken our whole planet hostage. In fact, our lives forfeited to him at the moment when Adam and Eve sold out to him in sin. In a single act of deception he disrupted humanity's relationship with their Creator-God. The ransom price for sin was death—to be paid for only with life. When Satan encountered Christ in the Judean wilderness, he tried unsuccessfully to negotiate the terms of the ransom so as to thwart God's plan for freeing the hostages. The plan held. It required both the Incarnation and the Crucifixion to free humanity. Jesus explained this to His disciples when He said that He had not come into the world to be served, but "to give up his life as a ransom for many" (Matt. 20:28, NEB).

It's as if Jesus has walked down the long corridor of the prison house of sin, throwing open all the doors, one cell after another. "Come out!" He cries. "You're free. The ransom payment has been made." Yes, He cared *that* much!

[*Thank You, Lord, for my freedom. Because I need no longer languish in captivity to the evil one, I give my praise to the Redeemer.*]

THE NAVIGATOR

In the main, the Hebrews were herders and farmers. As such, they had a congenital fear of the sea. It became a source of frightening images. Isaiah compared the wicked to "a troubled sea" (Isa. 57:20, NEB). Foreign nations invading Tyre came "as the sea brings up its waves" (Eze. 26:3, NEB). One of the anticipated glories of the new earth, according to John, was the fact that "there was no longer any sea" (Rev. 21:1, NEB). In general, the Bible regards the sea as hostile.

> HE DELIV-ERED THEM FROM THEIR DISTRESS. . . . AND HE BROUGHT THEM TO THEIR DESIRED HAVEN.
>
> PS. 107:28-30, RSV.

The Hebrews, nonetheless, recognized maritime skills—navigation being not the least among them. Lamenting over Tyre, Ezekiel referred frequently to seafaring matters: "Your own wise men, O Tyre, . . . became your pilots" (Eze. 27:8, NKJV). "Your sailors and your helmsmen . . . were flung into the sea on the day of your disaster" (Eze. 27:27, 28, NEB). Assuredly, whenever the helmsman or navigator drowns, all hope aboard a vessel vanishes.

Unique in Israel, Asher was the only tribe involved directly with maritime activities. In Canaan they received the fertile coastal lands below Mount Carmel. Thus they met the skilled Mediterranean merchants of Tyre and Sidon, as well as the rest of the sea peoples (Phoenicians, Philistines, Greeks, and others). Consequently, in the opinion of his fellow tribes, Asher's shrewd trade skills led not only to his affluence but also to a certain self-interested worldliness (Judges 5:17).

Our very lives depend on a reliable navigator. We trust him implicitly to get us from *here* to *there.* An ancient mariner steering his course by the stars. A general studying the map of his battlefield. A copilot reading the radarscope. A computer expert planning the fiscal course of a large corporation. A wife reading the road map while her husband drives. All of them need the skills of navigation. They must know where they want to go, and they have to find the safest and most direct route.

First, we must decide upon our destination. Then, as navigator, Jesus will show us exactly how to get there—provided that we give Him absolute authority to lead us there. Surely, we can undertake no more important journey than that of moving from "distress" here to a "safe haven" there!

[*I'm ready, my God, for the journey I will take with You to Your kingdom. I trust Your travel plans completely.*]

THE PILOT

A flat pancake of an island, Singapore fits like a tidy puzzle piece into the southern tip of the Malay Peninsula. When Sir Thomas Stamford Raffles claimed that swamp of Temasek for the British crown, he named it Singapore, "City of the Lion." Within 175 years it became the fifth-busiest port in the world, and now it is the real "Cinderella of the Orient," with one of the best airports anywhere.

HE AWOKE, AND REBUKED THE WIND AND THE TURBULENT WATERS. THE STORM SUBSIDED AND ALL WAS CALM.

LUKE 8:24, NEB.

A pleasant memory of my childhood, however, is Singapore Harbor, thick with freighters and ocean liners and interspersed with Chinese junks and sampans. Most of the big ships could not anchor at Clifford Pier. Instead, little pilot launches, lively as mosquitoes, ushered arriving ships past the breakwater to a safe harbor mooring. No sea captain, however experienced, would have dreamed of entering the harbor without the guidance of a pilot. Whenever our missionary friends arrived in or departed from Singapore, we would go to see them off, riding out to the ship with them and then returning to land after the "All ashore" call. During those years I learned something about pilots. A pilot is the one who knows the passage to safety, no matter how heavy the harbor traffic.

Matthew, Mark, and Luke all describe one great night storm in considerable detail. (The inland Sea of Galilee, but 13 miles long and 7 wide, has a long track record of sudden violent storms.) No earthly pilot, however excellent, could have saved the disciples, and they panicked. Even though Jesus, their master pilot, was with them in the boat, fear still overwhelmed them. He was asleep—apparently not on duty! "Get up and *do* something!" they cried. When He spoke, the elements calmed instantly. With no effort other than His immense innate power, He saw them through to the eastern shore.

If we have taken Jesus the Pilot into our boat with us, we can withstand any storm. Even at times when He appears not to be paying attention, He is still always there. He not only knows the way to the harbor but also has absolute power to save, whatever the violence of the storms we have to encounter on the way.

> "Jesus, Saviour, pilot me over life's tempestuous sea;
> Unknown waves before me roll, hiding rock and trech'rous shoal;
> Chart and compass come from thee: Jesus, Saviour, pilot me."
> —Edward Hopper

THE ANCHOR

One day on a street in London I had my usual difficulty in passing a woolen shop. Because woolen wear is hardly a necessity for a resident of southern California, I try to resist temptation. This time I failed. I went in and fell in love with a cardigan sweater, cream white with slate-blue anchors all over it. On a blue band around the bottom marched a procession of white seagulls with red feet. My love of the ocean and its creatures overcame me, so the sweater was in my bag when I left the shop— duly paid for, naturally. What occurred to me later was the fact that I had also bought into the anchors, one of the oldest and most beloved symbols in Christianity.

> WE HAVE THIS HOPE AS AN ANCHOR FOR THE SOUL, FIRM AND SECURE.
>
> HEB. 6:19, NIV.

The first anchors (found worldwide) were indented or pierced stones dropped on a rope to secure a ship in shallow water. By the first century A.D., however, anchors had begun to look quite modern, with an iron crossbar, flukes (hooks), and lead weights.

The New Testament, however, mentions the anchor only twice. First we have the dramatic, detailed account of the wreck of the Alexandrian grain ship on which the apostle Paul rode as a passenger. "The sailors tried to abandon ship; they had already lowered the ship's boat, pretending they were going to lay out anchors from the bows" (Acts 27:30, NEB). Through Paul's intervention the Roman soldiers forced the cowardly sailors to remain aboard, and everyone finally arrived safely in Malta.

The allegorical reference to the "anchor of the soul," however, harks back to the seafaring Greeks, for whom the anchor was a symbol of hope. Early Christian art abounds with the anchor, always signifying salvation and hope. It served as a favorite decoration on the tombs of pagans, Christians, and of pagans recently turned Christian. No wonder it became so beloved, speaking as it did of hope in the afterlife.

As the mystical "anchor of the soul," Christ is unrivaled. All of the other material and philosophic anchors we may cast forth to secure our lives will ultimately let go and cause us to shipwreck on some rocky shore. Jesus alone holds us in safety.

> *I've anchored my soul in the haven of rest,*
> *I'll sail the wide seas no more;*
> *Though tempests may sweep o'er the wild stormy deep;*
> *In Jesus I'm safe evermore.*

THE PIONEER

The fragmentation of modern society has given us a renewed interest in our roots. We like to identify those people whose bloodline we share. Some of us trace our ancestry back centuries. Others can barely see past grandpa or great-aunt Sarah. A few of our families emigrated to new lands with distinction. Others arrived as convicts, slaves, indentured servants, stowaways, or soldiers of fortune.

FOR IT IS FITTING THAT HE . . . SHOULD MAKE THE PIONEER OF THEIR SALVATION PERFECT THROUGH SUFFERING.

HEB. 2:10, RSV.

Those pioneers struggled against long-established oppression. After sailing uncharted oceans in frail boats, they carved farms out of forests and crossed boundless wildernesses. They fought unknown enemies and died in massacres, enduring hunger, thirst, and disease. Many buried husbands, wives, parents, or children in unmarked graves and coped with loneliness so intense that it sometimes destroyed the mind and seared the soul. In a word, the pioneers have always shared sacrifice and hardship.

They have passed on to us not merely hard-won material gains, but more important, they set us an example in faith, hope, and incredible strength. It is no accident that the most vigorous nations in the history of the world have been peopled literally with the sons and daughters of the pioneers, with adventure and toughness bred into the very fiber of their culture.

The author of the book of Hebrews was particularly fascinated with the picture of Jesus as "the pioneer of [our] salvation" (Heb. 2:10, RSV) and "the pioneer and perfecter of our faith" (Heb. 12:2, RSV). In this role Jesus suffered all of the hardships of pioneering—but on a celestial scale (verses 2, 3).

Pioneers, however, also enjoy rewards. We tell and retell their stories within the family or on a national scale. Perhaps we erect monuments and celebrate their memory with holidays and public tributes. By patterning our lives after Christ the Pioneer, we become living monuments to Him. Our keeping of the Sabbath day is a tribute to His pioneering work. Our legacy as His spiritual descendants enables us to share His place in heaven. And when we emigrate there, that divine country will not need to be cleared, fought over, or civilized. Jesus has already done all of that for us. He simply asks us now to come and take possession of our inheritance.

[*I am proud to be a child of Christian pioneers. But I am even more proud and secure in being also a child of the pioneer Christ.*]

THE ALMIGHTY

The type of hero we admire is an index to the health and the direction of not only our own lives but also of our entire nation. We have always understood, instinctively, that the virtues inherent in heroism must be exalted, publicized, and recorded. Nothing inspires us more than that independent and courageous human spirit that transforms a man or woman into a hero. The exploits of gods, "demigods," and "larger-than-life" kings and warriors abound in the myths and legends of every culture. They have parallels in the spiritual and moral realm by Christian knights and martyrs, missionaries, and other heroes of faith.

"I AM . . . [THE ONE] WHO IS AND WHO WAS AND WHO IS TO COME, THE ALMIGHTY."

REV. 1:8, NKJV.

Now at the end of the twentieth century, however, changes in values have brought us to such a confusing array of heroes that we are hard pressed to sort out what really motivates our choices. The current roster of American candidates for adulation includes sports heroes, film stars, rock groups, technocrats, politicians (fleetingly), playboy types, millionaires, and even criminals. What this tells us about ourselves is downright embarrassing. Hero worship is not, however, just a teenage infatuation. It is a necessity that follows us through our lives, though, hopefully, we become more selective and bring it under more rational control as we mature. We are programmed to admire someone who is what we cannot be, who has what we cannot have.

From time to time, philosophers have told us that war, not peace, is humanity's natural condition. It, of course, rises from our natural instinct for self-preservation. Therefore, everyone exalts acts of physical bravery. True, Confucianism gave the Orient a special regard for the intellectual, the poet, and the artist. But the tendency in the West has been to celebrate the muscle below the ears rather than what is above the ears. When in danger, however, everyone looks to the brawny fighting man.

One sixteenth-century philosopher's assertion that "might makes right" has not only spawned dictatorships but has also enhanced our faith in raw strength. Knowing our dependency on power, God identified Himself with "might." But He went one step further when He declared Himself as the "All-Mighty." That is, when He exerts His power in our behalf, it will supply *every* type of need—physical, moral, and spiritual.

> I rest, my God, in Your all-encompassing strength and capability.

THE LIBERATOR

The soft greens of tropical plants and grasses now cover the site of the notorious Los Banos Concentration Camp, south of Manila in the Philippines. As if in an effort to dull the last memories of those vicious days of World War II, creepers try to cover what remains of the old Japanese cement bunkers and blend them into the banks lining the trails marking the old roads. Here Americans and Filipinos, missionaries and businessmen alike, shared the privations of imprisonment. They never knew from one day to the next which would be their last, whether from starvation or from the firing squad.

Liberation day began on the morning of February 23, 1945. Enraptured, the internees (most on the brink of extermination) stood outside their barracks to watch General MacArthur's rescue campaign begin. Even today it moves the visitor when he or she stands in the now open field looking toward those hills. Over that rise nine American planes swooped in to drop the first paratroopers into the camp. When they realized what was happening, the prisoners took refuge under their bunks while the Americans and the Japanese fought it out. Then still under fire, the Americans transported them in tanks to the smoking ruins of Manila. The liberation of Los Banos Camp has long since become a legend of valor.

> "I WILL . . . GIVE YOU AS A COVENANT TO THE PEOPLE . . . TO BRING OUT PRISONERS FROM THE PRISON, THOSE WHO SIT IN DARKNESS FROM THE PRISON HOUSE."
>
> ISA 42:6, 7, NKJV.

The prophet Isaiah speaks metaphorically of the hopeless condition of sinners "hidden in prison houses." They are, he says, "trapped in holes, lost to sight in dungeons, carried off as spoil without hope of rescue" (Isa. 42:22, NEB). That is, until their Liberator comes. When the prophet fully grasps the vision, he sees that there *is* One sent to "proclaim liberty to captives and release to those in prison" (Isa. 61:1, NEB).

And the gift of freedom comes not just as a governor's pardon. Nor through the carelessness of a prison guard. And certainly not by the crafty intelligence of a prisoner plotting his own escape. Rather Christ Himself has entered our concentration camp guarded by Satan's minions. He throws open the doors and carries us out to everlasting safety.

> [*I wait for that day when You, the great Liberator, fling open the door to our dark prison house and usher us into Your freedom and light.*]

THE FREEDOM FIGHTER

The freedom fighter is not unknown in Western culture, but currently he survives most spectacularly in the Middle East. We have a steady succession of modern-day zealots who give their lives for their causes in car bombings and other suicidal missions. Their intense patriotism and fearless courage make them unconquerable terrorists. Indeed, when a person has decided to give up his or her life, we can do little to stop him or her. Such warriors are the descendants of those bold rebels known in Jesus' time as the Zealots. In fact, at least one of them, Simon, became a disciple and apparently retained his reputation for zeal throughout his ministry (Luke 6:15; Acts 1:13).

CHRIST SET US FREE, TO BE FREE MEN. STAND FIRM, THEN, AND REFUSE TO BE TIED TO THE YOKE OF SLAVERY AGAIN.

GAL. 5:1, NEB.

With Palestine under Roman rule, Jesus found His ministry surrounded by two groups of fanatics—the Zealots, who were ready to die in the overthrow of the foreign government, and the Pharisees, who eagerly desired the same end but envisioned liberation coming as a result of total obedience to God's law. Young Jews devoted to a mighty cause, the Zealots never hesitated to use intrigue, violence, force, and deception to achieve their political ends. They received inspiration, no doubt, from their forebears Simeon and Levi who had led a murderous expedition against the Shechemites centuries earlier (Gen. 34:4ff).

No opposition, however powerful, nor the prospect of any kind of death, has ever deterred a Zealot. In this respect, Jesus is also just such a freedom fighter. He imprisoned His divine self in the shackles of humanity in order to combat Satan on his own ground. Fascinated by the situation of the prisoners of sin, Zechariah described their being "set free from the waterless pit" and then returned "to the stronghold, [as] . . . prisoners of hope" (Zech. 9:11, 12, NKJV).

In this complete and dramatic portrait of deliverance, Christ changes the whole scene for us. First, He leads us out into the clean, sunny freedom of His mercy. Then He transfers us to the eternal "stronghold" of His love. There we, who were once prisoners of despair and doomed to death, become "prisoners of hope." No other freedom fighter has accomplished as much!

[*I thank You, Lord, not only for delivering me but also for securing my eternal safety afterward. I'm not just on parole, but will never have to serve a sentence again.*]

THE DELIVERER

Arecent film, *Schindler's List,* set before the world
once more the horrors of World War II and the
Holocaust. The viewer returns to the Jewish
ghettos in Poland and then on to the massacre, followed by the loaded boxcars headed off either to the
labor camps or to the gas chambers at Auschwitz. An
enterprising Nazi industrialist, Oskar Schindler, exploits
the chaos to acquire a Jewish workforce to run his factory. A gifted entrepreneur, he becomes so rich that
even the military administration cannot ignore him.
Time goes by, and the rather unprincipled Schindler
evolves into a secret humanitarian. Before the war
ends, he has sacrificed his entire fortune to "buy," literally, the lives of 1,100 factory workers. He reunited old
couples, parents and children, friends and colleagues.
The people he saved had known all too well the groan-
ing of prison life and the appointment they had with
death. In keeping with this mood, the entire picture,
except for a few scenes and the epilogue of the film, is
starkly filmed in black and white. The grayness of despair, the cold murky paleness of oppression, the blackness of impending
gloom—it is all there. Today the "Schindler Jews," the survivors and descen-
dents from the original factory workers, number about 6,000 people.

[THE LORD]
LOOKED
DOWN . . .
TO HEAR
THE GROAN-
ING OF THE
PRISONER,
TO LOOSE
THOSE AP-
POINTED TO
DEATH, TO
DECLARE
THE NAME
OF THE
LORD IN
ZION.

PS. 102:19-21, NKJV.

From the beginning of time untold multitudes have languished in
prison. Not just prisons of the body, but of the mind and the spirit as well.
The panorama of human suffering seems to extend out into infinity. Over
the millennia God has listened to anguished prayers, cries of pain, and ago-
nizing pleas for deliverance. We hear war stories and rejoice for those few
who survive. More often, however, imprisonment leads to its natural (or
rather unnatural) conclusion.

That dark chorus of human grief arising out of the prison house, however, has been heard. God has a plan. He has paid the price for each life,
and He has the power to deliver. We need have no fear should the first
death take us, for our Deliverer has total control over the second death—
and nothing else is required.

[*Whatever should happen to me today, I am determined to look at it from the
eternal point of view. Even my human death would be a secondary concern,
compared with the permanent escape that the great Deliverer provides for me.*]

THE FORTRESS

Modern nuclear warfare being what it is, the fortresses and strongholds of other times are now only picturesque ruins dotting the landscape for romantically minded tourists to photograph.

THE LORD IS MY STRONG-HOLD, MY FORTRESS.

PS. 18:2, NEB.

Primitive castle fortresses were simply hilltops encircled by a ditch and/or an earthen wall. The Norman invaders of Britain introduced the great stone "keeps" surrounded by double stone walls fortified with towers. In the late thirteenth century, King Edward I of England built 17 castles in Wales to consolidate his claim to tribal lands there. The feisty Welshmen, however, took up the "stone arms race" and built their own fortresses. Hence, the green meadows and rocky ranges of Wales display the best in fortress-building.

Because a fortress had to be self-supporting in order to survive a siege, the storming of a castle posed serious challenges. If the invaders survived the arrows, spears, and rocks that rained down upon them from the battlements, they could try several approaches—tunneling under the walls or scaling them with ladders, hurling boulders and fiery missiles over the walls, or using a battering ram to demolish the gate or some vulnerable section of stonework. Getting past one wall, however, usually let the enemy into only the outer court—with a second wall to penetrate. After that, the defenders might *still* hold out indefinitely in the central keep (tower). Ultimately, ancient strategists found that the best way to take a castle was to intercept supplies going in or by poisoning the water supply. God as a fortress has inspired prophets and poets alike for centuries. Affliction invariably drives us to seek the protection of a stronghold. In the midst of his tribulations, Jeremiah cried, "O Lord, my strength and my stronghold, my refuge in the day of trouble" (Jer. 16:19, RSV). Here is the prayer of one forsaken, lonely man to the only God. Centuries later, amid the turbulence of the Reformation, Martin Luther declared:

"A mighty fortress is our God, a bulwark never failing;
Our helper He, amid the flood of mortal ills prevailing."

Our enemy comes at us with catapults and battering rams and may even scale some of our ramparts. He tries to cut off our supplies, both material and spiritual. But God's wholly self-sufficient keep secures us, for He Himself is the heart of the fortress.

[*Thank You, Lord, for the fact that You have equipped me to withstand the strongest siege. I take You to heart.*]

THE WALL OF FIRE

Building a wall is an effective means of self-protection, either domestically or militarily. Our ancient walled fortresses have given way to walled compounds and a variety of security-gated communities. Moreover, we surround ourselves with other less tangible walls—property, investments, family connections, alarm systems, and insurance against all kinds of misfortune. None of them, however, can *fully* protect us.

Fire is unlike any other element. Neither plague nor pestilence can get through it. Not only does it destroy utterly, but it also sucks oxygen out of the air so that those not even touched by the flames may also die. (California's recent progression of drought, earthquakes, firestorms, and floods certainly have given us all a new respect for fire.)

I WILL BE A WALL OF FIRE ROUND HER, SAYS THE LORD, AND A GLORY IN THE MIDST OF HER.

ZECH. 2:5, NEB.

For total coverage for the many evils awaiting us at every turn, we need a "wall of fire." At one point in the Scandinavian epic *The Volsunga Saga* the warrior maiden Brunhild sleeps within a ring of fire. Any suitor wishing to win her would have to ride through the wall of fire. The hero, Sigurd, manages to do so on his magic horse. Walls of fire do afford special kinds of protection, and it takes supernatural power to pass through them.

When Nehemiah had almost completely enclosed Jerusalem—except for the gates—he received a message from his enemy Sanballat to come to "one of the villages in the plain of Ono." Knowing that his enemies "thought to do [him] harm," the great wall builder flatly refused to go (Neh. 6:1, 2, NKJV). The city of Jerusalem would, of course, ultimately outgrow its walls—cities always do. Men, families, and livestock would abandon the ramparts as villages spread themselves out into the open countryside, where there could be no walls. Out there only the presence of God could defend. That's why Jehovah promised to be the flaming wall and the glory of Zion (Isa. 4:5).

Fire also purifies and illuminates. God's invincible position as a "wall of fire" makes Him a veritable powerhouse of spiritual energy. In this capacity He protects us after our human efforts have failed. Sin cannot intrude in His presence. Then to keep the protective fire burning, He will purify our hearts and illuminate our minds.

[*I want always to stay within, not outside of, Your wall of fire. I don't want to spend my energy constantly trying to get out of Your protection.*]

THE CHAMPION

In medieval times a "champion" was far more than a warrior or a winner of the first prize. He was one who "took to the field" (Latin, *campus*) in defense of persons unable to bear arms themselves. One medieval legal document authorized "a woman, a sick man, or a man who has passed the age of 60" to hire a champion. People scorned "mercenary" champions, however, for simply going around the countryside looking for a fight or a lucrative deal.

> "THE LORD IS MY . . . CHAMPION."
> PS. 18:2, NEB.

At his coronation banquet, an English king would have his *campio regis* (king's champion) ride into Westminster Hall, clad in complete armor. Three times the knight would challenge anyone who would dispute the king's right to reign, throwing down his gauntlet and imperiously awaiting a response. Then the king would drink a pledge to his honored champion and present him with the gilt cup. Should a fight ensue, the champion would also be entitled to the armor he wore and the horse he rode (always the second best in the royal stables). This picturesque ceremony last took place in 1820 at the crowning of George IV.

We have many ancient records of two rival armies sitting "in the bleachers," as it were, while two champions did the fighting. Such a practice prevented a general slaughter while thrilling the spectators with games of strength and prowess. When Goliath took the field as champion for the Philistines, Saul had a hard time finding a Hebrew champion to match the fierce giant. With reluctance he finally settled for David—who rejected his king's armor for the confrontation.

As Champion, Jesus has "taken to the field" before the whole world. He stands between the forces of good and evil—but this is neither a ceremony nor a sport. He has bought our sinful human race with His own life, and now He challenges the right of anyone to prevent His taking us into His heavenly kingdom. In such a conflict not one of us could hope to survive. We can only appoint Him our personal champion. Meanwhile, always subversive, Satan cowers in the shadows. Only before God's holy city will he finally take up Christ's challenge—and be destroyed. And that battle will be fought before us all—the saved and the lost.

> The issues are too great, and I am too weak. I give over my struggle to my peerless Champion.

THE WATCHER

Today a number of technological inventions have usurped the traditional work of the watchman. Unquestionably efficient and comprehensive, they include radar, infrared sensors, X-rays, "night vision" viewing devices, electronic burglar devices to protect homes, special telephone numbers for emergencies, steel clubs and alarm systems for our cars. When all is said and done, however, nothing quite takes the place of neighborhood watch groups, in which people accept the responsibility of looking out for one another.

> "NOW WILL I WATCH OVER THEM [ISRAEL] TO BUILD AND TO PLANT."
>
> JER. 31:28, NEB.

One of the most vivid of Isaiah's poetic prophecies is a dramatic interchange among the watchmen of Israel with the seer's own profound reaction to what he beholds in the vision (Isa. 21, 22). It is a song of doom, for Babylon will invade Judah. From the Tigris and Euphrates the enemy comes sweeping across the desert like "whirlwinds in the Negeb." The Lord speaks: "Go, set a watchman, let him announce what he sees" (Isa. 21:6, RSV). In a surrealistic leap in time, we hear another voice: "Upon a watchtower I stand, O Lord, continually by day, and at my post I am stationed whole nights" (verse 8, RSV). As he observes files of horsemen coming, the prophet cries out in alarm. Next comes an agitated mixture of voices from all sides: "Watchman, what of the night? What of the night?" He advises them to wait for the next dispatch. Thus we catch the tension as the voices call from tower to tower across the desert, relaying troop movements.

A watchman sees, interprets, and warns. God Himself marks the watches we must keep in the night of sorrow in which we live. No alarm system we know of can meet such needs. So thorough is the surveillance of the divine Watchman, however, that we will have security and time "to build . . . and to plant." Peace! He has promised it, and He never trades shifts or goes off duty. So, like the ancient watchers on the hills of Zion, we too may look to the eastern sky in hope and not despair.

[*May my ear be always tuned to hear dispatches from Your divine watchtower.*]

THE HORSEMAN

The domestication of the horse entirely changed the character of ancient warfare. In this animal human beings found an intimate and intelligent companion. When the Hyksos invaders introduced the horse and chariot into Egypt's middle kingdom, the event was comparable to the inauguration of the nuclear bomb. Traditionally, owning a horse was the monopoly of kings and lords (peasants made do with asses). David's 100 chariots with Arabian horses (2 Sam. 8:4) and Solomon's 4,000 stalls and 12,000 horses (2 Chron. 9:25) indicated Israel's military strength.

Unquestionably, to sit upon a great horse magnifies anyone's image immensely. When kings and the nobility commissioned artists to make statues or portraits, they favored the equestrian, or horse-mounted, figure. Napoleon, that ego-crazed, would-be world conqueror, had several equestrian portraits made. Certainly, he *needed* to be on a horse, for he was short in stature. Mounted on a handsome, spirited horse, a small man looks a great deal better. A big man seems even more impressive. And a king will, assuredly, appear at his imperial best. Despite our twentieth-century preoccupation with technological warfare, the picture of the horseman is still an immense celebration of life and power, a grand blend of beauty and nobility.

Jesus is the royal rider on the white horse! We have seen Him as the gentle shepherd, as the suffering servant, and as the crucified prisoner. And at His first coming He appeared among us as a helpless baby. Now, triumphant at His second coming, the conquering Christ assumes the role of a magnificent horseman. With the immortal cavalry of heaven He sweeps away all His enemies before Him and shatters the heavens on judgment day.

> THEN I SAW HEAVEN OPENED, AND BE-HOLD, A WHITE HORSE. AND HE WHO SAT ON HIM WAS CALLED FAITHFUL AND TRUE, AND IN RIGHTEOUS-NESS HE JUDGES AND MAKES WAR.
>
> REV. 19:11, NKJV.

[
"Ride on, King Jesus to victory, ride on,
Till Heav'n and earth shall own Thee Lord,
O, conq'ring One, ride on."
]

THE WARRIOR

I happen to be one who neither wishes to hear noise nor to make it. I consistently prize the gentler passages of life that leave us time and space at least to think. Fans yelling at a ball game, crowds screaming at a rock concert, supporters whooping it up at a political rally—all tend to paralyze me. Despite my personal dislikes, however, I must admit that people cheering at a parade, giving a boisterous standing ovation, or rooting for a contestant in the boxing ring must all have a purpose. We note that those who practice the martial arts do a considerable amount of grunting and shouting. Does noise, then, stimulate better performance?

THE LORD GOES FORTH LIKE A MIGHTY MAN, LIKE A MAN OF WAR HE STIRS UP HIS FURY; HE CRIES OUT, HE SHOUTS ALOUD.

ISA. 42:13, RSV.

Beowulf is the epic hero of an eighth-century Anglo-Saxon poem. This Norse hero embodies in his own person the ideals of Germanic culture. Along with his integrity, loyalty, and valor, he does a remarkable amount of boasting to King Hrothgar. He proposes to personally and singly destroy the monster Grendel, who has preyed unremittingly on Denmark. Beowulf's bragging is so loud, incredible, and unceasing that even the reader grows weary. We can only imagine what it was to sit in an ancient mead hall and listen to the blustering warriors exchange heroics.

Such reckless boasting preceded the bloodthirsty cries on the battlefield, and all tended to whip up courage. Having made a loud and large announcement of one's self, of course, would encourage anyone to try hard to stay alive. The adrenaline flow would, hopefully, stimulate bravery. We recall that in the confrontation between Goliath and David (1 Sam. 17:9-11), however, the giant did all the shouting, but the young lad did the killing.

Why does Isaiah give us this rather earthy picture of the Lord going into battle like any other "mighty man of valor"? God's work is not always accomplished by a still small voice. To be sure, His second coming will be something to shout about: "The Lord will soon march forth like a mighty warrior. He will give the battle cry and triumph over His enemies" (Isa. 42:13, Clear Word).

[*Great Captain, help me always to believe in the ultimate victory of Your cause.*]

THE CAPTAIN OF THE HOST

Joshua assumed the leadership of Israel following the long administration of Moses. That tense time of transition and conquest tested Joshua's skills to the limit. Then he had to attack the powerful fortress city of Jericho. The task not only called for keen military prowess but also for the powers of persuasion to convince the erratic, emotional Hebrews that they should cooperate with his plans.

One day as Joshua sized up the city, "a Man stood opposite him with his sword drawn in His hand" (Joshua 5:13, NKJV). "Are You for us or for our adversaries?" Joshua asked.

The Stranger replied, "No, but as Commander of the army of the Lord I have now come" (verse 14, NKJV). Knowing himself to be in the presence of his divine Commander, Joshua immediately fell down and worshiped. Then the Captain gave him a detailed battle plan for the conquest of Jericho.

What are the characteristics of a successful captain? First and foremost, he or she is a leader. A captain should know how to manage people, how to build morale, and how to secure cooperation. Second, a captain should be a talented strategist and organizer chosen for such abilities. Third, a captain should display above-average courage and willingly take risks. Finally, being a captain entails certain status privileges. The position has heavy responsibilities to those above him or her as well as to those below.

Captains carry badges of rank and authority. Making complex plans and implementing them, they report to their superiors and see to the welfare of those enlisted below them. Their courage and ability ensure victory.

In assigning the rank of captain to Himself, Jesus touches upon an enormous human need. The warfare with evil permits no neutrality. Whoever is not on Jesus' side is automatically against Him (Matt. 12:30). Those who survive into eternity will be those who submit to the will of their heavenly Captain, as Jesus submitted to His Father.

Jesus has not failed us in any of the requirements of captaincy. Therefore, our place is to fall down and worship Him, even as Joshua did before the walls of Jericho.

GOD HIMSELF IS WITH US FOR OUR CAPTAIN. . . . O CHILDREN OF ISRAEL, FIGHT YE NOT AGAINST THE LORD GOD OF YOUR FATHERS.

2 CHRON. 13:12.

[*O divine Commander, let me never fail to be Your faithful soldier.*]

THE SWORD

Our continual need for weapons is one of sin's major legacies—with but one result: destruction and death. When used offensively, they vanquish our enemies. But when employed defensively, they protect us. Fighting and weaponry have been with us from the time when Cain dealt his brother the first death blow to our present dilemma over the management of the nuclear warheads we have stockpiled. The idea of fighting and killing is so embedded in our consciousness that youngsters are busy at cops-and-robbers games and space wars almost before they learn to walk.

Although now obsolete as a combat weapon, the sword has an ancient and honorable history. It is a personal instrument, effective only in hand-to-hand combat. Therefore, the skill and courage required for its use could distinguish an individual—and even make him a hero. Every aristocratic lad in the Age of Chivalry dreamed of owning his sword and of learning the art of swordplay—attack and defense.

No one has brought sword culture to a finer point than the Japanese. Their weapons have been works of art ever since the time of the shoguns. Ancient Japanese religion taught them absolute loyalty to their nation and to the emperor. Under their code of chivalry, each samurai (warrior class) wore two swords—a long one with which to fight, and a short one they could also use to commit harakiri (honorable suicide) in case of defeat or dishonor. For the knights of Christian chivalry, on the other hand, the blade and guard of each sword formed the shape of the cross.

The similarity in modern English between *sword* and *word* is more than accidental. The Word of God as a two-edged sword has always been a double metaphor deeply ingrained into the consciousness of the Christian church. Just as a sword physically hacks through "joints and marrow," so our obligations to Christ, the living sword, can "pierce the spirit" and probe the heart. In so doing, though His Word may wound us, it also defends and liberates.

FOR THE WORD OF GOD IS LIVING AND ACTIVE, SHARPER THAN ANY TWO-EDGED SWORD, PIERCING TO THE DIVISION OF SOUL AND SPIRIT, OF JOINTS AND MARROW, AND DISCERNING THE THOUGHTS AND INTENTIONS OF THE HEART.

HEB. 4:12, RSV.

[*Lord, give me the knowledge and spirit to wield Your word with telling power.*]

THE ARCHER

One day, amid the crowds surging through Tokyo's Harujuku train station, I saw four young girls carrying large bows, much taller than themselves. Dressed in smart school uniforms, they were off to practice *Kyudo,* the traditional Japanese style of archery. More than six and a half feet high and crafted from wood and bamboo, the bows require arrows a yard long—quite a challenge for teenagers.

HE MADE ME A POLISHED ARROW, IN HIS QUIVER HE HID ME AWAY.

ISA. 49:2, RSV.

Such classical training in archery has been handed down from the days of the shoguns (warlords), when it was used ceremonially and as a competitive sport. The demanding practices of Zen meditation have made *Kyudo* a spiritual discipline. The archer literally "thinks" the arrow to the target (up to 200 feet [60 meters] distant). As the Western world learned in World War II, the Japanese soldier can be terrifying in his single-mindedness and overpowering in his drive to conquer. His practice with his weapons has its roots in the powerful concentration of mind required by Zen Buddhism. Thus the man and his bow, sword, gun—whatever it is—are bonded into a lethal unit. Add to this his devotion to his country and fearless attitude toward death, and you have an irresistibly effective fighting man.

Predating even the sword, archery was effective for hunting wild animals and equally useful for disposing of one's enemies. (A rain of arrows— particularly those with poisoned heads—was bound to hit something.) It enjoyed a long and successful battle history (especially in England) simply because soldiers cannot accomplish certain things just through hand-to-hand combat.

Archery called up a familiar and dramatic picture. One of the psalmists used the metaphor of archery as a symbol of the extending of life. Anciently, parents considered their future to lie in their children: "Like arrows in the hand of a fighting man are the sons of a man's youth. Happy is the man who has his quiver full of them" (Ps. 127:4, 5, NEB). Isaiah made the more profound application when he saw himself as a "polished arrow" hidden in God's quiver. He stood ready for use in any of the Lord's battles. Likewise, in the conflict between good and evil every Christian also becomes an efficient weapon in the arsenal of God, swift and sharp in the hand of the divine Bowman.

> [Lord, give me such love and devotion to You
> that I may be a swift arrow in Your hands.]

THE SHIELD

Ancient literature abounds in descriptions of the weapons of prominent warriors, often individualized with their own proper names. An indispensable and versatile piece of armor, the shield was carried on the arm and swung into position to shelter whatever part of the body was most vulnerable. At first shields consisted of wood covered with leather. The elaborate account of the shield of Achilles, however, in *The Iliad* (ninth century B.C.) indicates that the Greeks had mastered the art of fine metal craft.

BUT YOU, O LORD, ARE A SHIELD FOR ME.
PS. 3:3, NKJV.

In feudal Europe, when strange knights in full armor showed up at a castle looking for hospitality, they could identify and defend themselves by the insignia on their shields. Those colorful shields of the past have now become obsolete—except for the fact that in heraldry most coats-of-arms appear emblazoned upon shields. The shields employed by riot police today, however, lack the romance and artistry of other times. Functional, yes, but not impressive—especially when one recalls the grand aspirations and religious fervor of the Crusaders going off to the Holy Land proudly wearing the cross of Christ on their shields.

Shields held a significant place in the history of Israel. Skill in their handling ranked with the other martial arts of swordsmanship and archery. In his roster of "mighty men," Jeremiah spoke of the Ethiopians and Libyans as being particularly adept in the use of the shield (Jer. 46:9, NKJV). Shields hung in armories as trophies of victory, the tower of David being adorned with 1,000 of them (S. of Sol. 4:4). Solomon ordered 200 large shields and 300 small shields of solid gold (1 Kings 10:16, 17). Later, however, after the king of Egypt stole them, Rehoboam had to replace them with brass shields—a commentary on the decline of the kingdom (1 Kings 14:26, 27).

Scripture elevates the shield from the battlefield to the higher plane of spiritual meaning. The point is that we use the shield exclusively for self-defense. Therefore, when God repeatedly presents Himself as the shield of His people, He makes a very simple statement. He is available to each individual *separately,* providing protection according to the personal need of every believer. In bearing this shield into our battles, we, like modern Crusaders, proclaim our identity and our allegiance. With confidence we display His insignia.

> *Great God, help me ever to make*
> *Your truth my shield and buckler.*

THE AX

Homer's epic hero Odysseus returned home after 20 years away at the Trojan War. He found his house full of suitors attempting to woo his wife and thereby seize his kingdom, the island of Ithaca. The climax of his homecoming is the "Contest With the Great Bow" during the evening feast hour. Disguised as a beggar, the wily Odysseus suggests that each man aspiring to wife and kingdom pass a test. He has a line of perforated axheads set up, and each suitor is to take the mighty bow of Odysseus himself and shoot an arrow through the socket ring of all 12 iron axheads. Failure will result in the men renouncing all hopes of marriage (to anyone) and in their being evicted from the kingdom. The terms are too stiff, and all the suitors decline.

Then they stare in horror as Odysseus himself picks up the huge bow with practiced familiarity. "He drew the string and grooved butt of the arrow, aiming from where he sat upon the stool. Now flashed arrow from twanging bow clean as a whistle through every socket ring, and grazed not one."* Thus Odysseus reclaims his own throne and summarily destroys his rivals.

The ax was first an instrument of test and later of retribution. Scripture describes the ax as a weapon of war—and a primitive one it is (Jer. 51:20). Also, it is an implement for felling trees and trimming timber. Isaiah saw the Lord of hosts able to "lop [off] the boughs with terrifying power" and "cut down the thickets of the forest with an axe" to make way for the coming of the Messiah (Isa. 10:33, 34, RSV). John the Baptist at the Jordan River applied the same imagery to Jesus, who was about to appear among the people. Christ would destroy the old system. He would lay the ax to the root of every unprofitable tree (Matt. 3:10).

The use of the ax requires enormous power. A fitting picture of final (sometimes even brutal) judgment, it sets the record straight as no other weapon can do—whether flailing over the open battlefield or hacking at the roots of living trees.

> **"EVEN NOW THE AXE IS LAID TO THE ROOT OF THE TREES; EVERY TREE THEREFORE THAT DOES NOT BEAR GOOD FRUIT IS CUT DOWN AND THROWN INTO THE FIRE."**
>
> MATT. 3:10, RSV.

[*God, I accept the hewing of the ax as a necessary part of Your cosmic plan. I pray only to pass the test of fruitfulness.*]

*Homer, *The Odyssey*, book 21.

THE REFUGEE

When David cried "With thee, O Lord, I have sought shelter, let me never be put to shame" (Ps. 31:1, NEB), he pointed out our painful need for shelter—both physical *and* emotional. First, we instinctively want to live and not die. Second, we want to do both with honor and respectability. We need places of refuge for at least three important reasons. Sorrow is always with us. Also, because we are sinners in a sinful world, guilt always accuses us. Then adversaries surround us. Although they may not destroy us outright, they misunderstand and hurt us continually.

Interestingly, God Himself commanded Joshua to build the cities of refuge, and then He gave specific instructions as to their use (Joshua 20:9). The laws of Deuteronomy also outline the function of the cities, their strategic placement, and their role in the administration of justice (Deut. 19:1-13). They served any person in the country, foreign or local (Num. 35:5-15). The cities were not, however, intended for career criminals. Rather they served the large number of persons who daily made tragic mistakes.

Perhaps the only counterparts we have had since then to Israel's cities of refuge were the medieval monasteries and abbeys. Or the old Spanish missions of western America. Such places of solitude provided shelter for broken people who needed not only to recover life and health but also to find again their sense of self-worth.

Israel's six refuge cities were simply a material demonstration of what Jesus as a refuge can do for us. He guarantees our emotional safety. And even though death may interrupt our physical security, it is but an interlude before we arrive at eternity and stand at the gates of the ultimate city of refuge.

> THESE SIX CITIES SHALL BE FOR REFUGE FOR THE PEOPLE OF ISRAEL, AND FOR THE STRANGER AND FOR THE SOJOURNER AMONG THEM.
>
> NUM. 35:15, RSV.

[*"Hide me, O my Saviour, hide, Till the storm of life is past."*]

THE CAPTOR

A young man I know recently had a chastening experience. He came from a well-to-do professional family. His father, however, had an extremely independent turn of mind. For his entire life, apparently, he'd ignored parking tickets. Since he was a busy man, he felt it acceptable to leave his car wherever it best suited his purposes and ignored any police opinion to the contrary. In the large city where they live, however, the purveyors of parking tickets had lately decided to put teeth into their traffic regulations. Influenced by the fact that his father had gotten away with it so long, the son paid no attention to his parking citations—until he'd amassed a bill of nearly $600.

THE LORD IS AMONG THEM. . . . YOU HAVE ASCENDED ON HIGH. YOU HAVE LED CAPTIVITY CAPTIVE.

PS. 68:17, 18, NKJV.

Suddenly, at work in the office where he was employed, the police came and arrested him. They just walked in, handcuffed him, and took him to jail. Embarrassed and mortified beyond speech, he spent the night and the next day in captivity. He loves to read—but now he had no books. Although he has a passion for music—no music. And he enjoys his friends—but no friends were with him in jail. No one, of course, has since dared make sport of his time in jail—but he now pays attention to where he parks his car.

To be in captivity, even for a minor offence, is traumatic. The pain thrusts deep into the human psyche. Perhaps that's why so many children's games involve hiding, seeking, capturing—and escaping. Even ball games have an element of restraint and imprisonment about them.

For centuries captives taken in war have automatically become slaves. But the agony goes beyond physical abuse. The emotional and mental anguish leaves a mark for life. The triumphal arches built throughout the Roman Empire reflect for all time the military victories of the generals. They cut a grand figure sweeping through these specially prepared archways in their chariots, trailing strings of humiliated captives in chains. Knowing the anguish of such processions, proud soldiers have sometimes chosen suicide in preference to being taken prisoners of war.

The chains, solitary confinement, starvation, beatings—even the death sentence—Jesus has it all in hand. Just as He will say to death "Thou shalt die," so He will "take captivity captive." He will remove that blot from the universe.

[*Make me captive, Lord, and then I shall be free.*]

THE BANNER

J ust a piece of cloth hanging from a pole? No, much more than that. A flag has deep emotional meanings. Banners, ensigns, and standards have begun and ended wars. They identify military divisions and armies and signal messages. At first they were not fabric embossed with an emblem. Instead, they were images of animals, birds, or the brightly painted figures of gods carried at the forefront of battle or attached to the prows or masts of fighting ships.

Although it originated in Babylon and Egypt, Israel picked up the proud tradition of banners and standards upon their way to Canaan. The Exodus was, to all intents and purposes, a military campaign. Moses gives a detailed picture of the organization of Israel in the desert. "Everyone of the children of Israel shall camp by his own standard, beside the emblems of his father's house" (Num. 2:2, NKJV).

HE WILL LIFT UP A BANNER TO THE NATIONS FROM AFAR, AND WILL WHISTLE TO THEM FROM THE END OF THE EARTH.

ISA. 5:26, NKJV

An "ensign" was a rallying point for people, usually placed in some conspicuous high point. Here was something on which they could focus their hopes. After his victory over Amalek, Moses built an altar of thanksgiving and named it *Jehovah Nisi*—"The-Lord-Is-My Banner" (Ex. 17:15, NKJV). This type of standard includes the fiery bronze serpent that Moses raised to be the rallying point of salvation and healing for Israel (Num. 21:8, 9).

The psalmist speaks of the Lord's enemies who also "set up their banners for signs" (Ps. 74:4, NKJV). Christ's hearers were always looking for little "signs." The Pharisees said, "Master, we should like you to show us a sign." Jesus rebuked them. They'd have nothing but "the sign of the prophet Jonah"—and *that* referred to Himself (Matt. 12:38-41, NEB).

Christ is not just a minimal sign. He's the banner itself, the central rallying point. He's the one who draws humanity out of destruction and leads it to victory. Christian soldiers are called to enlist under His standard, to march to war against the powers of evil.

> "Brightly gleams our banner, pointing to the sky,
> Waving wand'rers onward, to their home on high;
> Journ'ying o'er the desert, gladly thus we pray,
> And with hearts united, take our heav'nward way."
> —Thomas J. Potter*

*Thomas J. Potter, "Our Banner," *Christ in Song*, No. 657.

THE EPIDEMIOLOGIST

Epidemiology is a relatively new specialty in medicine. Its scientists investigate the causes of epidemic diseases and seek to control them. As a result, practitioners of preventive medicine today have a great deal of advice to offer the public about healthful living. Whereas the ancients attributed their sufferings to the vengeance of discontented gods, modern science now has comprehensive new insights into the nature and genetic implications of germs, viruses, plague, and the like.

WASH AWAY ALL MY GUILT AND CLEANSE ME FROM MY SIN.

PS. 51:2, NEB.

Simple cleanliness turns out to be one of the prime requisites for good health, one that fortunately we crave instinctively. A baby wants a clean diaper. A toddler enjoys playing in the mud, but will usually submit to a bath and the cozy comfort of clean pajamas at bedtime. No matter how dirty and disorderly the task before us, as soon as we complete it we head for the shower. Commerce trades on this basic desire of ours and spends billions of dollars annually advertising soap to us.

We would not, of course, dream of criticizing the trend toward cleanliness—it is too important for health and for social respectability. The sad fact is, however, that ever since the coming of sin, we have had a hard time keeping things clean. We scrub our clothes, but not our religion. It quickly gathers the stains of superstition. We sterilize every utensil in the house, but selfishness tarnishes our relationships with our neighbors. Although we scour our floors, our basic philosophy of life remains polluted. While we may wash our windows, we let our integrity and our high ideals get corrupted. And though we bathe ourselves and shampoo our hair, the thoughts of our hearts may still be filthy.

Longing to be clean and well again, King David emerged from the affair with Bathsheba intensely aware that the disease of sin caused his symptoms of guilt. "Though you wash yourself with lye and use much soap," a later biblical writer lamented, "the stain of your guilt is still before me" (Jer. 2:22, RSV). God has, however, been practicing epidemiology ever since the disease of sin broke out in the Garden of Eden. The blood of His own Son is the *only* agent that can cleanse our habits, thoughts, and intentions.

> *"Wash me thoroughly from mine iniquity, and cleanse me from my sin" (Ps. 51:2).*

THE GREAT PHYSICIAN: HEALER OF SICKNESS

Physicians earn their title from the Greek *physike*, meaning "nature." Ideally, they are supposed to restore people to the sound minds and bodies the Lord designed for the Garden of Eden—or something close. Now, however, we are so far from Edenic health that we begin to wonder if anyone remembers what perfect health feels like.

The other day I visited an old friend in a nursing home. Amid the wheelchairs in the lobby and the listless patients with vacant faces, I glimpsed a poster:

"I think today's going to be a good day.
I woke up this morning and nothing new hurt."

More and more, as time goes by, we need a doctor on call to help us cope with our failing bodily functions.

JESUS WENT THROUGHOUT GALILEE, TEACHING . . . AND HEALING EVERY DISEASE AND SICKNESS AMONG THE PEOPLE.
MATT. 4:23, NIV.

The practice of medicine, however, has not always been the prestigious occupation that it is today. King Asa of Judah came down with some malady in his feet, perhaps gangrene. After his marvelous victories over the Ethiopians and Libyans, he should have known better, but he "sought help from physicians" instead of the Lord (2 Chron. 16:12, RSV). Three years later he died. His mistake lay not in seeking medical advice, but in trusting to the local "quacks"—physicians who practiced magic instead of the healing arts derived from an understanding of God's laws.

Despite the corruption and evil reputation of much "medicine," Jesus presented Himself as the Great Physician. He spent the largest proportion of His time healing the sick rather than either teaching or preaching. Since medical practice as we know it was still in its infancy, the needs were enormous. The throngs of invalid people had no hope of a cure and no prospect even for the partial relief of pain. Jesus' practice, however, was to go far beyond "primary care." That's always the way with Him—we get so much more than we ask for. We *want* to be included.

Jesus' qualifications as a physician we may divide into at least seven specialties—all of them having surprisingly contemporary descriptions.

> *"Pass me not, O gentle Savior,*
> *Hear my humble cry;*
> *While on others Thou art calling,*
> *Do not pass me by."*

THE GREAT PHYSICIAN:
THE FAMILY PRACTITIONER

A story tells about an ambitious young medical resident who returned to his home for a visit. He called upon the town doctor to tell him of the wonders of the great city hospital where he worked. "And did you say you are specializing in ENT [ear, nose, and throat]?" the hometown doctor inquired.

"Oh, no!" The youth regarded the simple old man with superiority. "Only the nose, sir."

"I see. And may I ask," the general practitioner replied stiffly, "have you yet decided which nostril it will be?"

> "THE BLIND RECEIVE SIGHT, THE LAME WALK, THOSE WHO HAVE LEPROSY ARE CURED, THE DEAF HEAR."
>
> MATT. 11:5, NIV.

The humble hometown doctor who used to live among us is now virtually extinct. Family doctors delivered successive generations of babies and made house calls, sometimes daily. (Nowadays it is expedient to become ill only during office hours.) They would tramp through a blizzard to sit with a patient at midnight and see him or her through "the crisis." Making friends with their patients, they knew families intimately and often listened to their troubles. People expected family doctors to know everything about everything, for they had no specialist within reach to whom to refer difficult cases. Saving some and losing some, family doctors simply did their best until the day when they wore out and passed their practice on to some bright young person who had a sense of self-sacrifice and a vision for helping the world.

Recently family practice as a "specialty" has again become a viable alternative for new doctors wishing more breadth of experience than a narrow field offers. In fact, I had a young physician tell me the other day that relieving some poor sufferer of the pain of an ingrown toenail gave her as much satisfaction as performing complicated brain surgery could do—and probably more.

As the greatest General Practitioner, Jesus never needs to refer a case to anyone else. No hurt exists that He cannot heal, no bleeding that He cannot staunch, no sickness that He cannot diagnose and cure. One touch from Him heals any possible disease of the soul. Like His faithful human counterpart, who held most of the town's secrets in confidence, Jesus is also ready to hear about our every problem.

[*O loving Healer, help us to trust in*
Your healing, however severe our pain.]

THE GREAT PHYSICIAN: PREVENTION

Since the time Moses relayed God's health laws to Israel, people have probably never had a keener interest in healthful living than they do today. Schools of public health and government health agencies multiply without number. Determined smokers find fewer and fewer places to do so. The highway patrol has determined how much drinking is too much for the road. Red flags appear on every side in the world of diet. Scientific research, the popular press, and television keep health concerns constantly before us. They are preaching much "good news" to the "poor"—poor addicts of every variety. In a surge toward whole and healthful living preventive medicine has finally come of age. The old adage "Prevention is better than cure" makes sense *wherever* you apply it. The vision of "making people whole" has become a significant part of medical practice.

> "THE GOOD NEWS IS PREACHED TO THE POOR."
>
> MATT. 11:5, NIV.

Many of the fathers of the early Christian church, however, devalued the human body as an instrument of sin, an encumbrance to shake off as soon as possible. But they were wrong. Christ Himself regarded His human body as a temple, worthy of all the dignities accorded a holy place (John 2:21). Paul inquired of the immoral Corinthians: "Do you not know that your body is the temple of the Holy Spirit who is in you?" (1 Cor. 6:19, NKJV).

Jesus is the ultimate practitioner of preventive medicine. Creator of the human mind and body, He has written the maintenance manual for preserving both in optimum condition. He has given us but one body in which to live. While we cannot stop age, accident, and death, much illness *can* be prevented. Even though the body can sustain a remarkable amount of abuse, the earlier we follow our Physician's practical prescription—sunlight, water, fresh air, good diet, and exercise—the better.

To these five physical habits, however, we must add a sixth. Without it, complete healing is not possible. The greatest specialist in preventive medicine, Jesus insists that we have trust in divine power. Such faith not only enables us to practice the other five components of "wholeness" but it also consecrates the body temple. And that is the *rest* of the good news.

[*Dear Jesus, make me always conscious of my sacred duty toward my body temple.*]

THE GREAT PHYSICIAN: THE SURGEON

Modern surgery has advanced to such great heights that even the patient about to undergo it can understand little of what is to be done. We have acquired enormous faith, however, in the efficacy of surgery. Many people, when they face some mysterious internal affliction, are likely to say, "Well, can't you just cut it out and let me get on with my life?"

COME, LET US RETURN TO THE LORD. HE HAS TORN US TO PIECES BUT HE WILL HEAL US; HE HAS INJURED US BUT HE WILL BIND UP OUR WOUNDS.

HOSEA 6:1, NIV.

Such an attitude has given rise to dark tales of busy, knife-happy doctors who annually do millions of dollars of unnecessary cutting. Nonetheless, the most honest in the profession will be the first to admit that the best any doctor can do is set up the most favorable conditions he or she can. Ultimately the cure takes place as the body heals itself. And that, of course, is in God's department—though He gets little enough credit for the wonderful power inherent in our bodies. Christian surgeons are the first to testify that their hands seem literally to become the hands of God as they do their work.

At the other end of the spectrum are those who for religious or whatever reasons refuse to consult a doctor because they declare that God will heal them. So they remain disabled, continue in suffering, or die of their disease while they wait for a miracle.

Still, no matter how often you have been there, facing surgery never really becomes a commonplace event. With all the help we now have from drugs and anesthesia, it astounds us how patients faced surgery in ancient times. Many, of course, self-administered their anesthetic by going into shock from the pain. And often they died.

Living in those times of the most primitive forms of surgery, Hosea was still able to envision God as a kindly surgeon. The "injury" and the act of being "torn in pieces" was the essential prelude to healing. Then, the prophet assures us, the divine Surgeon stands by to "bind up the wounds" and to "heal." Today not even the most celebrated surgeon of them all could expect to accomplish more than that.

[*Father, help me to trust You still, despite Your wounding. We wait until You see fit to heal us by Your power.*]

THE GREAT PHYSICIAN:
THE CARDIAC SURGEON

Some of us still remember clearly what happened on December 3, 1967. That day world news services carried the story of Dr. Christiaan Barnard, in South Africa, performing the first heart transplant operation. We all know that hearts wear out, but the idea of a transplant hit the public imagination like a meteor. Instantly elevated to stardom, Dr. Barnard enjoyed the adulation usually reserved for football players and film personalities. The fact that his 55-year-old patient lived only 18 days did not tarnish the glamour much. A month later he did it again—and that time the patient lived for more than 18 months. We had arrived in a brave new world!

> A NEW HEART I WILL GIVE YOU, . . . AND I WILL TAKE OUT OF YOUR FLESH THE HEART OF STONE AND GIVE YOU A HEART OF FLESH.
>
> EZE. 36:26, RSV.

Now, some 25 years later, heart transplants are commonplace. We have become accustomed to the whole idea of transferring organs from one body to another. Or, failing that, some animal may have something to offer us. And while the patient waits, medical science might provide him or her with a mechanical device to function until an organ becomes available. Although the possibility of rejection of the transplanted organ always lurks in the shadows, drugs have been fine-tuned to the point where even that difficulty can usually be overcome. Certainly we do clever things in the line of heart surgery.

In His role as a heart surgeon, however, Christ deals not merely with defective organs. He works on fossilized hearts. They are dead, turned to stone. While none of us would deliberately *choose* heart disease, the cases with which Christ works are self-inflicted and terminal. According to Zechariah, disobedient Israel deliberately "made their hearts like flint" (Zech. 7:12, NKJV). Transplanting a heart from another defective person would cure nothing. Jesus has to repeat the process of creation, melting the stony heart back into flesh. Only regular appointments with the Surgeon will prevent our hearts from reverting back to stone.

> *"Create a pure heart in me, O God, and give me a new and steadfast spirit"* (Ps. 51:10, NEB).

THE GREAT PHYSICIAN: HEALER OF THE MIND

Any doctor who does not take into account the powerful relationship between mind and body should turn in his or her credentials. The bond between the two is amazingly strong. The mind of the hypochondriac can create physical disease. An overpowering "death wish" can kill as certainly—if not as rapidly—as a plane crash. On the other hand, long unrelieved pain can break the spirit of even the most courageous person. As a terminal illness draws to its close, the often unremitting suffering can cause such a personality change that it turns a loved one into a total stranger.

HE HEALS THE BROKEN-HEARTED AND BINDS UP THEIR WOUNDS.

PS. 147:3, NIV.

While we have long spoken of "my doctor," nowadays we are equally likely to refer to "my psychiatrist" or "my therapist." Health of the body is linked with the health of the mind.

The psychologist Abraham Maslow theorized that human needs differ in urgency. As each one gets satisfied, a higher one emerges and dominates. Our supply of food, water, and air, along with our safety, takes precedence over everything else. We all know that it requires only moderate pain or a degree or two of fever to make us totally lose interest in work or recreation. When we are in health, however, we "wear" our bodies lightly. Something as simple as a bruised toe or a torn fingernail, however, can intrude itself into even our loftiest enterprises.

Christ's frequent miracles, then, were not simply to arouse the interest and increase the faith. He intended them to bring people to a degree of health that would enable them to be open to the truths of the kingdom. At this point our Great Physician steps in to make the patient "whole."

In treating the broken heart as well as the wounded body, Jesus has made some specific recommendations. Confessing sin in order to be free of guilt, we pray for one another to escape the blight of selfishness (James 5:16). We love because "perfect love casts out fear" (1 John 4:18, NKJV). Thus the Healer of the mind preserves us from that ultimate death that will finally destroy *both* body and spirit.

> [*"Restore unto me the joy of thy salvation; and uphold me with thy free spirit"* (Ps. 51:12).]

THE PHYSIOTHERAPIST

After recent back surgery I fell into the hands (literally) of the physical therapists. When the surgeon has done his best, and when you have taken as many drugs as you care to risk, you turn to physical medicine. And you count yourself fortunate to find those who still believe in hydrotherapy and therapeutic massage. They speak of swimming and walking, diathermy and diet, steam baths and such.

O LORD, . . .
I AM WEAK;
HEAL ME,
MY VERY
BONES ARE
SHAKEN.

PS. 6:2, NEB.

Your presurgical MRI gave you a lot of bad news. Therefore, knowing that you really have no other option, you adjust your mind to achieve the rest of your healing by means of these slow and simple methods. Nonetheless, if you are one of those all-systems-go "A type" personalities, you find yourself faced with real difficulty in cooperating with your therapist—easy as the task would appear to be. You spend hours lying prone on the table, being stretched and pulled about at odd angles. Often the pain is pure torture. "Relax . . . Just relax! . . . Push down . . . One-two-three-four-five . . . Relax." The voice of the long-suffering treatment giver begins to sound like a disembodied recorded message.

Truly, you do *try.* "Relax. Just let go and let *me* do it." Just when you think you have done it, however, your muscles tense up again. "Don't help me, or I can't make the treatment work. It won't do any good."

Sometimes it takes us a long time to reach that point of spiritual pain at which we willingly turn ourselves over to Jesus the Physiotherapist. Trying everything else first, we hope for an awesome surgical procedure or some miraculous drug. Something that will cure us today—if not yesterday, then today. We're always in a hurry.

Our Physical Therapist, however, waits for us patiently. He promises nothing instantaneous. It is going to be the work of weeks, months—and years, perhaps. God knows that we will inherently resist Him, so we hear His gentle voice: "Relax. Just let Me do it. Relax."

You would be surprised how relaxing such *hard* work can be—indeed, a long learning process. Only by submitting to the Therapist's treatment, however, can we find healing and freedom from pain.

[*Help me this day, my Creator, to let go. Let me rest in the knowledge that You will choose the most effective treatment for my pain.*]

THE GREAT PHYSICIAN:
THE HEALER OF DEATH

Death is the ultimate disease over which no physician has power. Medical science can only postpone it or make the passing easier. Theoretically, for the Christian death is *not* the worst possible circumstance.

If by desire, effort, and prayer any of us could keep alive those we love, we would, no doubt, be surrounded by crowds of sick, wretched old people who were hundreds of years old. The thought is appalling! The philosophers of many times and places have understood that immortality on human terms would be nothing but a terrible curse. Many have told their doctor or friends, "If I had known I was going to live this long, I would have taken better care of myself."

HE WILL SWALLOW UP DEATH FOREVER. THE SOVEREIGN LORD WILL WIPE AWAY THE TEARS FROM ALL FACES.

ISA. 25:8, NIV.

Moreover, today's medical skills keep many patients alive far beyond what they could wish. Consequently, euthanasia has become a major ethical issue. Jesus, though, would have us see that death, horrible as it is, still offers the believer a precious gift. It spares us from much suffering. It lets us sleep in His arms, safe from all harm and heartache. But that is not all. Oh, no! Our Great Physician, in addition to everything else, heals death itself. He vanquishes the last enemy. For Him the cure is not complicated. And when He gives us immortality at His advent, He combines with it eternal youth and health. We will have not only eternal life, but eternal youth and health.

The poet portrayed the joyous destiny awaiting each one of us who accept Jesus' gift of salvation.

> "Death, be not proud, though some have called thee
> Mighty and dreadful, for thou art not so. . . .
> One short sleep past, we wake eternally,
> And Death shall be no more: Death, thou shalt die!"
> —John Donne (1633)

THE BALM IN GILEAD

The word "balm" derives from "balsam" plants and refers to the fragrant oily or sticky gum that trickles out of certain trees when you make a cut in the bark. Although we know that ancient medicinal remedies must have had herbal origins, Scripture actually mentions very few of them. The balm of Gilead seems to have been one of the most prized and was an item of trade among Arab and Phoenician merchants. It reputedly healed wounds and cured stomach disorders. Josephus, the Jewish historian, says that King Solomon grew the balm of Gilead tree from seeds brought to him by the queen of Sheba. He is supposed to have planted them in his gardens at Jericho.

The rolling hills and rich pasturelands of the tribe of Gad were proverbial for health and prosperity. Their beautiful land lent itself to some of the loveliest spiritual imagery in the Bible. "Gilead is mine," God said (Ps. 60:7). To the royal house of Judah He paid the compliment: "You are as Gilead to me" (Jer. 22:6, RSV). Most important, it became the home of the balm that every sick person craved.

The plaintive question haunts us: Is there no balm, even in Gilead, "to heal the sin-sick soul?" Like the discouraged, chronically ill patient, many have mourned, confessed, and resolved. But they fall again—until they are without hope. Indeed, they didn't really expect a change anyway.

Hope, then, is one of the first things doctors need to cultivate in their patients. If the physician fails to do so, despair will undermine all other treatments. Thus it is that some people die long before their time, while others—with all of the odds against them—live far beyond anyone's expectations. Those with hope can sometimes defy even the most dismal prognosis medicine can give them.

Jesus is the Balm of Gilead, always available and accessible. He is well known in the marketplace, to be sure. Many people, knowing of His infinite value, imagine that the price must be beyond their reach. Still, He pleads, "I am here. Freely. Why do you still suffer when there *is* hope?"

> IS THERE NO BALM IN GILEAD, IS THERE NO PHYSICIAN THERE? WHY THEN IS THERE NO RECOVERY FOR THE HEALTH OF THE DAUGHTER OF MY PEOPLE?
>
> JER. 8:22, NKJV.

[*O Balm of Gilead, help me never to doubt Your healing power.*]

THE EYESALVE

One Saturday night in a back alley of Taipei I accompanied friends to observe some Chinese folk medicine. At the Snake Restaurant we found a large menu of snake steaks and soups available. Out front two young men were at work opening crates of deadly poisonous serpents. After breaking the reptiles' necks across the edge of the table, they would hang the wriggling creatures on a ceiling hook and slit their bodies from neck to tail. From each snake's surprisingly prominent gallbladder they would drain off the bile, pour it into glasses, add a little wine, and offer it to the spectators—a guaranteed cure for eye trouble.

"SO I ADVISE YOU TO BUY FROM ME . . . OINTMENT FOR YOUR EYES SO THAT YOU MAY SEE."

REV. 3:18, NEB.

A stranger standing next to me bought a small glass for a large price. As he drank the loathsome brew, I could hear him swallowing repeatedly just to keep it down. "See?" the snake doctor said to us, reasonably enough, "you are all wearing glasses. Buy, drink, and become well!" Unprofitable clients that we were, we declined and moved on.

Today medical science can correct many eye problems. We have worn glasses and then contact lenses. Now radial keratotomy and laser surgery can correct our eyesight almost to perfection. Glaucoma can be treated. Surgeons can remove cataracts. For most of us, blindness seems an unlikely and remote possibility.

Until quite recently, however, it was a continual threat. The Bible world teemed with blind beggars. They were victims of punishment and disease. Also, age took its toll. Little medication other than the usual eyesalve was available, and that relieved only the superficial troubles.

Society celebrated blind poets and blind musicians, however. Supposedly, those cut off from physical distraction could allow their spirits to soar. But Christ made a specialty of opening the eyes of the blind, always connecting the physical healing with deliverance from ignorance and spiritual blindness.

When the heavenly Eye Specialist tells us to buy eyesalve, He intends to treat both physical and spiritual blindness. We do well to follow His prescriptions precisely.

[*Lord of the Light, open the eyes of my soul that I may see Your way.*]

THE POULTICE

Europe made a painful discovery during the Crusades. It discovered that the Muslims were centuries ahead of the West in mathematics, astronomy, and medicine. Moreover, the Muslim diet, dress, and standard of living made the Frankish strongholds look like harsh, bleak prisons— which they were. Defending their honor, the Crusaders fiercely defamed their foes on every issue. (As we know, when one's argument is weak, one tends to shout louder.)

Usamah Ibn Muniqidh (A.D. 1095-1190), a friend of the great Saladin, was revolted by the coarseness of the Franks and their deplorable medical practices. In *Kitab al-I'tibar* (Book of Reflections) he describes the visit that a Muslim physician made to the Christian camp. Among the patients he saw a knight with a large abscess on his leg. His services accepted, the Arab applied a simple poultice, and in a few days the festering sore started to heal over.

> HE SPAT ON THE GROUND AND MADE A PASTE WITH THE SPITTLE; HE SPREAD IT ON THE MAN'S EYES.
>
> JOHN 9:6, NEB.

Then the Frankish doctor arrived "Do you let a heathen touch a Christian?" he shouted. "This man knows nothing about treating him." He turned to the terrified patient. "Which would you prefer, living with one leg or dying with two?"

"To live with one leg," the knight whispered.

"Bring me a strong knight and a sharp ax," the doctor ordered. They laid the patient's leg on a block of wood. "Now strike it off with one blow." The physician stood back.

The first blow only partially severed the leg. But with the second, Usamah tells us, "the marrow of the leg flowed out and the patient died on the spot."

Sorrowfully the Arab physician went his way, mystified at the violence and perverseness of the Christians.

A poultice was the recommended treatment for King Hezekiah's deadly lesion, and Christ also used it in healing at least one blind man.

In treating spiritual ailments, our Great Physician may choose gentle remedies (such as the poultice) to do His work as painlessly as possible. Drawing us close to Himself, He tries to help us drain all the infection of sin out of our lives. The slow, quiet power of a poultice is irresistible.

[
"Purge me with hyssop, and I shall be clean:
wash me, and I shall be whiter than snow" (Ps. 51:7).
]

THE MAKER

"YOUR MAKER IS . . . THE LORD ALMIGHTY."

ISA. 54:5, NIV.

Some time ago I paid an afternoon visit to a rather affluent friend whom I had not seen for several years. Sitting in her airy, spacious home and facing the beach with the turquoise-blue Caribbean beyond, I wondered what it would really be like to "have everything." As we chatted, however, I noticed a large playpen in the corner of the patio. Her two children having outgrown it, the pen was filled to overflowing with toys. Seemingly it contained everything ever invented to tempt parents. But were the little boys playing with them? No. Squatting out in the driveway, they were utterly absorbed in building their own world with sticks, rocks, and gravel.

It made me think about how life today is steadily robbing us of one of our most precious legacies—that of "making" things. With each new technological breakthrough, more and more people lose a little more of their creative potential. Time was that if you wanted to hear music, you probably had to make it yourself. If you wanted to put a picture on the wall, you either painted it yourself or worked and saved enough money to pay an artist to do it. Someone has defined football as a game played by 11 people who desperately need rest and watched by 50,000 people who desperately need exercise. Television is creative only for the actors and producers. The viewers usually degenerate into lethargic spectators, or, to use a common term, "couch potatoes."

God must have looked down to the end of the twentieth century and seen what we've done to ourselves. Therefore, He set before us this vivid, sharp image of Himself as *maker*. He would like to share His creative vigor with each of His children. True, some old women still make quilts and a few grandfathers still turn wood. But almost everyone else pushes themselves to distraction by driving cars, "hanging out," or watching other people do things.

Modeling Himself as a maker, however, God opens the wonderful door of craftsmanship for us. His business is making saints out of sinners, and that activity, in turn, should motivate us to be makers. He would have us *make* a difference in our world; *make* peace, not war; *make* beauty, not ugliness; *make* confidence, not fear.

> *"My Maker and my King,*
> *To Thee my all I owe."*

THE BUILDER

While Christ's accusers could comprehend the "destruction of the Temple" in only the most literal and ludicrous terms, we should consider exactly what Jesus' master plan for building is. When the Jews returned from exile, their rebuilding project fell into three phases: the Temple, the walls, and the houses—strictly in that order.

1. *The Temple.* As Ezra supervised the restoration of the Temple services, he offered the exiled Hebrews two special opportunities. Vertically, they found the lifeline to their God. Horizontally, they could relate peacefully to one another. Although the slogan "All human beings are equal" is a fine democratic concept, history has shown it to be a somewhat unrealistic ideal. Too many variables shape our lives. Actually, we have true equality only at the hour of physical birth and then at death. In between we are equal only when we stand together before God in worship.

2. *The walls.* Although modern military warfare has made walled cities obsolete, walls still serve important purposes. They keep conflicts *out.* There is only one proper way to pass through a wall—that is to go through the gate built for that purpose. (More than likely, guards will oversee it.) Walls also protect and keep good things *in.* Finally, walls are also a point of decision-making. One can sit there, consider both sides of a problem, and then come down on either side.

3. *The houses.* The private houses of the people came last. While we might well have reversed the order, God plans otherwise. Had house building come first, the people would have had nothing to equalize and unify them. They might well have spent their energies worrying about who had the biggest house and the best land—and greed would have been difficult to curb. As it was, the land-allotment came in a peaceful manner *after* the establishment of the Temple services and the building of the walls (Neh. 11; 12).

When God the builder goes to work, it pays to notice the order in which He proceeds through His master plan for creating in us His holy character.

> TWO [FALSE WITNESSES] CAME FORWARD AND DECLARED, "THIS FELLOW SAID, 'I AM ABLE TO DESTROY THE TEMPLE OF GOD AND REBUILD IT IN THREE DAYS.'"
>
> MATT. 26:61, NIV.

[*Master Builder, may I never forget that I am Your building and that my foundation is Christ my Lord.*]

THE REMODELER

The other day a friend and I had occasion to stay in a bed-and-breakfast in Ouray, Colorado. The little town with its hot spring sits in the bottom of a valley with breathtaking mountain scenery above and all around. No wonder it has become a popular (and therefore, expensive) resort. I was curious to see how the more rare bed-and-breakfasts in America compare to those homey, creative lodgings one finds everywhere in England and Ireland.

The Victorian Rose delighted me. Pressed securely up against the cliffs, it offered a charming guest suite. Our hosts were a newly married couple who had re-modeled a plain boxy little house and extended it into a gracious Victorian home, complete with tower. They showed us pictures and also the books and magazines they had studied to reproduce the proper period decor. It pleased them to find us as interested as we were in what they had done. And breakfast in the morning was in the same spirit—color-matched place settings and a delicious cooked meal.

Some people, of course, want brand-new houses filled with designer furniture—nothing but the latest! Others, like our friends in Ouray, dearly love an old house. They thrive on the challenge of taking a 100-year-old house, healing its wounds, strengthening its weaknesses, and loving it back into cozy homelikeness. After they fill it with antiques, suddenly it's mellow with memories. To be sure, remodeling homes has become a national pastime. Even in a relatively new house a bathroom, the kitchen, or something needs to be redone. Maybe for no other reason than the fact that we don't like the wallpaper our predecessor left behind. Always from our viewpoint it could be *better*.

God shares our passion for remodeling. Doing it since the beginning of time, He Himself prepared the guidebook for such work. He's done some amazing renovations—you have seen some of them yourself. You might be thinking of cooperating with Him on such a project. It might involve a room or two, or it might call for working over the entire house, expanding the space, installing new windows, repairing old furnishings—whatever.

> **"I, THE LORD, HAVE REBUILT THE RUINED PLACES, AND REPLANTED THAT WHICH WAS DESOLATE."**
>
> EZE. 36:36, RSV.

[*Father, I marvel at the remodeling work I have seen You do. I have some restoration work that needs doing in my life, and I ask Your help.*]

THE DRAFTSMAN

When teaching in Jamaica, I despaired of ever getting Jocie through freshman English. She was a lovely girl in every way, except that she simply couldn't cope with academic affairs. Meanwhile, Jocie dressed almost all of the girls at college. Evidence of her expert designing and sewing appeared all over campus. I've never seen a more skilled seamstress. You could show her a picture of what you wanted, draw an awkward sketch, or tell her "sort of like this but you figure it out." Promptly she'd be back with a garment exactly right for you. She had an utterly uncanny sense of design. As far as I know, Jocie never finished college. Last I heard, she'd gone home to Costa Rica and opened a highly successful dress shop. Good for her!

Drafting patterns for clothing, blueprints for buildings, plans for city improvements—all of them are highly demanding efforts. Even using computers for design does not diminish the necessary skill of the draftsman. Indeed, it may well be more rigorous than the old chalk, ruler, and compass method. Our world consists of three kinds of people. The gifted few, the draftsmen who make the patterns. Then the many people who can read, understand, and create whatever object the pattern is designed to produce. Finally, another crowd who can't or won't follow a model. They're the ones who will read the directions only after they've tried everything else.

The apostle Paul adopted the picture of "God the draftsman" to make a bold statement about God and also about himself. First, God has drafted the pattern for salvation—He and His Son worked it out "from the foundation of the world," attending to every detail. Those who will follow the model explicitly can acquire a life fit for heaven. Then Paul said what only a courageous, confident Christian could. He invited us to look at *him*. "He [God] wanted to display His mercy through me, the worst of sinners, as an example to others so they, too, would see God's great love, accept the Lord Jesus Christ and receive eternal life" (1 Tim. 1:16, Clear Word).

> FOR THIS REASON I OBTAINED MERCY, THAT IN ME FIRST JESUS CHRIST MIGHT SHOW [ME] ALL LONG-SUFFERING, AS A PATTERN TO THOSE WHO ARE GOING TO BELIEVE ON HIM FOR EVER LASTING LIFE.
>
> 1 TIM. 1:16, NKJV

[*My Designer of Life, I thank You for setting the pattern so clearly before me. Help me to clarify the guidelines to others around me.*]

THE CARPENTER

As a youngster growing up in Singapore, I used to watch carpenters at work. I had my own private reasons for lingering about the sawdust pits. My thick, dull-brown hair hadn't the least suggestion of a curl in it. Because of the equatorial heat, my mother bobbed it extremely short. Nonetheless, I dreamed, hopelessly, of long, wavy tresses, the color of shimmering spun gold. The idea so obsessed me that I would go wherever on the school compound the carpenters were at work. As the long curly shavings peeled off under their planes, I would pick them up and pin them into my hair—convinced, if only temporarily, of my loveliness. Even today (for entirely different reasons) I revel in the scent of wood shavings, the smoke of a wood fire, the smooth perfection of a fine wood carving, and the polish of a piece of well-crafted furniture.

"IS THIS NOT THE CARPENTER, THE SON OF MARY . . .?" AND THEY [THE CITIZENS OF NAZARETH] WERE OFFENDED AT HIM.

MARK 6:3, NKJV.

"I wish I had been His apprentice,
To see Him each morning at seven,
As He tossed His gray tunic about Him,
The Master of earth and of Heaven.
When He lifted the lid of His work-chest,
And opened His carpenter's kit,
And looked at His chisels and augers,
And took the bright tools out of it;
When He gazed at the rising sun tinting
The dew on the opening flowers,
And He smiled at the thought of His Father
Whose love floods this fair world of ours;
Then fastened the apron about Him,
And put on His workingman's cap,
And grasped the smooth haft of His hammer
To give the bent woodwork a tap,
Saying, 'Lad, let us finish this ox yoke,
The farmer must finish his crop.'
Oh, I wish I had been His apprentice
And worked in the Nazareth shop."—*Author Unknown**

[*O Master, may I be Your faithful*
apprentice to help You rebuild lives.]

---

* "In the Carpenter Shop," in Cynthia P. Maus, *Christ and the Fine Arts* (New York: Harper Brothers, 1950), pp. 255, 256.

THE NAIL

I have long had a fascination with Jael, that bold desert woman who killed Sisera, commander of the army from Hazor. Judges 4 gives a prose account of the conflict between Israel and Jabin, king of Canaan. Judges 5 elaborates the same story in poetry. We shall not discuss whether she enticed Sisera into her tent or not. That is another issue. What interests me is the way she drove that nail home.

> I WILL FASTEN HIM AS A NAIL IN A SURE PLACE.
>
> ISA. 22:23.

I don't handle tools well. Indeed, my overall mechanical abilities border on retardation. Yes, I can (with effort) hammer in a nail. If left to my own management, however, the nail may or may not be in "a sure place." But think of Jael. She has fed the mighty soldier and given him a place to rest. Then she takes a tent peg and a hammer and drives "the peg into his temple, till it went down into the ground" (Judges 4:21, RSV). (Pardon the details of this gory story, but they're important.) Sisera, of course, didn't just lie there and die. He apparently tried to struggle to his feet—more than once. As she crushed his head, "he sank, he fell, he lay still at her feet" (Judges 5:27, RSV). Jael had to get it right the first time, for she would never have a second chance. Such a thing would have challenged a strong man. Alone, this remarkable woman accomplished the task with equal strength and skill.

Isaiah's prophecy continues the symbol of the nail. At the human level the symbol suggests the duties and authority of a prime minister—one who will eventually be removed. "I will fasten him firmly in place like a peg. On him shall hang all the weight of the family, down to the lowest dregs" (Isa. 22:23, 24, NEB). The picture has a more extended application, however, as it foreshadows Jesus' work in the carpenter's shop of Nazareth. You can imagine Him handling the wood—bronzed, muscled, and bare-armed, driving the nails home, probably with a single blow.

A nail either holds things together or exhibits an item hung up for display. Those are its two basic functions. Seldom do I get a nail into a "sure place." But Jesus has an unfailing stroke. He drives it home permanently.

> *Dear Lord, make me a nail upon the wall to hold a picture of Your face.*

THE NARROW GATE

Recently I had occasion to go on a concert tour with the New England Youth Ensemble and Chorale in China—a China that has not yet fully recovered from its former restrictions. The greatest inconvenience was airport departure. Our group visa required that all 95 of us line up in alphabetical order and pass through narrow gateways into small already-crowded rooms, barely one person wide. But we had to go through with all of our luggage and the musical instruments. The officials would sit placidly surveying the chaotic scene—a seething mass of people and bags interspersed with lumpy cellos, fat tympani, the tuba, and the double basses raising their heads like dinosaurs above the confusion. We almost couldn't get through the narrow gates.

Passing through narrow gates is all a matter of how much luggage we carry. Whatever travel adviser said "Take half the clothes and twice the money you planned on" was absolutely correct. I have a colleague who takes his favorite pillow with him when he goes on long journeys. He distrusts most hotel pillows. Although at times circumstances force him to leave his pillow behind, by and large it works out. Taking his pillow, of course, forces him to leave other things behind. Most of us carry too much luggage anyway.

> "ENTER BY THE NARROW GATE. THE GATE IS WIDE THAT LEADS TO PERDITION . . . AND MANY GO THAT WAY; BUT THE GATE THAT LEADS TO LIFE IS SMALL AND THE ROAD IS NARROW, AND THOSE WHO FIND IT ARE FEW."
>
> MATT. 7:13, 14, NEB.

As we consider the narrow gate, we begin to realize that we can't take with us the pillows that spare us the more uncomfortable realities of life. We're going to have to leave behind our amassed material treasures and the self-importance of credentials, certificates, and professions. The opening is so narrow that we have no room to carry through it selfishness, greed, craving for fame, or any such trivia. We need to repack with lighter and less bulky items—compassion, generosity, faith, humility. The matter requires much thought and effort, for Jesus says, "Many, I tell you, will try to enter and will not be able to" (Luke 13:24, NIV).

Not only have we been carrying too much luggage; we have been packing the wrong things.

[*Keeper of the Narrow Gate, I want to repack the luggage of my life. Help me choose only those things that I can carry through to the end of my journey.*]

THE DOOR

A visit to central California should prompt the curious-minded to visit the Winchester Mystery House in San Jose. It is the fantastic creation of Sarah Winchester, heiress of the inventor of the Winchester rifle. Obsessed with the occult, she "communicated" with the ghosts of those killed by the "gun that won the West." Because they told her that if she kept building on the house she would not die, she spent her fortune of $20 million on the Victorian monstrosity. For 38 years the sound of the workmen pounding did not cease day or night. The result of her neurotic enterprise was a bizarre conglomeration of 160 rooms set in six acres of gardens. It featured staircases ascending into blank walls, windows set in the floor, a chimney stopping 18 inches short of the ceiling, upside-down posts, and doors opening into nothing. Vast effort also went into modern heating and sewer systems, gas lights, and elevators— to say nothing of 47 fireplaces, Tiffany glass windows, inlaid parquet floors, and gold-and-silver chandeliers. Finally, of course, Sarah Winchester *did* die—in 1922 at age 82.

> **"I AM THE DOOR. IF ANYONE ENTERS BY ME, HE WILL BE SAVED."**
>
> JOHN 10:9, NKJV.

A door opening into nothing? Madness, to be sure! Doors must go somewhere. Presuming the existence of an "inside" and an "outside," the door is such a simple, homely metaphor. It may be as weak as a fiber curtain or iron strong and able to withstand a battering ram. The door may offer access to a cottage or palace, a fortress or torture chamber, a church or a royal treasury. We may open it by a simple latch that a child can lift, or it may be bolted and barred. A door may stand open to all comers, or it may lock away mysterious secrets to be revealed only by the correct key.

Jesus called Himself the door in the setting of His being the "door of the sheepfold." Thus He allegorically secures the safety and privileges of the sheep. He stands guard against the threat of thieves and false shepherds. When Paul and Barnabas "opened the *door of faith* to the Gentiles" (Acts 14:27, NIV), they exemplified Jesus' divine purpose as the door. Christians, though, should beware of opening Winchester-type doors that lead nowhere.

> *Master, who knows how I should go, I'm glad that You are the Way.*

THE MASON

While masonry is something quite beyond my ability, I am a great admirer of artistic stone and brickwork—a tidy wall with ivy trailing over the top of it, brick planters in a flower garden, a gateway with low, curved block walls ushering the visitor in. I once watched an Indian mason build just such an entranceway. Immaculately clad in an ironed and creased sports shirt and not perspiring, even in the fierce heat, he squatted at his task, executing an excellent piece of work. He never moved once from his position except to go for his siesta. Two bedraggled little women carried the sand and gravel on their heads for his use. They mixed the mortar and placed the cement blocks within his easy reach. Any tool he needed, one of them put into his hand at just the right moment. Almost he seemed to be a nonparticipant in the very work he was doing. Quite a lordly affair, the whole thing. The result, however, was a handsome, single-colored pair of walls.

> COME, AND LET YOUR-SELVES BE BUILT, AS LIVING STONES, INTO A SPIRITUAL TEMPLE.
>
> 1 PETER 2:5, NEB.

Christ the Mason has something else in mind, I believe.

During our years in the Philippines we took vacations in Baguio. A few old mission bungalows remained available to us as an escape from the unrelenting Manila heat. Cool mountain air, poinsettias growing wild in massive hedges, tall whispering pines—where else should we go for Christmas? Each house had a dull, smoky-gray fireplace made of hundreds of more-or-less egg-sized stones. One year, having found a number of paint cans out in the shed and having long evenings to spend together, my family and I painted all the stones, each one a different color. The smooth surfaces took our multicolored efforts nicely. We were pleased, especially the children. Some of our friends said, "Great!" The more conservative said, "What!"

Nonetheless, our rustic Baguio fireplace is more like the model Christ had in mind. Moreover, He is actively involved in every part of the work. So we come, no two of us alike, all with different abilities, backgrounds—and colors. Some smooth, some rough. He invites us to let ourselves "be built" into His temple as "living stones."

> *Father, You have a master plan for Your spiritual temple. I would have You fit me into the place that You see is right for me.*

THE FOUNDATION

Probably nowhere else in the world can you stand on a firmer foundation than in the Forbidden City in Beijing, China. Today anyone and everyone can wander freely through the grounds, looking at the golden throne room, bedrooms, stately halls, and all the rest. The huge palace has lost some of its glamour, because today few nations can maintain such a level of extravagance. Still, enough remains to recall the former glory. Yet, like other royalty, the emperors found themselves driven by fear. They took a special precaution. Under the spacious courtyards with their marble porches and staircases, the emperor ordered 19 thick layers of foundation laid. As far as we know, no one ever tried to enter the palace by tunneling in under the walls—it would have been futile.

NO OTHER FOUNDATION CAN ANYONE LAY THAN THAT WHICH IS LAID, WHICH IS JESUS CHRIST.

1 COR. 3:11, RSV.

The necessity of a strong foundation is elementary knowledge in any culture. Jesus' parable about the house built on bedrock as opposed to the one on the sand was a tale of the obvious—a lesson even the most backward could grasp (Matt. 7:24-27). Several ancient peoples took further precautions. They sought to strengthen their building projects by the addition of human sacrifices. A ruthlessly ambitious emperor of the Chin dynasty had certain artists and philosophers sealed up in the Great Wall of China so that their spirits might increase the impregnability of the fortification. Babylonian records show that human sacrifices sometimes accompanied the laying of a foundation.

Perhaps the story of Hiel's rebuilding of Jericho is a reference to such a loathsome practice. Joshua had specifically cursed whoever would try to restore the fallen city (Joshua 6:26). When Hiel did it, "laying its foundations cost him his eldest son Abiram, and the setting up of its gates cost him Segub his youngest son" (1 Kings 16:34, NEB). Some scholars dismiss both deaths as "accidents," but others feel that Hiel sacrificed the boys to ensure the success of his project. That is possible, considering that the event occurred during the evil days of Ahab.

[*Dear Father, how strongly You have built Your church. I rejoice to think of it enduring all the way into eternity.*]

THE REJECTED CORNERSTONE

In earliest times builders used the "cornerstone" to join two walls. They tied the courses of long stones in walls, the joints filled with smaller stones, at the corner by the cornerstone. Although the foundation stones we now see are merely ornamental, in ancient times the survival of any kind of stone building depended on the quality of its cornerstones. In the same connection, David entreated God for beautiful daughters "as corner stones, polished after the similitude of a palace" (Ps. 144:12). In Palestine, however, people did not use much cut (quarried) stone until Solomon built the Temple and King Ahab constructed his palace in Samaria—the two foremost architectural achievements of early Israel. (Solomon's remaining foundation stones may still be seen today at the base of Jerusalem's Wailing Wall.)

> THE STONE WHICH THE BUILDERS OF THE TEMPLE REJECTED AS WORTHLESS WAS THE VERY STONE NEEDED AS THE CORNER-STONE.
>
> PS. 118:22, CLEAR WORD.

Jesus applied the psalmist's picture of the "rejected stone" to Himself. Uneasily, the Jews knew the story of the rejected stone to be historical. "When the temple of Solomon was erected, the immense stones for the walls and the foundation were entirely prepared at the quarry; after they were brought to the place of building, not an instrument was to be used upon them; the workmen had only to place them in position. For use in the foundation, one stone of unusual size and peculiar shape had been brought; but the workmen could find no place for it, and would not accept it. It was an annoyance to them as it lay unused in their way. Long it remained a rejected stone. But when the builders came to the laying of the corner, they searched for a long time to find a stone of sufficient size and strength, and of the proper shape, to take that particular place, and bear the great weight which would rest upon it. . . . Several stones had at different times been chosen, but under the pressure of immense weights they had crumbled to pieces." Only when the builders went back to the rejected stone that had withstood years of weather did they discover it to be an exact fit in the essential position of cornerstone.*

We do well to look about ourselves and see if we have overlooked something vital to our life-building.

> [*Lord, I lay my building plans before You. Help me make the best choices of materials to put into my life.*]

*Ellen G. White, *The Desire of Ages* (Mountain View: Pacific Press Pub. Assn., 1940), pp. 597, 598.

THE CAPSTONE

God the Builder-Creator once inquired of Job: "Where were you when I created the world? If you know so much, tell me about it. Who stretched the measuring line over the globe and decided how large it should be? . . . What does the earth rest on? Who laid its cornerstone . . .?" (Job 38:4-6, Clear Word). Many other prophets picked up this familiar cornerstone imagery to point to the work of the Messiah. As we've seen, Jesus applied it to Himself directly. "What then is this that is written: 'The stone which the builders rejected has become the chief cornerstone'?"(Luke 20:17, NKJV). Mark adds: "Haven't you noticed what the Scriptures say in the psalm that we sing as a hymn of thanksgiving? 'The stone which the Temple builders rejected is the stone needed to support the corner'" (Mark 12:10, Clear Word).

"THE STONE THE BUILDERS REJECTED HAS BECOME THE CAPSTONE."

MATT. 21:42, NIV.

While most translations give Matthew's text as "cornerstone," several modern renderings use the word "capstone"—which gives yet another dimension to our metaphor drawn from architecture. Masons use a capstone to finish the top of a wall. Laid in a series along the top, it protects the joints of the stones. It may also crown the top of a tower or other structure.

Zechariah was one prophet fascinated with building operations. After the Babylonian captivity (in which Israel, as a nation, had been nothing but a despised "stone"), he describes Zerubbabel taking charge of rebuilding Israel's sacred house, the Temple, in Jerusalem. No longer could anyone despise "the day of small things" (Zech. 4:10, NKJV). The laying of the last stone called for celebration. "He [Zerubbabel] shall bring forth the capstone with shouts of 'Grace, grace to it!'" (verse 7, NKJV). Later the same prophet celebrated the supremacy of the royal tribe in a series of curious metaphors: "From Judah will come the cornerstone, from him the tent peg, from him the battle bow, from him every ruler" (Zech. 10:4, NIV). While the last two pictures refer to political power, the cornerstone and tent peg guarantee the security of strong foundations.

The existence and support of the kingdom of God depends on Christ. As the Cornerstone, He sustains. As the Capstone, He is the finishing touch, the supreme glory of the church.

[*Lord of the kingdom, I would be a citizen, a dweller, in Your spiritual house.*]

THE BONDING STONE

In the hands of the apostles, the familiar image of the cornerstone acquires new meanings. Standing with John before the Sanhedrin, Peter, filled with the Holy Spirit, laid the blame precisely where it belonged: "The stone you builders rejected . . . has become the capstone. Salvation is found in no one else" (Acts 4:11, NIV).

To the Ephesians, Paul presented Christ as the capstone, without which the wall would be incomplete and weak. The Jewish authorities rejected Him as Messiah-cornerstone. Yet only He could unite Jews and Gentiles in one vast and glorious spiritual building—the Christian church.

When Christian believers come to Christ the Cornerstone as to the "living stone," laid in Zion, they themselves become "living stones" to be built up in "a spiritual house." They find Jesus to be "elect, precious." Referring to the disobedient, however, both Peter and Paul again echo Isaiah when he declares that Jesus becomes not just "a stone of stumbling," but a great "rock of offense" (1 Peter 2:4-8, NKJV; Rom. 9:33; Isa. 8:14).

Jesus' life reflects the cornerstone in three ways. First, He was quarried and chiseled for His part in the plan of salvation. The events of His human life prepared Him for the Saviour He was to become. Second, those who could find no use for Him in their blueprints rejected Him. And they were the very ones who prided themselves on "building God's temple on earth." Third, Christ is to be honored as the foundation of God's church on earth. His Father will set the petty builders aside to ensure the triumph of His Son. This recovery of the rejected stone also emphasizes how God's grace may come as a surprise to humble people—rejected people. When they believe in Him they find themselves elevated to amazing responsibilities.

Finally, as Redeemer and Judge, Jesus fits both pictures—the foundation-cornerstone and the capstone.

> [YOU ARE] BUILT ON THE FOUNDATION OF THE APOSTLES AND PROPHETS, WITH CHRIST JESUS HIMSELF AS THE CHIEF CORNERSTONE. IN HIM THE WHOLE BUILDING IS JOINED TOGETHER AND RISES TO BECOME A HOLY TEMPLE IN THE LORD.
> EPH. 2:20, 21, NIV.

[*Heavenly Architect, I will study Your blueprint for my life. Preserve me from letting pride blind me to Your purposes in my life.*]

THE STUMBLING BLOCK

In the developing countries you change your driving habits. Cars are but a fraction of the traffic on the roadways—mostly it is people, bicycles, donkeys and carts, chickens and goats, mats of drying rice, piles of gravel, lumpy baskets of produce, and broken-down trucks undergoing repair. And should you be in India, you'll find any number of sacred cows taking their ease in the middle of the busiest intersections. You have to be able to gauge distances by the thickness of paint on your own vehicle to come through this unscathed. So you drive cautiously, possibly at no more than a walking pace. Difficult as such conditions may appear, you find surprisingly few road accidents.

"BEHOLD I AM LAYING IN ZION A STONE THAT WILL MAKE MEN STUMBLE, A ROCK THAT WILL MAKE THEM FALL."
ROM. 9:33, RSV.

Americans, on the other hand, are accustomed to thousands of miles of open, high-speed freeways—excellent driving conditions. No one expects to find anyone or anything extraneous on the road. Consequently, when the unexpected takes place, few people are ready for it—and accidents are lethal. In a car or out of it, accidents face us every day—the crash, the headlong fall downstairs, the loss of balance, the skid on the wet sidewalk, the stumbling over a heretofore invisible rock on the path. In some way or another we've all had to face such accidents. They halt us in midflight, as it were.

Paul points out an unusual idea. God deliberately places a rock in our way to cause us to stumble. In his letter to the Corinthians, he specifies that that Rock is Jesus. "We preach Christ crucified, a stumbling-block to Jews and folly to Gentiles" (1 Cor. 1:23, RSV). Most of us are traveling too fast. We don't keep alert to the unexpected and may scarcely be reading the signs as we catapult down the freeway. In order to prevent our taking a wrong turn God puts up a "stumbling block." It may well cause an accident, and then we'll have to stop and rethink our priorities. Or we might swerve and miss the roadblock and continue on our headlong journey to damnation. Even so, God's intention is clear. In this light, then, we should be able to thank Him for the hardships that come our way. Time to slow down and think again!

[*Father, I travel a dangerous road and am going too fast. If need be, break me on the Rock You have set in my path so that I may be saved.*]

THE LADDER

From the beginning of time human beings have searched for ways to reach heaven, to be "at home" with God. Lacking any realistic knowledge of the nature of the universe, the tower builders of Babel thought to ascend to heaven brick by brick. In destroying their scheme, the Builder of the solar system must have smiled a little at their naivete.

A LADDER WAS SET UP ON THE EARTH, AND ITS TOP REACHED TO HEAVEN.

GEN. 28:12, NKJV.

Jacob's heaven-inspired dream of the ladder, however, did demonstrate a practical way by which humanity could reach God. Many of us, no doubt, have childhood memories of a picture in one of our Bible story books showing Jacob lying in the dark foreground, head on a stone, and beyond a brilliant ladder filled with angels. While the homeless man remained rooted to earth there at Bethel, the angels, like so many silver butterflies, fluttered about the ladder. Not that they, with their great feathery wings, *needed* a ladder! They seemed to be just waiting for the man to wake up and begin climbing. Each of them wanted to show him how to do it. At the top, in a blaze of light, waited the Lord Himself with a promise for Jacob's well-being.

The mystical ladder, which is Christ Himself, is what links us to the divine. Heaven and earth touch in two places—the horizon of the past and the horizon of the future. How, then, may we link ourselves with heaven in the present? For this we need Jacob's ladder. Three things bring it into our possession and set it firmly down in our lives:

1. God's daily providence supplies the necessary connection.
2. Jesus mediates in our behalf, a firm link between us and God.
3. Our own desire for spiritual things helps us value the ladder.

One must climb a ladder single file. Other people will be above and some below, but we have no room for a companion alongside us. That is, we must follow through with our decision to ascend the ladder entirely on our own, but the ascent brings us to a glorious destination at the top!

[*O Glorious One, help us as we climb the ladder.*
We must keep our eyes on You, our great reward.]

THE ACCESS ROAD

A huge piece of junk sits up on the hill behind where I live. The rusted derelict crane, abandoned up there on the hilltop some years ago, has long been a blemish on what is some of the most beautiful landscape in southern California. The residents have, therefore, complained and signed protests begging to have the ugly machine removed. And (after much too long a time) someone brought it down to the foot of the hill and parked it right by my fence. It took another couple months, but finally, in a rather humiliating scene for the old crane, it was hitched up and towed away to wherever dead cranes go. Its memory, however, remains a monument to a case of all too-human folly.

A NEW AND LIVING WAY OPENED FOR US THROUGH THE CURTAIN, THAT IS, HIS BODY.

HEB. 10:20, NIV.

A man owns that hilltop. It commands a marvelous circular view of lakes and valleys, and the place would certainly make a magnificent home-site. So sometime back before I moved into the area, the owner went ahead with his building preparations for his dream home. But he left one vital consideration to chance—and that was a fatal mistake. How would he build a road to reach his property?

The crisis came when no one in the whole valley would give him permission to build an access road. Since the reasons were perfectly defensible, his project came to an end. The only road he *might* have used would be a long, arduous one all the way down to the freeway. And that would have been at a price he would not pay. The cost would have been so great that he would have nothing left with which to build his mansion.

When He personally entered the human race, Jesus opened up an access road for us to attain the heavenly mansions He has already prepared. He planned our salvation down to the minutest detail. His body and His sacrificing of it literally became our escape route out of our sinful mortality. His access road has been very costly. Moreover, we must give all we have to make the journey. But think of the glorious destination!

[*No, none of the ransomed will ever know how dark the way was for You. But I thank You, Lord, for the costly road You made for us.*]

THE WAY

"Way" is a rather loose and generic old Anglo-Saxon word with more than 20 meanings and innumerable uses. We lose our way and then find it. Or we're "on the way," and then something gets "out of the way." Maps show us the way to travel, and parents tell us the way to behave. Psalmists and prophets sang of the way of holiness. Matthew's Gospel differentiates the broad way of sin contrasted with the narrow way of righteousness (Matt. 7:13, 14). Engineering highways and hiking along "byways," we declare there's "no way" we can be persuaded to a certain opinion. About 500 B.C. the Chinese philosopher Lao Tzu founded a religious system and assembled his teachings in the *Tao Te Ching.* Believers ever since have sought to follow the *Tao,* or the "way."

> "I AM THE WAY, . . . NO ONE COMES TO THE FATHER, BUT BY ME."
> JOHN 14:6, RSV.

In His farewell discourse to His disciples, Jesus announced that He was going to prepare a place for them. Then Thomas—Thomas with the inquiring mind—asked, "Lord, we do not know where you are going, so how can we know the way?" (John 14:5, NEB).

Christ's reply burned itself into the consciousness of His hearers. No governing prepositions, no enumeration of rules, no lack of focus, here. Just a single assertion: *"I am the way"* (verse 6, RSV). The metaphor appealed to the early Christians so strongly that they became known as "the people of the way."

Young Paul the persecutor headed off to Damascus, where he hoped to find "any who were of the Way" (Acts 9:2, NKJV). Later he confessed, "I persecuted this Way to the death, binding and delivering into prisons both men and women" (Acts 22:4, NKJV). Next Paul the missionary became embroiled in a riot at Ephesus because "there arose a great commotion about the Way" (Acts 19:23, NKJV). Finally, Paul the prisoner stood before Governor Felix in Caesarea. He argued that he worshiped the God of his fathers, but "according to the Way which they call a sect" (Acts 24:14, NKJV).

Perhaps no other portrait of Jesus is more streamlined or direct. "I have lived My life before you," He says. "I am the Way—and that is all anyone needs to know to find salvation."

> [*Thank You, Jesus, that You are the Way, the Truth, and the Life.*]

THE TOWER

oday's architects don't "think towers." Old World castles will, however, furnish you with tower experiences. The tower provides safety by both height and inaccessibility. Only a narrow circular staircase reaches it.

Even the luxuries of royalty must give way to the basic tortuous structure of the tower. Cardiff Castle in Wales features two specialties. A dozen large stone animal sculptures perch on the wall, looking down on the traffic of Castle Street with their eyes of semi-precious stone. Then there's the tower furnished as the bachelor quarters of the prince of Wales (King Edward VIII). At the rate of one room per floor, the prince must have done a lot of climbing. Even the toilet is very remote from the elegant bathroom, where fish worked in real gold cavort along the sides of the enormous bathtub. The smoking rooms and parlors are a frenzy of lavish Victorian taste.

All such decoration, however, was a rather futile effort to gild the basic purpose of tower building—and that is security. We cannot make a tower either comfortable or convenient, no matter how many golden fish we put on the bathtub tiles. The fact remains that residents had to climb endless rounds of stairs to move from one room to the next—and if two of them met on the way, one would probably have to back up or down.

Towers served as prisons and also as places of refuge. Watchtowers and defensive lookouts dominated the city walls and stood at the gates. Sometimes a tower crowned the citadel within the city. Abimelech died storming such a tower at Thebez, in which all the city inhabitants had taken refuge. As he approached the entrance to set the tower afire, a woman high on the roof dropped a millstone on his head. "Draw your sword and kill me," he commanded his armor bearer, "so that they can't say, 'A woman killed him'" (Judges 9:54, NIV).

Jesus is a "tower of salvation!"—a wonderful metaphor! In His stronghold we may not find living easy, but the advantages are immeasurable. We are secure, high above the attacking multitudes. And we have a sure defense against our enemies, even when they are beating at our very door.

> "HE IS THE TOWER OF SALVATION . . . AND SHOWS MERCY TO HIS ANOINTED."
>
> 2 SAM. 22:51, NKJV.

[*"Let thy mercy, O Lord, be upon us, according as we hope in thee" (Ps. 33:22).*]

THE TABERNACLE

Wonderful as they may be, temples cannot fulfill *all* of our spiritual need. We also require something celebrative, earthy, and movable. Something more our size!

Tabernacles fill that need. They were temporary shelters, often built of branches and leaves. Farmers built "booths" to have relief from the sun's heat by day and to shelter in while they guarded their crops by night (Job 27:18). Booths also accommodated domestic animals (Gen. 33:17). Jonah built one for his own comfort as he waited for the Lord to pour out His wrath on the city of Nineveh (Jonah 4:5). God designed the portable tabernacle in the wilderness as a "dwelling place" in which He could reveal Himself to Israel.

The seven-day Feast of Tabernacles was a joyous festival marking the end of the harvest season, a kind of ancient preview of American camp meetings. It combined the economy and practicality of the booths not only with sacrifices of thanksgiving but also the feasting, dancing, singing, and grand fellowship that went with the happy event.

Peter, always generous and impulsive, brought the humble tabernacle to its greatest height at the transfiguration of Christ. Excited by what he saw, he cried, "Lord, it is good for us to be here; if You wish, let us make here three tabernacles: one for You, one for Moses, and one for Elijah" (Matt. 17:4, NKJV). Perhaps they should have built six—to provide for himself, James, and John. But he thought nothing of himself there on the open mountainside. Peter wanted only to preserve the magnificent spiritual experience, to fit it into a "booth" somehow and save it!

But Peter's effort was not only impossible—it was also completely unnecessary. The word *tabernacle* is a verb as well as a noun. One goes "tabernacling" when one dwells in a temporary shelter. The early Church Fathers liked to speak of the "soul tabernacling in the body." Most important, however, Jesus has tabernacled with humanity. He left the temple-like magnificence of heaven to come and dwell with us in the temporary little shelters we have been living in ever since God had to evict Adam and Eve from Eden's garden. He meets us exactly where we are.

AND I HEARD A LOUD VOICE FROM THE THRONE SAYING, "NOW THE DWELLING OF GOD IS WITH MEN, AND HE WILL LIVE WITH THEM."

REV. 21:3, NIV.

[*Thank You, dear Jesus, for pitching Your tent here on earth with us.*]

PART FOUR

Liberal Arts

EDUCATION

COMMUNICATION

THE FINE ARTS

HEAVENLY WISDOM/KNOWLEDGE

Although knowledge and wisdom are comple-mentary, they are not interchangeable. The first is the mere accumulation of information, derived from education and experience. The second is the ability to *use* the knowledge we have acquired. Unfortunately, knowledge originates in a variety of places—some good, some bad.

The book of Proverbs, suitably enough, begins with some advice to the reader. Wisdom and common sense, we find, are rare. Wisdom—personified—goes out like an ordinary vendor to market her wares. She "cries aloud in the open air, she raises her voice in public places; she calls at the top of the busy street and proclaims at the open gates of the city" (Prov. 1:20, 21, NEB). Apparently, few listen.

> THE FEAR OF THE LORD IS THE BEGINNING OF WISDOM, AND THE KNOWL-EDGE OF THE HOLY ONE IS INSIGHT.
>
> PROV. 9:10, RSV.

But she makes magnificent promises to those who actively seek her—a relationship with God plus a keen understanding of justice, moral safety, prosperity, health, honor, long life, and much more (Prov. 2; 3:1-35).

Significantly, Solomon, the richest and most celebrated monarch of his time, began his glorious reign with one simple request. He asked God to give him wisdom—not knowledge, just "a heart with skill to listen" (1 Kings 3:9, NEB). All of the rest of his gifts then came later in natural sequence.

Our world abounds with high-tech capabilities that would have baffled us all even 15 years ago. The "information superhighway" now tells us more than we really needed to know about everything. A child in first grade is probably more computer-wise than his grandparent can ever hope to be.

None of this, however, has anything to do with wisdom. We do not necessarily, as we fondly say, grow wiser as we grow older. Instead, we simply become *old* fools, never attaining wisdom, maybe not even in a whole lifetime. (Scripture has an amazing amount to say about fools and their folly.)

The truth is that we have to look for wisdom in the right place. It is an attribute of God. Without it, our knowledge—however great the quantity—will only victimize us. As the wise man tells us: "Knowledge of the Holy One is insight." *This* learning must come before all other intellectual adventures.

[*Lord, I desire the rich fulfillment You have promised. Give me Your wis-dom so that I may make the best use of the knowledge I acquire day by day.*]

THE SOURCE OF WISDOM

Out of the rich legend of German culture comes the story of Dr. Faustus. He seems to have been based on the real-life character of a German necromancer, George Faust (1480-1538), a contemporary of Martin Luther. The *Faustbuch,* a collection of his achievements in both church and worldly courts, records his exploits. Literature, music, and art have celebrated Faust—and for good reason. His life became a terrible parable of craving knowledge at any price, of knowledge without wisdom.

OH, THE DEPTH OF THE RICHES BOTH OF THE WISDOM AND KNOWL-EDGE OF GOD!

ROM. 11:33, NKJV.

Faust's brilliant, questing mind causes him to sell his soul to the devil. In exchange, he will receive the services of Mephistopheles (an emissary from hell), who will supply Faust's every desire. The servant from hell will show the doctor the "small world" of personal feeling and experience, followed by the "great world" of history and politics. For such a gift, the professor signs the contract in his own blood and agrees never again to call upon the name of Christ. Twenty-four years later the final scene plays out in pure terror as Faust tries to turn to God in last-moment repentance. To no avail. He must, as contracted, give himself up to the claims of Lucifer. No wonder the Faust theme appears in so many different cultures.

It's the old story. What the serpent offered Eve in Eden was *knowledge* of good and evil. (God had designed only good within His new creation.) Wisdom provides us with the damage control we need to survive in an extremely difficult world. God is the ultimate source of wisdom. If derived from any other place, our wisdom will be counterfeit, and ultimately our secular knowledge will cause us to self-destruct.

We need to realize that even though we do not, like the obsessed Faust, sign a dramatic agreement with the evil one, we still stand in danger of selling out to him. We do so whenever we allow our search for knowledge—legitimate as it may be—to subvert our ultimate reliance upon God's wisdom.

Some of us still equate wisdom with knowledge. Others know the difference, but look for wisdom in all of the wrong places. Then, failing to find God, we find ourselves handicapped in our handling of knowledge.

[*Fill me this day, Lord, with Your wisdom—and no other. I would know You. Govern every decision I shall have to make, no matter how great or small.*]

THE WISDOM OF JESUS

Jeremiah's prophecies had a poor reception, and the rebellious Hebrews appealed to the three professional groups then known in the ancient East: "There will still be priests to guide us, still wise men to advise, still prophets to proclaim the word" (Jer. 18:18, NEB).

THE CHILD GREW AND BECAME STRONG IN SPIRIT, FILLED WITH WISDOM.

LUKE 2:40, NKJV.

The priests and prophets concerned themselves with communication with God and preparation for the next life. The wise men, however, addressed themselves to surviving in the present world. From observation and experience, they distilled practical advice as to what worked.

Although the traditions of conventional wisdom were useful—full of insightful admonitions—they still contained error. The "wisdom theory of rewards" was a case in point. Job's experience illustrates its flaws. He and his three friends were philosophers, faculty from the wisdom schools, if you please. Young Elihu, who appeared late in the discussion, was a talkative graduate student. Job's anguish grew out of the shattering of his belief in the wisdom theory—the concept that righteous people prosper and bad people suffer. Job's colleagues probed for his "sin" and insisted that he confess and repent of it. He *must* have done something, they declared, or he wouldn't be in the situation he was. As it turns out, it's a matter of timing. Anyone—good or evil—may receive an immediate reward. Often as not, however, it may delay for years—perhaps even into eternity. Therefore, at the end of Job's trial, God made it clear that his friends were dead wrong. They even needed Job to pray for them. Theirs had not been the wisdom of God.

Learning from the Holy Spirit at His mother's knee, Jesus did not attend the schools of His time. As a 12-year-old in the Temple, He tested His wisdom, challenging the wise men in debate. The results clearly showed the superiority of Jesus' wisdom—even in childhood. Later Matthew recorded His teachings in five "wisdom discourses": the Sermon on the Mount (Matt. 5-7); the commission to the disciples (Matt. 10); the parables of the kingdom (Matt. 13); the denunciation of hypocrites (Matt. 23); and a discussion of the end-time (Matt. 24)—all embodying His wisdom, His counsel for practical, everyday living. Society has always equated the acceptance of divine wisdom with piety—the inevitable result of such a choice.

[*Jesus, let me not be distracted this day by any other arguments that would turn me away from the gift of Your wisdom.*]

THE TEACHER

he title of rabbi was at first a term of respect for Jewish religious teachers. The scribes were rabbis, or "doctors of the law" (Matt. 23:3, NEB). Virtual spies, they dogged Jesus' footsteps throughout His public life, criticizing Him and arguing every possible point in His teachings. Nonetheless, Jesus assumed the title for Himself. To the disciples He said, "You must not be called 'rabbi'; for you have one Rabbi, and you are all brothers" (verse 8, NEB).

> JESUS WENT ABOUT ALL THE CITIES AND VILLAGES, TEACHING IN THEIR SYNA-GOGUES.
>
> MATT. 9:35, RSV.

Jesus' ministry, both in and out of the synagogues, did resemble the traditional work of the Jewish rabbis. Ironically, "He taught them [the Jews] as one who had authority, and not as their scribes" (Matt. 7:29, RSV). Indeed, the title carried with it the honor of being a master. Jesus' earliest disciples recognized the striking power in Him, addressing Him as "Rabbi, (which is to say . . . Master)" (John 1:38).

The warmer, more attractive interpretation of the word is simply "teacher." When he came to Christ in the night, Nicodemus the Pharisee was technically a peer. He carefully defined, however, the special kind of help he wanted from the Master. "Rabbi, we know you are a teacher who has come from God" (John 3:2, NIV). The risen Christ on His resurrection morning surprised Mary Magdalene in the garden by calling her name. She turned and said to Him in Hebrew, " 'Rabboni!' (which means Teacher)" (John 20:16, RSV).

Teachers have an enormous influence in our lives. They are the first persons of steady, strong authority to enter our lives after our parents. And if our parental background was less than ideal, their impact is all the greater.

Any teacher worth his or her salary (minimal as it may be) can impart knowledge. That is their business, what we hire them for. Moreover, in this age of technocrats, we dare not despise their youth. Since our lives must needs be a continuing learning process, we certainly require all kinds of teachers—all the way to the end.

This we do—with one proviso: that our teachers impart their knowledge along with the discretion of God's wisdom. But they will learn that only at the feet of Jesus, the Master Teacher.

> *My Master, I would learn from You. I want to be teachable. Let me recognize Your hand in every situation I face today.*

THE TUTOR

As a child I grew up thinking that everyone automatically went to college. That elementary school, high school, college, and university formed a natural sequence that all youths inevitably followed. I always lived on a school campus of one sort or another, and books were an absorbing way of life in our family. No wonder I made the mistake. My dad and I often discussed the day when I would go off to college. (He promised, among other things, to give me my own typewriter!)

Then one day he made a surprising remark. "Going to school has really never been all that popular. Many people just don't like it."

It stunned me. "Not like going to school?" Now who, I wondered, would want to be *that* boring! I soon learned, however, that the greater percentage of my schoolmates had other things in mind—getting away from home, making money, getting married, whatever. Others counted the days until they would be 16 and could leave school forever. No more forced learning.

The "tutor" or "schoolmaster" to whom Paul refers had charge of children to see that they arrived at school without getting detoured en route. Two hundred years ago in England no one expected travel to be fun. But then wealthy families began to send their young people on the "grand tour" of Europe to round out their education. The tutor was an academic who accompanied them.

Traditionally, governesses and other kinds of guardians have done tutorial work in affluent households. Tutors on college campuses offer study guidance to those struggling with a second language or with some other kind of academic deficiency. The tutor can give personal time to a student on a one-to-one basis, something not usually available from the classroom teacher.

A tutor is a teaching assistant, a counselor who prepares us for future responsibilities and privileges. He or she leads us from our "minority" to our final destination, the full experience of faith (Gal. 4:3, 5). In this respect, God's law is a fine tutor, acting in the absence of the Teacher Himself. But when "faith has come, the tutor's charge is at an end" (Gal. 3:25, NEB).

> THUS THE LAW WAS A KIND OF TUTOR IN CHARGE OF US UNTIL CHRIST SHOULD COME, WHEN WE SHOULD BE JUSTIFIED THROUGH FAITH.
>
> GAL. 3:24, NEB.

[*Father, I have so much to learn about faith yet. Let me never reject the assistance of Your Tutor, who will lead me into an understanding of grace.*]

THE MODERATOR

THEY SAW GOD, AND DID EAT AND DRINK.
EX. 24:11.

This curious little sentence is tucked away in the midst of the account of Israel's wilderness experience. Certain ceremonies had taken place in connection with God's confirmation of His covenant with Moses and Israel at Sinai. God issued a special invitation to Moses, Aaron, Nadab and Abihu, and 70 of the elders to come up onto the mountain. After sacrifices, a reading of the covenant, and a "purifying" of the ever-unstable congregation, the party set out to meet God in the mountain. There they "saw the God of Israel" standing upon "something like a pavement made of sapphire, clear as the sky itself" (Ex. 24:10, NIV).

And there they sat in His very presence, eating and drinking. Now we can respond to such a situation in three different ways.

First, we have those who eat and drink and never behold God. Because material delights preoccupy them, they can never glorify God. As Paul put it rather earthily to the Philippians, "Their god is their stomach" (Phil. 3:19, NIV).

Next are those who behold God but never "eat and drink." Such rigid—sometimes fanatical—persons divorce God from the common duties of life and regard Him with fear. They never find the correlation between the sacred and the secular, between service to God and ministry to humanity.

Finally, God the Moderator teaches us how to strike the balance. Like Moses' party atop Sinai, like Brother Lawrence among the pots and pans in his kitchen, we learn how to turn from the commonest tasks to look into God's face. We praise God in both body and spirit. Whatever we do—eating, drinking, or anything else—may and must be done "to the honour of God" (1 Cor. 10:31, NEB).

God would not have us be extreme in either the material or the religious. The truly spiritual experience will be a beautiful combination of God's natural world and His moral precepts. An insightful passage from the Talmud points to a fine balance between joy and judgment: "In the world to come each of us will be called to account for all the good things God put on this earth which we refused to enjoy."

[*My God, let me find Your divine balance. While I enjoy Your good earth, I would also see Your face.*]

THE WORD

Recently my son and I were bearing down upon Dulles Airport, Washington, D.C., bent on making it to our noon-hour flight. We saw what appeared to be a carpool lane. Intended to encourage people not to ride alone in their cars, carpool lanes in urban America offer motorists the possibility of bypassing the rush-hour traffic jam by driving in the far left lane with others who also share their vehicle with one passenger or more. Here in Maryland we saw the possible carpool lane labeled "HOV." For several miles we debated over what HOV might mean. Finally we decided not to risk using it. We didn't need a traffic ticket just as we were boarding the plane. Then just before we reached the exit for car rental returns, we learned that the letters stand for "high occupancy vehicle." It *was* a carpool lane after all! Finding mystifying official jargon on road signs so near the seat of federal government did not, of course, come as a surprise to us.

> THE WORD BECAME FLESH AND MADE HIS DWELLING AMONG US. WE HAVE SEEN HIS GLORY, THE GLORY OF THE ONE AND ONLY.
>
> JOHN 1:14, NIV.

The West, on the other hand, is more relaxed and straightforward. Los Angeles freeways pose no such uncertainty. They simply announce, "Carpool lane—two or more persons." At the same time it notifies drivers that the fine for ignoring carpool regulations is $271. Now, this information is absolutely clear. No question about the interpretation of *these* words.

Words have a life all of their own—a life rather like our own. They are born, live, grow old, and sometimes die. Having personalities and reputations, words may be honest and forthright or devious and evasive. But they *all* have power. They exist for just one purpose—to communicate.

When Jesus announced Himself as the Word, He made Himself the link of communication between heaven and earth. He thus embodies all that is both clear and beautiful in language. Jesus has no part in the pompous, muddled effusions of our officialdom, but is the exact, understandable, well-chosen, and beautiful Word! That is, indeed, an apt metaphor for the splendid "glory of the one and only Son."

> *"O Word of God Incarnate, O Wisdom from on high,*
> *O Truth unchanged, unchanging, O Light of our dark sky,*
> *We praise Thee for the radiance that from the hallowed page,*
> *A lantern to our footsteps, shines on from age to age."*
> —William Walsham How

THE WORD OF POWER

When "the preacher" of Ecclesiastes described the "word power" of the king, he wrote from the viewpoint of absolute monarchy. In ancient times rulers were preoccupied with the exercise of their "divine rights." Their word meant life or death. And since literacy was the exception rather than the rule, the spoken word took on a life of its own.

WHERE THE WORD OF A KING IS, THERE IS POWER.

ECCL. 8:4, NKJV.

Words once spoken, of course, cannot be recalled. They still retain great influence and power, but nowadays we want to get everything "in writing"—preferably in triplicate. We trust only what someone has written and signed. About the only significant use of the spoken word today is the taking of wedding vows. Judging from the prevalence of divorce, however, we assume that some of the potency must have vanished.

On the other hand, in former, more primitive cultures, a word spoken in either blessing or cursing had a fearful power. When the aged Isaac discovered that he had spoken the birthright blessing over Jacob instead of Esau, he exclaimed, "I have blessed him—and indeed he shall be blessed" (Gen. 27:33, NKJV). The words had gone out, and nothing could change that fact. Esau would be subservient to Jacob.

When Balak, at great expense and effort, brought Balaam to the high places of Moab to curse Israel, he wanted the prophet to proclaim only devastating words. Three times, without success, the king tried to get the curse said. At last, in despair and exasperation, he cried, "Neither curse them at all nor bless them at all!" In other words: "Just shut up!" Don't keep throwing words out into the air, because they will *happen!* (Num. 23; 24).

Jesus used the spoken word at the creation of the world. When He walked here among us, He employed the spoken word to convict His listeners and to work miracles. Through the Word He gave the assurance of forgiveness and emphasized the hope of the resurrection.

We have passed from the confusion of Babel to the miracle of Pentecost and are now learning the unified speech of heaven. By the Word of God, we may take the power of the King with us. His Word is His signet ring, His token of power and authority.

> *"Lord Jesus, once You spoke to men*
> *Upon the mountain and the plain,*
> *O help us listen now as then*
> *And wonder at Your words again."*
> —H.C.A. Gaunt

THE WORD: THE GREAT I AM

One of the responsibilities of language teachers is to induct students into the mysteries of verb tenses. First, one must *find* the verb, then come its forms—past, present, future, past perfect, future continuous, and so forth. Such technical material occupies many classroom hours. Moreover, dealing with verb tenses is a skill requiring periodic review. A teacher can never—even in the upper reaches of higher education—be absolutely certain that the student sitting in the back row *really* has verbs under control.

"BEFORE ABRAHAM WAS, I AM."

JOHN 8:58, NKJV.

All of which points to the enigma of time. Knowing that we can neither recall the past nor borrow from the future, we multiply maxims. "Dost thou love life?" Ben Franklin observed. "Then do not squander time; for that's the stuff life is made of." "Life is what happens to us while we're busy making other plans." "Making full use of today is our best preparation for tomorrow." "You can't change the past, but you can ruin a perfectly good present by worrying about the future."

Although we live in space, we enjoy relationships only in time. Elusive as it may seem, time is all that truly belongs to us. Even the people who have nothing else have at least that, and in it lie all the seeds of their tomorrows. Therefore, Jesus, as the great I AM, enters our lives in the urgent present tense. Unlike us, however, He sees the world from an immortal perspective, outside of time. For Him, human life is but a tiny segment on His scale of life that has neither beginning nor end.

God has designed us, however, to live in the joy of the "already" (present tense), His kingdom on earth. Here, at this precise point where He encounters us, we are to shoulder only the load of the moment. Never does He ask us to bear, all at once, the combined weight of the whole year, past and future.

At the same time, He has also implanted in us the hope and expectation of the "not yet," which is the future. It behooves us, then, not just to *spend* our lives in time. Rather the I AM points us toward *investing* our lives in eternity.

[*O God of the eternal present, give us the wisdom to understand Your eternal point of view.*]

THE MESSENGER

I lived for seven years without a telephone, either at work or at home. Nor did we have the prospect of ever having one there on the mission compound at the college in Manila, Philippines. Before you expend too much sympathy on our situation, however, I should tell you that it was not all bad. Indeed not! It meant that we didn't go to anyone's house or office, nor did anyone come to ours, without a definite purpose in mind. We had no salespeople, no vulgarity, no invasion of privacy, just blessed silence! In any case, ideas committed to paper tend to be taken more seriously than those just tossed out across the telephone line, so we did a lot of note writing.

> "THE LORD YOU ARE SEEKING WILL COME TO HIS TEMPLE; THE MESSENGER OF THE COVENANT, WHOM YOU DESIRE, WILL COME."
>
> MAL. 3:1, NIV.

When we did need to communicate, we sent messengers, employing students and our children for the purpose. Struck with a great sense of responsibility, the children thoroughly enjoyed such opportunities to trot through the campus to one another's houses. In fact, I still have a few of those witty little inter-compound notes I used to exchange with my neighbors. Because whatever we said lived on in writing, we could remember the message clearly.

In the main, being a messenger requires two characteristics. The first is loyalty and reliability. The sender must know that the message is going to get through. The second necessity is accuracy. The communication must be delivered with absolute clarity. At the death of Absalom, Ahimaaz eagerly asked to carry the message to King David. Joab, however, chose another to bear the sad news. Nonetheless, Ahimaaz ran, took a shortcut, and reached the king first. The gatekeeper could even identify him by the way he ran. When he arrived, however, he could report only having seen "a great tumult, but I did not know what it was about" (2 Sam. 18:29, NKJV). The zealous Ahimaaz had the loyalty, but could not relay the news when he arrived.

The divine "Messenger of the Covenant" is above reproach. He bears tidings from heaven, and there can be no question as to either His faithfulness to His Father or the accuracy of His message to us. Hear Him!

> *Lord, give me the loyalty and faithfulness*
> *to be a true messenger of Your covenant.*

THE HERALD

The herald has a colorful and bold task. After the Babylonian King Nebuchadnezzar set up his gold image on the plain of Dura, he called in a vast assemblage of officials from all over the kingdom. "Then a herald cried aloud: 'To you it is commanded, O peoples, nations, and languages, that at the time you hear the sound of . . . music, you shall fall down and worship the gold image" (Dan. 3:4, NKJV).

In feudal Europe this officer at arms went from being a shield-bearer in battle to announcing happenings in court and civil ceremonies. Remnants of this flamboyant figure still appear in England at contests among colorfully costumed town criers. Meanwhile, the authorities in the honored College of Heralds continue to monitor the uses of heraldic devices. The "marshaling of arms" and "differencing" is a highly technical arrangement. Interest in family roots today, however, has made the carefree modern descendants of the aristocracy display their escutcheons with a casual freedom that would surely shock the lords and ladies who first bore them.

Beginning in the fourteenth century, a family had its insignia embroidered on the surcoat that a knight wore over his coat of mail. When an unknown knight arrived at a joust or tournament, the herald had to *blasen* the stranger's coat of arms. After the blowing of a trumpet to gain attention, he then described in detail the stranger's bearings. Heraldic design included the *escutcheon* (shield), the *tincture* (gold, silver, colors, and background furs), the *charges* (ornamental figures, crosses, chevrons, animals, etc.), and the family motto (originally the war cry of the bearer).

When after 40 days in the Judean wilderness Jesus returned to Nazareth, "He went to the synagogue . . . and he stood up to read." Acting as His own herald, He read from the scroll of Isaiah: "The Spirit of the Lord is on me, . . . to preach good news to the poor. He has sent me to proclaim freedom for prisoners." Thus before the skeptics in His hometown of Nazareth, He "blazoned" Himself, giving His identifying features and announcing "the year of the Lord's favor" (Luke 4:18, 19, NIV).

> HE OPENED THE BOOK [OF THE PROPHET ISAIAH] . . . WHERE IT WAS WRITTEN, "THE SPIRIT OF THE LORD IS UPON ME, BECAUSE HE HAS ANOINTED ME TO PREACH GOOD NEWS TO THE POOR."
>
> LUKE 4:17, 18, RSV.

[*Father, help us to preach the good news, not only in words but in action.*]

THE GOOD NEWS

An insatiable appetite for news is part of our human condition. We want to hear whatever is novel or new. Originally, one picked up this kind of information at the well, the city gate, or in the city forum. Medieval town criers announced whatever events citizens had need of hearing. With the advent of the printing press, news sheets began to appear on the streets, followed by daily and weekly newspapers, as well as monthly magazines. The new reading public enjoyed philosophical discourse, but the news they heard was pretty much like what we have today—bad news. Still, those who did not wish to hear news did not have to. Today mass media have taken that option away from us.

AND THE ANGEL SAID TO THEM, "BE NOT AFRAID; FOR BEHOLD, I BRING YOU GOOD NEWS OF A GREAT JOY WHICH WILL COME TO ALL THE PEOPLE."

LUKE 2:10, RSV.

Years ago, during the Suez Canal crisis, the wife of British prime minister Anthony Eden sighed, "I feel as if the Suez Canal has been flowing right through my parlor." With the current inundation of television coverage, however, the "canals" not only pour through our living rooms, they flood over us and threaten to sweep away our very sanity. We all know far more than we ever wanted to know about everything. We have the choice, ad nauseam, of the despicable behavior of fictional film characters and real-life violence in every conceivable form. In most newscasts the anchorpeople *do* try to insert at least one fragment of hope with a "good news" story. Nonetheless, their main business is tracking criminal activities. Almost all news boils down to bad news—something that, sadly, reflects public taste. Naturally, those who pay for broadcasting news consistently give people what they want to hear. It is a depressing thought as we move steadily from one war scare, one sensational murder case, or one titillating scandal to the next.

What a miracle it seems when we look back to the angels' Christmas announcement: "The good news has arrived!" Two thousand years later, with technology literally drowning us in bad news, we cannot repeat that joyful cry too often—the good news is among us. We have only to listen.

[*The good news is that the most powerful One in the universe is also the One who is good. I thank You, God, for that.*]

THE ALPHABET

lthough we take it for granted, the alphabet is one of the great treasures of our civilization. At first our ancestors communicated orally, presenting everything by word of mouth. Then they set about "getting it in writing." Records to keep, messages to send, facts to remember, ideas to share—humanity moved into the thrilling arena of written language. What had at first been picture writing evolved into abstract alphabets.

"I AM THE ALPHA AND THE OMEGA," SAYS THE LORD GOD.
REV. 1:8, NIV.

We must remember at least five important facts about our alphabet. First, it is efficient, streamlined, and functional. We limit it only by our own lack of talent and purpose. Second, it is versatile, suiting every individual's need. Thus we may employ it for the preaching of truth, the singing of poetry, or the spreading of falsehood and filth. Third, because the alphabet is timeless, we need never complain that it is in need of updating. It can never wear out.

A most wonderful feature of the alphabet is that it is complete—nothing to add or take away. And above all, it is inexhaustible. We may say, "I've run out of ideas and can't go on" or "I am too busy/tired/frustrated to go on." But assuredly we can never complain that we had to stop because there weren't enough letters left in the alphabet.

It is one of the most striking portraits Jesus ever painted of Himself: "I am the alphabet. I am the Alpha [the first letter of the Greek alphabet] and the Omega [the last letter]." In other words, "I am the first and the last and all that lies in between—I can meet your every need."

Jesus works efficiently to make us productive people. His laws are timeless. He is versatile so that we never face a temptation or take up a responsibility He does not understand. Best of all, He is inexhaustible, for He brought into our world a great spiritual energy that nothing can ever deplete. Like the alphabet from which we daily take endless supplies of words, He provides blessings, power, and forgiveness in a flow that absolutely has no end.

> *"Praise God, from whom all blessings flow;*
> *Praise Him, all creatures here below."*
> —Thomas Ken

THE ORATOR

The people of classical times greatly admired oratory. The Latin philosopher Quintilian rightly defined the theory and practice of eloquent speech as that which would "instruct, move, and delight." He who has mastered rhetoric can play upon the minds of people as a conductor with an orchestra. Orators were much to be prized because of their potential influence. In describing Judah's impending exile, Isaiah listed four essential kinds of leadership that the nation would lose: " the mighty man," "the judge," "the prophet," and "the eloquent orator" (Isa. 3:2, 3). The New International Version renders "eloquent orator" as "cunning enchanter."

> AND SEEING THE MULTITUDES, HE WENT UP ON A MOUNTAIN. . . . THEN HE OPENED HIS MOUTH AND TAUGHT THEM.
>
> MATT. 5:1, 2, NKJV.

One of the more colorful (and horrific) episodes in Acts describes the oratory of King Herod. After a killing spree among the Christians, he next concentrated on his enemies in Tyre and Sidon. Attired in his royal robes and seated on his rostrum in Caesarea, he "harangued" the people in the grand style. The impact on the audience was electrifying. "This is the voice of a god," they cried, "not of a man" (Acts 12:20-22, NIV). Instantaneously, "an angel of the Lord struck him down, and he was eaten by worms and died" (verse 23, NIV).

Usually, however, it is the *anti*-rhetorical devices that truly move people. In Shakespeare's tragedy *Julius Caesar,* Mark Antony announced himself at Caesar's funeral as "a plain blunt man," and not an orator. His "low-key" speech carried the day.

To be sure, dramatic oratory can be exciting, but most of us are "plain" people. Jesus knew this as He addressed the peasant crowds who followed Him everywhere. Although not a trained orator in the classical tradition, He had a striking ability to instruct. After He had delivered His sermon on the mount, the people were astounded, for unlike their own teachers, He taught with a note of authority (Matt. 7:29). Reporting on another of Jesus' discourses, the Temple police told the Pharisees (their employers), "No one ever spoke the way this man does" (John 7:46, NIV). Thus Jesus drew His listeners to Himself, irresistibly leading them into life-changing decisions.

[*Master of the beautiful language of the heart, we listen for Your Word today and wait to hear Your voice.*]

THE AUTHOR OF SALVATION

Authoring is a challenging, sometimes over-whelming undertaking. Because it involves the creation of something new, the origination of something that did not exist before, it requires time and patience. Although we usually think of an author as a person who writes books and articles, the word actually applies to anyone who *makes* something. The old Latin *auctor* was one who increased the supply of things, who added to the sum total.

HAVING BEEN PERFECTED, HE BECAME THE AUTHOR OF ETERNAL SALVATION.
HEB. 5:9, NKJV.

One of the gifts that creative writers have is to sift through the chaos and disorder of our daily lives and distill meaning for us. Able to gather up scattered human experience and organize it into new patterns, they write a story, an essay, a sermon, and hand it back to us, saying, "This is the way life is."

After we have read or heard it, we have the "shock of recognition" and exclaim, "Why, yes, that *is* the way it is. Only I never thought of putting it that way before." Authors, then, increase our understanding and help us interpret life.

Authoring the plan of salvation that stretched from eternity to eternity was a cosmic undertaking. It originated something never before thought of, gathered up our fractured experience, and made human survival possible. What a vast act of creativity!

When we apply the word "author" to God, we tend to limit Him to His divine revelation in Scripture. Christ Himself, however, became the book. Through Him we may hear, see, and handle with our hands the Word of Life (1 John 1:1).

As the "author [Greek, *aitios*] of salvation" Christ points up another aspect of the authorial work. The meaning here has to do with *causing* something to happen. The universe exalts Christ as Saviour because the work He finished on earth now causes our eternal salvation to be possible. He is salvation itself (Luke 2:30; 3:6). Because He was the first to possess salvation, He could become the "Author" of it for others.

[*Author of Salvation, I would keep my attention fixed on You. I will read Christ the Book as I read nothing else.*]

THE AUTHOR OF FAITH

T he word "author" appears only twice in the Bible. The second instance (Greek, *archegos*), like the first, concerns the work of Christ. This time He's the "finisher" of faith. We talk a good deal about faith. Subject as we are to moods, however, we have difficulty in comprehending the life of faith because it deals with intangibles. As one would-be definer of faith puts it:

LOOKING UNTO JESUS, THE AUTHOR AND FINISHER OF OUR FAITH.

HEB. 12:2, NKJV.

"For those who believe, no explanation
is necessary.
For those who don't believe, no explanation is possible."

Dwight Moody once remarked lightly that the greatest example of faith we have must be that of "Jesus going away and not calling legions of angels to spread the gospel, but leaving it to Peter and the others." We've betrayed His faith in us often enough, to be sure—but that's another story!

In describing his transition from atheism to Christian belief, C. S. Lewis graphically describes the difficulty of dealing with our moods and feelings. When he was an unbeliever, he had times when Christianity "looked terribly probable." Conversely, when he became a Christian, he sometimes felt that the "whole thing looked very improbable." Such rebellious moods will come anyway, he says. And unless you get them under control, "you can never be either a sound Christian or even a sound atheist." Faith is the only virtue that can prevent you from becoming "a creature dithering to and fro," dependent, as Lewis says, on the weather and "the state of its digestion." Faith is simply "the art of holding on to things your reason has once accepted, in spite of your changing moods."*

We have only one place to turn in order to escape our human moods and despair, to rise above them. Jesus in His own person provides the first example of total faith. As the Author of life, He didn't receive life from another, but rather had it within His own person. Hence He is the originator of faith, the pioneer in the life of faith.

Faith must take Christ not only for its object but also for its supreme example. Moreover, faith is a gift—we cannot generate it alone. God has authored it and can give it to us on request.

[*God, I would acquire the habit of faith. I ask for that faith that enables me to reach out and grasp Your unseen hand, for faith that will permit me to go farther than I can see.*]

*C. S. Lewis, *The Joyful Christian* (New York: Macmillan Pub. Co., 1977), p. 130.

THE STORY

M oses' prayer speaks of human frailty and the brevity of life. Martin Luther (1483-1546) rendered the passage as "We bring our years to an end like empty talk." Miles Coverdale (1488-1569), an early English Bible translator, perhaps influenced by Luther, spoke of life's "tale." The English Book of Common Prayer preserves his version: "We bring our years to an end, as it were a tale that is told." The word "tale" has a double meaning here—as a numbering of our mortal years and as the ending of a story. Let's consider the latter picture.

WE FINISH OUR YEARS LIKE A SIGH.
PS. 90:9, NKJV.

The whole earth adores stories! Instinctively, we love to hear them, tell them, and pass them on. Nothing comes more naturally to us than storytelling. Indeed, as my church pastor, Smuts van Rooyen, pointed out recently, "narrative therapy" is an effective counseling technique to help people understand their motivations. The life story we carry with us is, in essence, what we have done with our lives. Every day presents us with a new turn in the plot.

The practice of good story writing demands that every story have four component parts. First, you must have a *character* (or more than one). Second, the characters must be given a *place*, a "setting" in which to act. Third, they must encounter a *problem*, a "complication," through which they must work. Finally, at the end there must be a *change*. If nothing happened and everything at the end were the same as at the beginning, then a story would have no point in its telling.

Paul entered into the story of Jesus so intensely that he actually said: "I have been crucified with Christ; it is no longer I who live, but Christ lives in me; and the life which I now live in the flesh I live by faith in the Son of God" (Gal. 2:20, NKJV). Incorporating such a story into his life enabled the persecuted apostle to rise above all of his circumstances.

We must choose how we shall "tell our tale" to conclude our story. Working it out for ourselves brings us to nothing but a bad end—indeed, a tragedy, because of the complications of sin. Our story endures only when we incorporate Jesus' story and let it change our plot.

> *"Live out Thy life within me, O Jesus, King of kings!*
> *Be Thou Thyself the answer to all my questionings;*
> *Live out Thy life within me, in all things have Thy way!*
> *I, the transparent medium Thy glory to display."*
> —Frances R. Havergal

THE ENGRAVER

My American grandfather taught elementary school for 60 years. One of the things he brought out of the Victorian Age was his insistence on excellent handwriting. Before I started school, he had me doing the long rows of loops and coils that were the preamble to the Palmer Method. Then my family went overseas, and because I didn't see Grandpa for the next eight years, my handwriting evolved into something between Babylonian cuneiform and Egyptian hieroglyphics. I'm sure it was a matter of disappointment to him that I never learned to write nicely. But now, in the computer age, I scarcely do anything other than affix my signature (such as it is) here and there.

I have artist friends who wonder why, as a writer, I don't relish that primal, creative act of putting pen to paper. But I don't. I find it sluggish and, if I'm pressed, painful. That is not to say, of course, that I don't admire calligraphy and appreciate the excellence of fine engraving. For my purposes, however, the computer fonts offer sufficient adventure in this line.

In order to grasp Paul's allusion to God as an engraver, we need to understand the writing methods available in his time—a time when writing was serious art. Few races or cultures progressed far toward civilization until they had a written language. Only thus could a people keep records, preserve laws, and deliver messages.

Three kinds of recording existed in his time. People inscribed a temporary message with a sharp-pointed instrument on a tablet covered with wax. Reed or bronze pens with split nibs (not unlike our modern pens) dipped in ink provided more permanent documents on papyrus or parchment (leather). People wanted the most important records and inscriptions, however, engraved on monuments or on stone or metal tablets. Then the engravers highlighted the letters with paint.

Paul's metaphor refers to the third and most permanent form. The instrument for engraving God's message on the human heart is, fittingly enough, the Holy Spirit. Thus the Christian should be highly readable to his or her associates—with an unerasable text.

YOU ARE A LETTER FROM CHRIST DELIVERED BY US, WRITTEN NOT WITH INK BUT WITH THE SPIRIT OF THE LIVING GOD, NOT ON TABLETS OF STONE BUT ON TABLETS OF HUMAN HEARTS.

2 COR. 3:3, RSV.

[*Send Your Spirit, Lord, to engrave Your message on my heart. Let me be always conscious of my need to keep my life clean and readable.*]

THE CREATIVE ARTIST

The artist—any kind of artist—is a "maker." Moreover, he or she cares intensely about the "making." Artists easily become obsessed with their creations, so much so that living with a highly creative person is more often than not a real challenge. The unpredictable moods, the irregular lifestyle, the withdrawn silences or constant talking—all have to be understood and coped with. At the same time, one admires an artist's strong powers of concentration, optimism, and insight. Above all, we prize the work of creators who understand the spiritual impact of their work and who are willing to share. Communication, therefore, is the Christian artist's goal.

IF ANYONE IS IN CHRIST, HE IS A NEW CREATION; THE OLD HAS GONE, THE NEW HAS COME!
2 COR. 5:17, NIV.

Creativity has at least a dozen facets. One's gifts may lie in painting or music, cooking or woodcrafting, graphic design or administration, counseling or writing. Like a series of mountain ranges receding into the horizon, the possibilities for using our creative energies are limitless. And it is in our moments of creativity that we come closest to understanding the character of God.

Here we discover Him in His most important function—that of Creator. The Old Testament opens with the creation of the world—the Father, Son, and Holy Spirit working together on a project that gave Them enormous satisfaction. One senses Their divine joy, Their almost gleeful exuberance, as They finished each day's work and declared it "good!" Then the New Testament opens with the coming of God to earth, His entering into human experience. The Incarnation was a tremendous multimedia event, with all the heavens bursting open with light and music. Here was a creative act beyond comprehension.

Yet one more divine achievement remains—the saving of a transgressor. Perhaps here is God the Creative Artist at His best. When David prayed "Create in me a clean heart, O God, and put a new and right spirit within me" (Ps. 51:10, RSV), he was doing more than just expressing the wish of a defeated man. He described a creative act that actually can and does happen—the producing of a newly transformed life. It has to be Christ's highest artistic achievement.

> *"Oh how great is thy goodness, which thou hast laid up for them that fear thee" (Ps. 31:19).*

THE CRAFTSMAN

I have a problem about my desks—the one in my office and the four that I have at home. People usually look at them and avert their eyes. I've posted here and there comforting and defensive little signs such as "A clean desk is a sign of a sick mind" and "My desk, my mess, my business." In the past I used to apologize about my difficulty, explaining that I just hadn't had time yet to clean up and organize. I don't say anything anymore, for I have had to accept the fact that the situation is permanent and will never get any better. A student at one of my writing conferences sent me a poster showing a distraught woman under her desk after its contents have overflowed from above and almost buried her. The caption reads "I'm more together than I look." And I do, indeed, have a certain pattern of organization. It is, however, entirely my own and not comprehensible to any onlooker.

FOR WE ARE GOD'S HANDI-WORK, CREATED IN CHRIST JESUS TO DEVOTE OURSELVES TO THE GOOD DEEDS FOR WHICH GOD HAS DESIGNED US.
EPH. 2:10, NEB.

Appearances notwithstanding, art is ultimately organization. Life is often random and chaotic, and art is the organizing principle for us. We instinctively move toward order and structure. Music focuses us powerfully upon a single emotion. The visual arts set a single moment in time before our eyes. The writer takes the raw material of human experience, distills it for us, and sets before us a poem, a story, an essay. "Why, yes! That's the way it is!" we exclaim. "Only I was never able to describe it like that!"

Now, all of these artists must master their crafts. To make an impact, to communicate an idea, to make people think and feel, they must study the techniques they need to use. They learn the rules, what works and what doesn't. While inspiration has a part, the notion that art arises solely from a flash of heavenly fire is absolutely wrong. Consequently, when God created humanity, much more was involved than simply the forming of yet one more beautiful creature. God the Craftsman built into us gifts enabling us to perform certain tasks and desires that continuously turn us back to Him to find their fulfillment.

Creator of all, thank You for letting me share a little with You in the joy of creativity. During such moments I can glimpse some of the glory of Your craftsmanship.

THE DESIGNER

God does not allow us to read very far into the book of Genesis before He makes clear that He had *planned* the whole of creation. That, indeed, humanity was not only designed to resemble its Maker, but that we were custom-made for very specific tasks. How infinitely comforting to know that for each of us God has "prepared in advance" our individualized assignments (Eph. 2:10, NIV)!

In our zeal to accomplish the good works necessary to the Christian life, however, we tend to think that every kind of work fits every person. We are "God's workmanship" (verse 10, NIV). The word "workmanship" implies that God designed us to fulfill our specific function. Then—and this is the exciting part—He has prearranged a task for each of us that matches that function. While we may from time to time become weary and perhaps even bored, we need not struggle with labors for which we have no talent.

> "LET US MAKE A MAN— SOMEONE LIKE OURSELVES TO BE THE MASTER OF ALL LIFE ON EARTH."
>
> GEN. 1:26, TLB.

I have no aptitude for things scientific. Also I have proved to be a complete failure at salesmanship, accounting, mechanics, and a number of other things. So I became a teacher. And he's a doctor . . . She's a musician . . . They're computer programmers . . . And so forth.

How infinitely comforting to know that for each of us God has "prepared in advance" a specific task. Thus we become complementary members of the body of Christ. Two things determine the perfect outworking of God's plan. First, that we each have our personal gifts, our individual tool kits, implanted in us even before birth. Our circumstances, however, constitute the second and more flexible part of God's "before-ordained" program. We have choices regarding education and work opportunities that affect the quality of our good works and the enjoyment we have in doing them.

Thus the Christian finds not tedium, but joy and rich reward in doing good works. Let us generously make space for one another so that we all may do the precise work "for which God has designed us" (verse 10, NEB).

> [*Dear Father, how grateful I am for the assurance I have that You have designed a specific task for me to do—one that I can enjoy performing. Show me the way to such fulfillment.*]

THE ART COLLECTOR

A widespread passion began during the late seventeenth century. Enthusiasts started collecting anything they could haul into their houses. Today our collections range from classic cars to buttons, from stamps to bottles. Collecting, however, calls for discrimination.

Paul pictures the potter classifying his or her vessels. Because of his or her skills in design and craftsmanship, the craftsman determines what he or she makes in the pottery studio. Once the artwork passes into the public marketplace, however, other things happen. The critics begin to talk about what they see and hear. Speculating on the future, serious art collectors pay high prices and expect to sell at even higher figures. They build special rooms to hold and display their collections. Perhaps they negotiate with museums and galleries. Everyone thinks about money—and few stop to look at and appreciate the art object itself.

HAS THE POTTER NO RIGHT OVER THE CLAY, TO MAKE OUT OF THE SAME LUMP ONE VESSEL FOR BEAUTY AND ANOTHER FOR MENIAL USE?

ROM. 9:21, RSV.

As we have seen, God is an artist and a designer. Also a critic and collector, He has collected all kinds of things—and He has done so with the abandon of the most reckless speculator. Collecting things living, dying, and dead, He organizes and displays His handiwork throughout nature. Running the cycle of the seasons, He finds things lost and broken and decides how to preserve them. He deals with stars, atoms, rays, living souls, and unwanted babies. Gathering up doubts and sins, He casts them away. Through His Holy Spirit He tracks the repentances of sinners, the thoughts of old men and women, the fears of children, the thousands of impressions that come to us daily. At Calvary He gathered the world's pain and then showed us how we could handle it.

Like the wise collector that He is, God knows what is of no value and must be destroyed. But He is also a happy enthusiast over His collections, delighting to present us in an attractive display before His universe.

[*What a privilege, Lord, to be part of Your collection.*
I rejoice in the value that You have found in me!]

THE SCULPTOR

The biographer of the Italian Renaissance* Giorgio Vasari declared that God sent to earth "a spirit . . . able to give form to painting, perfection to sculpture, and grandeur to architecture." That brilliant artist was Michelangelo Buonarroti (1475-1564), a giant born into an age of giants. A tormented genius driven by his art, he never found happiness, although in old age he did experience a profound religious conversion. The title of a novel about him, *The Agony and the Ecstasy,* has described him well.

> "REMEMBER THAT YOU MOLDED ME LIKE CLAY. WILL YOU NOW TURN ME TO DUST AGAIN?"
>
> JOB 10:9, NIV.

When he was about 35 years old, Michelangelo began a series of four statues for the tomb of one of his patrons. Before he finished *The Captives,* however, he abandoned them. Still, they remain for us seemingly empowered by a force from within. With every muscle flexed to the breaking point, those tortured figures have been trying for the past five centuries to escape from their rough-hewn stone prisons. Michelangelo peeled off layer upon layer of superfluous stone in search of the figures that he had already seen in his mind's eye lying locked within the block. Or to put it in the more earthy speech of the cartoon character Dennis the Menace as he watched a sculptor at work: "That's easy. You just take the chisel and knock off all of the pieces that don't look like a horse."

God the Sculptor employs two sculpting techniques. He may mold us in clay, building us up until we can be cast in bronze in the foundry of life. Or He may, more conventionally, carve us out of a stone block, excising all superfluities from our lives. In either case, He sees the possible perfection of our characters. Never in a hurry, He painstakingly takes all the time He needs to create the artwork He has in mind. Another word for His divine sculpting process is "sanctification."

> "Great Sculptor, hew and polish us, nor let
> Hidden and lost Thy form within us lie.
> Spare not the stroke; do with us as Thou wilt.
> Let there be naught unfinished, broken, marred.
> Complete Thy purpose that we may become
> Thy perfect image, O our God and Lord."
> —Horatius Bonar

---

*Giorgio Vasari, *The Lives of the Most Eminent Italian Architects, Painters, and Sculptors.*

CERAMICS: THE POTTER

One summer I worked as a member of an archaeology team at Caesarea Maritima in Israel. Out of bed at 3:30 a.m. and into the field long before dawn, we probed the secrets of King Herod's magnificent city. We moved and sifted tons of sandy soil, the Mediterranean breezes doing little to relieve the parching heat of the late morning. Using dental instruments, we meticulously uncovered the skeletons of the Christian Crusaders and the Muslims who had fought over the city. Along the way we found smooth pink-and-gray fragments of marble veneer, a few bits of jewelry, some coins, and pieces of rough Roman glass.

WE ARE THE CLAY, YOU ARE THE POTTER; WE ARE ALL THE WORK OF YOUR HAND.

ISA. 64:8, NIV.

Then one morning the monotony broke with the discovery of what must have been the potter's house. We uncovered a large number of handsome unbroken vessels—big and small, plain and fancy—scattered through the pottery rubble on the mosaic floor. A Jewish matron might well have come by just then to shop for her household, except that after 1,800 years the display was a little disorganized.

Pottery-making has always been a vital industry in the world of the Middle East, so naturally society highly prized the potter's skill. Since he was a judge of quality, the potter's decisions were final. The kings of Judah even allotted land to the potters near the royal estates, where the craftsmen could conveniently live and work for the king (1 Chron. 4:23).

Our archaeologists examined the pottery fragments we brought in from the dig site every evening. From the shards they could determine the date for all the artifacts found on that level. Sometimes they would put a piece of broken pottery in their mouths to detect the differences in the clay.

Repeatedly God has compared His relationship with humanity to that of a potter and his clay. He can expertly distinguish the differences among the vessels in His care and identify the needs of each one. As the potter has power over the clay, so the Creator of the universe has the right to rule human beings and nations and to shape their lives.

> "Have Thine own way, Lord!
> Have Thine own way!
> Thou art the Potter; I am the clay."

CERAMICS: THE POTTER'S HOUSE

When God sent the prophet Jeremiah down to the local potter's house, He was not sending him to a secluded artist's studio. It was the busy commercial center bustling with deliverymen, the craftsman's assistants, and the customers. Here the prophet sat down amid the crowd to watch. *The Living Bible* describes it graphically: "I . . . found the potter working at his wheel. But the jar that he was forming didn't turn out as he wished, so he kneaded it into a lump and started again" (Jer. 18:3). It always grieved God when, as the divine potter, He could not shape Israel as He would choose (verses 5, 6).

> "GO DOWN AT ONCE TO THE POTTER'S HOUSE, AND THERE I WILL TELL YOU WHAT I HAVE TO SAY."
>
> JER. 18:2, NEB.

Next the Lord ordered Jeremiah to buy a jar from the potter and break it before the people, saying: "This is what the Lord Almighty says: I will smash this nation and this city just as this potter's jar" (Jer. 19:11, NIV). Catching the same vision of God's decisive power, the psalmist cried: "You shall . . . dash them in pieces like a potter's vessel" (Ps. 2:9, RSV).

Yet herein lies divine mercy, a fragment of hope. Some broken pottery shards *can* be used again— to carry ashes from the fire, to dip water, and for writing material. Also, when finely ground, the shards made a waterproof plaster for lining cisterns. While a broken pot could not be useful again in its original form, God always has an alternative plan—one that we dare not challenge. "But who are you, O man, to talk back to God? 'Shall what is formed say to him who formed it, "Why did you make me like this?" ' Does not the potter have the right to make out of the same lump of clay some pottery for noble purposes and some for common use?" (Rom. 9:20, 21, NIV).

The afflicted Job found himself on the ash heap, withered as a rejected potsherd and pleading with the Divine Potter: "Remember that you molded me like clay. Will you now turn me to dust again?" (Job 10:9, NIV). Broken yet resolute like Job, we may all be restored to a new life.

> *As the divine potter, Lord, You have the skill to help me overcome my mistakes. If only I am willing, You will find new usefullness for me. Take my day into Your hands, please.*

CERAMICS: A WORK OF ART

Not only do I have an insatiable desire to visit china shops but also to look into the china cupboards of my friends and admire the lovely dishes there. I am never in England, Ireland, or Canada without dropping by a china shop or museum at least once to feast my eyes on the lovely displays of crystal and china. It is, to be sure, a purely objective and non-jealous taste. Since I have spent a lifetime in moving household goods and in international travel, and in being perpetually in restricted financial circumstances, I have no real expectation of owning very much of such gorgeous artwork. I simply look and enjoy.

The potter's task has always been to choose artistic decoration to suit the various vessels. Likewise, God has created us to be useful containers—full of necessary, precious, and beautiful things. Indeed, He has a specific plan for each of us vessels whom He has created at His "divine wheel."

WE ARE NO BETTER THAN POTS OF EARTHENWARE TO CONTAIN THIS TREASURE, AND THIS PROVES THAT SUCH TRANSCENDENT POWER DOES NOT COME FROM US, BUT IS GOD'S ALONE.

2 COR. 4:7, NEB.

"The Potter"

"The nail-scarred hands of the Potter
Are molding this vessel of clay
As in grateful submission
I yield to Him day by day.
On lumps of pride and selfishness
On knots of canker care,
The firm, strong hands of the Potter
Must often be brought to bear.
As I cry out in my anguish,
'Oh, gentle Potter, spare!'
He answers, 'The vessel I'm making
Must be exceeding fair.'
And so in humble submission
I yield to Him as before,
For soon the heavenly Potter
Will work on the clay no more."

—Marian H. Phillips

Jesus, I rest myself completely in Your hands today. Shape me as You choose.

CERAMICS: THE GLAZED VESSEL

Applying glaze to a raw clay surface is an artistic adventure. When you fire the clay in the kiln, the unpromising dullness of the glaze when first applied now forms a hard surface, often bursting into a blaze of color. From the delicately painted serving dish to the colorful flower pot, the lovely glazed exterior of a vessel holds promise of good things and many uses inside.

Still, glaze *can* be a gross deception. Though a royal prince, Isaiah knew about the discipline down in the potter's house. He described Israel's exile as a breaking "in pieces like pottery, shattered . . . mercilessly" (Isa. 30:14, NIV). Jeremiah described Coniah, king of Judah, as "a despised, broken pot, a vessel no one cares for" (Jer. 22:28, RSV).

As Master Potter, of course, God is a realist. Unlike a sentimental housewife, He never glues together a broken dish that can never be useful again. Instead, He may salvage a few broken shards out of the rubble to use for a different purpose. Or He may grind up the fragments to create something entirely new out of the dust.

Judas is the classic example of the deceptive vessel. Operating under a "glaze" of impressive talents, he turned out to be a blemished pot. Ironically, his 30 pieces of silver bought the "Potter's Field," the place where discarded potsherds were dumped. Since no crops could grow there, it became a cemetery for non-Jews. Not one of those unfortunate traveling Gentiles, however, could have been more tragic than Judas himself. A broken vessel, shattered beyond repair, not a single shard of his life remained to serve any future purpose.

As the Divine Potter, God desires that we understand that we are the pottery of His exclusive making. He wants us to acknowledge His absolute power and direction in our lives. We have the choice to submit wholly to His shaping influences, or we can, like Judas, destroy ourselves in rebellion and be cast out—eternally—into the Potter's Field.

> LIKE THE GLAZE COVERING AN EARTHEN VESSEL ARE SMOOTH LIPS WITH AN EVIL HEART.
>
> PROV. 26:23, RSV.

[*Take the broken fragments of my life, God, and create a new purpose, a new meaning to my journey down here on earth.*]

METALLURGY: THE REFINER'S FIRE

We have to deal with three kinds of fire. First, there is the relentless, violent fire of destruction, such as when invading armies put villages to the torch, when bombs fall, setting fires that blaze out of control. Or when arsonists—driven by the quirks of their own twisted minds—burn down churches, schools, thousands of acres of land in a forest fire, or even their own houses. Sheer terrorism, such fires have no acceptable reason or explanation. We can only stand by, watching firefighters risk their lives in heroic rescue operations and marveling at human perversity.

> "FOR HE IS LIKE A REFINER'S FIRE."
>
> MAL. 3:2, RSV.

Second is the tame domestic fire we make to serve ourselves: that in the furnace to warm the house, in the oven to bake the bread, and in the stove to simmer the soup. Such fire burns in the fireplace at which we sit and dream our dreams. The spark ignites the car engine or unleashes the power of the jet airplane. Confined and controlled, such fires are faithful servants, obedient to our commands. Domestic fires are, indeed, the hallmark of civilization.

Then we have the refiner's fire, the one that separates valuable metal from the slag. Not the senseless fire of destruction or the limited everyday fire we may use for our convenience, it is the fierce, all-consuming flame of the smelter.

Christ is the great refiner's fire, and "who can endure the day of his coming" (Mal. 3:2, RSV)? In this last definitive separation of good and evil, we are the crude metal. Most of us have discovered that the refining process can be hard to endure. Entering into the fiery furnace of purification must involve suffering and pain. As the process goes on, we pass from one trial to yet another, for refining is the work of a lifetime. We thus learn patience.

The pain notwithstanding, we must cling to our faith, for we realize that our lives can do nothing useful until the dross has been burned away. Indeed, we may take comfort in remembering that no one would waste time refining slag! And Jesus somehow finds that we are worth refining. Behind our plain faces, bad habits, annoying attitudes, persistent waywardness, and limited talents, He can see rich ore. For this, then, we must rejoice.

> [*Today may well hold a fiery furnace experience for me. Stand by me through it, Master.*]

METALLURGY: THE REFINER

The refiner sits patiently over the crucible while the heat of the fire purges away the dross.

Hour after hour the person works until one can see his or her own face reflected in the liquid gold or silver. Until the metal is thus purified, the artist can create no objects of beauty.

The Chinese craftsmen of the ancient Shang dynasty (1523-1028 B.C.) cast large bronze containers, not just for domestic use, but for ritual services in the temples. Fancifully shaped and wonderfully incised with religious inscriptions, the sacred vessels are now among China's most precious national treasures. The artisans who chose to create such bronzes had a high calling. Not only did they produce the purest molten metal for sacred purposes, but often they were expected to make a personal sacrifice in order to impregnate the vessel with a strong "spirit." To accomplish the mystical—but dreadful—task, the craftsman might throw wife or child into the molten metal to become, literally, part of the substance of the temple vessel. Occasionally, a refiner even threw himself into the deadly cauldron.

> HE WILL SIT AS A REFINER AND PURIFIER OF SILVER, AND HE WILL PURIFY THE SONS OF LEVI AND REFINE THEM LIKE GOLD AND SILVER.
>
> MAL. 3:3, RSV.

Full of all kinds of uncleanness, like the waste material that must be separated from valuable metal, our lives require much refining. Jesus' work as the great refiner is to burn away the dross, for we are now mixed with the slag of crime, superstition, fear, hate, and a hundred other pollutants. We bear little resemblance to the pure characters God intended us to be.

If we permit Him, Jesus will separate us from our sin, even as metal is separated from dross. We have to be patient, however, with what is likely to be a long process. Silver, we are told, must pass through at least seven firings. But at last the flame of God's love and grace will consume the evil out of our lives. Then—and only then—can He use us as fit vessels for His kingdom. Like the old artists of Shang, He has thrown Himself into the crucible of our humanity in order to make such beauty possible in our lives. Unlike them, however, He does not leave the finishing of the work up to others. Christ lives on to complete His work on His "vessels."

[*Separate me from the dross in my life, O Lord. I want Your likeness to be perfectly reflected in me.*]

MUSIC: THE SONG

No one understood better than the royal musician David the redemptive power of music. Repeatedly the king called for singing "a new song" to the Lord. Before we can sing the Lord's song, however, we must undergo extensive restoration and tuning.

On his deathbed in Jerusalem an old Russian pianist told his grandson of a wonderful antique piano with a tone so beautiful that it had been called the "harp of King David." Its richly carved case, people said, had been hewn of wood from Solomon's Temple. Although that part was legend, the piano itself was fact. Built about 1800, it stood in the palace of King Victor Emmanuel in Rome, an incredible work of art combining the gifts of a piano builder and a wood carver. The grandson, Avner Carmi, became a piano tuner and kept the story of the "harp of David" always in mind.

During a period of years he had a series of unbelievable encounters with the piano. He first found it encased in a rock-hard coating of plaster, scheduled for destruction at El Alamein at the end of the North Africa campaign in World War II. Looting German soldiers had apparently brought it down to the desert. A troupe of British entertainers then took it to Italy and later abandoned it in Tel Aviv. Next a beekeeper made it a beehive, a chicken farmer used it for an incubator, and a butcher stored meat in it. Finally Carmi acquired the old piano. When he removed the plaster, he realized that he had discovered the legendary "harp of David." Thereafter, he devoted his life to making the "harp" sing again. Its remarkable tone quality blended the diamond-point clarity of a harpsichord with the darker sounds from the modern piano.

We, like the antique piano, have repeatedly fallen to unworthy uses, been abandoned, and been scheduled for destruction. When Jesus removes yesterday's discord from our song of life, however, we will praise Him in music that is forever new and unrehearsed.

"THE LORD IS MY STRENGTH, MY SONG, AND MY SALVATION. HE IS MY GOD, AND I WILL PRAISE HIM."

EX. 15:2, TLB.

> "Great Master, touch us with Thy skillful hand,
> Let not the music that is in us die."
> —Horatius Bonar

MUSIC: THE SONG OF TRIUMPH

Only music can capture the Christian's existence. In his high and holy moments King David saw the earth itself breaking forth in song—the bursting harmonies of creation in seas, floods, and quaking hills. No solemn, chilly chant this! No bleak, single wailing voice here! David calls for singing psalms "in the Lord's honour with the harp, . . . with the music of the psaltery. With trumpet and echoing horn acclaim . . . the Lord" (Ps. 98:5, 6, NEB). The strong, unifying song that only the saints can sing, it heals and renews.

THE LORD IS MY STRENGTH AND SONG.

PS. 118:14, NKJV.

Medical science has long been intrigued by the effects (both good and bad) of music on the human mind. Altering emotions, music can either soothe or damage the nerves, and can stimulate circulatory and muscular activity. It can distract so as to alleviate pain or provide a creative outlet to release energy. But music is powerful, and it has a dangerous side as well.

In 1988 a physicist and neurobiologist experimented with the effect of music on mice. One group of rodents listened to Strauss waltzes for eight weeks. The second endured disharmonic sounds accompanied by constant drumbeats (at low volume). The control group lived in silence. After weeks of jarring noise and pounding rhythm, the disharmonic group of mice had suffered brain damage. They had difficulty even finding their food. Their brain tissue showed abnormal growth of the neurons and chemical imbalances. "We cannot preclude the possibility," the scientists concluded, "that disharmony may affect human brains as well."

The Indian poet and philosopher Rabindranath Tagore (1861-1941) had a keen awareness of the fine line between the material and the mystical. He knew how firmly the gift of music bonds us to our Maker in a mighty flowing channel of love: "God respects me when I work, but He loves me when I sing."

The music designed for the believer opens up fresh and deepening understandings of God. The Master enables us, singly and in unison, to take up the triumphant song of joy, heaven's ever-new music. He is the composer who turns our lives into symphonies of praise.

> *Teach me Your song now, dear Lord. I want to be in the rehearsal now for the singing of anthems in eternity.*

MUSIC: THE PRAYER SONG

Because the Hebrews were famed for their musical talents, the Babylonians knew how to hurt
them. "Our tormentors demanded songs of joy,"
one exile mourned. "They said, 'Sing us one of the
songs of Zion!' How can we sing the songs of the
Lord while in a foreign land?" (Ps. 137:3, 4, NIV).
How, indeed, does one learn to sing the Lord's song
in the despair of the night!

AND IN THE NIGHT HIS SONG SHALL BE WITH ME—A PRAYER TO THE GOD OF MY LIFE.

PS. 42:8, NKJV.

Yet nighttime is exactly when we most need
music. After several floggings, Paul and Silas found
themselves thrown into the Roman prison at Philippi.
At midnight, however, they "were praying and singing
hymns to God." The results of those songs in the night were threefold.
They encouraged the singers, as well as the other prisoners. Next they led
to the jailer's conversion. And finally they opened the way for more powerful Christian witness in that city.

Have you stopped singing lately? Has the night seemed so dark that
you could not find a song anywhere in it? Have your circumstances become
so strange that you cannot recall the Lord's song that you once knew?

John Donne, dean of St. Paul's Cathedral, London, was celebrated as a
clergyman, but even more so as a poet. As he faced his night of death, he
discovered that the song sung in the dark is a prayer. Just one week before
he died in 1631, he peered across the threshold into eternity and wrote
"Hymne to God My God, in My Sicknesse."

> "Since I am coming to that Holy roome,
> Where, with thy Quire of Saints for evermore,
> I shall be made thy Musique; As I come
> I tune the Instrument here at the dore,
> And what I must doe then, thinke here before."

The Christian becomes more than just the instrument for God's song.
His life is, indeed, the song itself. It requires daily practice for us to learn
that song—perhaps even in a new key. Only then will we be able to sing it
in the night at crisis times.

[*Heavenly conductor, help me rehearse my old songs
and teach me the new ones You have chosen for me.*]

THE HARP

The family of Cain, with good reason, has had much bad publicity. After the murder of Abel, the clan moved off into the "land of Nod, east of Eden" (Gen. 4:16, NIV). There they developed some special talents. One of Cain's descendants received credit as the first musician on record. Jubal, the sixth-generation grandson of Cain, invented the harp and flute (Gen. 4:21). The harp (*kinnor*) denotes the whole class of stringed instruments (one or more strings), while the "flute" covered the whole range of wind instruments (one and more pipes). Music makers ever since those primeval days have been improving and enlarging upon Jubal's skills.

THEREFORE MY HEART SHALL RESOUND LIKE A HARP FOR MOAB.

ISA. 16:11, NKJV.

The harp, the national instrument of the Hebrews, has come to be associated with the deepest expressions of the human soul. Describing the destruction of Moab, Isaiah cried, "My heart laments for Moab like a harp" (Isa. 16:11, NIV). David's harp music, Saul's courtiers hoped, would have therapeutic effects upon the king's insanity (1 Sam. 16:16). Finally, the sound of the redeemed standing before God in heaven was that of "harpers playing on their harps," a vast swell of music mixed with the sound of "rushing waters and like a loud peal of thunder" (Rev. 14.2, NIV). The sweet plaintive notes of the single harp have become the identifying feature of many people. Egyptian musicians favored the harp, and to this day the gentle harp is the favorite instrument of the Irish, the Welsh, and other Gaelic races.

Similarly, the Lord's song is to be found not just in the "loud" parts of nature described by David but also in quiet secret places as well. The plucked and bowed strings can speak quietly to us, even in the midst of sorrow. The American philosopher and poet Ralph Waldo Emerson (1803-1882) found a universal song in nature. The music arose, he declared, not just from the beautiful features of our world but also from "the mud and scum of things."

"But in the darkest, meanest things
There alway, alway something sings."

The Christian's faith enables him or her to take courage and exult with the poet. Whatever crises we must face, we can always find that "something that sings"—like the clear, pure note from the harp.

> Let me find a song to sing, even in the darkest night and in the most fearful silence.

THE ORCHESTRA

The conductor of a great symphony orchestra is a combination of demon and saint. He has dignified presence, an incredible memory, and vast wisdom. Administrator, actor, psychologist, and disciplinarian, he or she is a leader who tolerates no opposition. After all, he or she must keep a hundred or more players together (most of them believing that they could do a better job) and weld them into a precision unit. And then comes the magic. Taking a score that orchestras have played for the past 100 years, the conductor fills the air with magnificent new sound that no one has heard before. He or she conducts music rather than the orchestra, sweeping all along with him or her into the fierce joy of making music. "Play with your hearts," Toscanini used to say. "Not your instruments."

Even those who have never attained the concert stage can discover the peculiar thrill of making music together as a community. Finding and filling one's place in the overall harmonic design is a satisfaction not to be understood or appreciated by those who have missed the experience. Playing under the baton of a good conductor becomes high joy, even for an amateur.

An old folktale tells of an Empire of Music located in a remote mountain grove. It was rumored that when someone played the finest music with the greatest skill, the heavenly vision of the Palace of Peace would materialize. Musicians arrived from all over the world, each eager to be the one to usher in the age of peace on earth. One by one they came. They all played their hearts out, each trying to outdo all of the others, but the vision never came. Finally one youth, violin tucked under his arm, said, "Why don't we try playing *together*—in harmony?" They did. And at the first mighty chord, the glorious vision of the palace burst over their heads.

We all play different instruments with varying skills and different timbres. When the Divine Maestro assembles and trains His people, He draws the most perfect harmonies from their united praise.

PRAISE HIM WITH THE TRUMPET AND WITH LUTE AND HARP. PRAISE HIM WITH THE TAMBOURINES AND PROCESSIONAL. PRAISE HIM WITH STRINGED INSTRUMENTS AND HORNS. PRAISE HIM WITH THE CYMBALS, YES, LOUD CLANGING CYMBALS.

PS. 150:3-5, TLB.

> *Today, Master, I would concentrate on making harmony, not discord.*

PART FIVE

Abstract
Concepts

THE NAME

ABSTRACT CONCEPTS

THE NAME OF YAHWEH/ADONAI

What is in a name? A great deal, really. It's a major means of identity, and we take much care in giving names. Businesses and products need correct names so that they will "sell." Writers and editors mull over book and story titles at great length, the naming of their brainchild being almost as momentous as the birthing of a physical child. Prospective parents spend time discussing their name options long before the baby's birth.

Traditionally, shepherds have named their sheep and dairymen their cows. My grandfather named his chickens. Purebred horses, dogs, and cats carry aristocratic registered names. We often choose names to suit appearances and personalities. (Therefore, my black-and-white Pomeranian answers to the name of Patches simply because that is what he looks like.) Ancient warriors named their weapons in order to infuse them with spirit and strength. Some householders still individualize their homes with names. I have friends living in a house in Ireland called Late Naughton's—a name, no doubt, with its roots buried somewhere deep in the folklore of the Irish countryside.

"I APPEARED UNTO ABRAHAM, UNTO ISAAC, AND UNTO JACOB, BY THE NAME OF GOD ALMIGHTY, BUT BY MY NAME JEHOVAH WAS I NOT KNOWN TO THEM."
EX. 6:3.

As the name *Jehovah* implies, God is indeed strong, mighty, and distant. To the ancient Hebrews Yahweh was the sacred title that distinguished God from all the false gods. It stressed His faithfulness and His self-existence as the very source of life. For fear of profaning it, people gradually came not to speak it at all. Instead, they combined the name Yahweh with the vowels of Adonai to form Jehovah. It simply meant "Lord."

John applied many names to God and His Son, particularly in the book of Revelation—the "Faithful and True," "the Word of God," and superlatively, "the KING OF KINGS, AND LORD OF LORDS" (Rev. 19:11-21). In his translation of John's third letter, however, Phillips simply said, "They [the evangelists] set out on this work, as you know, for the sake of 'the name'" (3 John 7, Phillips). No need to say *whose* name, for there rises just "one Name above every name." It is for us to unfold its hidden meanings. Only then can we fully honor it.

[*In a world that speaks of You so casually, I would always honor the pure holiness of Your name.*]

THE NAME OF IMMANUEL

The name of Jehovah was awesome, even terrifying, to Israel. Upon His entry into our human circle, however, Jesus took up, in our behalf, the special name of Immanuel.

And a name is, indeed, a very special gift. A man shares his name with his wife and then passes it down to his children. Because we tend to like (or not like) a name according to the people we have known who bore it, we often name our children after favorite relatives or illustrious public persons. We emblazon our family name on a coat of arms, indicating our pride in a worthy heritage. Then we sign our names on thousands of documents (almost always in triplicate) to ensure the sincerity of our intentions. Our names, in fact, signify the essence of all that is peculiarly ours, separating us from everyone else on the one hand but also joining us to our family and nation on the other.

Whenever we let down the barriers and allow people to come close, we evidence the new intimate relationship by the name that we permit them to use. "For *you* the name is Dr. Smith," we intone. Or we say casually, "Just call me George." Or "In school my nickname was always Beanie." Or "Everyone in the family calls me Wes."

A university professor once gave some of us younger people the gift of his name. We had been his students and had long been impressed by his fame and brilliant scholarship, always addressing him as "Doctor" or "Professor." Then he retired and went guest lecturing and socializing among us. "Never mind that now," he would say. "Just call me Steve." Although he obviously wanted to feel closer to us, we could hardly overcome the years of classroom discipline. Every time we slipped back into the old terminology, however, he would pull us up short. "Please! Just call me Steve!"

Like the retired professor, God also longed to be near His people. Hence, the name Immanuel closed that distance, for it meant "God with us." Still, one more nearer and dearer name would be necessary. God would be born among us and would be named Jesus.

> "BEHOLD, A VIRGIN SHALL CONCEIVE AND BEAR A SON, AND HIS NAME SHALL BE CALLED EMMANUEL."
>
> MATT. 1:23, RSV.

"Given for us, and condescending
To be born for us below,
He, with men in converse blending,
Dwelt the seed of truth to sow."
—Thomas Aquinas (1227-1274)

THE NAME OF JESUS

Our personal name is a very special, very private possession—part of the very fiber of our lives, our identity. Even a child becomes angry when someone mocks his or her name. Humans and animals alike respond acutely and instinctively to a name's sound. Moreover, our name does more than simply identify us in a crowd. It often calls up a specific image and ties events, hopes, and joys to a certain person. For Christians the name of Jesus embodies all of our hope, salvation, and expectation of eternal life. It is all there in that single name. One of the ironies of history is that when Jesus stood trial before Pilate, the alternative prisoner offered to the Jews was *also* named Jesus. "Which would you like me to release to you," Pilate inquired, "Jesus Bar-Abbas, or Jesus called Messiah?" (Matt. 27:17, NEB).

"AND YOU SHALL CALL HIS NAME JESUS, FOR HE WILL SAVE HIS PEOPLE FROM THEIR SINS."

MATT. 1:21, NKJV.

At the time of His birth "Jesus" was actually a common name—virtually the equivalent of Tom, Dick, or Harry. Joshua, Jehoshua, and Jeshua were all variations. Its meaning of "God's salvation" or "God is my help" would make it a favorite choice for devout Hebrew parents. "Jesus the Messiah," however, is something else. Thus the title emphasizes, on the one hand, His commonness and availability, and on the other, His uniqueness. William Barclay writes: "It is no accident that our Lord was called by the name Jesus. That name sums up the things which he came into the world to do and which only he can do."*

Angel messengers announced God's appointment of the name Jesus before His birth. No one could mistake His identity when He arrived. He would have many titles, of course—each of the many names of God and His Son portrays a different aspect of divine character. None would be more personal, however, than "Jesus." He is never more accessible to us than when we call on that name. "Indeed, anything you ask in my name," He promises, "I will do, so that the Father may be glorified in the Son" (John 14:13, NEB).

> *"'Jesus,' oh, how sweet the name!*
> *'Jesus,' every day the same;*
> *'Jesus,' let all saints proclaim*
> *Its worthy praise forever."*

---

*William Barclay, *Jesus as They Saw Him* (Grand Rapids: Eerdmans, 1978).

THE NAME OF CHRIST

What is in a name, then? We repeat—*much!* It confers power and identity. From among all of the names of God, we have corporately adopted the name "Christian." The Greek *Christos* (meaning "the anointed one") implies separateness, a setting apart, a uniqueness, a promise, and a commitment.

> AND PETER ANSWERED AND SAID TO HIM, "YOU ARE THE CHRIST."
>
> MARK 8:29, NKJV.

God has double claim on us. Jesus has called us "heirs of the kingdom" by adoption. He has also presented Himself as the heavenly Bridegroom. In both cases He expects us to take on a new name—and we should be proud to do it before all of the world. By assuming the name of Christ and calling ourselves Christians, we announce our relationship publicly.

I know a number of bright, independent young women who have chosen to retain their maiden names when they marry. Most of their bridegrooms, it appears, agree to such an arrangement. There is no point to argue the pros and cons of the custom here. We need only to remind ourselves of the long tradition of a name change at the time of marriage and see how it applies neatly to biblical imagery. Proud and important men have gifted their less-privileged wives with names that automatically confer on them wealth, power, and prestige.

Those who share a name both have certain mutual rights and obligations. The title of "Christian" endows us with at least six wonderful gifts:

1. Power. "If you ask anything in my name, I will do it" (John 14:14, RSV).
2. Healing. "They shall never perish, and no one shall snatch them out of my hand" (John 10:28, RSV).
3. Joy. "I have spoken . . . that My joy may remain in you" (John 15:11, NKJV).
4. Forgiveness. "Repentance and forgiveness of sins should be preached in his name to all nations" (Luke 24:47, RSV).
5. New Life. "[By] believing you may have life in his name" (John 20:31, RSV).
6. Sharing. "I will praise thee among the Gentiles, and sing to thy name" (Rom. 15:9, RSV).

> [*To the name that brings salvation let the nations bow the head;*
> *Let them kneel in adoration when this name of names is said.* *]

*From a fifteenth-century hymn, translated by John Mason Neale (1818-1866).

THE NAME OF ELOHIM

At the risk of seeming a little overacademic, we need to look briefly at the name "El." This root word comes from the Acetin and Ugaritic and means "strength, power, and majesty." It became a poetic designation of the one and only true God of Israel. In certain Canaanite mythologies it also refers to a chief "father god." The Old Testament abounds in patriarchal variations on this word: *El Anna* ("the jealous God," Ex. 20:5); *El Lyon* ("most high God," Gen. 14:18); *El Roi* ("God the seeing one," Gen 16:13), and so forth. Sometimes the biblical writer used *Elohim* to imply the "royal plural," and it also referred to angels: "the sons of *Elohim*" (Job 1:6).

AND AT THE NINTH HOUR JESUS CRIED WITH A LOUD VOICE, SAYING, ELOI, ELOI, . . . MY GOD, MY GOD, WHY HAST THOU FORSAKEN ME?

MARK 15:34.

In view of its heritage, it's amazing how we've come to take such appalling liberties with the name of our God. Why do we cripple our minds with profanity and the trivializing of His name?

Of Jesus' seven dying cries from the cross, none has aroused more controversy in interpretation than *"Eli, Eli, lama sabachthani!"* Generations have puzzled over the Aramaic phrase and have not reached any agreement on its interpretation. From a devotional standpoint, however, perhaps we can make just two significant points.

First, "My God, my God, why hast thou forsaken me" is a direct quotation from David's Psalm 22:1. The passion of this song is, in effect, the prayer of a virtuous man who is suffering. More exactly, it is a Messianic psalm, linked directly to the ministry of Christ. It sounds like a cry of despair. That is until we remember His triumphant last words: "Father, into thy hands I commend my spirit" (Luke 23:46).

In His intense mental and physical suffering, Christ felt loneliness and perhaps even perplexity. It should not surprise the Christian, then, that he or she may face temporary moods of depression—but they aren't the last word ever. The final "loud cry" of Jesus was not a gasp of despair in the last moments of life in His broken body. Rather it was a confession of faith, a shout of victory.

> *"Glorious is Thy name, O Lord! Thou art mighty, Thou art holy,*
> *Glorious is Thy matchless name!"*
>
> —B. B. McKinney

THE UNKNOWN GOD

Paul's discovery of this inscription on Mars Hill is pathetic evidence of one of humanity's most deep-seated anxieties—the need to be bonded to God. Here is a gnawing fear that we might have overlooked something or someone—with eternally fatal results.

Long before the Athenians wrestled with this problem, however, the ancient Egyptians felt the same lack of security. A vivid painting in the tomb of Queen Nefertari shows the dead woman walking hand in hand with the goddess Isis to be justified before the great god Osiris. A scene in another tomb shows the "Broad Hall of the Two Justices," where the king, cowering behind a god, awaits his fate and watches his heart being weighed in the balances. Nearby a monster stands ready to eat him if he fails the test. Meanwhile, he cries out to the 42 gods, one by one, hoping that his name will be recognized. "I am pure! I am pure! . . . . I know the names of these gods. . . . . O Breaker-of-Bones, I have not told lies. . . . O Wide-of-Stride, I have not been covetous" (Book of the Dead, 1500-950 B.C.).

Not knowing one's God becomes pure panic. In similar terms Jesus described the tragedy of those uncommitted Christians who would plead, "Lord, Lord, did we not prophesy in your name?" They receive a terrible answer: "Then I will tell them plainly, 'I never knew you. Away from me, you evil doers!'" (Matt. 7:23, NIV).

Those who can step out in faith have a special advantage. After His resurrection Jesus said to Thomas: "Have you believed because you have seen me? Blessed are those who have not seen and yet believe" (John 20:29, RSV). Faith is what it takes to bridge the gap between our human reality and the mystery of God.

Unlike the ancient Egyptians, however, we do *not* have a severe, remote God. He is, in fact, constantly trying to make Himself known to us in a thousand ways. It is a wonderfully comforting thought to walk hand in hand with your God!

"AS I PASSED ALONG, AND OBSERVED THE OBJECTS OF YOUR WORSHIP, I FOUND ALSO AN ALTAR WITH THIS INSCRIPTION, 'TO AN UNKNOWN GOD.'"

ACTS 17:23, RSV.

> [*I know and honor Your name, Lord, and You know mine.*
> *Let there never be any mistaken identity between us.*]

THE HOLY ONE

The word *holy* derives from an old Anglo-Saxon word meaning "sacred and consecrated."

Whenever we celebrate any "holiday"—whether a relaxing or riotous one—we are recalling those far-off days when the only respite people had from their daily labors was a religious festival, a "holy day."

Through the centuries the word has accumulated a wide range of connotations. Today it may call up feelings of the unapproachable and distant, even the forbidding. We feel threatened by unattainable standards of holiness. On the other hand, the word has generalized itself into common slang, as in our random exclamations of "Holy mackerel!" and "Holy cow!"

"FOR I AM THE LORD, YOUR GOD, THE HOLY ONE OF ISRAEL, YOUR SAVIOR."

ISA. 43:3, NIV.

The "Holy One of Israel," however, is neither threatening nor frivolous. He has four unmistakable characteristics:

1. Holy things come from God, and holy people are bonded to God. Apart from Him, no one can find the truly sacred. Any other source of "holiness" dooms the seeker.

2. Holiness is a condition of refreshing, saving purity and spiritual perfection. Nothing but divine grace and forgiveness, however, can fill the great abyss between holiness and our poor human frailties.

3. Holy things and holy places are to be reverenced—all the way from Moses' burning bush in the desert to the modern church where you worship. Religious rites and acts must be directed to the worship of the holy God.

4. Because holiness is beautiful, it satisfies our deep need to find loveliness in our lives. Thus the holy nurtures our inner spirituality.

From the start, all of these traits appeared in Jesus' ministry. Even a crazed lunatic in the synagogue in Capernaum could recognize pure holiness. Over the heads of the astonished congregation, he cried to Christ: "I know who You are—the Holy One of God!" (Mark 1:24, NKJV).

Understanding true holiness, then, the Christian honors *all* of the names of God, for Jehovah is a "jealous" God regarding the use of His names. Yet His promise to the faithful holds: "I will dwell in the midst of the people Israel for ever. And the house of Israel shall no more defile my holy name" (Eze. 43:7, RSV).

[*"Holy, holy, holy! Lord God Almighty!*
All Thy works shall praise Thy name in earth and sky and sea."]
—Reginald Heber

SHILOH

On his deathbed Jacob delivered his final message to his family. To Judah he promised personal royal supremacy "until Shiloh comes." The name "Shiloh" means "peace giver," "rest giver," or "a place of rest." Understandably, Israel, weary from wilderness wanderings, named their first sacred tabernacle site Shiloh.

Picture that secluded little settlement in the Ephraim hills, just off the highway between Bethel and Shechem (Judges 21:19, 20). There the ark rested, and the holy place prospered throughout the times of the judges. The priests conducted services, and the people made annual pilgrimages. Eli ministered at Shiloh as high priest, and there at the tabernacle young Samuel grew to manhood (1 Sam. 1-3). Then a national disaster occurred. The Philistines captured the ark during the battle of Aphek (1 Sam. 4:1-11).

After the Israelites recovered it, however, the ark did not return to Shiloh, an indication that the Philistines had destroyed the beloved religious center (1 Sam. 6:21-7:2). Its mass of shapeless ruins was not rediscovered until 1838, the destruction being dated at about 1100 B.C. Five hundred years later Jeremiah remembered the place only as a ruin. "Go to my shrine at Shiloh," Jehovah told him. "I made [it] a dwelling for my Name" (Jer. 7:12-14, NEB). It had become "an object of ridicule to all nations" (Jer. 26:9, NEB). In other words, Israel had lost rest and peace—both materially and spiritually.

The time of His birth having been predicted, "Shiloh" came after the Hebrew monarchy had expired and the Romans had annexed Palestine. The aged prophets Simeon and Anna hailed His presentation at the Temple with the joyous assurance that the "glory of Your people Israel" had indeed arrived (Luke 2:32, NKJV).

But there is more. We also discern signs of the second coming of Shiloh today. Meanwhile, He is the maker, giver, and bringer of peace, settling the discordant elements in our lives. He does so, however, under specific conditions. His dominion is absolute, and peace can come only through obedience. Only when we obey the peace giver shall we find "the peace that passes all understanding."

> **"THE SCEPTER SHALL NOT DEPART FROM JUDAH . . . UNTIL SHILOH COMES; AND TO HIM SHALL BE THE OBEDIENCE OF THE PEOPLE."**
>
> GEN. 49:10, NKJV.

[*Bringer of peace, repair and renew the ruins of my heart today. I would make it a shrine to Your honor once more.*]

THE INVISIBLE GOD

Invisibility is a tantalizing idea. Children fantasize about it. "The Emperor's New Clothes" is a case in point. You'll recall that a pair of con men came to sell the emperor some "marvelous fabric that only intelligent people could see." Of course, though no such fabric existed, the proud ruler wouldn't admit that he saw nothing. So the men pretended to make a new suit of clothes and fit them on him. Meanwhile, the townspeople turned out to watch their lord parading through the street, wearing the clothes that only intelligent people could see. Everyone admired the fabulous "clothes," until one honest child in the crowd blurted out, "But he hasn't got any clothes on!"

> **HE IS THE IMAGE OF THE INVISIBLE GOD, THE FIRSTBORN OVER ALL CREATION.**
>
> COL. 1:15, NIV.

The demand to see "the invisible" has also entered spiritual matters. A famous picture of the American Shaker community demonstrates the difficulty. The drawing shows the Shakers, men and women on opposite sides, in formal dance around the tree of life in the center of the picture. All you see, however, is a small, empty fenced-in area. The "tree" is visible only to righteous, saved persons, so if you can't see it, then you the viewer have a problem.

Our times have conditioned us to associate reality with what we can see, what we can measure in a test tube. At one end of the scale, more and more people are becoming involved with the occult. In contrast, many others dismiss the supernatural as nonsense. Believers themselves cover about the same range. Imagine a "spectrum of faith." At one end is the extreme of invisibility—God is a Spirit, a universal force, a mystical presence. At the opposite end is the idol worshiper who must have a "humanized" god of wood or stone, a tangible reality. We're all somewhere on that scale.

Since God is (and always has been) invisible to us, then faith must take a leap beyond the physical and the material. After the Resurrection, Jesus put a very pertinent question to His disciple Thomas: "Have you believed because you have seen me? Blessed are those who have not seen and yet believe" (John 20:29, RSV).

We belong to the latter group.

> "Immortal, invisible, God only wise,
> In light inaccessible hid from our eyes,
> Most holy, most glorious, the Ancient of days,
> Almighty, victorious, Thy great name we praise."*

*W. C. Smith (1824-1906), in *Jubilate Hymns*.

NUCLEAR ENERGY

August 6, 1945, marked a turning point in human history. After that day the threat of nuclear warfare has never left us. We eye one another suspiciously, waiting for some nervous politician to push the button. That first atomic bomb destroyed 60 percent of the city of Hiroshima, Japan, bringing the Pacific war to an earlier but costly end. Subsequently, the Japanese dedicated the international Peace Memorial Park on "ground zero" where the bomb struck.

Greek mythology marks the beginning of civilization with Prometheus giving divine fire to humanity. Fearing that the technically wise humans would revolt, the other gods severely punished Prometheus for his error in judgment. The after-Eden world of Genesis called for other necessary measures. Fire was one, first revealed, perhaps, in the consuming of sacrifices. Since then we've moved from wood fires to fossil fuels such as coal and oil. Then came gunpowder and TNT—a huge menu of explosives. Meanwhile, electricity had changed our lives.

God, however, has supreme "nuclear capability." Indeed, He invented it! He kept the secret long hidden in the heart of His mighty universe. Then about 100 years ago scientists glimpsed the possibilities of radioactivity. They found that enormous energy lay in either the splitting or the fusing of atomic nuclei. Peaceful uses notwithstanding, the horror of Hiroshima became our first knowledge of what nuclear energy could do. All this power in *our* extremely unsteady hands?

Since then we've become too familiar with the death-dealing effects of radioactive fallout. We've been shown what "nuclear winter" after an atomic war looks like when all life is threatened. And we are beginning to grasp the force of total annihilation that leaves *nothing* behind. The divine Nuclear Scientist has given us some small, modest previews of His power—at the gate of Eden and certainly at Jesus' resurrection.

The main nuclear event, however, lies ahead. The Lord will come "with clouds, and every eye will see Him" (Rev. 1:7, NKJV)—a burst of power seen round the world. And as Peter adds, "All these things are thus to be dissolved." So then "what sort of persons" ought we to be (2 Peter 3:11, RSV)?

> HIS APPEARANCE WAS LIKE LIGHTNING. . . . THE GUARDS WERE SO AFRAID OF HIM THAT THEY SHOOK AND BECAME LIKE DEAD MEN.
>
> MATT. 28:3, 4, NIV.

[*God, the vast resources of Your cosmic power and energy are beyond my comprehension. Not for one moment would I stray from Your protection.*]

THE ANCIENT OF DAYS

Our opinion of exactly who or what is "ancient" modifies as we grow older. Do you remember when you thought anyone in their 20s had done just about all the growing up they could do? When your parents were in their 30s, do you remember how you felt sorry for them because they had so little left to look forward to? When you yourself reached 40, do you remember hoping you were only in the prime of life? And after that, well, what can we say? I once had a professor friend who diligently guarded her age all of her life. Actually, *no one* ever knew how old she was until she had her one hundredth birthday—then she confessed.

> "THE ANCIENT OF DAYS CAME, AND JUDGMENT WAS GIVEN FOR THE SAINTS OF THE MOST HIGH."
>
> DAN. 7:22, RSV.

Reticence about aging is tied to our Western "culture of youth." It's a fine thing to be young in America, but it's even better to be old in the Orient, where age and experience have honor. White hair is prestigious, and the accumulation of years indicates wisdom.

The peculiar expression "Ancient of Days" appears only once in Scripture—in one of Daniel's visions. The word "ancient" derives from the Hebrew verb "to move." Hence, it is an elegant Semitic expression for one who has "advanced" through many days.

Daniel offers us a dramatic picture of the Ancient of Days, as the Father and Son confer in the celestial throne room. The appearance of Jehovah in judgment would arouse supreme reverence in the Eastern mind: "[Jehovah's] garment was white as snow, and the hair of His head was like pure wool. His throne was a fiery flame" (Dan. 7:9, NKJV). Now Christ appears before His Father to be enthroned and to receive His imperial jurisdiction over the eternal kingdom—a kingdom that will overcome the transitory empires of the four beasts of the vision.

The Ancient of Days and His Coregent merit all possible honor. For the first time in history we receive a preview of Christ's unique divine-human nature when He will enter into earthly time. He comes girded with clouds to hide the glory of His divinity, but He is also human, the "Son of Man" (Dan. 7:13, NKJV).

[*I live in time, Father, and I know what old age means. But only in You can I begin to learn the thrill of seeing life from Your perspective in eternity.*]

THE DESIRE OF ALL NATIONS

Stunned by what he saw of human suffering when he left his princely life some 1,500 years ago in India, Siddhartha Gautama sought a solution to the problem. When he did, he became the Buddha, "the enlightened one." He started expounding his *four noble truths:* (1) "life is suffering," (2) "suffering is caused by desire," (3) "suffering can end only by extinguishing desire [Nirvana]," and (4) "the Eightfold Noble Path [a self-help design for righteous living] leads to attainment of Nirvana." From Gautama's day to ours, uncounted millions of people have striven to overcome desire and thereby find peace and happiness.

On the other hand, God has programmed us with desires. They are what drive us to achieve, make us compassionate, give us dreams and hopes, and shape our personality. With his usual virile energy, the Christian poet Robert Browning wrote: "Ah, but a man's reach should exceed his grasp, or what's a heaven for?"* Indeed, when God created desire within us, He left that strange but very real empty place that can be filled only by Himself. An earlier English poet described the bond. In pouring out blessings on the earth, the Creator withheld just one—contentment.

David wrote, "Lord, all my desire is before You" (Ps. 38:9, NKJV). Because He implanted them, God knows our desires even when we cannot verbalize them, even when we dare not share them with a friend, even when we have ideals so high that they frighten us. Moreover, desire directed toward Him never misses gratification. A fatalistic acceptance of a kind of "nirvana," then, destroys our capacity for experiencing our most "desirable" moments with Him.

He would lead His saints into that most far-reaching of all of our holiest desires—for loving our fellow travelers, for seeing the glory of Christ, for believing in the second coming of the King, and finally for entering into Paradise itself. We have been created to crave the Desire of all nations.

"THEY SHALL COME TO THE DESIRE OF ALL NATIONS, AND I WILL FILL THIS TEMPLE WITH GLORY," SAYS THE LORD OF HOSTS.

HAGGAI 2:7, NKJV.

[*I would not deny my desires, Jesus. I pray that they may be fulfilled according to Your plan.*]

---

*Robert Browning, "Andrea del Sarto."

THE AMEN

"A men" is an interesting word. It can be the ending to a simple prayer, or it may come in a hearty chorus from a congregation responding to their preacher's sermon. Or again it may have an elaborate musical setting, with dozens of amens in many voices climaxing an anthem or concluding public worship. In whatever circumstances we hear the ancient Hebrew word, the meaning remains the same. "Amen" declares that all that has gone before is certified to be "true, faithful, and certain."

"THESE ARE THE WORDS OF THE AMEN, THE FAITHFUL AND TRUE WITNESS, THE RULER OF GOD'S CREATION."

REV. 3:14, NIV.

Saying it at the end of a prayer commits the worshiper to a solemn pledge to what has been presented to God, meaning, "Let it be so" or "So shall it be." Also, we catch the exuberance as each of the five books of the Psalms ends with exuberant double amens. And hear John's thrilling exclamation at the end of the vision of Revelation: "Amen. Come, Lord Jesus!" (Rev. 22:20, NEB). Then too the force of the amen can verify negative events, like the twelvefold curse Moses passed on to the Levites in Deuteronomy 27:15-26.

God has chosen this, one of the most powerful words in Scripture, to describe Himself. Isaiah speaks literally of "the God of the Amen" (Isa. 65:16) as a means of emphasizing Jehovah's utter reliability and trustworthiness.

The Word tells us other reassuring things about Him. First, as the True Witness, Jesus leads us into a vital (but most difficult) kind of knowledge—the knowledge of self. He has always known what was in us. Now we too must know. It takes much courage to tear away our masks of self-deception and face truth. Only when we stand before the great Amen can we begin to know our innermost selves.

At the same time we find great security in being able to accept Jesus' view without question. In a world in which few certainties remain, we stand here on firm ground, for He has long established His total dependability. Then we accept His sustaining power as He surrounds us with His protection and support. Finally, when we lay hold of the faithfulness of God, we have cause for continual praise and rejoicing—even in the times when we must walk through dark, distressful valleys.

[*Yours, Lord, will ever be the last word in my life. Therein lies my refuge and my only hope.*]

THE YES

Almost the first word a child learns, it seems, is "no." That's the watchword through the "terrible twos" and well beyond. All part of growing up and asserting our individuality, we tell ourselves. Contrary to appearances, however, yes and no are both neutral responses. The outcome is dependent entirely on the question asked.

FOR ALL THE PROMISES OF GOD FIND THEIR YES IN HIM.

2 COR. 1:20, RSV.

Moreover, in the question-asking process, sometimes neither yes nor no is acceptable. We know the familiar inquiry: "Have you stopped beating your wife yet?"

The answer? "Yes [I was doing it, but now I quit]." Or "No [I'm still abusing her]." Neither reply is satisfactory.

I once had an excellent professor in graduate school. "Being able to ask the right questions," Professor Sullivan declared, "is just as important as being able to answer them." Although we faced a stout examination at the end of the course, each class period required us to produce at least one question based on our assigned readings. It was, of course, beneath our dignity to ask hopeless, trivial questions such as "May I have a week's extension on my term paper?" or "What's my final grade going to be?" Instead (because we took ourselves seriously), our questions actually fostered deep insights and lively class discussions.

When God announces Himself as "the yes," we see all kinds of possibilities opening up to this strong, positive answer. And so we should. We expect *anyone's* yes to be secure and encouraging. God's yes, on the other hand, is immeasurably more reliable.

Nonetheless, we must ask the proper questions—totally free from any hidden agenda. For some inquiries God will never come forward with the promised yes. "Can You forgive me my sins? But I just cannot tolerate my neighbor." Or "Will You give me material security? I faithfully support the church."

Instead, we need to discover the eternal questions of life and death—the ones for which Scripture assures us a resounding yes. "I commit myself to total faith in Jesus. Will He renew me and make me fit for heaven?" "I have so many limitations. Can You use my hands to minister to others today?" "I am facing a huge crisis in my life. I am asking You for patience and strength to see it through."

Yes! Yes! A thousand times yes!

[*Lord, Your promise of the yes answer encourages me. Teach me how to ask the correct questions. Sometimes I can't see far enough ahead to make the right request.*]

THE BEGINNING

For the benefit of us mortals who live in finite time, God, who is eternal, sets two important propositions before us. "I am the beginning." "I am the end."

Remember your first day at school? the place where you first learned to ride a bicycle? your first date with the person you married? what you bought with the first paycheck you had from your new job? the birth of a new baby? the occasions when you first realized that you were your own person and that your opinions could be as valid as anyone else's? (Complete this list as you choose.)

Acquiring something new is always a tremendous morale booster. Women know what a new dress can do for them, even though they still have other good ones left in their closets. A new car has approximately the same effect on men. The beginning of a new school year offers hope for students whose records the previous year were perhaps less than admirable.

We must have new beginnings because we daily face destruction and failure. New opportunities give us a second chance to set the record straight, to try it again, to work harder and get it right.

"I wish that there were some wonderful place
Called the Land of Beginning Again,
Where all our mistakes and all our heartaches
And all of our poor selfish grief
Could be dropped like a shabby old coat at the door,
And never be put on again."*

Yet at the same time beginnings can be frightening. Are we strong enough? Will we be able to finish the project? Is anyone going to stand by us? But beginnings are absolutely essential to our survival. The Chinese philosopher Lao-tzu (604-531 B.C.) observed that "a journey of a thousand miles must begin with a single step."

At our lowest ebb, Jesus, who is the essence of "beginning," steps in to show us where we stand. In 1942 at one of Britain's lowest points during World War II, Winston Churchill spoke to the nation about the battle in North Africa: "This is not the end. But it is perhaps the end of the beginning."

[*Lord of beginnings, show me where I stand. Make it clear. Am I nearing an ending, or do I look to starting again? Which?*]

*Louisa Fletcher, "The Land of Beginning Again," in Hazel Felleman, *Best Loved Poems of the American People* (Garden City, N.Y.: Garden City Pub. Corp., 1936), p. 101.

353 ❋ ABSTRACT CONCEPTS

THE END

I once visited a newly remodeled church in southern California. Having recently come from an overseas assignment, I was wholly unaccustomed to seeing such gracious and ample worship provisions. Inviting stone benches stood under spreading shade trees in the courtyard. The sanctuary shone in blue and white, full of light. Live plants grew inside and out so that one could hardly tell where the interior ended and the outdoors began. Children's facilities offered every possible attraction. The fellowship hall had a huge stone fireplace that must have been a wonderful center around which to visit. And the kitchen? State-of-the-art, gleaming with stainless steel, glass, and yards of counter space.

> "'I AM . . .
> THE END,'
> SAYS THE
> LORD."
> REV. 1:8, NKJV.

I turned to compliment the pastor on the beautiful facility. His reply surprised me. "When we were all raising the funds and doing the work, we had a great spirit in the church," he said. "But now that it's finished and paid for, people have started quarreling. Our membership is even going down."

Surprised? Maybe not. Endings, work completed, can lead to death. Even good endings are, of themselves, static and lifeless. Everything's known, and there's nothing more to do. With the adventure over, boredom and discouragement can easily set in. Nothing challenges anymore. The secret, then, is to *move on.* I once heard a college president complain of the inept performance of a certain faulty member: "He's not had 33 years' experience, as he claims. The man's just had one year's experience 33 times."

An English poet* aptly describes this complexity: "What we call the beginning is often the end, and to make an end is to make a beginning. The end is where we start from." This is where Jesus, the manager of endings, steps in to tell us a secret—that an ending is only a beginning in another guise.

> *"Today the journey is ended,*
> *I have worked out the mandates of fate;*
> *Naked, alone, undefended,*
> *I knock at the Uttermost Gate.*
> *Behind is life and its longing,*
> *Its trial, its trouble, its sorrow;*
> *Beyond is the Infinite Morning*
> *Of a day without a tomorrow.*†

---

*T. S. Eliot, "Little Gidding," 5.

†Wenonah Stevens Abbott, "A Soul's Soliloquy," in *America's Best Loved Poems* (Garden City, N.Y.: Garden City Pub. Corp., 1936), p. 78.

THE SOURCE

Australian children of my generation were fed sago pudding. While Auntie May's lemon sauce helped, eating sago pudding could still be tiresome. It used to be set before us in large, flat-bottomed soup bowls. Trained to clean up our plates at any cost, we worked at the task faithfully—no one could fault us there, even if we did get silly at the table. But I can still see that pale, transparent mass there on my place. With every mouthful, the stuff just spread itself around and never seemed to diminish. We named it "everlasting pudding."

I doubt that any of us seven youngsters knew what "everlasting" really meant. The mystery of eternity is enough to challenge even the greatest adult mind.

But how long *is* "everlasting"? Humanity has always been trapped in time. We've known nothing else, seeing history as a sequence of events, a chronology. Our lives are linear, punctuated with the beginnings and endings of episodes—some good, some bad. God, on the other hand, has an entirely different viewpoint. Without either beginning or end, time, as we know it, need not be part of God's reckoning.

We live on earth in that segment of time that we call our "lifetime," beginning it *after* our ancestors and usually finishing it *ahead* of our children. Our individual time-space overlaps with others who become our friends—or sometimes opponents. At birth we enter the tiny allotment of eternity that is ours now, and which we leave at death—when time ceases to mean anything more to us.

At that point Jesus, the eternal source of life, takes over. Like the cycle of seasons that He sends upon our earth, He programs eternal life on a *circular* track that has no beginning and no end. He wants to receive us back into that wonderful dimension in which He lives—between two everlastings.

> LORD, YOU HAVE BEEN OUR DWELLING PLACE IN ALL GENER-ATIONS. . . . EVEN FROM EVERLAST-ING TO EVERLAST-ING, YOU ARE GOD.
>
> PS. 90:1, 2, NKJV.

"God, grant that I may never be
A scoffer at Eternity—
As long as every April brings
The sweet rebirth of growing things:
As long as grass is green anew,
I shall believe that God looks down

Upon His wide earth, cold and brown,
To bless its unborn mystery
Of leaf, and bud, and flower to be:
To smile on it from tender skies—
How could I think it otherwise?"*

*"A Prayer for April."

THE DESTINATION

Amid stories of hijackings, bombings, airline price wars, employee strikes, and general mayhem in the air, the news this week turned up an odd bit of information. A major American airline sent a planeload of passengers off to Europe—destination, Frankfurt, Germany. Nothing unusual here. Shortly before landing, however, many people watching the electronic map at the front of the cabin saw that they were approaching Brussels, Belgium. Perhaps some of them were also able to look out the window and say, "Hey! *This* isn't Frankfurt." At some point the control tower must have asked, "Where do you think you're going? This is Brussels. We weren't expecting you."

> "I GO AND PREPARE A PLACE FOR YOU . . . SO THAT WHERE I AM YOU MAY BE ALSO; AND MY WAY THERE IS KNOWN TO YOU."
>
> JOHN 14:4, NEB.

Well, since the mistake occurred in peaceful airspace and not a war zone, the plane was not shot down. The error, of course, involved expense and embarrassment for the airline. And doubtless many passengers had their personal time schedules seriously disrupted. As for the crew, apparently they didn't know what was going on until they landed. "They're grounded," the airline spokesperson announced, "until an investigation has been made."

To have no sense of direction and to be careless, unwilling, or unable to read a map is a fearful disability. In the matter of arriving at our final life-destination, however, we have no room for making mistakes—not even one. It is not merely inconvenience—such as taking the wrong exit off the freeway or landing in the wrong airport. We face everlasting life-and-death issues here.

With His inerrant focus on His destination, Jesus gave His disciples a final directive at the end of the Last Supper. He knew "that He had come from God and was going to God" (John 13:2, NKJV). A little later in the conversation, He offered Thomas the doubter (and others like him) special assurance. " 'Lord,' " Thomas had asked, " 'we do not know where You are going, and how can we know the way?'

"Jesus said to him, 'I am the way. . . . No one comes to the Father except through Me' " (verses 5, 6, NKJV). Thomas and the others, however, would have to pass through the tumultuous events of the Crucifixion, Resurrection, and Ascension before they could fully comprehend what the Master had said.

> [*Keep me alert, Lord, with my eyes fixed on the destination You have prepared for me.*]

VIGILANCE

E ven a cursory study of non-Christian religions, in general, points up one common denominator. Gods other than the God of Israel tend to be "absent." They simply are not paying attention. It takes an enormous amount of effort for their worshipers just to be noticed.

"THE LORD HAS BEEN MINDFUL OF US."

PS. 115:12, RSV.

Following three years of drought and famine, Elijah proposed that King Ahab call for a contest atop Mount Carmel (1 Kings 17, 18) in order to identify conclusively who the true God was. The time had come to stop "limping with two different opinions" (1 Kings 18:21, RSV). Thus Elijah and the priests of Baal built two altars and made sacrifices. Fire from heaven promptly responded to Elijah's. The 850 pagan priests and prophets, on the other hand, danced in a frenzy all morning (the optimum time of day for Baal and Ashtoreth). Nothing happened.

With fine sarcasm Elijah suggested, "Call louder, for he is a god; it may be he is deep in thought, or engaged, or on a journey; or he may have gone to sleep" (verse 27, NEB). Or, as older translations put it, "he has gone aside" (RSV)—a euphemism for the need to relieve himself.

Other Old Testament prophets satirized the entire system of idolatry in a similar manner. Isaiah mused on the incongruity of a tree (nourished by God's rain) being cut down. Then the carpenter builds furniture and fuels his fire to bake bread and keep himself warm. At last, with the remaining wood, he carves an idol, falling before it and pleading, "Deliver me; for thou art my god!" (Isa. 44:17). No wonder the ancient Chinese proverb reads: "He who carves the Buddha never worships him." The god-makers *know* that the deity really isn't there!

To the best of my knowledge, I know of no gods on record who ever promised their presence to their worshipers. Jehovah, on the other hand, has repeatedly assured His followers that He is present. He is aware and available to us, able to attend to our needs. We have only to ask in faith. This we can do calmly, for He is always alert and on duty.

[*Ever-present God, I rest in Your promise. You are paying attention to what concerns Your children.*]

JUST ONE

One of the laws of language is that the singular is always more powerful than the plural, the superiority of the *one* over the *multitude*. Knowing how plurality dissipated impact, Jesus began His pithy little parables thusly: "There was a certain landowner . . . a woman . . . a sower." Significantly, none of them begin: "There was a committee . . . a group of merchants . . . a consortium of government agencies . . ." When medieval European monarchs began referring to themselves in the mode of the royal "we," they undoubtedly added to their pomposity, but gained little in effectiveness.

WE HAVE BEHELD HIS GLORY, GLORY AS OF THE ONLY SON FROM THE FATHER.

JOHN 1:14, RSV.

Individuality is a basic principle of God's creation. It is a mind-teaser to consider what happened when that certain combination of genes and chromosomes came together to create *you*. That special blend of cells that became your body and your personality could never again be repeated—not even if you had an identical twin. The precise pattern would never be reused—not even in "cloning." Nowhere in the universe, never at any future time, could there be another person like you. For this reason, when a child is lost, he or she can never find a replacement in the parents' hearts through any number of other brothers and sisters. Therefore, if you try to become someone other than yourself, that special God-made "you" will be forever lost.

This fact of creation leads naturally to two fundamental Christian truths. First, there is but *one* God, the only begotten of the Father, the "Holy and Righteous One" (Acts 3:14, RSV). He presents Himself in perfect focus as a single divine person, not as a fuzzy, ill-defined "cosmic force." Instead of inviting us to get lost in some kind of "universal consciousness," He promises us an eternal personal identity. Second, God so values each one of His single creations that if all the rest of the 5 billion people on the planet disappeared, leaving only me, Jesus would have still come to die for my salvation alone.

No matter what our limitations or circumstances, then, the glory of "just one" nurtures hope and self-esteem in us. Our uniqueness itself makes us of great value in God's eyes.

[*Dear Father, today let me find joy and not despair in the individuality You have given to me.*]

THE SURPRISE

G ranny Weatherall is a creation of the Pulitzer Prize-winning American story writer, Kathryn Anne Porter.* Granny "weathers all" in her struggle to tame the harsh land and rear five children alone. She succeeds despite the fact that George jilted her on their wedding day—a calamity for which she never forgives him. Then she marries John, but he dies early, leaving her with the young family. The story climaxes in a heart attack. Confused but still feisty, Granny talks to her family around her bed. A lifetime of unremitting toil is all she can remember—toil is the only thing she's ever trusted. Suddenly she realizes that she's actually dying. "I'm not going," she cries. "I'm taken by surprise. I can't go." But go she must. Jilted for the third time, she discovers that God cannot accept work in place of love. Her unforgiving spirit has disqualified her from joining her heavenly Bridegroom.

> "IF YOU DO NOT WAKE UP, I WILL COME LIKE A THIEF, AND YOU WILL NOT KNOW AT WHAT TIME I WILL COME TO YOU."
>
> REV. 3:3, NIV.

We usually interpret the warning about the "thief in the night" as the hour of Christ's second coming arriving as a surprise. God may always be present in our lives, however—often in unrecognized ways and unexpected places. On the road to Edom to meet Esau, Jacob paused at the ford of the Jabbok. That night he wrestled with God by the stream (Gen. 32:22-32).

After the Crucifixion, two disciples returning home to Emmaus didn't realize that the Christ they mourned walked with them. Suppertime revealed Him to them (Luke 24:13-31). After they reported their encounter to the 11 disciples, suddenly Jesus stood among *them* also—calming the room with His familiar greeting, "Peace be with you" (verse 36, NIV).

How we love those *happy* surprises—the birthday party, the remembered anniversary, the appreciative letter, the loving phone call, and all the rest. But surprise can also be risky. The thief-in-the-night image also implies the possibility of grievous disappointment. Like Granny Weatherall, many who feel ready to enter the kingdom must be told, "I never knew you" (Matt. 7:23, NIV)! An eternally fatal surprise, this!

[*Help me to be open today for whatever surprising encounters my Lord has in store for me. Let me recognize the new within the old, hope within despair. Keep my path to heaven clear before me, for I would not lose my way.*]

*In *The American Short Story* (New York: Dell Pub. Co., 1980), vol. 1, pp. 228-237.

JOYOUS LAUGHTER

Laughter is one of the most delightful manifestations of Christ. It may surprise some to see that humor is a legitimate and specialized branch of Christian joy. Indeed, the Bible contains far more of it than most of us suspect. Laughter relieves tensions, paves the way to friendship, and enables us to tolerate life's absurdities—our own and those of others. In his book *For God's Sake Laugh,* Nelvin Vos points out that there is a "relevancy of humor" that "almost amounts to revelation. . . . Only the serious can laugh. The rest only giggle."

> "HE WILL YET FILL YOUR MOUTH WITH LAUGHTER AND YOUR LIPS WITH SHOUTS OF JOY."
>
> JOB 8:21, NIV.

It is in laughter and high humor that human beings manifest their freedom. We are told that St. Francis of Assisi sang and danced in the streets only after he had given himself up entirely to God—just as David had done before the ark centuries earlier (2 Sam. 6:14-16). Christians never use humor as a mask to hide from themselves and others. Their laughter is self-confident because the truth has made them free (John 8:32). Free from guilt, free from fear, they have a sense of inner release.

The raw material of laughter rests on two fundamental principles: surprise and incongruity. The Bible is laced through and through with the familiar reactions of human beings—people like ourselves who must deal with the absurdities that life daily sets before us, and who are, from time to time, caught in the act of being themselves. The teachings of Jesus embodied a wit that, no doubt, drew appreciative chuckles and sometimes peals of laughter from His listeners. Moreover, it could never have been a somber, humorless God who created the giraffe and the bullfrog. In the solemnity of our times we cannot afford to forget laughter. In planting His gift within us, God has shared a wonderful part of Himself.

What's more, He is planning a tremendous surprise—a whole eternity for joy and laughter. But the greatest rejoicing in that day will not be over the arrival of the "righteous" in heaven. Rather, it will be the homecoming of the unexpected ones—all of us poor fallible mortals who, incongruously—by God's grace—have *also* arrived.

[*I'm so small and inadequate, Lord. It seems laughable to think that You can fit me for citizenship in Your kingdom. But I know You can, God of joy. Please do it.*]

DERISIVE LAUGHTER

Not always lighthearted, God is also a purposeful satirist who "laughs at the wicked." The ancient Romans perfected the technique of satire as a political device. Juvenal wrote bitter tirades against his native city that had sent him into exile. Comfortably settled on his Sabine farm, Horace wrote pleasant, gentle mockeries of his neighbors' follies. In either mode, satire works.

> **BUT THE LORD LAUGHS AT THE WICKED, FOR HE KNOWS THEIR DAY IS COMING.**
>
> PS. 37:13, NIV.

Probably we know no suffering quite so intense as that of being laughed at. The satirist, therefore, hopes to correct human error by exposing people to ridicule and laughter. The Old Testament prophets found satire an effective weapon against idolatry. Isaiah portrayed the irrational plans of the craftsman who cut down a tree, used a portion of it for warmth and bread-baking, and then employed the remainder to carve an idol.

Jesus used satire against the self-righteousness of the Pharisees. He corrected the excesses of their authority and invited us to learn to laugh at what is truly foolish. This same subtle vein of humor also ran through His encounters with other people. While a lesser teacher would have resorted to dull moralizing, Christ made truth sparkle forth in clear-cut, often ludicrous images: the false prophets in sheep's clothing (Matt. 7:15); the lighted lamp hidden under the bed (Mark 4:21, 22); curious crowds trooping out to the wilderness to see "a reed shaken with the wind" (Matt. 11:7); a little man's frustration in trying to "add one cubit unto his stature" (Matt. 6:27); and much more.

Descriptions of Jesus' trial and crucifixion reveal the events to have been a high comedy scene for many spectators. To see the One who claimed to be the Son of God clad in a tawdry robe, crowned with thorns, and finally hanging under a mocking sign, "King of the Jews"—all of this seemed very funny. But they bought their sport that day at a tragically high price—just *how* high they have yet to discover. Only God fully knows the end of their folly.

[*God, I would share Your sense of humor and, at the same time, be spared the bitterness of being sarcastic.*]

REST

Humanity has always envisioned—somehow, somewhere—the perfect life. The Greeks told of a lost Golden Age, when human beings and gods communicated together. Political victims dreamed of governments that dispensed perfect justice. Poor people expected immeasurable wealth. Hungry people anticipated an abundance of food. Everyone looked for an endless age of peace. And unnumbered multitudes anticipated *rest*. Indeed, we must all be very tired—tired of both physical work and inactivity, mental pressures and anxiety, controversy and bondage.

"COME TO ME, ALL YOU WHO LABOR AND ARE HEAVY LADEN, AND I WILL GIVE YOU REST."

MATT. 11:28, NKJV.

The idea of rest has two subdivisions. First, we have sleep. The Lord "grants sleep to those he loves" (Ps. 127:2, NIV). Continually we coerce our bodies into overtime. Over the years I've observed the sleep habits of hundreds of college students. At examination seasons many of them shift into panic gear. They go for days without sleep. I meet them "spaced out" in the halls. "I haven't slept for three days," they croak, staring hollow-eyed. "I just haven't been to bed at all!"

Then we get older, and a film of tiredness settles over our days, thickening in proportion to the amount of sleep we lose. Knowing our needs, God blesses us with sleep. "Sweet is the sleep of a laborer, . . . but the surfeit of the rich will not let him sleep" (Eccl. 5:12, RSV). He even heals our guilty consciences and lack of trust with sleep.

Finally, death comes as a release, for sin has rendered our human bodies wholly unfit to bear the weight of immortality. In the case of Jairus' daughter, for instance, Jesus dismissed the professional mourners with "Depart, for the girl is not *dead but sleeping*" (Matt. 9:24, RSV). They laughed—not realizing that sleep and death both respond to precisely the same life-giving energy. The first awakes us from rest to the beginning of another day's work. The second calls us to resurrection and the health and vigor of eternal life.

God, the total rest-giver, does more than drug our senses. He *Himself* is the rest into which we must enter. We weary pilgrims have only to accept Him, to work, and then to find true rest. That soul rest that can refresh us even on our sleepless nights.

[*Dear God, I live in this troubled, restless time between Your two paradises, Eden and the new earth. I must thank You not only for soul rest but also for Your practical gifts of sleep and death.*]

GOODNESS

I have always admired Harry M. Tippett, an English professor of a former generation. In browsing through some of his old notes the other day and following the classroom trails of his astute mind, I encountered a provocative idea. He was speaking of aesthetic experience, the theory of the fine arts, and of people's responses to them. After we have satisfied our basic physical and social needs, he suggested, we next follow our deeply ingrained desire to surround ourselves with beauty and virtue.

"NO ONE IS GOOD EXCEPT GOD ALONE."

LUKE 18:19, NEB.

Aesthetics, Tippett pointed out, consists of five elements: goodness, beauty, truth, power, and devotion. Next he showed that the five names that Isaiah gives to Christ coincide almost perfectly with these basic aesthetic principles: "For unto us a child is born . . . and his name will be called Wonderful Counselor, Mighty God, Everlasting Father, Prince of Peace" (Isa. 9:6, RSV). For the next few days, then, we shall consider the aesthetic aspects of Christ's life.

"Altruism" is the more technical word for what we more commonly call simple "goodness." Having lived now for hundreds of generations and thousands of years, embroiled in all the many manifestations of evil, we have become distrustful and cynical. From most ancient times philosophers and prophets have been assuring us that ours—in whatever time and place—is the "worst of all possible worlds." And evil does proceed unabated. Some have even surmised that to be in a state of violence and war, to live by the laws of the jungle, is, in fact, humanity's natural condition.

God's goodness, however, provides the "Prince of Peace," who breaks down the walls of division among us (Eph. 2:14). Therefore, we may all "rejoice in . . . goodness" (2 Chron. 6:41, RSV). Not only does Jesus promise His eternal kingdom of peace and goodness, but He enables us to find peace within ourselves and in others. Virtue *is* discernible among us. Let not the media emphasis on violence, crime, and corruption blind us to the fact that we may daily discover the good fruits of the Spirit in the lives of those who are committed to Christ—and even in the lives of those who have not yet fully understood the true nature of our Prince of Peace.

[*Lord, help me train my eye to discern the pure goodness You have placed here in my sin-ridden world. Help me believe that it's there.*]

TRUTH

I have always enjoyed wandering through old grave-
yards. It is in no way a morbid hobby. Indeed, it
points back to a time when we had a more personal, more empathetic view of death than we do
now. Old statuary often holds drama in itself. The epi-
taphs are sometimes long and poignant, often realistic,
and occasionally humorous. In other words, the graveyard breathes of character. It delineates circumstances
and conflicts, and portrays the affairs of real people,
thus preserving human stories.

> "I AM THE
> TRUTH . . .;
> NO ONE
> COMES TO
> THE FATHER
> EXCEPT
> BY ME."
>
> JOHN 14:6, NEB.

Modern funeral practices have robbed us of a
pleasure that earlier generations once bequeathed to us. Our contemporary
bronze or marble plate in the grass (buried at just the right level so that
power lawn mowers can do their work) says little to us other than the arrival and departure times of those who lie in the coffins below. Cremations
offer even less.

In his quaint little collection of homespun lore,* Douglas Jerrold describes an unusual graveyard visitor: "If the devil ever takes churchyard
walks, how he must chuckle and rub his brimstone hands when he reads
some of the tombstones—eh? How he must hold his sides at the 'loving
husbands,' 'affectionate fathers,' 'faithful friends,' and 'pious Christians,'
that he sees advertised there! For he knows better—*he* knows better."

"I am the Truth." It is one of the grandest, most shining claims Jesus
ever made about Himself. For thousands of years philosophers and theolo-
gians have debated—to the point of abstraction—the question of truth. We
daily admonish one another about truth. In courtrooms witnesses swear to
tell the truth. Parents try to instill a sense of truth in their children. Awash
as we are, however, in a murky swamp of hypocrisy, corruption, and outright lies (both black and white), we hardly dare trust anyone or even voice
an opinion as to where we think the truth might lie.

At this point we can only look to the One who, in His own Person, *is*
Truth. In and through Him truth, in all its transparent simplicity, has its
source. We find thousands of applications to our daily lives. Only thus do
we find the way to freedom and to the Father.

[*God, You are the embodiment of truth. Let no falsehood,
however attractive, tempt me from my attachment to You.*]

*Tom Hood and Douglas Jerrold, *Wisdom and Wit* (London, n.d.), p. 80.

BEAUTY

An unprepossessing man may appear dignified and handsome when standing at the marriage altar. Even a very plain girl can be lovely—marvelously so—as she walks down the aisle to meet her bridegroom. Every detail of the wedding is planned to have a beautiful effect. The vivid impressions of one's wedding day never fade. When we read that Christ shall be called "Wonderful," we know that *beauty* is what evokes feelings of wonder—joyous wonder!

HE IS ALTO-GETHER LOVELY.

S. OF SOL. 5:16, NIV.

In speculating on Jesus' personal appearance while here on earth, artists and writers have wavered between presenting Him as an anemic pious sufferer and a severe judge who will not permit one single sin to go unrecorded. In between lies the Jesus of beauty, the heavenly bridegroom. Overwhelmed with happiness, the Shulammite bride of the Song of Solomon cries out, "He is altogether desirable" (S. of Sol. 5:16, RSV). The ecstatic beauty of this wedding poem gives rise to the thrill of finding perfect union between the bridegroom and the bride. Many Bible interpreters have found the song to be a picture of the bond between Christ and His church—and every individual believer within that church.

David's choirmaster Asaph sang to the "Mighty One, God the Lord," who shines forth "out of Zion, the perfection of beauty" (Ps. 50:1, 2, RSV). A thoughtful reading of the Psalms strikes us with the vitality, the vibrant joy, and the sheer exuberance that prevailed among the Hebrews. David wanted to "dwell in the house of the Lord all the days of [his] life," and then declared his eager purpose "to behold the beauty of the Lord" there (Ps. 27:4).

Some of us may ask, "How come *I* don't feel that way about going to church?" Has the way been stripped bare of the beauties of spiritual experience? Have legalism and misplaced emphases emaciated the joy of worship?

> "For hearts that sing through sunshine or through rain,
> And praise Thee in the dull grey mists of pain—
> I thank Thee, King of Beauty."*

[*In Him lies the cure for all the deformities and ugliness inherent in our characters.*]

---

*Minnie Hardwick, cited in Rita Snowden, *While the Candle Burns* (London: Epworth Press), p. 21.

POWER

EVERYONE WHO IN-VOKES THE NAME OF THE LORD WILL BE SAVED.

ROM. 10:13, NEB.

Because we begin to discover our limitations early in life, we always admire strength and power wherever we find it. Remember those episodes in the schoolyard at recess time when someone bullied you into submission? And you threatened, "I'm gonna tell my big brother on you!" Or when you fell to the dust in defeat? Still you lifted your defiant head to your oppressor. "My dad's bigger 'n' your dad, and he can beat you up!"

Yes, it is imperative for us to know where our reserve sources of strength lie. Otherwise, we will never know a moment of security. There's power in education. In technology. In social connections. And—ever and always—in money! Above all, however, one must rely on the strength of one's God. From the beginning of time we have peopled our worlds with gods—tens of thousands of them. The bottom line has always been: "Is my god strong enough to defend me against the machinations of other spirit powers?" Plagued with anxiety, worshipers have laid on more sacrifices, offered more appeasements, and even invented additional new and more specialized gods to be sure that they have covered all the bases.

Above this vast confusion created by innumerable nations of "god-makers" rises Jehovah, the Lord God of all Scripture. It is not surprising that Scripture should emphasize His superiority over all other gods. "Power belongs to God" (Ps. 62:11, NKJV). "The thunder of His power who can understand?" (Job 26:14, NKJV). He makes "His mighty power known" (Ps. 106:8, NKJV). And no one could ever gainsay Christ's claim: "I have power to lay [my life] down, and I have power to take it again" (John 10:18, NKJV). In all ages the theme of God's power has been an unending anthem of praise among the saints.

Christ's last two aesthetic features, power and devotion, are the natural results of the work of His primary "trinity of absolutes": goodness, truth, and beauty. From the vast powerhouse of God's energy we draw our own strength—physical and spiritual. And God the Father and Jesus the Elder Brother are never more than a word away from our call for help.

[*Today, Jesus, I will be strong. I will remember Your power in my behalf, whatever challenges face me.*]

DEVOTION

AND HIS NAME WILL BE CALLED . . . [THE] EVERLASTING FATHER.

ISA. 9:6, NKJV.

When barely 17 I had one of the most memorable aesthetic experiences of my life, a real "rite of passage." My family joined my uncle and his family to hear Handel's *Messiah* in the Royal Albert Hall in London. Did our fathers sense that this night would be a significant experience for their teenagers? In any case, they took the seven of us to a box with a wonderful view of the stage, where we sat on a level with the nobility. Although brought up in "classical music homes," we adolescents had been, as usual, more enamored with the popular tunes of our generation. None of us, I think, had yet had a true spiritual encounter with great sacred music.

After that night, however, I was never the same again. Through the entire performance I shared the feelings of the composer himself when he testified that in the 24 days during which he wrote the oratorio, "I saw all heaven opened before me." The huge organ and the orchestra under the baton of Sir Malcolm Sargent sent glorious sound swirling through the gilded arches and up into the tiers of balconies. I could hardly breathe for the intensity of the event—the bell-like soprano arias, the mellow alto, the sweet tenor recitatives, and the resonant bass solos, all mingling with the orchestral instruments and then bursting into anthems, with storms of power. As usual, everyone stood for the "Hallelujah Chorus." Wonderful as it was, it was, in my book, surpassed by "For Unto Us a Child Is Born," ending with all 500 voices at full volume exulting again and again "the Everlasting Father! The Prince of Peace!"

In a daze, I left the hall. I don't remember any of us saying much as we walked to the underground station to take the train back to Bracknell—speech seemed quite superfluous.

The functioning Christian is the one whose understanding of the first four aesthetic attributes of the Godhead leads him or her inevitably to the fifth—worship. The One who is both "everlasting" and our "Father" merits all praise and devotion. Thus worship becomes a natural response as we view God in His glorious totality.

[*Let me be sensitive, my God, not only in the grand times when I see You, but also in the quiet, private moments like this one, here at the beginning of my day.*]

WISDOM

More than 1,400 years ago Emperor Justinian I employed two gifted architects to build what became the chief landmark of Constantinople (Istanbul, Turkey). Anthemius and Isidorus worked for five years to create one of Christendom's most magnificent churches. Four great arches top a massive square base. Rising 185 feet above the pavement, the vast central dome seems to float over an ethereal circle of light. Shimmering mosaics and polished marble veneer sheath the interior walls. (The early Christian churches were plain outside and beautiful within, symbolizing the precedence of the interior spiritual life over the visible and external material life.) Devoted Christians dedicated the church in A.D. 537, naming it *Hagia Sophia,* the Church of Holy Wisdom.

> CHRIST [IS] THE POWER OF GOD AND THE WISDOM OF GOD.
>
> 1 COR. 1:24, RSV.

"Holy Wisdom" is what delivers us from sterile knowledge and the foolishness that goes with it. Perhaps it's no accident that we label the second-year college student a "sophomore"—a Greek word meaning "a wise fool." Given time, he or she will, hopefully, become a wise person before graduation.

Every race and nation has its proverbs and wisdom—the practical resources gleaned from experience and experiment, a guide to what works and what does not work in our present life. Someone has defined wisdom as "truth for living." It is not, however, just an abstract philosophy. You not only know something but you also *do* something. Jesus said, "God's wisdom is proved right by its results" (Matt. 11:19, NEB).

In describing Christ as the "wisdom of God" Paul brought Solomon's personification of Wisdom (Prov. 1-9) to its ultimate glory. By centering our lives on Jesus, we combine holy wisdom with all our practical knowledge. Then as the sunshine filters through those dome windows and illuminates the beautiful interior of Hagia Sophia, so divine wisdom brightens our lives, making us all lovely within, no matter how plain and dull our exteriors may be.

> "He is the Ancient Wisdom of the World,
> The Word Creative, Beautiful and True,
> The Nameless of Innumerable Names,
> Ageless forever, yet Forever New."*

*Charles Carroll Albertson, "The Holy Child."

HUMILITY

Uriah Heep is probably one of the most famous characters in Victorian English literature. In Charles Dickens' *David Copperfield* (1849) he is Mr. Wickfield's odious clerk. His constant groveling focuses everyone's attention on the fact that he's so "'umble." Actually, he is a manipulative, malignant tyrant who blackmails his employer and aspires to marry the daughter of the house. His name has come to imply ambition and malice cloaked in the guise of false humility.

Although the hymns of Isaac Watts improved Protestant hymn-singing immeasurably, one of his best-known songs contained a troublesome phrase—now usually edited out: "such a worm as I?" "I won't use that hymn," my father would say. "I am not a worm, and I won't ask anyone else to say those words either."

AND BEING FOUND IN APPEAR-ANCE AS A MAN, HE HUMBLED HIMSELF AND BE-CAME OBE-DIENT TO DEATH— EVEN DEATH ON A CROSS!

PHIL. 2:8, NIV.

What then are the earmarks of *true* humility? It doesn't mean having a low opinion of your own gifts. Rather it is freedom from being preoccupied with yourself at all. Truly humble people:

1. Are mature. A "small" person cannot contain the truly humble spirit.
2. Don't grovel, because that's a symptom of pride.
3. Are usually kind and affectionate—easy to love.
4. Are fully aware of the strengths and limitations of their abilities.
5. Can admit when they've made a mistake (but they won't say they're worms).
6. Know they're responsible for their work, but realize they can't control all of the results.
7. Acknowledge both failure and success, criticism and flattery alike. Thus they free themselves from the debilitating effects of anxiety.
8. Don't announce their humility. Totally unself-centered, they don't even think of themselves as "humble."

Our prime source of humility is the habit of constantly realizing the presence of God and our relationship to Him. We have no other way to detach our souls from centering on ourselves. In order to ensure the success of the plan of salvation, Jesus humbly took every step required of Him without ever saying one word about His condescension.

[*Today, I would take one more step forward in learning a hard lesson. I will respect myself and, at the same time, detach myself from all self-interest.*]

INNOCENCE

In 1789 and 1794 an eccentric but spiritually minded Englishman, William Blake, published collections of poems called *Songs of Innocence* and *Songs of Experience*. The first group represents the naive outlook of children in a protected world. They believe everything told them by their elders and think reality is simply what they see around them. In "The Lamb," the best-known pair of the poems, the gentle animal, with "such a tender voice" and "softest clothing, woolly, bright," feeds meekly by the stream.

> "For He [Jesus] calls Himself a Lamb. . . .
> I a child, and thou a lamb,
> We are called by His name.
> Little Lamb, God bless thee!"

A terrifying "song of experience," however, follows this gentle picture with the portrayal of a flaming, wrathful tiger who replaces the lamb. The child must mature. Now comes materialism, poverty, oppression, disease—and responsibility.

> "Did He smile His work to see?
> Did He who made the Lamb
> make thee?
> Tyger! Tyger! burning bright
> In the forests of the night."*

Jesus advises us to become as little children, "for to such belongs the kingdom of heaven" (Matt. 19:14, RSV). It is not an injunction to perpetual childish dependence, but rather an invitation to the recovery and maintenance of innocence. Innocence means freedom from sin and guilt, freedom from cunning and deception—simplicity. Finding the balance between mature responsibility and purity is a lifetime undertaking.

Titus assures us that we can recover innocence. The necessity of purification indicates that we have been corrupted by too much experience. Only when Christ removes the stains do we become fit for His kingdom.

> JESUS CHRIST . . . GAVE HIMSELF FOR US TO REDEEM US FROM ALL INIQUITY AND TO PURIFY FOR HIMSELF A PEOPLE OF HIS OWN WHO ARE ZEALOUS FOR GOOD DEEDS.
>
> TITUS 2:13, 14, RSV.

[*I have done so many things to lose my purity and disqualify me for Your eternal kingdom. Fulfill in me today Your promise to recover my innocence.*]

*William Blake, *Songs of Innocence* and *Songs of Experience,* in the *Norton Anthology of English Literature* (New York: W. W. Norton and Co., Inc.), pp. 51, 57, 58.

SUFFERING

At certain shrines in Japan you observe an interesting rite. You find hundreds of folded pieces of rice paper tied to the twigs and branches of trees in the temple courtyard. Worshipers go to the Shinto priest, from whom they choose lots. Then he gives them a paper describing the "fortune" they've drawn. If they like what they got, they simply go home and wait for good things to happen. If, however, the paper predicts trouble, they roll up the rice paper and tie it to a tree. This constitutes a request to the gods to take back the trouble and give it to someone else. A further stipulation requires the worshiper to tie the paper to the branch *using only one hand.*

In real life, however, pain follows many to the grave. We have no way to transfer the burden to someone else's shoulders. Suffering is a major hazard of being human.

When pain comes, the first question we ask is "Why? Why me? I don't deserve it." The more Christian inquiry is "Why not me? Is there any reason why I should be exempt from the human lot of suffering?" God, however, doesn't always take us out of our problems. Sometimes He enters in *with* us—as he joined the three Hebrew exiles in Nebuchadnezzar's fiery furnace. Jesus is our model. His rejection, pain, and suffering worsened, ending only at the cross. As Peter pointed out in his sermon at Solomon's portico, the full spectrum of suffering and misery was "thus fulfilled."

She who has been a widow knows how to comfort the girl whose bridegroom gets killed by a drunken driver a month after their wedding. He who has been unjustly imprisoned will know what another victim of corruption needs to hear. Parents who have lost a child will be the first to step forward when a child down the street is abducted.

Can it be then that the suffering is part of our necessary education in our highly imperfect world? Is it the means that enables us to help one another toward the kingdom?

> "THOSE THINGS WHICH GOD FORETOLD BY THE MOUTH OF ALL HIS PROPHETS, THAT THE CHRIST WOULD SUFFER, HE HAS THUS FULFILLED."
>
> ACTS 3:18, NKJV.

[*Help me, God, to remember that my suffering, whatever it may be, is only temporary. It may last a day, a week, or a year. Or even to the day I die. But freedom and joy lie beyond.*]

THE MAN OF SORROWS

Manila is the largest, most congested place in the Philippines. Traffic defies description. Normally it takes an hour or more just to cross the city. Except for one day in the year—Black Saturday, the day between Good Friday and Resurrection Sunday. Then you can drive north, south, east, or west with amazing ease, for the streets are empty. Even the horses, stray dogs, and chickens disappear. Regardless of weather, it's a dark, dangerous day, for God is "dead." People take shelter in their houses while God is "off-duty."

"HE [WAS] . . . A MAN OF SORROWS AND ACQUAINTED WITH GRIEF."

ISA. 53:3, NKJV.

The Philippines has many religious festivals. Throughout the year the people honor a cycle of martyred saints. The events of the Lenten season outdo even Christmas. Dance, drama, and innumerable processions reenact the scenes of Passion Week and the Crucifixion. All in all, the various rites represent the "Man of Sorrows" in so many different ways that He overshadows the resurrected Lord. Easter Sunday comes almost as an anticlimax after all the grief, pain, and discouragement that have preceded it.

Since the Middle Ages Christian art has placed emphasis on the tragedy of sin and the train of grief that has followed in its wake. While we feel that this picture of the Man of Sorrows needs to be balanced by His many other bright and cheerful aspects, the grief of Jesus certainly merits our contemplation. Isaiah paints a vivid picture of the Man of Sorrows without "form or comeliness," having "no beauty that we should desire Him" (Isa. 53:2, NKJV). We must, however, read to the end of the passage. What is it that made Him this way? Certainly not He Himself. He was the king of heaven, so glorious that mortal eyes have never been able to look upon Him directly. Then what happened? We did it. Erratic, death-bound, proud, selfish human beings—we despised Him. That's what happened! "He has borne *our* griefs and carried *our* sorrows" (verse 4, RSV). Each of us made Him look that way.

In that case we should not be critical of those who for centuries have emphasized the grieving face of Christ. While it's only part of the story, it's still a scene upon which we *must* dwell. At this precise point we can most honestly evaluate ourselves.

[*My Jesus, I don't want to be excused from my responsibility. In my heart I look upon Your face and trace the lines that I have put upon it.*]

THE ALL-IN-ALL

Phocion was an Athenian soldier, statesman, and student of Plato who lived some 400 years before Christ. Throughout antiquity people celebrated him for his integrity and justice in counsel, his bravery on the battlefield, and his eloquence in debate.

Now for a visual parable. During the seventeenth century the French artist Nicolas Poussin painted a picture entitled *The Funeral of Phocion.* Hanging in the Louvre, in Paris, it merits a little time spent in contemplating it. In the background of the classical landscape we see a walled village dominated by a church tower. In the middle distance the peasants tend their sheep. An oxcart passes. Other people take their leisure under the trees. Their backs are turned to us, however, for they face the town. In the center foreground, following a curving path to our right, two lone men carry a stretcher. On it lies the enshrouded body of Phocion, with no procession, no mourners—just the stark reality of death. No one cares or pays attention.

The message is strikingly poignant. No matter how full and successful our lives, we find in the end that all we ever wanted wasn't enough. We are doomed to incompleteness in this life. Therefore, the most fulfilling service we may render to others is simply to supply to them, in any manner we can, a piece missing from their lives.

The apostle Paul asserted that "all things" exist "*from* him [the Source of life] and *through* him [a channel of grace for us], and *to* him [Creator, Provider, and Redeemer]" (Rom. 11:36, RSV). Like a mighty tide all life flows back to the throne of God.

> *My All-in-All, I ask that You fulfill my incompleteness every day, including the emptinesses of which I am not even aware. In turn, may I contribute at least one small piece today toward the building up of someone else's life.*

THERE CANNOT BE GREEK AND JEW . . . BARBARIAN . . . SLAVE, [OR] FREE MAN, BUT CHRIST IS ALL, AND IN ALL.

COL. 3:11, RSV.

FORGIVENESS

C ontrary to his usual cynicism, Mark Twain once remarked that "forgiveness is the fragrance the violet sheds on the heel that has crushed it." A picture delicate as springtime, but as difficult to achieve as hard labor.

> "FATHER, FORGIVE THEM; FOR THEY KNOW NOT WHAT THEY DO."
>
> LUKE 23:34, RSV.

Europeans distinguished themselves for being sensitive to matters of honor and revenge. Their feuds lasted for centuries—long after the participants had forgotten the original injury or insult. Hostilities often began in remote places in which the warring parties had no recourse to regular legal controls. Although modern governments have long since declared such private wars to be illegal, family feuds continue to break out and fester. An amazing number of families are not on speaking terms with each other. The famous century-long dispute between the Hatfields and McCoys of Kentucky and West Virginia has become part of American folklore.

Many people *cannot* forgive. Whether it's family prejudice or their personal grievance, they simply can't give it up. Nothing is more stubbornly "earthbound" than an unforgiving spirit that still seeks revenge. And when we "forget" (overlook) wrongs that have been done to us, we put ourselves into a position of extreme vulnerability. The ability to forgive is the true mark of a highly mature person.

God alone has the ability to forgive *and* forget. We humans cannot do it. While devout people may forgive, they can seldom shed the offense from their memories. It's a marvelous thing that God's forgiveness is absolute and everlasting! Sin can actually be erased—put off the record and out of mind. Therefore, no mistake has to be final. We are saved because we're forgiven. And we're forgiven simply because we're loved.

Jesus' supreme act of forgiveness from the cross may make us wonder to whom the "they" refers. The soldiers driving in the nails? The administrators of Jewish law? The Romans as occupation forces in a difficult land? We whose continued transgressions have gone on for almost 2,000 years? Or is it the whole motley multitude? Only the divine Judge can see justice done.

Failure to forgive exacts a severe penalty. "Forgive, and you will be forgiven." "If you do not forgive [one another], neither will your Father in heaven forgive your trespasses" (Luke 6:37, NKJV; Mark 11:26, NKJV).

[*Dear Father, teach me the fine art of forgiveness. Because of my own need of Your forgiveness, it is something I must learn and practice.*]

THE HOPE OF ISRAEL

Some four centuries of enslavement in Egypt left the children of Israel short on hope. Later after corrupting themselves with idolatry and then straggling off into exile, hope was again in short supply. Both nations and persons experience such low moments. The phrase "Hope of Israel," however, implies that the Master, who would present Himself as hope personified, can bring hope, no matter what the situation.

"O HOPE OF ISRAEL, ITS SAVIOR IN TIMES OF DISTRESS.

JER. 14:8, NIV.

A widespread and often unrecognized disease, depression strikes its victims in strange times and places. Rita Snowden, a devotional writer of another generation, offers a prayer for special circumstances. We could all make our own additions and elaborations:

> "For all whose labor is without hope . . .
> For all whose labor is without honor . . .
> For all whose labor is without interest . . .
> For all who have too little leisure . . .
> For all women workers . . .
> For all who work at dangerous trades . . .
> For all who cannot find work . . .
> For all who will not work . . .
> For those who are intemperate, luxurious, or cruel . . .
> Dear Lord, great Lord, for these we pray."*

Have you ever wondered why Olympic athletes are such good-looking people? They have youth on their side, of course, but it's not quite that simple. They carefully nurture their health. Unless they practice clean living, discipline, and concentration, they're lost. But beyond that, they have a purpose—a goal to which they have been looking for most of their lives. It drives them to spare nothing in time or training. Above all, they have hope, hope of attaining that medal. Why are Olympic athletes such good-looking people? Hope literally shines in their faces. If you saw them on the street, it is possible that you might miss some of them because their features can be quite plain. On the athletic field, however, all of that changes. They are transfigured, faces radiant with hope.

> [*Make my face shine today. I lay hold of Your gift of hope!*]

*Rita Snowden, "A Prayer for Hope," *While the Candle Burns* (London: Epworth Press, 1942), p. 78.

OUR HOPE

The Greeks enjoyed sportsmanship for itself. From his travels through the Greco-Roman world the apostle Paul obviously learned a good deal about their Olympic games. "Do you not know that in a race all the runners compete, but only one receives the prize? . . . Every athlete exercises self-control in all things" (1 Cor. 9:24, 25, RSV).

PAUL, AN APOSTLE . . . OF CHRIST JESUS OUR HOPE.

1 TIM. 1:1, NIV.

I wish Paul could have seen the 1994 Winter Olympics. He would have understood Dan Jansen, champion speed skater. Haunted by the death of his sister and a series of defeats, Jansen repeatedly missed an Olympic medal—even though he still won other honors and was reputedly the strongest ice skater in the world. Finally, surrounded by friends and family, Jansen took to the ice at Lillehammer, Norway, for his last Olympian attempt. Missing the 500-meter sprint, he had his last opportunity in the 1,000-meter race. Amid indescribable tension, viewers hoped and prayed, hardly daring to look as that sleek, muscular body, arms flailing, flew low, curve after curve. But he did it! He won the gold.

For an instant we watched Jansen's clean-cut young face as it reflected a lifetime of self-discipline, years of hopes dashed and rewards deferred. Hours torn between confidence and fear. Days spent wondering what life would be afterward—with or without the medal. At first he did not realize he had won. Then the arena exploded. Emotions surged through in waves, with tears, screams, laughter, and faces transfigured with joy.

As I said, Paul might have enjoyed this spectacular. "I told you so! You must fix your eyes on the goal and run to obtain the prize," he would tell us. "I am in training myself. I don't want to be disqualified." Moreover, athletes "do it to receive a perishable wreath, but we an imperishable" (verse 25, RSV).

Jesus is our goal, the hope that carries us through disappointment and hardship. Like Olympians going for the gold, we concentrate on Him. . . . Then let your mind run ahead to the awards ceremony. Think what it will be to stand up to receive the medal while a choir of angels sings the national anthem of heaven.

> *I face another day of training. Whatever setbacks I encounter, let me not waver. I'm going for the gold!*

VALOR

A story is told of Captain Russell Smith, master of Queen Elizabeth II's private yacht, *Britannia*. On a cruise one night the captain had just completed dinner with Her Majesty and returned to the bridge. Peering ahead, he was startled to see a fast-approaching light dead ahead. He barked an order to the signal master. "Tell that ship to alter its course."

THE RIGHT HAND OF THE LORD DOES VALIANTLY.

PS. 118:16, RSV.

The light ahead flashed back the answer: "You alter *your* course."

What insolence! Didn't the other ship's crew understand who they were? He replied: "My name is Captain Russell Smith. This is Her Royal Majesty's private yacht, and the queen is aboard. This is a royal command. You will alter your course!"

A pause. Then: "My name is Tom Johnson. I've been in charge of this lighthouse for 16 years. You will alter *your* course."

Valor combines a number of strong ingredients: self-confidence, loyalty, decisiveness, and commitment. We must never confuse such virtues with arrogance, selfishness, possessiveness, and tyranny—all of which can masquerade as courage. Two alternatives operate here.

First, if we have embarked on a false or dangerous enterprise, we need to be smart enough and humble enough to step back and say, "I was wrong. I don't need to get into this problem." To plow ahead is sheer recklessness.

Second, when we do face a crisis, we will need faith. Like the manna of Israel's wilderness years, courage is not something that we can stockpile. As we look ahead to some threatening situation, anxiety and fear almost overwhelm us. We approach the event with both prayer and fear. Will we survive? Then just when we need the strength, God reaches down and implants sufficient courage in us to see us through. As in the case of the priests of Israel carrying the ark, the turbulent waters of Jordan did not part until they actually stepped into them. Afterward we look back on our trials and realize that God came near and implanted us with exactly the spirit we needed to face the challenge.

A potent commodity, valor must be handled with care. We need to know when to back off before we shipwreck on the rocks. When we're on course, however, we desperately need to be in touch with heaven's supply of faith.

[*Captain of my soul, I take Your commission to me with pride and faith. Help me hour by hour to distinguish between Your causes and my own selfish opinions. I want to know when to use my courage.*]

DEPENDABILITY

We have always had a universal shortage of reliable people. The parable of the talents (Matt. 25:14-30) confirms this fact. In the same vein we find a curious little plea in the old English Book of Common Prayer (1662). The quaint language reads:

> "Help me, Lord, for there is not one godly
> man left;
> For the faithful are minished from among
> the children of men."

"THE LORD, WHO IS FAITHFUL, THE HOLY ONE OF ISRAEL, . . . HAS CHOSEN YOU."

ISA. 49:7, RSV.

The question of loyalty, faithfulness, and dependability extends itself across a broad range—from the obsessive to the "flaky" (as the current usage goes). Some of us seem to be congenitally equipped to be dependable. A sense of responsibility, loyalty, care, and concern is bred into our very marrow. At the other end of the scale are those who cheerfully fail to show up to work, who let down even their best friends, and who resort to an endless sequence of excuses as to why they failed to do whatever it was that they were supposed to do.

For example, the phenomenon of "being sick" fascinates me. The fact that people call in sick in order to go shopping, to play on the beach, or to stay home and sleep is amazingly common. Students too frequently explain their negligence by saying, "I was sick." Teachers, on the other hand, sometimes wonder, "Why am I here today? I don't feel well either."

The ploy works because we are intimidated by the fact that every once in a while people really *do* get sick—and one does not wish to be unreasonable. We all realize, however, that often as not we are being had.

Where is the spirit of service, of loyalty, of promises kept? In a word, faithfulness? Shifting values have become an ethical quicksand all across our social landscape. Abandonment of moral standards has turned into a mass exodus of self-gratification.

Having repeatedly shown Himself to be the "faithful one," God searches for those who aspire to the same high standard of living. "The eyes of the Lord run to and fro throughout the whole earth" to discover "those whose heart is blameless toward him" (2 Chron. 16:9, RSV). How wonderful to find responsible men and women like that!

> *God, I would build my life upon Your great faithfulness. Whatever else my reputation may include, let me always have the honor of being an unchangingly faithful person—both to You and to my fellows.*

INTELLIGENCE

Among his many other fine qualities I remember my father well for his keen intelligence and irrepressible sense of humor—a mind like the proverbial steel trap. He came by it naturally, I suppose, from his Anglo-Irish heritage. Then he sharpened those gifts in a lifetime of active academic pursuits and his insatiable love for talking to people about ideas. *Ideas* excited him, and I can't remember anyone else who surpassed him on it.

At one time in his professional life my dad, peaceable man that he was, found himself at odds with a certain administrator. Always champion of the underdog, he eventually provoked the overbearing chairperson to retaliation. During one meeting the latter delivered a tirade against my father. Even though he named no names, everyone present knew who the victim was. In the profound silence that followed the outburst, all waited to see what Dad would do. Promptly, calmly, and without the least rancor, he delivered a single sentence: "I deny the allegation, and I defy the alligator."

With that, the committee broke up in laughter. They were unable to conduct any more business that afternoon. For perhaps the first time that dictatorship had met its match!

Minds, like bodies, can be fit and healthy or sluggish and diseased. A "sound mind" is one of God's greatest gifts. As the Creator of all intelligence, He has given His creatures varying degrees and types of mental ability. On us human beings He has bestowed a portion of His best talents, programming our minds to learn, to laugh, to make decisions, to change course, to feel compassion, and so forth. Birds and animals, on the other hand, though blessed with practical instincts, have limitations. For example, God has made the ostrich "forget wisdom, and given her no share in understanding" (Job 39:17, RSV).

In his counsel to young Timothy, Paul described the tremendous scope of an intelligent mind: self-confidence, influence, "self-control," as well as the ability to love and to champion right. How dare we then abuse such magnificent power within us by allowing anything we see, hear, or do to corrode our strength? To weaken our bond with God Himself?

> FOR GOD HATH NOT GIVEN US THE SPIRIT OF FEAR; BUT OF POWER, AND OF LOVE, AND OF A SOUND MIND.
>
> 2 TIM. 1:7.

[*Creator of all gifts, I praise You for the mind You have given me. Let me do nothing to impair its function in any way. Show me, Lord, how to improve it daily.*]

THE MODEL

I n the White Mountains of New Hampshire you can see a huge outcropping of rock with the distinct profile of a man's face. It is a tourist attraction, of course, especially when the sunlight picks out its rugged granite features. But if you read Nathaniel Hawthorne's tale entitled "The Great Stone Face," you'll find that he gives this curious work of nature a profound moral meaning.

The story tells of a little boy, Ernest, who grows up and lives under the noble, kindly features of the face. His mother has relayed to him an old Indian prophecy that said that a child would be born who would become the "greatest and noblest personage of his time." In manhood his face would exactly resemble the Great Stone Face of the Franconia Notch. Years passed, and great men came and went: Mr. Gathergold, a wealthy merchant; a famous, bemedaled Army general (Old Blood-and-Thunder); and an illustrious politician (Old Stony Phiz). One and all, they purported to be the looked-for champion of virtue. None of them could ever match the strong, noble face in the mountain. Year after year the village people were disappointed. The expected one had not come. Finally a poet arrived, one whose songs pointed to the majesty of God's natural world. He was the one who made the amazing discovery. "Behold! Ernest is himself the likeness of the Great Stone Face!" By living his industrious, simple life in the daily presence of the Great Stone Face, he had become changed.

> WE ALL, WITH UNVEILED FACE, BEHOLDING THE GLORY OF THE LORD, ARE BEING CHANGED INTO HIS LIKENESS FROM ONE DEGREE OF GLORY TO ANOTHER; FOR THIS COMES FROM THE LORD.
>
> 2 COR. 3:18, RSV.

Paul describes our modeling upon Jesus as a progression. The veils, the barriers, must come down. Next we "are being changed into his likeness," moving from one "glory" to another. It is never a static situation. Like Ernest, we need to spend a lifetime in the presence of His face. Fame, fortune, all the other gifts, must be secondary to the quiet development that we achieve in His presence.

Indeed, it is a marvelous plan that will carry on throughout eternity. If learning, growing, blossoming, fulfilling, loving, and all the rest is a "glory" here on earth, what must it be like in the everlasting context of heaven?

Heavenly Father, I want to live every hour in Your presence, under Your influence. Whatever else I seek to achieve, let me consciously keep the divine Model before me.

RED FOR FORGIVENESS

We, as well as the Egyptians and probably some of the Israelites, find ourselves rather put off by the Passover requirement to spatter the doorposts and lintel with the blood of the sacrificial lamb (Ex. 12:22). Throughout the rest of Scripture, however, Jesus constantly associated Himself with the sprinkled blood, from His wounding for our transgressions (Isa. 53:3-5) to John's vision of Him "clad in a robe dipped in blood" (Rev. 19:13, RSV).

Color symbolism is universal, and people have consciously used it in worship, art, and literature. Red is the first of the seven primary colors of the rainbow spectrum. Signifying pulsing blood and purifying fire, it is active and life-giving. It also stands for passion and surging emotions. Human beings anciently stained with blood any object they wanted to bring to life, and the color red features largely in tribal decorations.

Medieval Christian scholars pictured the path of spiritual growth in an ascending scale of colors: black for penitence, white for purity, red for love and compassion, all tracing the way in which we pass from darkness to light.

White and red frequently appear together, giving us a striking combination. In celebrating roses, the flowers of love, a Christian poet interprets the colors:

> "The roses of joy are red,
> The roses of pain are white;
> But I think, when the day is sped
> And I stand by the gate at night,
> I shall know just this, when the day is dead:
> That a rose is sweet, be it white or red.
> —Percy Ainsworth.*

The prophet Isaiah, however, elevated the red-and-white combination to its greatest possible height. "Though your sins are like scarlet, they shall be as white as snow" (Isa. 1:18, RSV). In other words, Christ voluntarily wore the red so that we might eventually wear robes of white.

[*Your loving sacrifice ensures my salvation. Let me never forget the great value You have put upon my life.*]

"I HAVE TRODDEN THE WINEPRESS ALONE; FROM THE NATIONS NO ONE WAS WITH ME. . . . THEIR BLOOD SPATTERED MY GARMENTS, AND I STAINED ALL MY CLOTHING."

ISA. 63:3, NIV.

Poems and Sonnets (London: Epworth Press).

WHITE FOR PURITY

I never saw my Australian grandmother—she died when my father was only 17. She reared six children, however, and kept a green-grocer's shop to sell produce from the family orchard and vineyard. A delicate and petite woman, she recorded in her diary, late at night, her spiritual life and her dreams of reading and music. She often berated herself for being discontented within the narrow confines in which she lived back at the turn of the century. One March evening she wrote:

HIS CLOTHES WERE WHITE AS SNOW.
MATT. 28:3, NIV.

"We keep only one cat down here [at the shop], and she is a beautiful pure white with one bright blue eye and the other grey. I love pure white things. I like white horses, white pigs, white fowls, white cats, white bedrooms, white dresses on babies and young girls. I am a great lover of white. It may be a queer fancy, but I have often thought if I had a farm of my own I would like to have all white fowls and cattle. I even like plates, cups, and saucers of white."

The purity of white fascinates us. As the distillation of all of the colors in the spectrum of light, we often contrast it with its opposite, the lack of light altogether. Day and night, life and death—a number of dualisms come to mind. The wearing of white clothes and the blackening of faces were part of many primitive rites. For instance, the white garments worn by dancers in medicinal ceremonies have been passed on to our modern medical profession. As the ceremonial color for christenings, confirmations, and brides, white makes its own statement. Some places still consider white the only proper attire for baptism, church attendance, and burial.

John's revelation of Christ as the magnificent rider on the white horse is a kind of symphony of whiteness, celebrating purity and illumination. The vision then moves on to the armies of heaven following Him "on white horses and dressed in fine linen, white and clean" (Rev. 19:14, NIV) and thence to the "great white throne and him who was seated on it" (Rev. 20:11, NIV).

Because white has such an instinctive and universal appeal, its use places Jesus among some of His most attractive symbolic associations.

[*I thank You for white, because it shows up the least stain or blemish. And I need to be able to see those things that offend You.*]

BLUE FOR OBEDIENCE

A few places remain in the world where the urban-bound, smog-infested citizen can still enjoy pristine *blue sky*. One is in the northern reaches of Canada, where the high dome of heaven still arches over virgin forests, rolling wheat fields, and icy lakes. Flying across the Northwest Passage on a clear day is an event unmatched anywhere else in the world. Spread out below is a breathtaking mosaic of blue sky and ocean. Snowy coastlines textured with wrinkled mountains harbor jagged icebergs sailing in dark ultramarine seas.

Blue, as another of the primary colors, seems to be almost everyone's favorite. And God's too. He has used it so lavishly, in every conceivable shade, for the sky above and ocean below. Expansive and upward tending, cool blue, then, stands for spiritual feeling and sympathy, reason and intellect, devotion and innocence.

Since it was not one of the common earth tones achieved by natural desert pigments, blue was used in Bible times with pride and distinction. During the building of the Temple, Solomon sent for "a man skilled to work . . . in purple, crimson and blue yarn" (2 Chron. 2:7, NIV). Xerxes had his palace garden hung with "white and blue linen" (Esther 1:6, NIV), and the honored Mordecai wore "royal garments of blue and white" (Esther 8:15, NIV). Pagans dressed their idols in blue and purple (Jer. 10:9), and young Assyrian warriors, "clothed in blue," seduced Israel (Eze. 23:6, NIV). Mercantile Tyre imported "beautiful garments, blue fabric" and boasted "awnings . . . of blue and purple" (Eze. 27:24, 7, NIV).

When Jehovah, in ordering the garments for the priests, chose blue tassels, He selected the rarest and most significant color then possible—so unusual that the people would *remember* when they saw it. Thus blue exemplified the importance of obedience to God's commands.

THE LORD SAID TO MOSES, "SPEAK TO THE ISRAELITES AND SAY TO THEM: . . . 'YOU ARE TO MAKE TASSELS ON THE CORNERS OF YOUR GARMENTS, WITH A BLUE CORD ON EACH TASSEL. YOU WILL HAVE THESE TASSELS TO LOOK AT AND SO YOU WILL REMEMBER ALL THE COMMANDS OF THE LORD.'"

NUM. 15:37-39, NIV.

[*So many of us surround ourselves with blue. It's our favorite color—and Yours too. (You've used so much of it in Your creation.) Thank You for emphasizing its spiritual meaning.*]

THE RAINBOW

The rainbow is a magnificent culmination of God's self-portrait. Its breathtaking loveliness invariably stops us, wherever we are. For an instant we preview heaven itself, our human eyes peering beyond our earthly landscape. No wonder the rainbow has captured our imagination.

But rainbows are elusive. Sometimes we see them doubled. Other times only one end will show itself against a shadowy hillside, floating in a fragile blend of light and dark air. Under the right conditions we may see it from the air, a complete circle, with the shadow of our plane caught in its middle. To prevent it from becoming commonplace, probably the Creator arranged the weather conditions so that we can catch it only in a moment of time. He wants us to see and remember it.

A rainbow usually has three components—clouds, rain, and sunlight. A spiritual rainbow forms in the same way. First may come a cloud—bereavement, regret, discouragement. Perhaps even a solemn moment of conviction. Second, rain falls. Drops of sorrow are inevitable. Without them the rainbow cannot occur. Then, prismlike, the raindrops catch and unravel the sunbeams for us. The sunshine bursts upon the cloud and rain—God's own light breaking through our grief. Behold—a rainbow and a promise.

God sent the first rainbow to Noah as a promise. His family, eight weary refugees cast upon the ravaged slopes of Ararat, looked up into the clouds and saw the sun break through. At that moment the rainbow appeared, and with it the promise that never again would God judge His world by flood. John the revelator closes Scripture with another view of the rainbow, this time encircling God's throne (Rev. 4:3). God never forgets, and the book of Revelation comforts all of us weary pilgrims waiting here at the end of time. Heavenly judgment is upon us, if not our own mortality, and Christ is about to return.

> **"WHENEVER . . . THE RAINBOW APPEARS IN THE CLOUDS, I WILL REMEMBER MY COVENANT BETWEEN ME AND YOU AND ALL LIVING CREATURES OF EVERY KIND."**
>
> GEN. 9:14-16, NIV.

[*"Even so, come, Lord Jesus."*]